APPLYING IFRS FOR SMEs
Second Edition

Authors
Bruce Mackenzie

Professor Danie Coetsee

Raymond Chamboko

Tapiwa Njikizana

Edwin Selbst

Blaise Colyvas

Brandon Hanekom

Emile Nel

Tobie Oosthuizen

W. CONSULTING

Disclaimers and copyright

All examples, illustrative disclosures and financial statements are based on specific, fictional facts and circumstances. In some cases, further interpretation will be required to apply the IFRS for SMEs to an entity's specific transactions, events and circumstances. Users are cautioned to read this publication in conjunction with the original text from IFRS for SMEs, Illustrative Financial Statements Presentation, Disclosure Checklist and Basis for Conclusions as issued by the International Accounting Standards Board. We recommend that preparers of financial statements in terms of IFRS for SMEs consult with a professional advisor when they are not certain of the appropriate accounting treatment for significant transactions, events and balances.

This publication is not a replacement for such professional advice and services, and it should not be acted on or relied upon or used as a basis for any decision or action that may affect you or your business.

Whilst every effort has been made to ensure the accuracy of the information contained in this publication, this cannot be guaranteed, and neither W Professional Learning (Pty) Ltd, nor any related entity shall have any liability to any person or entity that relies on the information contained in this publication. Any such reliance is solely at the user's risk.

No responsibility for loss occasioned to any person acting or refraining from action as a result of any material in this publication will be accepted by the authors or publisher.

ISBN: 978-0-620-67618-2

Published by W.consulting, 10th Floor, Sinosteel Plaza, 159 Rivonia Road, Sandton, Johannesburg, South Africa.

Desktop publishing and proofreading by Gouri Barua, 082-441-7697, www.gouribarua.com.

Printed and bound in South Africa by Interpak Books.

Contents

Foreword

Increasingly, policymakers are recognising the critical role of small- and medium-sized entities (SMEs) in the growth of developed, and perhaps more especially, developing economies. This recognition has been accompanied by significant support for the activities of SMEs at both the national level, and, through the guidance of international financial institutions such as the World Bank, at a global level. A key part of this support is ensuring that the regulation of these businesses occurs at a level that, whilst robust and supportive of the general goals of the economies, is nonetheless not overly burdensome. Indeed, one of the main focuses of recent changes in the business environment in many countries has been the removal of impediments and barriers to the establishment of SMEs and toward encouraging their subsequent growth.

Why an IFRS for SMEs is needed

One of the regulatory requirements applied to almost all small entities is the requirement to prepare financial statements. Financial statements are considered key, not just for the measurement of activities within an economy, but also for more directly beneficial activities such as facilitating the raising of capital, the granting of financing, and the enhancement of trade activities. The IFRS for SMEs, published in 2009, recognises the need for SMEs to prepare financial statements, but also acknowledges the need to reduce the burden on these smaller entities. The Standard is self-contained, tailored to the needs and capabilities of smaller businesses, and understandable across borders. As such, it is in line with the growing trend of facilitating the establishment of SMEs.

The IFRS Foundation has in recent years developed and posted profiles about the use of IFRS in individual jurisdictions. By June 2015, the Foundation had completed profiles for 140 jurisdictions, including all the G20 jurisdictions. Seventy-three of those jurisdictions require or permit the IFRS for SMEs. The Standard is also currently under consideration in a further 14 jurisdictions. This widespread uptake for a Standard that has only been in existence for six years is evidence both that the Standard addresses a real need, and that it is successful in doing so.

What changes have been made in the second edition

The publication of this second edition of Applying IFRS for SMEs coincides with the May 2015 publication by the IASB (the Board) of revisions to the IFRS for SMEs following the completion of a comprehensive review of the Standard. Given the success of the IFRS for SMEs to date, an immediate question is: why did the Board consider it necessary to make changes?

When originally considering the development of a separate standard for SMEs, the Board expressed a view that changes to related requirements for SMEs should be proposed concurrently with each exposure draft of the corresponding IFRS or Interpretation. The effective dates of the new or revised requirements for SMEs would then probably be the same as the effective date of the new or revised IFRSs. However, our constituents did not agree. They explained that because SMEs do not have internal accounting resources or the ability to hire accounting advisers on an ongoing basis, the IFRS for SMEs should be updated only periodically, perhaps only once in two or three years. On balance, the Board found these arguments persuasive. In concluding this, the board acknowledged that, compared to full IFRS, there is a considerable greater need for a stable platform in the SME environment.

Consequently, at the time of issuing the Standard, the Board undertook to only update the IFRS for SMEs on a periodic basis, and noted its plan to perform an initial comprehensive review within two or three years. The objective of the review would be to assess the experience entities had had in implementing the Standard and to consider whether practice indicated a need for amendments.

This review commenced in 2012, and was completed with the publication of amendments in 2015. By design, these amendments have been limited. The Board felt that, given that this was the first review since the initial publication of the IFRS for SMEs, and that in many jurisdictions, the Standard has only been effective for a short period of time, there was an even greater need for stability during this review than there may be in future reviews. The effective date of these amendments is January 2017.

How often will changes be made to the IFRS for SMEs

Although not part of the formal Standard, the IASB also detailed its approach for future reviews of the IFRS for SMEs. In accordance with this approach, the next review of the Standard will commence in 2019, approximately two years after the effective date of the existing amendments. This should allow time for SMEs to apply the amendments, and for interested parties to identify and comment on any implementation issues or unintended consequences that result from those amendments. Additionally, the Board will shortly decide whether there is a need for an interim review to consider any new and revised IFRSs not yet incorporated or any urgent amendments that have been identified.

The Board is of the view that this process will mean that amendments to the IFRS for SMEs will not be expected to be more frequent than approximately once every three years.

In the foreword for the previous edition of this publication, Paul Pacter wrote 'An important public interest is served when those who provide capital have good information on which to base their lending, credit, and investment decisions. The IFRS for SMEs will bring those benefits to South Africa and the rest of the world.'. It is my belief that this continues to be the outcome of the SME Standard. In our efforts to ensure this, we will continue to work with preparers, users, educators, regulators, and others involved in the process in those jurisdictions where the IFRS for SMEs has already been adopted. We will also continue to encourage the adoption of the Standard in those jurisdictions where it has not yet been adopted.

Darrel Scott
IASB Board Member
International Accounting Standards Board
August 2015

Preface

Applying IFRS for SMEs is based on the International Financial Reporting Standards for Small and Medium-Sized Entities (IFRS for SMEs or *the Standard*) as issued by the International Accounting Standards Board in May 2015. The book is a comprehensive review of the Standard, providing the principles and guidance contained in the Standard. It has been written by subject matter experts, training and applying the Standard in practice.

The publication can be used by practitioners and preparers applying IFRS for SMEs, as well as for academic purposes.

The aim of *Applying IFRS for SMEs* is to assist in the application of the Standard in practice and provides insights on certain interpretative issues. This is achieved by:

- Examples showing certain transactions and events.
- Figures illustrating more complex issues in the form of a diagram.
- Tables providing lists and points.
- Our insights and opinions on the appropriate treatment for certain transactions and events.
- Extracts from the IFRS for SMEs and full IFRS.
- Highlights of main points.
- A summary of the major points at the end of each chapter.

To identify extracts, highlights, insights and opinions the following symbols are used:

Extracts from the IFRS for SMEs and full IFRS.

Highlights or to emphasise issues.

Our insights or opinions on issues where there is no guidance, or where there may be more than one interpretation.

Abbreviations used

FIFO	First-in-first-out
Framework	IASB's Framework for the Preparation and Presentation of Financial Statements
FV	Fair value
GAAP	Generally Accepted Accounting Principles
GBP	Great Britain Pound Sterling
IASB	International Accounting Standards Board
IFRIC	International Financial Reporting Interpretations Committee
IFRS (Full IFRS)	International Financial Reporting Standards
IFRS for SMEs	International Financial Reporting Standard for Small and Medium-Sized Entities
IRR	Internal rate of return
JV	Joint venture
NCI	Non-controlling interest
OCI	Other comprehensive income
P/L	Profit or loss
PPE	Property, plant and equipment
SCF	Statement of cash flows
SCI	Standard Interpretations Committee
SIC	Standard industrial classification
SIRE	Statement of income and retained earnings
SME	Small and medium-sized entity
SPE	Special purpose entity
The Standard	IFRS for SMEs
USD	United States Dollar

Chapter 1
Scope of the IFRS for SMEs

Contents

1.1   General scope

The IFRS for Small and Medium-Sized Entities (IFRS for SMEs, "the Standard") is an independent standard that prescribes financial reporting guidance for small and medium-sized entities (SMEs). The Standard was originally issued in 2009, with the first set of amendments being made to the Standard in 2015. The effective date for these amendments are for the years beginning on or after 1 January 2017. The Standard is applicable to SMEs that:

- Do not have public accountability; and
- Publish general purpose financial statements for external users.

The Standard does not provide any quantitative measures, such as revenue, expenditure, assets or number of employees, to determine whether or not the Standard may be used. The Standard states that each jurisdiction needs to determine which entities may apply the IFRS for SMEs.

1.2   Definitions

1.2.1   General purpose financial statements

General purpose financial statements are defined as financial statements aimed at the general financial information needs of a wide range of users who are not in a position to demand reports tailored to meet their particular information needs.

The IFRS for SMEs allows general purpose financial statements to be published for external users, including:

- Owners who are not involved in managing the business.
- Existing and potential creditors.
- Credit rating agencies.

1.2.2   Public accountability

An entity has public accountability if:

- Its debt or equity instruments are **traded in a public market** or it is in the process of issuing such instruments for trading in a public market.
- It holds assets in a **fiduciary capacity** for a broad group of outsiders as one of its primary businesses.

Meeting any one of the above two requirements is regarded as public accountability, which results in an exclusion from the scope of the Standard.

1.2.3   Traded in a public market

Publicly traded is defined in the Standard as 'registered with a securities commission or other regulatory organisation for the purpose of sale in a public market'. Public accountability is not only when an entity's debt or equity instruments are actually traded in public market, but also when the entity is in the process of issuing such instruments for trading in public markets.

The Standard states that public markets include domestic or foreign stock exchanges or over-the-counter markets, whether local or regional.

Entities whose memorandum of incorporation or other incorporation documentation allows for the offering of any of its securities to the public will not be regarded as having public accountability until they actually start taking steps to issue such instruments for trading in a public market.

The Standard is not intended for small publicly-traded entities. Due to the special needs of capital markets, the use of full IFRS is required for small publicly-traded entities. All entities whose debt or equity instruments are traded in public capital markets, regardless of size, have chosen to seek capital from outside investors. Usually, these investors are not involved in the management of the business and are not in a position to demand specific information. Full IFRS is developed to serve the capital markets, and with this in mind, require specific disclosures, which may not be included in the IFRS for SMEs.

1.2.4   Fiduciary capacity

To be excluded from the scope of the Standard, entities must hold assets in a fiduciary capacity for a broad group of outsiders as one of its primary businesses. The requirement *as one of its primary businesses* is essential. Some entities may hold assets in a fiduciary capacity because they hold and manage financial resources entrusted to them by clients, customers or members not involved in the management of the entity. However, if they do so for reasons incidental to their primary business, they are not considered to be publicly accountable – they can apply the Standard.

The Standard provides the following examples of entities that may be excluded from the scope of the IFRS for SMEs because they hold assets in a fiduciary capacity. An analysis of their operations, and the markets in which they operate, would be needed to confirm whether they are excluded from the Standard. The list includes:

- Banks.
- Credit unions.
- Insurance companies.
- Securities' dealers.
- Mutual funds.
- Investment banks.

The Standard provides the following examples of entities that may apply the IFRS for SMEs because they hold assets in a fiduciary capacity incidental to their primary business:

- Travel or real estate agents.
- Schools.
- Charitable organisations.
- Co-operative enterprises requiring a nominal membership deposit.
- Sellers that receive payment in advance of delivery of goods or services (eg utility companies).

Example 1-1: Purchase of an asset management company

Soweto is the holding company of a diverse group of entities. Currently, the Soweto Group has no public accountability as defined. The board of directors recently had their quarterly strategy meeting. As a result the financial director had various questions about the application of the IFRS for SMEs.

The board of directors identified a small asset management company for possible acquisition that will provide them with various strategic options in the future.

The financial director is uncertain if the asset management company will be able to apply the Standard and, if not, what the implication would be for the consolidation process of the Soweto group.

Required
Provide the financial director with advice with regard to applying the Standard with reference to the possible acquisition and its implications on the Soweto group.

Suggested solution
The asset management company receives funds and then invests them on behalf of its clients for a fee. The asset management company therefore has public accountability as it holds assets in a fiduciary capacity for a broad group of outsiders as one of its primary businesses.

With respect to the Soweto group, as one of its subsidiaries will not be eligible to apply the IFRS for SMEs, the group can therefore not apply the Standard in its consolidated financial statements.

1.3   Application to parent companies

A parent entity must assess its eligibility to apply this Standard to its own separate financial statements (refer to *Chapter 5*) on the basis of its own status. A parent entity that does not have public accountability and publishes general purpose financial statements may elect to present its separate financial statements under this Standard, even if it is required to present consolidated financial statements under full IFRS, or any other GAAP. Where it elects to do so, it should clearly distinguish financial statements prepared under this Standard from financial statements prepared in accordance with any other framework.

Example 1-2: Parent entity with a listed subsidiary

Grand Baie is a parent entity that owns 80% of a listed subsidiary, Moka. Grand Baie Ltd has no public accountability in its own right, and elects to prepare general purpose, separate financial statements.

Required
What framework can Grand Baie Ltd use to prepare its financial statements?

Suggested solution
As Moka has public accountability (ie it is a listed entity), the Grand Baie group would be required to prepare consolidated financial statements under full IFRS, or any other applicable GAAP. For Grand Baie's separate financial statements, it could elect to apply the IFRS for SMEs standard as its basis of preparation as it is within the scope of the Standard.

1.4   Application to subsidiary companies

A subsidiary whose parent uses full IFRS, or that is part of a consolidated group that uses full IFRS, is allowed to use the IFRS for SMEs in its own financial statements provided that it does not have public accountability.

Example 1-3: Acquisition by an international investment entity

The current shareholders of Berlin were approached by an international investment company regarding a possible purchase of a majority shareholding in Berlin.

The financial director has concerns – the international investment company is currently applying full IFRS as its financial reporting framework; Berlin uses the IFRS for SMEs. He is uncertain if Berlin would be allowed to continue applying the IFRS for SMEs if its potential new holding company does not apply the IFRS for SMEs.

Required

Provide the financial director with advice on applying the IFRS for SMEs and the implications of consolidating Berlin.

Suggested solution

The IFRS for SMEs states that a subsidiary whose parent uses full IFRS, or that is part of a consolidated group that uses full IFRS, is not prohibited from using the IFRS for SMEs in its own financial statements if that subsidiary does not have public accountability.

Berlin may, therefore, continue to apply the IFRS for SMEs in its own accounting records.

Full IFRS requires all entities included in consolidated financial statements to have uniform accounting policies. The international investment company would therefore need to convert Berlin's IFRS for SMEs' financial statements to full IFRS financial statements for consolidation purposes.

1.5   Application by micro-entities

The IASB states that this standard would be appropriate for all entities without public accountability preparing general purpose financial statements, irrespective of their size. This would include micro-sized entities (with less than 10 employees) and owner-managed businesses. If such an entity prepares financial statements solely to submit to income tax authorities for the purpose of determining taxable income or to a credit provider to obtain finance, such financial statements must not be deemed to be general purpose financial statements.

The guidance in the Standard is clear and concise. The guidance may cover some transactions or circumstances that micro-entities do not typically encounter, but the IASB did not believe that this imposes a burden on such entities. The structure of the Standard will make it easy for micro-entities to identify those aspects of the Standard that are relevant to their circumstances.

The IASB acknowledged that an extensively simplified and brief set of accounting requirements for micro-entities (with general principles of accounting, specific recognition and measurement principles for only the most basic transactions and limited disclosure requirements) might result in relatively low costs to micro-entities in preparing financial statements. The IASB concluded that such simplified requirements for micro-entities would not meet the aim of general purpose financial statements and might not improve the micro-entities' ability to obtain capital. Therefore, the IASB has not pursued a project to develop such a standard.

1.6 Changes to full IFRS

The IFRS for SMEs has not been written as a 'lighter' version of full IFRS. Where changes have and continue to be made to full IFRS, these have not and may not necessarily be incorporated into the IFRS for SMEs standard. The IFRS for SMEs is designed as a stand-alone document. Entities applying this Standard should not anticipate that changes made to full IFRS will be incorporated into the IFRS for SMEs standard in the future. The IASB will consider these when it next amends the IFRS for SMEs standard, but it is not obliged to incorporate them. An entity using this Standard should also note that it does not have the option of adopting accounting treatments in full IFRS into its IFRS for SMEs accounts unless these do not conflict with the IFRS for SMEs. The only exception to this is the option to adopt IAS 39, Financial Instruments, instead of the financial instruments chapter in the IFRS for SMEs (refer to *Chapter 17*).

1.7 Summary

- The IFRS for SMEs is applicable to small and medium-sized entities that do not have public accountability, and publish general purpose financial statements for external users.
- An entity is deemed to have public accountability if:
  - Its debt or equity instruments are traded in a public market or it is in the process of issuing such instruments for trading in a public market; or
  - The entity holds assets in a fiduciary capacity for a broad group of outsiders as one of its primary businesses.
- The Standard clarifies that where entities hold assets in a fiduciary capacity as an incidental part of their business activities, this does not make them publicly accountable. Entities that fall into this category may include travel agents, schools or charities.

Chapter 2
Concepts and pervasive principles

Contents

2.1   Objective of financial statements of SMEs

The stated objective of financial statements of SMEs is to provide information about the financial position, performance and cash flows of the entity that is useful for economic decision-making by a broad range of users, some of who may not be in a position to demand reports tailored to meet their specific needs. Such financial statements are commonly referred to as *general purpose financial statements*.

As a further objective financial statements also show how management has managed the entity's resources.

Figure 2-1: The objective of financial statements

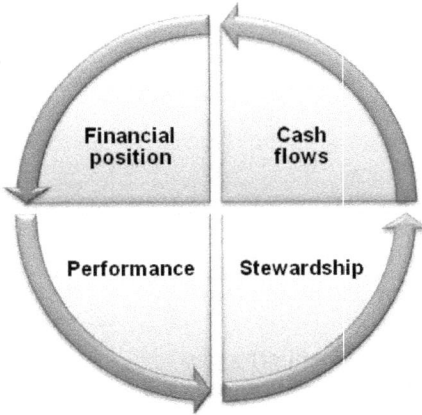

2.2   Qualitative characteristics of information in financial statements

Ten qualitative characteristics of information in financial statements are identified in the Standard without ranking them or explaining how the qualitative characteristics relate to each other or identifying some of them as constraints. These qualitative characteristics are:

- Understandability.
- Relevance.
- Materiality.
- Reliability.
- Substance over form.

- Prudence.
- Completeness.
- Timeliness.
- Balance between benefits and cost.

In the detail of the qualitative characteristics and in the discussion of the application of the qualitative characteristics to the development of accounting policies (refer to *Chapter 7.2.2*), certain links between the qualitative characteristics are created and certain of these qualitative characteristics created boundaries (also known as constraints). Due to these links and boundaries, these qualitative characteristics are identified as main or linked qualitative characteristics, and others as constraints in *Table 2-1*.

Table 2-1: Qualitative characteristics and constraints

Main characteristics	Meaning and interpretation	Characteristics linked	Meaning and interpretation
Understandability	Means comprehensibility by potential users with reasonable understanding and knowledge of accounting. This does not mean that information that is difficult to understand may be omitted.		
Relevance	Information is relevant when it is capable of influencing the economic decisions of users. Normally, only material items are relevant, but judgement must be applied to determine which items are immaterial items.	Materiality	Depends on the size of the item and the influence of its omission or misstatement. Omission or misstatement could influence economic decision-making of users of the financial statements.
Reliability	Means free from material error and bias and represents the information faithfully. Faithful representation is created through the linked characteristics of substance over form, prudence and completeness.	Substance over form	In accordance with the substance and economic reality and not merely the legal form.
		Prudence	Appropriate use of caution in the exercise of judgement.
		Completeness	Complete within the bounds of materiality and cost (refer to the constraints below).

Table 2-1: Qualitative characteristics and constraints *(continued)*

Main characteristics	Meaning and interpretation	Characteristics linked	Meaning and interpretation
Balance between relevance and reliability (not identified as a qualitative characteristic)	Accounting policies are developed through an appropriate balance between relevance and reliability (refer to *Chapter 7*).	Timeliness	Provide information in the period of relevance. Balance the relative merit between timely reporting and the provision of reliable information.
Comparability	Financial statements should be consistent from one period to the next, and between different entities.		Goal is to identify trends in financial position, performance and cash flows.
Boundaries			
Materiality	Depends on the size of the item and the influence of its omission or misstatement.		
Balance between benefits and cost	Benefits must exceed the cost of providing it.		
Undue cost and effort exemption	Depends on entity's specific circumstances and on management's judgement. Applicable if the incremental costs of obtaining information substantially exceed the benefits of expected users.		Assessment must be made at initial and subsequent measurement, if applicable. If the exemption is applied, that fact must be disclosed stating why it has been applied.

2.3 Financial position

2.3.1 Basic principle

The financial position of an entity is the relationship of its assets, liabilities and equity as at a specific date as presented in the statement of financial position (SFP) (balance sheet).

The elements that make up the financial position of an entity are defined as follows:

- An **asset** is a resource controlled by the entity as a result of past events, and from which future economic benefits are expected to flow to the entity.
- A **liability** is a present obligation of the entity arising from past events, the settlement of which is expected to result in an outflow from the entity of resources containing economic benefits.
- **Equity** is the residual interest in the assets of the entity after deducting all its liabilities.

2.3.2 Clarifying the definition of assets

The Standard does not explain the main characteristics of the definition of an asset, such as resource, control or past event. Only the following additional guidance is provided:

- The future economic benefit of an asset is explained as the potential to contribute, directly or indirectly, to the flow of cash and cash equivalents to the entity. The cash flows may arise from the use or disposal of the asset.
- Physical form is not essential to identify the existence of an asset. Assets may be intangible, eg broadcast licences or databases.
- The right of ownership is not essential to determine the existence of an asset, eg a leased asset could be capitalised if an entity controls the future benefits expected to flow from it.

However, for an item to be recognised as an asset or a liability in the statement of financial position it must not only meet the definition of an asset or liability, it must also meet the recognition criteria (refer to *2.7*).

2.3.3 Clarifying the definition of liabilities

Only the present obligation and settlement characteristics of the definition of a liability are explained further in the Standard.

To meet the definition of a liability, an entity must have a present obligation to act or perform in a particular way. Similar to full IFRS the obligation may be either a legal or constructive obligation. A **legal obligation** is commonly evidenced by a binding contract or by statute. A **constructive obligation** is defined as an obligation that is derived from an entity's actions where:

- By an established pattern of past practice, published policies or a sufficiently specific current statement, the entity has indicated to other parties that it will accept particular responsibilities; and
- As a result, the entity has created a valid expectation on the part of those other parties that it will discharge those responsibilities.

A present obligation may be settled or extinguished by other means, such as a creditor waiving or forfeiting its rights, or by any of the following means:

- Payment of cash.
- Transfer of other assets.
- Provision of services.
- Replacement of the obligation with another obligation.
- Conversion of the obligation to equity.

2.3.4 Equity

The definition of equity is not further clarified in the Standard. The Standard states that equity may be sub-classified in the statement of financial position. For example, in a corporate entity such sub-divisions may include:

- Share capital contributed by shareholders;
- Retained earnings; and
- Other reserves.

The Standard does not describe how, when, or if amounts may be transferred between components of equity.

2.4 Performance

2.4.1 Basic principle

Performance is the relationship of the income and expenses of an entity during a reporting period. The Standard allows entities to present performance in a single financial statement (a statement of comprehensive income (SCI)) or in two financial statements (an income statement and a separate statement of comprehensive income).

> The main indicators of performance are profit or loss and total comprehensive income.

Total comprehensive income and profit or loss are frequently used as measures of performance or as the basis for other measures, such as return on investment or earnings per share. There are of course many other measures of performance that are used in practice, some of which are based on sub-elements of the above measures.

2.4.2 Definition of income and expenses

Income and expenses is defined as follows:

- **Income** is increases in economic benefits during the reporting period in the form of inflows or enhancements of assets, or decreases of liabilities that result in increases in equity, other than those relating to contributions from owners.
- **Expenses** are decreases in economic benefits during the reporting period in the form of outflows or depletion of assets, or incurrence of liabilities that result in decreases in equity, other than those relating to equity investors.

In the Standard, the definitions of income and expenses are derived from the definitions of assets and liabilities, thus creating a focus on a financial position.

2.4.3 Clarification of the definition of income

The definition of income applies both to revenue and gains.

- **Revenue** is income that arises in the course of the ordinary activities of an entity and is referred to by a variety of names including sales, fees, interest, dividends, royalties and rentals.
- **Gains** are other items that meet the definition of income but are not revenue.

When gains are recognised they are usually displayed separately as they differ in nature from revenue in that they may not result from the ordinary activities of an entity – knowledge of this is useful in making economic decisions. Linked to performance, as discussed above, some users of financial statements may wish to assess the performance of an entity excluding gains, or assess specifically the impact of gains on overall performance.

2.4.4 Clarification of the definition of expenses

Expenses apply to losses as well as expenses that arise in the course of the ordinary activities of the entity.

- **Expenses** usually take the form of an outflow or depletion of assets.
- **Losses** are other items that meet the definition of expenses and may arise in the course of the ordinary activities of the entity. When losses are recognised, they are usually presented separately and, like gains, they may not result from the ordinary activities of the entity – knowledge of this may be useful for assessing the performance of an entity and for economic decision-making.

2.4.5 Total comprehensive income and profit or loss

The concepts of comprehensive income and profit or loss are not separate elements, and no recognition criteria are provided.

Total comprehensive income is the arithmetical difference between all income and expenses. **Profit or loss** is the arithmetical difference between income and expenses, excluding those included in other comprehensive income (OCI) (refer to *Chapter 3*).

2.5 Accrual basis

Except for cash flow information, the accrual basis is the basis on which financial statements are prepared under the Standard. On this basis, items are recognised as assets, liabilities, equity, income or expenses when they satisfy the definitions and recognition criteria for those items (refer to *2.7*).

2.6 Pervasive recognition and measurement principles

The recognition and measurement principles of the Standard are based on pervasive principles that are derived from the IASB Framework for the Preparation and Presentation of Financial Statements and from full IFRS. In the absence of a requirement in the Standard that applies specifically to a transaction or other event or condition, the specific guidance in the section dealing with the development of accounting policies needs to be followed to develop an appropriate treatment. These guidelines are based on the qualitative characteristics and a decision hierarchy is provided (refer to *Chapter 7*).

> Pervasive recognition and measurement principles are derived from full IFRS.

A fall-back to full IFRS or other financial reporting standards is not required. As part of the decision hierarchy, an entity considers the definitions, recognition criteria and measurement concepts for assets, liabilities, income and expenses, and the pervasive principles set out in the Standard.

> Where the wording in the Standard is the same as full IFRS, any related explanation in full IFRS, in the absence of an explanation in the Standard, may be considered as a practical solution.

2.7 Recognition of assets, liabilities, income and expenses

2.7.1 Recognition

Recognition is the process of incorporating in the financial statements an item that meets the definition of an asset, liability, income or expense (refer to *2.3* and *2.4*), and satisfies both the following recognition criteria (refer to *Figure 2-2*):

- It is probable that any future economic benefits associated with the item will flow from or to the entity.
- The item has a cost or value that can be measured reliably.

Figure 2-2: Recognition criteria

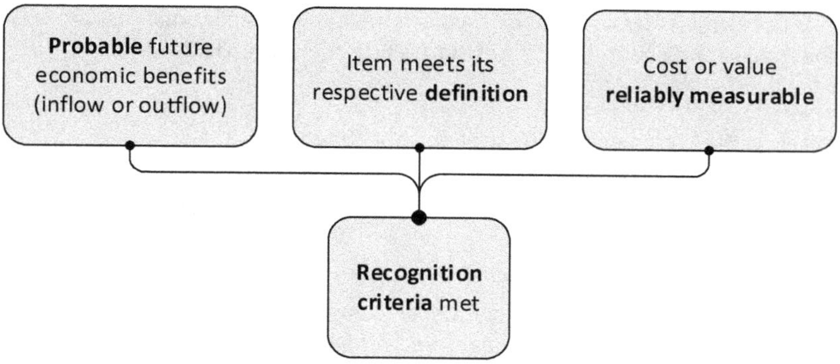

```
┌─────────────────────┐   ┌─────────────────────┐   ┌─────────────────────┐
│  Probable future    │   │   Item meets its    │   │   Cost or value     │
│ economic benefits   │   │ respective definition│   │ reliably measurable │
│ (inflow or outflow) │   │                     │   │                     │
└──────────┬──────────┘   └──────────┬──────────┘   └──────────┬──────────┘
           └──────────────────┬──────┴──────────────────────────┘
                    ┌─────────┴─────────┐
                    │   Recognition     │
                    │   criteria met    │
                    └───────────────────┘
```

The failure by an entity to recognise an item that meets the criteria cannot be rectified by inserting additional disclosures either as accounting policies, notes, or in any other form.

2.7.2   The probability of future economic benefits

The concept of **probability** refers to the degree of uncertainty associated with the future economic benefits. The degree of uncertainty is based on evidence of conditions available at the reporting date. Those assessments are made either:

- Individually for individually significant items; or
- For a group, where there is a large population of individually insignificant items.

2.7.3   Reliability

To be recognised in financial statements, an item needs to have a cost or value that can be measured reliably. The cost or value may be known, but in many cases it must be estimated. The use of reasonable estimates is an essential part of the preparation of financial statements and does not undermine their reliability. When a reasonable estimate cannot be made, no recognition takes place.

2.7.4   Failure to meet the recognition criteria

An item that fails to meet the recognition criteria at the reporting date may be recognised at a future date as a result of new circumstances or events. A failure to meet the recognition criteria at the reporting date may warrant additional disclosure when knowledge of it is relevant to the evaluation of the financial position, performance and prospects of an entity.

2.7.5   Recognition of assets

An asset is recognised in the financial statements when it is probable that the future economic benefits will flow to the entity and the asset has a cost or value that can be measured reliably. An asset is not recognised for expenditure incurred if it is unlikely that economic benefits will flow to the entity beyond the current reporting period. Such a transaction results in the recognition of an expense.

A **contingent asset** must not be recognised as an asset, as the probability of the inflow of economic benefits is not sufficient. Consequently, when the inflow of economic resources is virtually certain, the item is not a contingent asset, and is accordingly recognised.

2.7.6 Recognition of liabilities

A liability is recognised in the statement of financial position when:

- The entity has an obligation at the reporting date as a result of a past event;
- It is probable that the entity will be required to transfer resources containing economic benefits in settlement; and
- The settlement amount can be measured reliably.

A **contingent liability** is either a possible obligation or a present obligation of uncertain amount. Contingent liabilities must not be recognised as liabilities, with the exception of contingent liabilities acquired in a business combination (refer to *Chapter 6*).

2.7.7 Recognition of income

The recognition of income results directly from the recognition and measurement of assets and liabilities. Income is recognised for an increase in future economic benefits arising from an increase in an asset, or a decrease of a liability, other than contributions by owners.

2.7.8 Recognition of expenses

The recognition of expenses also results directly from the recognition and measurement of assets and liabilities. Expenses are recognised for a decrease of future economic benefits arising from a decrease in an asset or an increase of a liability, other than distributions to owners in their capacity as equity contributors.

2.8 Measurement

Measurement is the process of determining the monetary amounts at which assets, liabilities, income and expenses are stated in the financial statements. Three common measurement bases used in the Standard are historical cost, amortised cost and fair value.

2.8.1 Historical cost

Historical cost is defined for an asset as the amount of cash or cash equivalents paid or the fair value of the consideration given to acquire the asset at the time of its acquisition.

The historical cost of liabilities depends on whether there are uncertainties regarding the amount required to settle the liability, or if an amount was received that needs to be repaid. In case of uncertainties, the historical cost is the amount of cash or cash equivalents expected to be paid, or the fair value of other assets expected to be distributed, in settling the liability. When an amount was received that needs to be repaid, the historical cost is the amount of proceeds of cash or cash equivalents received, or the fair value of non-cash assets received at the time the obligation is incurred.

2.8.2 Amortised cost

Amortised historical cost is derived from historical cost. Amortised cost is the actual cash flows of an asset or liability, including initial and subsequent cash flows. It is adjusted for the time value of money by applying the effective interest rate method to arrive at the present value of cash flows.

2.8.3 Fair value

Fair value is defined as the amount for which an asset could be exchanged, or a liability settled, between knowledgeable, willing parties in an arm's length transaction. Elements of this definition are not explained further in the Standard. Under full IFRS the elements are explained as follows:

- *Knowledgeable* means that both the willing buyer and the willing seller are reasonably informed about the nature and characteristics of the asset, its actual and potential uses, and market conditions at the reporting date.
- A **willing buyer** is motivated but not compelled to buy. This buyer is neither over-eager nor determined to buy at any price. A **willing seller** is neither an over-eager nor a forced seller, prepared to sell at any price, nor one prepared to hold out for a price not considered reasonable in current market conditions. The willing seller is motivated to sell the asset at market terms for the best price obtainable.
- An **arm's length transaction** is one between parties that do not have a particular or special relationship that makes prices of transactions uncharacteristic of market conditions. The transaction is presumed to be between unrelated parties, each acting independently.

2.9 Measurement at initial recognition

At initial recognition, assets and liabilities are measured at historical cost unless the Standard requires otherwise (refer to *Table 2-2*).

2.10 Subsequent measurement

Different measurement bases are used for the subsequent measurement in the Standard. For instance, non-financial assets that are initially recognised at historical cost are subsequently measured on other measurement bases. The Standard requires such other measurement bases to ensure that an asset is not measured at an amount greater than the expected recovery from the sale or use of the asset. The different measurement bases that are applicable to different assets and liabilities are set out in *Table 2-2*:

Table 2-2: Measurement bases of assets and liabilities

Classification of asset or liability	Initial measurement	Subsequent measurement
Non-financial assets		
Inventories	Lower of cost or estimated selling price less cost to complete and sell.	Lower of cost and estimated selling price less cost to complete and sell.
Investments in associates	Transaction price (including transaction cost if subsequently measured at cost or equity method).	Cost less accumulated impairment, equity method less accumulated impairment or fair value.
Investments in joint ventures (JVs)	Transaction price (including transaction cost if subsequently measured at cost or equity method).	Cost less accumulated impairment, equity method less accumulated impairment or fair value.
Investment property	Cost.	Fair value is the default measurement basis. If, however, the fair value cannot be determined without undue cost or effort, the property is classified and accounted for as property, plant and equipment.
Property, plant and equipment	Cost.	Cost less accumulated depreciation and accumulated impairment. An option to revalue is available.
Intangible assets	Cost.	Cost less accumulated amortisation and accumulated impairment.
Goodwill	Amount calculated at original acquisition of business combination.	Cost less accumulated amortisation and accumulated impairment.
Biological assets	Fair value less cost to sell.	Fair value less cost to sell is the default measurement basis. If, however, the fair value cannot be determined without undue cost or effort the assets are accounted for at cost.
Agriculture produced harvest	Cost at harvest or slaughter (as inventories) = fair value less cost to sell.	Lower of cost and estimated selling price less cost to complete and sell.
Provisions and other non-financial liabilities	Best estimate of amount required to settle the liability.	Best estimate of amount required to settle the liability.

Table 2-2: Measurement bases of assets and liabilities *(continued)*

Classification of asset or liability	Initial measurement	Subsequent measurement
Financial assets and financial liabilities		
Basic financial instruments	Transaction price including transaction cost.	Amortised cost is the default measurement basis. However, certain basic financial instruments are measured at fair value.
Other financial instruments	Fair value.	Fair value.

2.11   Offsetting

An entity is not allowed to offset assets and liabilities, or income and expenses, unless required or permitted by the Standard. Measuring assets net of valuation allowances (provision for obsolescence stock or provisions for uncollectible receivables) is not deemed to be offsetting. Examples of items that may be offset are:

- Current tax assets and liabilities, or deferred tax assets and liabilities, when the entity has a legally enforceable right to set off the amounts and it intends either to settle on a net basis or to realise the asset and settle the liability simultaneously.
- In the statement of comprehensive income, a reimbursement amount receivable from another entity in respect of a provision may be offset against the expense created in recognising the provision.

Gains and losses on the disposal of non-current assets (including operating and investment assets) are reported net, by deducting from the proceeds on disposal the carrying amount of the asset and related selling expenses – except if an entity's normal operating activities include buying and selling such non-current assets.

2.12   Summary

- The objective of a set of accounts prepared under the Standard is to provide information on the financial position, performance and cash flows of the entity. Another objective is also stewardship.
- The following qualitative characteristics need to be met: understandability, relevance, materiality, reliability, substance over form, prudence, completeness, comparability, timeliness, and a balance between benefit and cost.
- The undue cost and effort exception depends on specific circumstances and management's judgements.
- Recognition criteria for assets, liabilities, income and expenses include the probability of a flow of economic benefits and the reliability of measurement.
- Pervasive principles include basic guidance for initial and subsequent measurements of assets, liabilities, income and expenses.
- Measurement at initial recognition is generally at historical cost except where the Standard requires fair value.

Chapter 3
Financial statement presentation

Contents

3.1   Presentation overview

The complete set of financial statements consists of the following sections:

- A statement of financial position (SFP).
- A single statement of comprehensive income, which may be separated into an income statement and a separate statement of comprehensive income (SCI).
- A statement of changes in equity (SCE).
- A statement of cash flows (SCF).
- Notes to the financial statements.

In limited circumstances, the Standard allows the statement of comprehensive income and the statement of changes of equity to be combined in a single statement of income and retained earnings (SIRE). This would be the case if the only changes to equity are profit or loss, payment of dividends, corrections of prior period errors, and changes in accounting policy.

Other titles for the principle financial statements may be used if they are not misleading.

> 👁 The Standard does not address the presentation of segment information, earnings per share or interim financial reports. When such presentations are provided, the basis on which such information has been prepared and presented should be disclosed.

3.2   Overall considerations

Seven overall considerations are provided for in the Standard and these must be observed in the preparation and presentation of financial statements and any additional related disclosure that may be required. These considerations are in addition to the qualitative characteristics provided in the chapter on Concepts and Pervasive Principles (refer to *Chapter 2*).

3.2.1   Fair presentation

The objective of financial statements, as stated in *Chapter 2*, is to present fairly the financial position, financial performance and cash flows of an entity. Fair presentation is defined as the faithful representation of the effects of transactions, other events and conditions in accordance with the definitions and recognition criteria for assets, liabilities, income and expenses in line with Concepts and Pervasive Principles (refer to *Chapter 2*).

Specifically, the application of the IFRS for SMEs is presumed to result in financial statements that achieve fair presentation if applied by an entity that has no public accountability. Additional disclosures are permitted by the Standard if the prerequisite disclosure set out in the Standard does not provide sufficient information to enable users of the financial statements to understand the effect of particular transactions, events and conditions on the entity's financial position and performance. For example, additional disclosure for discontinued operations may enhance the understandability of the financial statements. Preparers of financial statements must always consider whether additional disclosures are needed to achieve fair presentation.

3.2.2 Compliance with the Standard

An explicit and unreserved statement of compliance with the IFRS for SMEs is required in the notes. This statement may only be included in the financial statements if there is compliance with all the requirements of the Standard. Only in exceptional circumstances may an entity depart from this requirement, eg if management concludes that compliance with the IFRS for SMEs would be so misleading that it would conflict with the objective of fair presentation of the financial statements. However, it should be noted that such a departure may only be applied when it is not specifically prohibited by any regulatory framework that is relevant to the entity.

Should management arrive at the conclusion that such a departure is warranted, the entity is required to disclose the following information with a repetition of the disclosure in subsequent years if it affects the amounts recognised in those years:

- A conclusion has been arrived at that the financial statements present fairly the entity's financial position, financial performance and cash flows.
- That the financial statements comply with the IFRS for SMEs, except to the extent of the particular departure, which has been necessitated by the need to achieve fair presentation.
- The nature of the departure, including:
  - The required treatment of the Standard.
  - The reason why that treatment would be so misleading in the particular circumstances of the entity and thus conflict with the objective of achieving fair presentation.
  - A description of the treatment subsequently adopted and applied.

If the applicable regulatory framework prohibits departure, and management concludes that compliance with a requirement of the Standard would be misleading, the perceived misleading aspects of compliance are reduced by disclosing:

- The nature of the requirement of the Standard.
- The reason why management has concluded that complying with that requirement is so misleading in the circumstances that it conflicts with the objective of financial statements.
- For each period presented, the adjustments to each item in the financial statements that management has concluded would be necessary to achieve a fair presentation.

3.2.3 Going concern

Financial statements are prepared on a going concern basis and the assumption by a reader of the financial statements is that the company will continue to operate for the foreseeable future if the financial statements have not been prepared on an alternative basis.

To achieve this and thus prepare the financial statements on an appropriate basis, an assessment of an entity's ability to continue as a going concern must be made by management each time financial statements are prepared. In terms of the Standard, an entity is considered to be a going concern unless management either intends to liquidate the entity or to cease operations, or has no realistic alternative but to wind up its operations. In assessing the going concern assumption, management takes into account all available information about the future for at least 12 months from the reporting date.

Disclosure is required in respect of:

- Any material uncertainties relating to events or conditions that cast significant doubt upon the entity's ability to continue to operate as a going concern.
- If the financial statements are not prepared on a going concern basis:
  - This fact.
  - The basis on which the financial statements are prepared.
  - The reason why the entity is not considered to be a going concern.

Example 3-1: Disclosure about uncertainty of going concern

Basis of presentation

The change in the market profile of the products that the company is producing has placed doubt on the company's ability to continue to operate as a going concern. The company is investigating different options to ensure the continued sustainability of the company. The directors are of the view that there are sufficient financial resources to ensure the ability to sustain the company for the foreseeable future.

3.2.4 Frequency of reporting

A complete set of financial statements (including comparative information) is presented at least annually. When annual financial statements are presented for a longer or shorter period, the entity is required to disclose the following:

- The fact that the financial information has been prepared for a longer or shorter period.
- The reason for changing the length of the accounting period.
- The fact that comparative amounts presented are not entirely comparable.

3.2.5 Consistency of presentation

The presentation and classification of items should remain the same from one period to the next. Changes in presentation are only allowed when:

- The Standard requires a change in presentation; or
- There has been a significant change in the nature of the entity's operations or a review of its financial statements that necessitates the use of another presentation or classification deemed to be more appropriate.

Comparative amounts need to be adjusted for changes in presentation, unless the reclassification is impracticable. A situation is seen to be impracticable if the entity cannot apply it after making every reasonable effort to do so. If reclassification of comparatives is impracticable, the reasons for this are required to be disclosed in the financial statements.

When comparative amounts are reclassified, the following information is disclosed:

- Nature of the reclassification.
- Amount of each item or class of items that is reclassified.
- Reasons for the reclassification.

Example 3-2: Disclosure regarding the presentation of information

Because the company has changed its focus from the provision of services to financial services, it has decided to present assets and liabilities in the statement of financial position based on liquidity, and not a current and non-current basis. The presentation based on liquidity is considered to provide more reliable and relevant information in understanding the company's new focus. All items in the statement of financial position, except for equity, have been reclassified accordingly.

3.2.6   Comparative information

Comparative information is disclosed for all amounts presented, except when the Standard permits or requires otherwise. Comparative information for narrative and descriptive information is only provided when it is relevant to understanding the current period's financial statements.

3.2.7   Materiality and aggregation

The basic principle is that each material class of similar items must be presented separately. Therefore, items of a dissimilar nature or function are presented separately unless they are deemed to be immaterial.

The Standard specifically states that omissions or misstatements could also influence the fair presentation of financial statements. Omissions or misstatements are regarded as material when they influence the economic decisions of users. Materiality in this context depends on the size and/or nature of the omission or misstatement judged in the surrounding circumstances.

Omissions or misstatements could also influence fair presentation.

3.3   Identification of the financial statements

Financial statements must be presented with equal prominence and clearly identified from other information. For identification purposes also disclose:

- The name of the reporting entity and any change in the name.
- Whether the financial statements are individual or consolidated financial statements.
- The closing date of the reporting period.
- The period covered.
- The presentation currency.
- The level of rounding of amounts presented.

The following additional information is required in the notes:

- Domicile and legal form of the entity, its country of incorporation, and the address of its registered office (or principal place of business).
- Description of the nature of the entity's operations and its principal activities.

Illustrative disclosure 3-1: Additional disclosures

Notes to the Financial Statements for the year ended 31 December 20X2.

20. General Information

Country of incorporation and domicile	South Africa
Nature of business and principal activities	Jewellery and watch retailer
Registered office	40th Floor Jewellery Building
	1 10th Avenue
	Sandton
	South Africa
Postal address	P.O. Box 9000
	Sandton
	1000

3.4   The statement of financial position

3.4.1   The nature and information required

The statement of financial position (also known as the balance sheet) presents assets, liabilities and equity at a specific reporting date. The items in *Table 3-1* are the minimum that should be presented in the statement of financial position:

Table 3-1: Minimum presentation items

Assets
Cash and cash equivalents.
Trade and other receivables.
Financial assets.
Inventories.
Property, plant and equipment.
Investment property carried at fair value through profit or loss.
Investment property carried at cost less accumulated depreciation and impairment.
Intangible assets.
Biological assets carried at cost less accumulated depreciation and impairment.
Biological assets carried at fair value through profit or loss.
Investments in associates.
Investments in jointly controlled entities.
Current income and deferred tax assets.

Liabilities
Trade and other payables.
Financial liabilities.
Current income and deferred tax liabilities.
Provisions.

Equity
Non-controlling interest (NCI), presented separately in equity.
Equity attributable to the owners of the parent.

Note: All deferred tax balances are classified as non-current assets and liabilities in the statement of financial position.

The Standard does not prescribe the sequence or format in which items are to be presented in the statement of financial position. However, as stated before, additional line items may be included when separate presentation is relevant to an understanding of the entity's financial position. These line items may be amended based on the nature of an entity's activities and in assessing the following:

- The amounts, nature and liquidity of assets.
- The function of assets within the entity.
- The amounts, nature and timing of liabilities.

Illustrative disclosure 3-2: Statement of financial position			
Financial Statements for the year ended 31 December 20X2			
Statement of Financial Position			
Figures in Rand	Note(s)	20X2	20X1
Assets			
Non-Current Assets			
Property, plant and equipment	2	4,445,386	2,690,020
Intangible assets	3	5,333,333	5,866,666
Investments in subsidiaries	4	1,120	1,120
Investments in associates	5	677,422	612,745
		10,457,261	9,170,551
Current Assets			
Inventories	6	24,073,911	20,442,372
Loans to group companies	7	103,000	112,000
Trade and other receivables	8	2,898,559	1,648,670
Cash and cash equivalents	9	1,306,510	1,131,682
		28,381,980	23,334,724
Total Assets		38,839,241	32,505,275
Equity and Liabilities			
Equity			
Share capital	10	100	100
Retained income		17,346,868	13,004,658
		17,346,968	13,004,758
Liabilities			
Non-Current Liabilities			
Loans from shareholders	11	3,226,217	3,145,631
Other financial liabilities	12	4,093,294	3,672,284
Finance lease obligation	13	1,369,419	734,884
Operating lease liability		531,100	489,777
Deferred tax	14	665,518	508,425
		9,885,548	8,551,001

Illustrative disclosure 3-2: Statement of financial position *(continued)*			
Current Liabilities			
Other financial liabilities	12	729,137	827,920
Current tax payable		99,334	258,368
Finance lease obligation	13	567,966	126,175
Operating lease liability		233,678	141,312
Trade and other payables	15	9,439,554	9,023,051
Provisions	16	537,056	572,690
		11,606,725	**10,949,516**
Total Liabilities		**21,492,273**	**19,500,517**
Total Equity and Liabilities		**38,839,241**	**32,505,275**

3.4.2   Current/non-current distinction

Normally, a current and non-current distinction is provided for assets and liabilities in the statement of financial position. A presentation based on liquidity is optional when it provides information that is reliable and more relevant. Then all assets and liabilities are presented in order of liquidity (ascending or descending).

An asset is classified as current when it:

- Will be realised in the normal operating cycle of the entity;
- Is held primarily for the purpose of trading;
- Will be realised within 12 months after the reporting date; or
- Is cash or a cash equivalent whose realisation is not restricted for a period longer than 12 months after the reporting date.

A liability is classified as current when it:

- Will be settled in the normal operating cycle of the entity;
- Is held primarily for the purpose of trading;
- Will be settled within 12 months after the reporting date; or
- Does not have an unconditional right to defer settlement of the liability for at least 12 months after the reporting date.

All other assets and liabilities that do not meet any of these criteria are classified as non-current. When the entity's normal operating cycle is not clearly identifiable, there is a rebuttable assumption that its duration is 12 months and thus the first criteria set out under both assets and liabilities is disregarded.

Example 3-3: Normal operating cycle
Timbuktu is a construction company that builds high-rise buildings. As its business involves the construction and sale of buildings that on average take 24 months to complete, its normal operating cycle is regarded as 24 months.
All Timbuktu's assets and liabilities that are expected to be realised or settled within the normal cycle of 24 months will be classified as current.

3.4.3 Sub-classification

The Standard requires that additional information be provided, either in the statement of financial position or in the notes, relating to the sub-classifications of the line items presented:

- The different line items that make up the balance of property, plant and equipment reflected in a manner that is relevant to the entity.
- Different trade and other receivables distinguishing between trade, related parties and other.
- Inventories, distinguishing between finished goods, work-in-progress and consumables.
- Different trade and other payables, distinguishing between trade suppliers, related parties, deferred income, and accruals.
- Provisions for employee benefits and other provisions.
- Classes of equity, such as share capital, share premium, retained earnings and other reserves.

3.4.4 Share capital and reserves

The following must be disclosed for each class of share capital, either in the statement of financial position or in the notes:

- The number of shares authorised.
- The number of shares issued and fully paid, and issued but not fully paid.
- Par value per share, or that the shares have no par value.
- A reconciliation of the number of shares outstanding at the beginning and at the end of the period for the current period only (ie no comparative reconciliation needs to be disclosed).
- The rights, preferences and restrictions attached to that class, including restrictions on the distribution of dividends and the repayment of capital.
- Shares in the entity held by the entity or by its subsidiaries or associates.
- Shares reserved for issue under options and contracts for the sale of shares, including the terms and amounts.

A description of each reserve within equity must be provided.

Entities without share capital must disclose information similar to the requirements for share capital as discussed above. These disclosures must provide information about changes for all categories of equity and all rights, preferences and restrictions attached.

Example 3-4: Presentation of equity

The following presentation of the equity of a partnership will adhere to the disclosure requirements:

Capital and reserves	20X2	20X1
Partners' contributions	500,000	500,000
Reserves	250,000	250,000
Undrawn profits	65,000	125,000
	815,000	**875,000**

3.4.5   Binding sale agreements

Where an entity has entered into a binding sale agreement for the disposal of a major asset or a group of assets and liabilities, it must disclose the following information:

- Description of the asset or the group of assets and liabilities.
- Description of the facts and circumstances of the sale or plan.
- Carrying amount of the assets or, if the disposal involves a group of assets and liabilities, the carrying amounts of those assets and liabilities.

Example 3-5: Disclosure of a binding sales agreement

A binding sale agreement was concluded before the reporting date to sell the service division of the company in the following financial year. Management has decided to dispose of the service division to focus on the core activities of the company.

The service division handles the repairs, maintenance and service activities of the company's products, ie after-sales service.

The service division will be transferred on 31 July 20X1 for an amount of CU400,000. The carrying amounts of the assets and liabilities of the service division at the reporting date consist of:

Property, plant and equipment	350,000
Trade receivables	200,000
Inventories	170,000
Total assets	**820,000**
Trade payables	(580,000)

3.5   Statement of comprehensive income and income statement

The statement of comprehensive income presents the total comprehensive income for a period, which is separated into profit or loss and other comprehensive income. These statements provide information about the performance of the entity for the period. Performance is defined as the relationship of the income earned and expenses incurred during a period of time, typically one year.

Refer to the decision tree in *Figure 3-1* to help determine what performance statement to use.

Figure 3-1: Selection of performance statements – decision tree

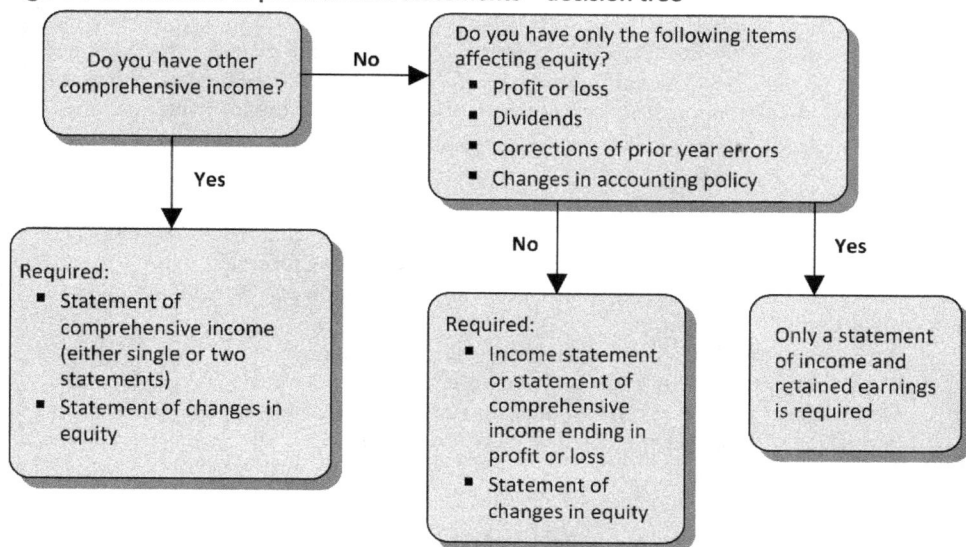

3.5.1   Presentation of total comprehensive income

Total comprehensive income may be presented in a single statement of comprehensive income, or in two statements – an income statement and a statement of comprehensive income. In a single statement, profit or loss is presented first and immediately followed by other comprehensive income. In the two-statement approach, the income statement presents all items of income and expense up to profit or loss, and the statement of comprehensive income presents the other comprehensive income items. A change from the one approach to the other is regarded as a change in accounting policy (refer to *Chapter 7*).

> ! Other comprehensive income are items of income and expense that are not permitted or required to be recognised through profit or loss. The Standard allows for the recognition of items in other comprehensive income only in the following instances:
>
> - Changes in fair values of certain hedging instruments.
> - Actuarial gains and losses.
> - Where another section of IFRS for SMEs requires a gain or loss on a non-monetary item to be recognised in other comprehensive income, the related exchange difference must also be recognised in other comprehensive income.
> - Foreign currency translation differences on the translation of a foreign operation to the presentation currency.
> - Where an entity elects to revalue its property, plant and equipment.
> - If an entity chooses to select *IAS 39 – Financial Instruments – Recognition and Measurement* as its accounting policy for financial instruments, movements in the fair values of available for sale and cash flow hedges will be recognised in other comprehensive income.

The Standard requires that items of other comprehensive income be split into those that will be reclassified subsequently to profit and loss, and those that will not. It is important to remember that not all items reported in other comprehensive income will eventually be included in profit and loss. The Standard only allows the amounts relating to hedging (and available for sale financial assets where IAS 39 is adopted) to be reclassified when the relevant transaction impacts profit or loss (or the available for sale financial asset is sold under IAS 39).

Example 3-6: Other comprehensive income

Tamarin Group has a 31 December year-end. The group has to account for the following items in its statement of comprehensive income:

- **The group has a foreign subsidiary. The FCTR movements for the FCTR are as follows:**
  - 20X1: (CU50,000)
  - 20X2: (CU75,000)
- **The group has a defined benefit pension fund. The group accounts for all actuarial gains and losses through equity. The movements are as follows:**
  - 20X1: CU125,000
  - 20X2: CU350,000
- **The group applies hedge accounting for its fixed rate loan. Tamarin has taken out an interest rate swap, which has been designated as a cash flow hedge in its accounts. The movements on the interest rate swap are as follows:**
  - 20X1: CU85,000
  - 20X2: CU35,000

Example 3-6: Other comprehensive income *(continued)*

For each of the above years, the following amounts were reclassified as the interest was recognised:
- 20X1: CU15,000
- 20X2: CU5,000

- **Tamarin has a 25% associate investment in Ebene Ltd. For the 20X1 and 20X2 years, the following items appeared in Ebene's statement of comprehensive income:**
  - 20X1: Revaluation of equipment CU100,000
  - 20X2: Revaluation of equipment CU200,000

Required
Prepare the statement of comprehensive income for the 20X1 and 20X2 years.

Solution

Statement of comprehensive income	20X2	20X1
Profit or loss		
Revenue	XXX	XXX
Interest (including hedge reclassification)	5,000	15,000
Profit or loss	**XXX**	**XXX**

Other comprehensive income	20X2	20X1
OCI not reclassified		
FCTR	(75,000)	(50,000)
Changes in defined benefit fund	350,000	125,000
Share of associate: Revaluation of equipment	50,000	25,000
OCI to be reclassified		
Effective portion of derivative in cash flow hedge	35,000	85,000
Less: amount reclassified	*(5,000)*	*(15,000)*
Total other comprehensive income	**XXX**	**XXX**

The following line items are presented in the statement of comprehensive income irrespective of whether a single-statement or two-statement approach is followed:

- In profit or loss:
  - Revenue.
  - Finance costs.
  - Share of the profit or loss of investments in associates and jointly controlled entities accounted for using the equity method.
  - Tax expense excluding tax allocated to discontinued operations and items disclosed in other comprehensive income.
  - A single amount for discontinued operations totalling the post-tax profit or loss of the discontinued operations, and the post-tax gain or loss attributable to an impairment, or reversal of an impairment, of the assets in the discontinued operation, both at the

time and subsequent to being classified as a discontinued operation, and to the disposal of the net assets of the discontinued operations (see *3.5.2* below).
  - The profit or loss amount determined.
- In other comprehensive income:
  - Each item of other comprehensive income classified by nature and grouped into items that will be reclassified to profit or loss, and those that will not.
  - Share of the other comprehensive income of associates and jointly controlled entities accounted for by the equity method.
  - Total comprehensive income.
- Profit or loss and total comprehensive income are further allocated between:
  - Non-controlling interest.
  - Owners of the parent.

If no items of other comprehensive income exist for the period the single statement of comprehensive income may end with profit or loss. Additional lines, headings and sub-totals may also be added if such presentation is relevant to an understanding of the entity's financial performance. However, no income and expenses are allowed to be described as *extraordinary items*.

3.5.2 Discontinued operations

The Standard defines a discontinued operation as a component of an entity that either has been disposed of, or is held for sale, and which meets either one or more of the following criteria:
- It represents a separate major line of business or geographical area of operation.
- It is part of a single co-ordinated plan to dispose of a separate major line of business or geographical area of operation.
- It is a subsidiary acquired exclusively with a view to re-sell.

On the face of its statement of comprehensive income or statement of income and retained earnings, the entity must present the amount comprising the:

Total of the post-tax profit or loss of a discontinued operation.

Post-tax gain or loss attributable to an impairment, or reversal of an impairment, of the assets in the discontinued operation, both at the time and subsequent to being classified as a discontinued operation, and to the disposal of the net assets of the discontinued operations (refer to *Figure 3-2*).

Figure 3-2: Separate presentation of discontinued operations

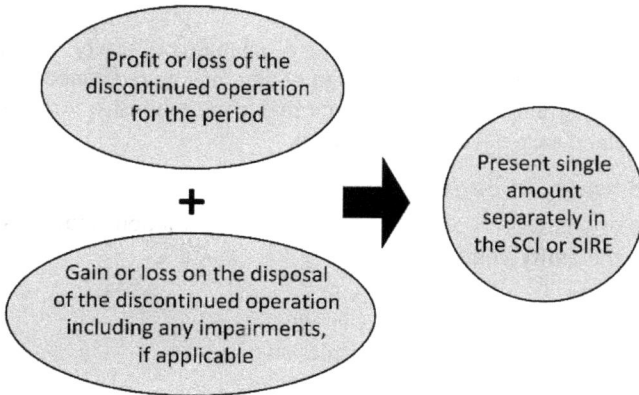

3.5.3   Analysis of expense

Expenses are analysed based on either the nature or the function of expenses, whichever provides information that is reliable and more relevant. Nature identifies specific expenses such as depreciation, materials acquired, transport costs, employee benefits and advertising costs, while function aggregates expenses in totals such as cost of sales, marketing or administrative expenses. Under the function method, the amount of the cost of sales incurred should be disclosed separately from other expenses at a minimum.

The method chosen should be disclosed as an accounting policy choice.

Example 3-7: Nature or function of expenses			
Statements of comprehensive income or income statement classified by function or nature are as follows:			

Classified by function		Classified by nature	
Revenue	10,000,000	Revenue	10,000,000
Cost of sales	(5,500,000)	Other income	250,000
Gross profit	4,500,000	Changes in inventories	(650,000)
		Raw material and	
Other income	250,000	consumables used	(4,100,000)
Distribution costs	(150,000)	Employee benefit expenses	(3,300,000)
Administrative expenses	(3,000,000)	Depreciation and amortisation	(600,000)
Other expenses	(120,000)	Other expenses	(120,000)
		Profit before taxation and	
Finance costs	(275,000)	finance costs	1,480,000
Profit before tax	1,205,000	Finance costs	(275,000)
		Profit before tax	1,205,000

3.6   Statement of changes in equity and statement of income and retained earnings

Effects of changes in equity are presented in the statement of changes in equity, but if certain conditions are met, profit or loss and other changes in equity may be combined in a statement of income and retained earnings. If an entity has other comprehensive income, the statement of income and retained earnings may not be used.

3.6.1   Statement of changes in equity

The purpose of the statement of changes in equity is to present information about the effects of the following items on the entity's equity:

- Profit or loss for a reporting period.
- Other items of income and expense recognised directly in equity.
- The impact of changes in accounting policies and the correction of errors.
- The amounts of investments by owners in their capacity as owners
- Dividends and other distributions to owners in their capacity as owners.

The following information is presented in the statement of changes in equity:

- Total comprehensive income for the period, with a distinction made between the amounts attributable to the holding company and to non-controlling interests.
- The effects of retrospective application of changes in accounting policy or errors.
- A reconciliation of the carrying amount of each component of equity and specifically for:
  - Profit or loss.
  - Each item of other comprehensive income.
  - The amounts of investments by investors.
  - Dividends and other distributions to owners in their capacity as owners.

The following should also be shown separately in the statement of changes in equity, if applicable:

- Amounts attributable to parents and non-controlling interest.
- Issues of shares.
- Treasury share transactions.
- Dividends and other distributions to owners.
- Changes in ownership interests in subsidiaries that do not result in a loss of control.

3.6.2   Statement of income and retained earnings

The statement of income and retained earnings combines an entity's profit or loss and changes in retained earnings for a reporting period. The combined statement may be used if the only changes to equity during the period arise from:

- Profit or loss.
- Payment of dividends.
- Corrections of prior period errors.
- Changes in accounting policy.

> 🛈 If the entity does not have any other comprehensive income, or any changes to equity other than retained earnings, it may present a statement of income and retained earnings.

The following is presented in the statement of income and retained earnings, in addition to the information required in the income statement:

- Retained earnings at the beginning of the reporting period.
- Dividends declared and paid or payable during the period.
- Re-statements of retained earnings for corrections of prior period errors and changes in accounting policy.
- Retained earnings at the reporting date.

Example 3-8: Statement of retained income and retained earnings

In the statement of retained income and retained earnings the following is provided at the bottom of the income statement after profit or loss for the period:

	20X2	20X1
Profit for the year	1,200,000	900,000
Retained earnings at start of year	400,000	200,000
Dividends	(1,500,000)	(700,000)
Retained earnings at end of year	**100,000**	**400,000**

3.7 Statement of cash flows

The statement of cash flows provides information about the changes in cash and cash equivalents for a reporting period by showing separately changes from operating activities, investing activities and financing activities. Since detailed guidance is provided on how these different activities are identified and presented, the statement of cash flows is discussed separately in the next chapter (refer to *Chapter 4*).

3.8 Notes

The purpose of the notes is to provide additional information, narrative descriptions or disaggregation of items presented in the principal financial statements, and information about transactions or events not recognised. The notes are presented in a systematic manner and should be cross-referenced to any related information in the rest of the financial statements. The order of the notes is not prescribed and may be presented as follows:

- A statement that the financial statements have been prepared in compliance with the IFRS for SMEs.
- Information about the basis of preparation of the financial statements.
- A sequential representation of information supporting items presented in the primary financial statements.

- Any other disclosures that are deemed appropriate and relevant to facilitating an understanding of the financial statements of the entity.

> ☝ Any additional information relevant to the understanding of the entity's financial statements needs to be disclosed.

3.8.1 Disclosure of accounting policies

In the accounting policies, the measurement basis (or bases) used in preparing the financial statements and other accounting policies that are relevant to an understanding of the financial statements are disclosed.

3.8.2 Information about judgements

Any judgements management has made in the process of applying the accounting policies (that have a significant effect on the amounts recognised in the financial statements) must be disclosed in the accounting policies, or elsewhere in the notes.

Example 3-9: Disclosure in accounting policies – Estimates and assumptions

Estimates and assumptions about future positions are used in the preparation of financial information. The estimates are based on the use of available information and the application of judgements. The areas where significant judgments are applied are the impairment of intangible assets and the measurement of provisions. Judgement is also required in determining whether arrangements contain leases and the classification of such leases as either operating or financing.

3.8.3 Information about key sources of estimation uncertainty

Information about the key assumptions concerning the future and other key sources of estimation uncertainty must be disclosed. These are uncertainties that have a significant risk of causing a material adjustment to the carrying amounts of assets and liabilities. The nature and the carrying amount at the reporting date need to be disclosed.

Example 3-10: Disclosure in accounting policies – Estimation uncertainty

Information about key assumptions concerning the future and other key sources of estimation uncertainty are disclosed in the notes to the financial statements, where applicable. These include discount rates, the best estimate of the outcome of a pending lawsuit, and the useful lives and residual values of property, plant and equipment.

Note: This disclosure in the accounting policies is often combined with the previous disclosure regarding estimations (refer to Example 3-8).

3.9 Summary

- To describe a set of financial statements as compliant with the IFRS for SMEs, all the requirements of the Standard must be complied with.
- Financial statements must be presented at least annually, be consistent with prior years, include comparative prior-year information, and include all material items.
  - A complete set of financial statements includes a statement of financial position;
  - Either:

- A single statement of comprehensive income; or
- A separate income statement and separate statement of comprehensive income.
- A statement of changes in equity;
- A statement of cash flows; and
- Notes to the financial statements.

- A combined statement of income and retained earnings can replace the statement of comprehensive income and statement of changes in equity if the only movements in equity for the period relate to profit or loss, dividends, errors and changes in accounting policy.

Chapter 4
Statement of cash flows

Contents

4.1   Nature of the statement of cash flows

Changes in cash flows for a period are presented in the statement of cash flows to provide an overview of the impact of the activities of an entity on its cash resources. These activities are presented as operating, investing, and financing activities. The movement in cash and cash equivalents from the beginning to the end of the period is reconciled by reflecting the cash impact of these activities.

4.2   Definitions and clarifications of definitions

4.2.1   Cash equivalents

Cash equivalents are defined as short-term, highly liquid investments that are readily convertible to known amounts of cash, and that are subject to an insignificant risk of changes in value. Cash investments are included in cash and cash equivalents when they are both:

- Held for short-term cash commitments and not for investment or other purposes.
- Have a short maturity. The term *short*, as used in this context, is a period of three months or less.

Although bank overdrafts are normally regarded as financing activities, similar to borrowings, they may be included in cash and cash equivalents if they are repayable on demand and form an integral part of an entity's cash management.

4.2.2   Operating activities

Operating activities are the entity's principal revenue-producing activities. Assets that are held for dealing and trading purposes are classified as operating activities. Examples of cash flows from operating activities are:

- Cash receipts from normal revenue activities – the sale of goods and rendering of services.
- Cash payments to suppliers, excluding purchases of capital assets.
- Cash payments to and on behalf of employees.
- Cash payments or refunds from income tax.
- Cash payments on financial instruments for dealing or trading purposes, including most derivatives.

Although in principle, cash flows from operating activities generally result from transactions and other events and conditions that are included in the determination of profit or loss, certain items included in profit or loss are not operating activities. Gains and losses on investment and financing activities, such as profit or loss on sale of plant and investments, are not classified as operating activities.

4.2.3   Investing activities

Investing activities are defined as activities undertaken in the acquisition and disposal of long-term assets and other investments that do not meet the definition of cash equivalents. This classification normally incorporates all cash flows arising from non-current assets.

The Standard provides the following examples of cash flows from investing activities:

- Cash payments to acquire property, plant and equipment, intangible assets, and other long-term assets.
- Cash receipts from the sale of property, plant and equipment, intangibles, and other long-term assets.
- Cash payments to acquire investments in equity or debt instruments, and investments in JVs.
- Cash receipts from sales of such equity or debt instruments.
- Cash advances and loans made to third parties and the re-payments of such advances and loans.
- Cash payments and receipts relating to certain derivative contracts.

Remember if any of the items in the list are classified as cash equivalents or held for dealing or trading they cannot be classified as investment activities. The cash flows from derivative contracts accounted for as hedges are classified in a manner similar to the nature of the cash flows of the underlying hedged item.

4.2.4   Financing activities

Financing activities are defined as activities that result in a change in the size and composition of the contributed equity and borrowings of an entity. This classification normally encompasses all cash flows that result from movement in all long-term debt and equity accounts of the entity. The Standard provides the following examples of cash flows from financing activities:

- Cash proceeds from share capital issued.
- Cash payments to re-purchase or redeem share capital.
- Cash proceeds from long-term debt instruments issued and other short- or long-term borrowings.
- Cash repayments of amounts borrowed.
- Cash repayments of finance leases.

4.3   Reporting cash flows from operating activities

Cash flows from operating activities are presented using either the indirect or the direct method.

The Standard does not prefer one cash flow presentation method over another.

4.3.1   Indirect method

The indirect method adjusts profit or loss to establish the net cash from operating activities. The method starts with the profit or loss amount recognised for the period and then adjusts it for the effects of:

- Non-cash transactions (such as depreciation), unrealised foreign currency gains and losses, changes in provisions, movements in deferred taxes, non-controlling interests, and the undistributed profits of associate entities.

- Changes in the balances of any deferrals or accruals of operating cash receipts or payments (inventories, receivables and payables).
- All other items of income or expense that relate to investing or financing activities.

Example 4-1: Indirect method of presenting cash flows from operating activities	
Here is an example of the indirect method of presenting the operating activities in the statement of cash flows:	
Cash flows from operating activities	
Profit for the year	795,000
Non-cash finance costs	(45,000)
Non-cash taxation	(65,000)
Adjustments:	
Non-cash item – Depreciation	1,200,000
Non-cash item – Impairment of investment	80,000
Cash generated from operations	**1,965,000**
Movement in working capital:	
Change in inventories	495,000
Change in debtors	(300,000)
Change in creditors	(150,000)
Dividends paid	(2,000,000)
Net movement in working capital	**(1,955,000)**
Cash retained from operating activities	**10,000**

4.3.2 Direct method

The direct method focuses on cash transactions, and not the adjustment of profit or loss. Major classes of gross cash receipts and gross cash payments are disclosed. The information may be obtained directly from the accounting records or by adjusting line items in the statement of comprehensive income such as sales, cost of sales and other items for the same adjustments as under the indirect method. Line items are therefore also adjusted for:

- Movements between the opening and closing balances of inventories, receivables and payables.
- Other non-cash items.
- All other items of income or expenses that relate to investing or financing activities.

Example 4-2: Direct method of presenting cash flows from operating activities

Here is an example of the direct method of presenting the operating activities in the statement of cash flows:

Cash flows from operating activities	
Cash receipts from customers	8,700,000
Cash paid to suppliers and employees	(6,635,000)
Cash generated from operations	**2,065,000**
Taxation	(65,000)
Finance costs	(45,000)
Finance income	-
Other income	55,000
Dividends paid	(2,000,000)
Other operating cash flows	**(2,055,000)**
Cash retained from operating activities	**10,000**

4.4 Reporting cash flows from investing and financing activities

Major classes of gross cash receipts and gross cash payments arising from investing and financing activities are presented separately. Specifically, the aggregate cash flows arising from the acquisition of and the disposal of subsidiaries or other business units are presented separately, and classified as investing activities. The acquisition and disposal of such businesses are regarded as the sale of an asset structure and thus are not specifically allocated to the various classifications that they may intuitively belong to, eg the inclusion of borrowings held by the business unit being disposed of are not included in the movement of financing activities of the group.

👁 The Standard does not specifically address how cash flows from such acquisitions and disposals should be calculated and disclosed. *Example 4-3* illustrates a possible method of accounting and presenting an acquisition of a subsidiary.

Example 4-3: Acquisition of a subsidiary

Barcelona purchases 100% of the share capital of Zurich on 30 June 20X1. The consideration was CU4,500,000 and the transaction was financed through a long-term loan. No cash was acquired as part of the business combination.

The financial manager has asked for your opinion on the classification of the cash flows in the statement of cash flows.

Required
Present the transaction in the statement of cash flows.

Suggested solution
Extract from Barcelona's statement of cash flows, assuming no other investing or financing cash flows for the year, and that Zurich holds no cash or cash equivalents.

Cash flows from investing activities	
Investment in subsidiary	(4,500,000)
Cash expended on investing activities	**(4,500,000)**
Cash flows from financing activities	
Financing of acquisition of subsidiary	4,500,000
Cash expended on investing activities	**4,500,000**

4.5 Foreign currency cash flows

Foreign currency cash flows are recorded in an entity's functional currency by applying the exchange rates at the dates of the respective cash flows to the foreign currency amount. The functional currency is the currency of the primary economic environment in which the entity operates as defined in *Chapter 25*. The same principle applies to the translation of the cash flows of foreign subsidiaries.

All cash and cash equivalents held in foreign currency are translated at reporting date exchange rates. Unrealised gains and losses arising from such translation are not cash flows. However, to reconcile cash and cash equivalents at the beginning and the end of the period, the effect of exchange rate changes on foreign cash and cash equivalents needs to be presented in the statement of cash flows. Such unrealised gains or losses must be presented separately from cash flows arising from the operating, investing, and financing activities of the group.

Cash and cash equivalents held in foreign currency are translated at reporting date exchange rates, with the resulting unrealised exchange gains and losses not accounted for as cash flows.

4.5.1 Presentation and disclosure

Such unrealised gains or losses must be presented separately from cash flows arising from the operating, investing, and financing activities of the group.

Example 4-4: Cash and cash equivalents held in foreign currency	
Unrealised exchange difference on cash and cash equivalents are presented as follows in the statement of cash flows:	
Net increase in cash and cash equivalents	32,445
Cash and cash equivalents at beginning of period	24,688
Unrealised gain on transfer of foreign cash equivalents	1,677
Cash and cash equivalents at end of period	**58,810**

4.6 Interest and dividends paid and received

Cash flows from interest and dividends received and paid are presented separately. These items must be consistently classified from one period to the next. *Figure 4-1* may be used as a guide in the classification of such cash flows in the statement of cash flows.

Figure 4-1: Classification of dividends and interest received and paid

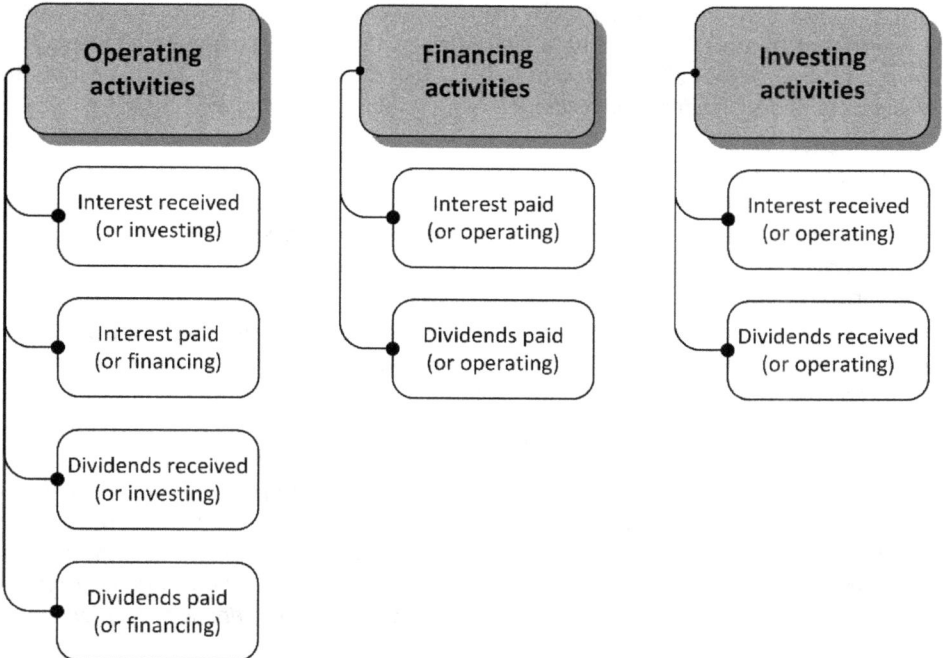

Interest paid and received may be classified as operating activities, as they are presented in profit or loss. The entity also has the option to present the same items as financing or investing activities respectively, as it can be argued that they arise as a result of having sourced funds to finance the entity, or are a return on investments made by the entity. Neither classification would be seen to be incorrect provided that there is consistency of application from one period to the next.

Dividends paid and received may be classified as operating activities because they are paid out of operating cash flows. The entity also has the option to present the same items as financing or investing activities respectively, as it can be argued that they arise as a result of having sourced funds to finance the entity, or are a return on investments made by the entity.

The classification chosen should be applied consistently from one period to the next.

4.7   Income tax

Cash flows arising from income tax are presented separately and classified as cash flows from operating activities unless they can be specifically identified with financing and investing activities. If tax cash flows are allocated over more than one activity, the total amount of tax cash flows should be disclosed in a note.

4.8   Non-cash transactions

Non-cash transactions are excluded from the statement of cash flows. Non-cash financing and investment transactions must be disclosed elsewhere in the financial statements in a manner that ensures that all the relevant information about their nature and impact on the financial statements is understood. Examples of non-cash transactions are:

- Impairment of an asset.
- Imputed interest on a financial instrument.
- Fair value adjustment of a financial instrument or investment property.
- Acquisition of assets through finance leases or other debt arrangements.
- Acquisition of a business funded by the issuing of shares.
- Conversion of debt to equity.

Although these items do not have a direct impact on current cash flows, they affect the capital and asset structure of an entity. Therefore disclosure of changes in these non-cash items is required, but is excluded from the disclosures made in the statement of cash flows.

4.9   Components of cash and cash equivalents

All components of cash and cash equivalents that are presented on the face of or in the notes to the statement of cash flows should be reconciled to the amounts that are reflected in the statement of financial position. *Note: This reconciliation is only required if the amount of cash and cash equivalents presented in the statement of cash flows differs from the amount of cash and cash equivalents on the face of the statement of financial position.*

4.10   Other disclosures

The amount of significant cash and cash equivalent balances that are held by the entity, but are not available for its use, is required to be disclosed. Such disclosure is required to be accompanied by a write-up from management explaining the restriction in access to these funds. In some instances, an entity may hold interests in a business that is encumbered by foreign exchange controls or legal restrictions, and as such, may not be able to access the cash resources held in such a business.

4.11   Summary

- Cash flows must be split into operating, investing, and financing activities.
- Operating activities may be presented using either the direct or indirect approach.

Chapter 5
Consolidated and separate financial statements

Contents

5.1 Scope

This chapter provides guidance on when and how **individual** and **consolidated financial statements** should be prepared with related disclosure. Guidance on the preparation of **separate financial statements** and **combined financial statements** is also provided. Individual or consolidated financial statements are required, while separate and combined financial statements are optional (refer to *Figure 5-1*).

Parent companies must prepare consolidated financial statements.

Figure 5-1: Mandatory and optional financial statements

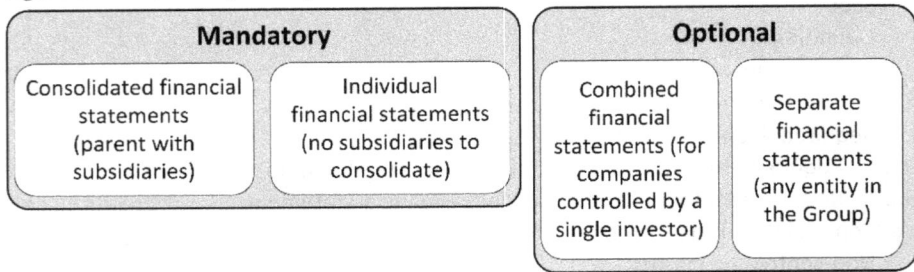

Mandatory		Optional	
Consolidated financial statements (parent with subsidiaries)	Individual financial statements (no subsidiaries to consolidate)	Combined financial statements (for companies controlled by a single investor)	Separate financial statements (any entity in the Group)

5.2 Definitions

5.2.1 Subsidiary and control

A subsidiary is defined as an entity that is controlled by the parent and includes an unincorporated entity such as a partnership. *Control* is the power to govern the financial and operating policies of an entity so as to obtain benefits from its activities.

Control could be established through ownership (voting power), 'auto-pilot' or other indirect influence.

Control could be established through ownership (shareholding) or through special purpose entities (SPEs). A SPE is set up to accomplish a narrow and well-defined objective, and is consolidated when the substance of the relationship between the entity and the SPE indicates that entity controls the SPE. Refer to *5.2.2* for further guidance regarding the consolidation of special purpose entities. The indicators of control are set out in *Figure 5-2*.

Figure 5-2: Sources of control

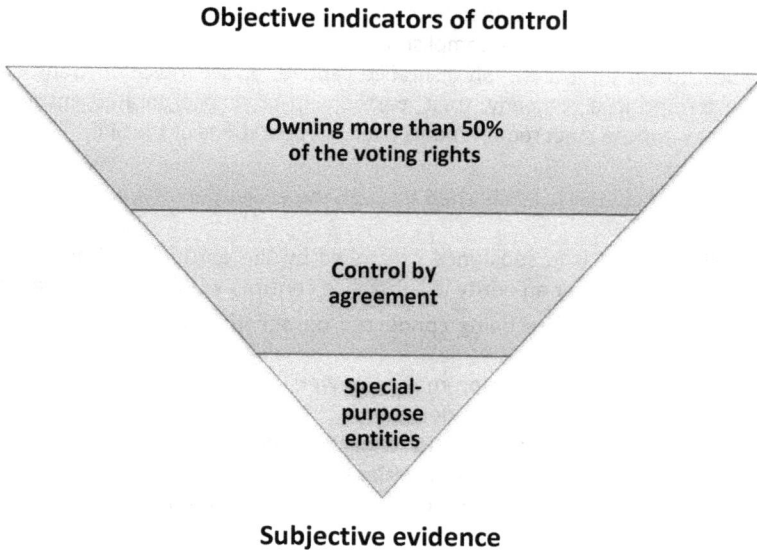

Objective indicators of control

Owning more than 50%
of the voting rights

Control by
agreement

Special-
purpose
entities

Subjective evidence

Based on ownership, control is presumed to exist when the parent owns, either directly or indirectly through subsidiaries, more than half of the voting power of an entity. This presumption may only be rebutted in exceptional circumstances when it can be clearly demonstrated that a shareholding of more than 50% of the voting power does not constitute control.

Besides ownership, control also exists when the parent holds half or less of the voting power of an entity but control is established through any one of the following:

- Power over more than half of the voting rights through an agreement with other investors.
- Power to govern the financial and operating policies through a statute or an agreement.
- Power to appoint or remove the majority of the members of the board of directors or equivalent governing body where control is situated in that board or body.
- Power to cast the majority of votes at meetings of the board of directors or equivalent governing body where control is situated in that board or body.

The Standard further states that control can also be achieved by having options or convertible instruments that are currently exercisable or by having an agent with the ability to direct the activities for the benefit of the controlling entity. The entity should consider whether currently exercisable options or convertible instruments, which when added to existing voting rights will give the entity more than 50% of the voting rights, constitutes control. Control based on the evaluation of options, convertible instruments and the involvement of agents could be very subjective, therefore all facts should be considered to establish control in such circumstances.

5.2.2   Special purpose entities (SPEs)

No specific definition of a SPE is provided in the Standard. However, the Standard explains that such an entity may be created to accomplish a narrow objective (for instance to undertake certain activities, to set up a lease, an insurance captive, or securitisation transaction). The entity may be formed in a company, trust, partnership or unincorporated entity. The legal arrangements may impose strict requirements over the operations of the SPE.

> The substance of control is established through the evaluation of indicators.

A SPE is consolidated if it is in substance controlled by the entity. The Standard identifies indicators to evaluate whether an entity in substance controls a SPE. These indicators are:

- The activities of the SPE are being conducted on behalf of the entity according to its specific business needs.
- The entity has the ultimate decision-making powers over the activities of the SPE even if the day-to-day decisions have been delegated.
- The entity has rights to obtain the majority of the benefits of the SPE and therefore may be exposed to risks incidental to the activities of the SPE.
- The entity retains the majority of the residual or ownership risks related to the SPE or its assets.

The above indicators are only broad indicators that are not discussed further in the Standard. All facts need to be considered to determine whether these indicators are applicable in any circumstances. Under full IFRS, SPEs were addressed in SIC 12 Consolidation – Special Purpose Entities. This interpretation has subsequently been withdrawn from full IFRS with the issuance of IFRS 10, Consolidated Financial Statements. The guidance in the IFRS for SMEs standard is, however, drawn from this interpretation, which further explained these indicators. The crux of the additional guidance in SIC 12 is:

- Normally the controlling entity is involved in setting up the SPE for its specific business needs.
- The evaluation of the decision-making powers is based on substance, ie whether in substance, the reporting entity has the decision-making power to control or to obtain control of the SPE or its assets. Such decision-making powers may be determined up-front, through 'autopilot mechanism' or come into existence after the SPE's formation.
- The rights to benefits could be obtained through a statute, contract, agreement, trust deed or any other means. Normally, the rights to benefits should be specified in favour of the controlling entity.
- The risk indicator is evaluated by considering the risks of all entities involved. Normally, the entity that retains the majority of the residual or ownership risks are regarded as controlling the SPE.

The indicators for identifying SPEs are applicable were control could not be established through voting powers or other powers. The focus is on how the SPE is set up, who benefits from the SPE, and who ultimately retains the residual or ownership risk. These indicators are sometimes referred to as *risk and reward* indicators that are applied when the normal principles to establish control are not applicable.

The consolidation principles relating to SPEs are specifically not applicable to post-employment benefit plans or other long-term employee benefit plans (refer to *Chapter 20*).

5.3   Required financial statements

5.3.1   Requirement to present individual financial statements

Individual financial statements are required for entities without any subsidiaries *(Figure 5-3)*, or where all the subsidiaries are acquired with the intention of selling or disposing of them within one year. In the individual financial statements, any investments in associates and jointly controlled entities are accounted for on the basis of including the reported results of the investees. Any entity may also elect to present separate financial statements (refer to *5.11.1*).

Figure 5-3: Individual financial statements

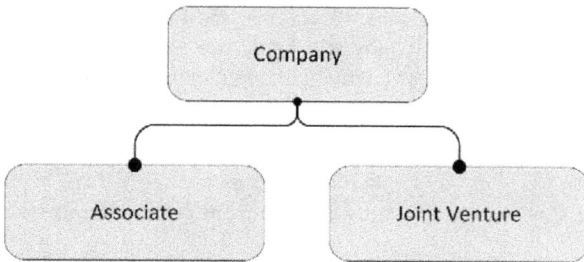

5.3.2   Requirement to present consolidated financial statements

In terms of the Standard, consolidated financial statements must be prepared when a **parent has one or more subsidiaries** *(Figure 5-4)*. In the consolidated financial statements, any investments in subsidiaries are accounted for on the basis of including the reported results and net assets of the investees. It may also elect to present separate financial statements (refer to *5.11.1*).

Figure 5-4: Consolidated financial statements

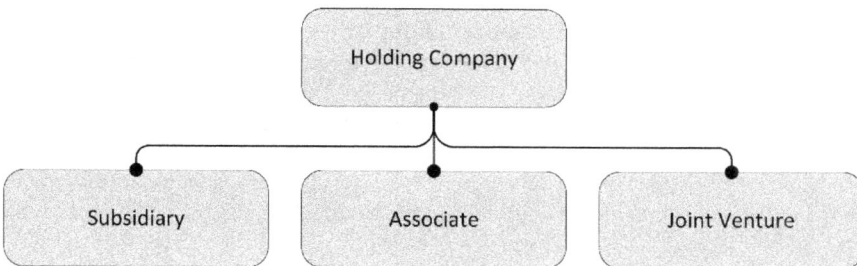

> ！ There are certain exemptions from the requirement to present consolidated financial statements exist.

A parent would be **exempt** from preparing consolidated financial statements when the parent itself is a subsidiary and any of its parents (ultimate or intermediate) produces consolidated financial statements that comply with full IFRS or the Standard.

The Standard also provides an **exemption** from consolidating a subsidiary when the parent holds a subsidiary that was acquired with the intention of selling or disposing of it within one year from the acquisition date (ie the date on which the parent obtained control of the subsidiary). Such a subsidiary is recorded in the financial statements at fair value, or otherwise at cost less impairment (see *Chapter 17* for guidance on accounting for financial instruments). Where a subsidiary was previously excluded from consolidation under this exemption, and it was not disposed of within a year of its acquisition, the parent must consolidate the subsidiary from its original acquisition date. If this was in the prior year, then the parent will be required to restate its comparative financial statements to reflect the acquisition in the prior year. If the delay in disposing of the subsidiary under this exemption was as a result of events or circumstances beyond the parent's control, and the parent is still committed to disposing of the subsidiary, the parent may still apply the exemption from consolidation for that subsidiary. Note that the parent would need to demonstrate that there is sufficient evidence to support its assertion that it still intends to sell the subsidiary.

If a parent only has subsidiaries that are exempt from consolidation, it does not prepare consolidated financial statements.

The Standard specifically clarifies that subsidiaries are not excluded from consolidation for any of the following reasons:

- The investor is a venture capital organisation or similar entity.
- The business activities of the subsidiary are dissimilar.
- The jurisdiction the subsidiary operates in imposes restrictions on transferring cash or other assets.

5.4   Consolidation procedures

The purpose of consolidated financial statements is to present financial information about the group as a single economic entity. Therefore, in the consolidation process:

- The assets, liabilities, equity, income and expenses of the parent and subsidiary are combined on a line by line basis, and this information is obtained from the separate financial statements or other sources. The income and expenses of subsidiaries are included in the consolidated financial statements from the date of acquisition until the date on which the parent ceases to control the subsidiary.
- The carrying amount of the parent's investment in each subsidiary is eliminated against the parent's portion of the equity of each subsidiary. Goodwill is recognised as explained in *Chapter 6*.
- Non-controlling interest is recognised separately (refer to *5.5*).

- The effect of any change in the holding of a subsidiary and related non-controlling interest during the year is also adjusted (refer to *5.9*).

> ♪ Consolidation is the process of combining, eliminating and establishing the non-controlling interest.

In the consolidation process the following must also be considered and adjusted:
- Unrealised profits or losses and intercompany transactions (refer to *5.6*).
- Any additional depreciation or amortisation due to the accounting of the fair values of the assets and liabilities of the subsidiary at the date of acquisition, and the calculation of goodwill on the acquisition of a subsidiary (refer to *Chapter 6*).
- Adjustments for different accounting policies (refer to *5.8*).
- Adjustments for significant transactions where the reporting dates are different (refer to *5.7*).

5.5   Non-controlling interest

Non-controlling interest (also known as minority interest) is defined as the equity in a subsidiary not attributable, directly or indirectly, to a parent. Therefore, non-controlling interest is presented in equity, separate for the equity of the owners of the parent.

> ♪ Non-controlling interest is a separate classification in equity. Non-controlling interest is also known as minority interest.

Non-controlling interests in the net assets of any subsidiary consist of the amount of the non-controlling interests at the date of acquisition plus the non-controlling interest's share of changes in equity (profit or loss and other comprehensive income) since the date of acquisition, adjusted for any changes in the non-controlling interest holding.

The balance of non-controlling interest at the reporting date is calculated as follows:
- Obtain the non-controlling interest share of the assets and liabilities of each subsidiary at acquisition. These amounts are included in the elimination of the parent's investment on consolidation. A calculation must be done for all new acquisitions during the period and the amount for previous acquisitions is obtained from the previous years' working papers.
- Obtain the non-controlling interest in the profit or loss and other comprehensive income since acquisition to the beginning of the year, from the previous years' working papers.
- Determine the non-controlling interest in the profit or loss and other comprehensive income for the year.
- Any other change in the non-controlling interest, such as increases or decreases in the relative holding, must also be adjusted.

Example 5-1: Non-controlling interest

Los Angeles purchases a 60% interest in Seattle. On the date of acquisition, the carrying value of the net assets of Seattle was CU5.4 million and the fair value of the net assets was CU7.4 million.

The non-controlling interest in the consolidated financial statements at the date of acquisition of a subsidiary is the non-controlling shareholders' share of the fair value of the net assets, ie CU2.96 million (40% of CU7.4 million).

The non-controlling interest's share in the net assets and liabilities of a subsidiary is determined based on existing ownership interests. Possible exercise of options or conversion of options or convertible instruments is specifically excluded from this determination.

Example 5-2: Potential voting rights

Bangkok has a 60% interest in Mumbai. Bangkok also has an exercisable option to acquire another 10% interest in Mumbai. The exercisable options of 10% are ignored to determine the non-controlling interest in the consolidated financial statements. The non-controlling interest is thus 40%.

Any change in the non-controlling interest of a subsidiary that does not result in the loss of control of a subsidiary is an equity transaction, the result of which will be presented in the statement of changes in equity.

Example 5-3: Sale of shares without loss of control

Riyadh has an 80% interest in Dubai. At the reporting date, Riyadh sold a 20% interest in Dubai for CU2 million, thus reducing its interest to 60%. At the date of sale, the carrying amount of the investment in Dubai in Riyadh's separate accounting records amounted to CU4 million. The consolidated carrying value of the 80% interest in Dubai amounted to CU6.4 million. The CU2.4 million difference in the carrying amount consists of Riyadh's share of the post-acquisition profits of Dubai recognised in the consolidated financial statements (of which CU2 million represents Dubai's profits recognised up until the beginning of the current period and CU400,000 the current period's profits until the date of sale).

Required

Determine the profit on the sale of the 20% interest in both Riyadh's separate and consolidated financial statements. Provide the journals to record the sale transaction in the consolidated financial statements. Ignore any tax effect.

Suggested solution

The profit on the sale of the 20% interest in the subsidiary in the **separate financial statements** of Riyadh is:

Selling price	2,000,000
Carrying amount of direct equity investment in subsidiary	1,000,000
(20% / 80% x CU4 million)	
Profit on the sale of shares in a subsidiary	**1 ,000,000**

Example 5-3: Sale of shares without loss of control *(continued)*		
The profit on the sale of the 20% interest in the subsidiary in the **consolidated financial statements** is:		
Selling price		2,000,000
Carrying amount of consolidated investment in subsidiary		1,600,000
(20% / 80% x CU6.4 million)		
Consolidated profit on the sale of a subsidiary		**400,000**
The journals in the consolidated financial statements:		
Dr Profit on sale of investment (Parent - SCI)	1,000,000	
Dr Investment in subsidiary (Parent - SCI)	1,000,000	
Cr Profit on sale to non-controlling interest (Group - equity)		400,000
Cr Acquisition by non-controlling interest (Group - equity)		1,600,000
Sale of interest to non-controlling shareholders.		
Since the parent only holds 60% of the subsidiary at the reporting date, the non-controlling interest will be consolidated at 60% at the reporting date.		

The Standard does not establish any limitation on the recognition of debit balances of non-controlling interest when the non-controlling interest in the share of losses of a subsidiary exceeds its investments. The Standard only states that non-controlling interests may create a deficit. However, any restrictions on the allocation of losses to non-controlling interest created through a specific contract or agreement should be considered.

5.6 Intra-group transactions and balances

The following principles are established for all intra-group transactions and balances:

- All income, expenses and dividend transactions are reversed in full.
- All unrealised profits are eliminated.
- Intercompany balances are eliminated in full.

In the elimination of these transactions, the related income tax effect and the effect on non-controlling interest must be considered. Any intra-group losses in assets that are eliminated may indicate that the related asset might be impaired and that an impairment loss be recognised in the consolidated financial statements.

Example 5-4: Intra-group transactions

During the year, Lagos, a wholly owned subsidiary, sold inventories to its parent, Nairobi, at a profit mark-up of 25%. 50% of the inventories are still on hand in Nairobi's records, at the reporting date. The total amount of such sales for the year: CU5 million. Ignore taxation.

The elimination journals in the consolidated financial statements:

Dr	Revenue (Subsidiary - SCI)	5,000,000	
Cr	Cost of sales (Parent - SCI)		5,000,000

Elimination of the intercompany sales.

Dr	Cost of sales (Subsidiary - SCI)	500,000	
Cr	Inventories (Parent - SFP)		500,000

Elimination of unrealised intercompany profit included in the closing inventories.
(CU2,500,00 x 25 / 125)

5.7   Uniform reporting date

Reporting dates should be uniform for the consolidation of the financial statements of the parent and its subsidiaries unless it is impracticable to do so. It would be regarded as impracticable when an entity cannot apply the requirement after making every reasonable effort to do so. In a situation where there are different reporting dates, the parent should consolidate the subsidiary using the most recent financial statements of the subsidiary. These should then be adjusted for the effects of any significant transitions or events that have occurred between the date the subsidiary's financial statements were prepared, and the date of the consolidated financial statements.

5.8   Uniform accounting policies

Uniform accounting policies are used for the consolidation of similar transactions and events. If the accounting policies adopted by any member of a group differ from the consolidated accounting policy financial statements, the Standard states that appropriate adjustments are to be made to the financial statements. Preferably, the adjustments will be made to the financial statements before they are included in the consolidation working papers.

5.9   Disposal of subsidiaries

A subsidiary is disposed of when control is lost. Any change in a parent's interest in a subsidiary that does not result in a loss of control, is a transaction with non-controlling shareholders and the effect should be presented in the statement of changes in equity.

5.9.1   Calculation of profit or loss on disposal

Profit or loss on disposal is included in profit or loss.

On disposal of a subsidiary, the profit or loss on disposal is calculated and recorded in profit or loss. The consolidated profit or loss on the disposal of a subsidiary is the difference between the proceeds from the disposal of the subsidiary and the consolidated carrying amount at the date of disposal. The consolidated carrying amount of the subsidiary is:

- The original acquisition cost (ie the cost of the investment) plus the parent's share of profit or loss of the subsidiary included in the consolidated financial statements since acquisition (excluding the cumulative amount of exchange differences that relate to a foreign subsidiary recognised in equity as required by the section dealing with foreign currency translation differences – refer to *Chapter 25*).

The above calculation of the profit or loss on disposal should specifically exclude the effect of any foreign currency translation reserve (FCTR) recognised in equity. Therefore, any balance in the FCTR on the date of sale should not be included in the calculation of profit or loss.

In the calculation of the profit or loss on disposal of a subsidiary, the parent's share of the profit or loss of the subsidiary should include any adjustments to the subsidiary's profit or loss in the consolidated financial statements. These adjustments represent:

- Any unrealised profits or losses, and income and expense on intergroup transaction recognised in the financial statements of the subsidiary since acquisition.
- Any additional depreciation or amortisation of the assets and liabilities of the subsidiary recognised since acquisition due to the determination of the fair value of assets and liabilities on the date of acquisition and the calculation of goodwill.

5.9.2   Investment retained

Any interest retained after the disposal of a subsidiary is regarded as a financial asset provided it does not become an associate or a jointly controlled entity. The classification of the remaining interest as a financial asset depends on the normal classification of a financial asset (refer to *Chapter 17*). The cost of the financial instrument, associate or jointly controlled entity retained on the date of sale of the subsidiary is the carrying amount of the investment in the subsidiary at the date of the disposal. However, the carrying amount of the investment in the parent's separate financial statements will differ from the consolidated financial statements.

In the parent's separate financial statements, the carrying amount of the investment will be the proportionate share of the original consideration. However, in the consolidated financial statements, the deemed cost of the investment will include the proportionate share of the income and expenses of the subsidiary included in the consolidated financial statements since the date of the acquisition.

Therefore, the deemed carrying value of the parent's share of the subsidiary calculated above needs to be allocated between the portion sold and retained to create the value of the investment retained. The new financial asset, associate or jointly controlled entity will thus not be recognised at its fair value on date of sale of the subsidiary, although the investment could be carried subsequently at fair value depending on how it is classified as a financial instrument.

Example 5-5: Disposal of subsidiary

Windhoek has an 80% interest in Lusaka. At the reporting date, Windhoek sold a 40% interest in Lusaka for CU3.6 million thus reducing its interest to 40%. At the date of sale, the 80% investment amounted to CU4 million in the separate financial statements of Windhoek, and the consolidated value of the 80% interest amounted to CU6.4 million (ie including post-acquisition profits). The CU2.4 million difference between the investment cost and carrying amount in the group financial statements consists of CU2 million profit of Lusaka recognised in the consolidated financial statements until the beginning of the current year and CU400,000 of the current year's profits.

Required

Determine the profit on the sale of the subsidiary in both the separate and consolidated financial statements. Provide the journals to record the sale of the subsidiary in the consolidated financial statements. Ignore any tax effect.

Suggested solution

The profit on the sale of the subsidiary in the separate financial statements of Windhoek is:

Selling price	3,600,000
Carrying amount of direct equity investment in subsidiary	2,000,000
(40% / 80% x CU4 million)	
Profit on the sale of a subsidiary	**1,600,000**

The profit on the sale of the subsidiary in the Windhoek group's **consolidated financial statement** is:

Selling price	3,600,000
Carrying amount of consolidated investment in subsidiary	3,200,000
(40% / 80% x CU6.4 million)	
Profit on the sale of a subsidiary	**400,000**

Note: Since the subsidiary is sold it will not be consolidated and its assets and liabilities will not be included in the consolidated financial statements at the reporting date. That is why the profit of the subsidiary is included in the opening retained earnings (only the parent's share) and for the year until the date of sale (gross less non-controlling interest). 50% of such profits are capitalised as part of the 40% investment in the associate retained.

Example 5-5: Disposal of subsidiary *(continued)*

The journals in the consolidated financial statements:

Dr	Profit on sale of investment (Parent - SCI)	1,600,000	
Cr	Profit on sale of subsidiary (Group - SCI)		400,000
Cr	Accumulated profits beginning of the year (Group - equity)		2,000,000
Cr	Profit for the year (Group - SCI) *(100%/80% x CU400,000)*		500,000
Dr	Non-controlling interest (Group - SCI) *(20% x CU500,000)*	100,000	
Dr	Investment in associate (Parent - SCI) *(40% x CU2.4 million)*	1,200,000	

Sale of subsidiary and recognise post-acquisition profits not sold in the carrying amount of the investment in associate.

5.10 Disclosure

The following disclosure is required in consolidated financial statements:

- The fact that the statements are consolidated statements.
- The basis for establishing control when control is not established by more than half of the voting power.
- Any difference in the reporting date of the financial statements of the parent and its subsidiaries.
- The nature and extent of any significant restrictions on the ability of subsidiaries to transfer funds to the parent in the form of cash dividends or to repay loans.

Where a parent has not consolidated a subsidiary under the exemption in 5.3.2 above, the subsidiary is accounted for as a financial instrument, and the parent should apply the disclosures applicable to financial instruments (see *Chapter 17*). In addition to these disclosures, the parent shall disclose the carrying amount of such investments in subsidiaries not consolidated in total on the face of the Statement of Financial Position or in the notes.

5.11 Optional financial statements

5.11.1 Separate financial statements

5.11.1.1 Basic requirement

The basic requirement of the Standard is that a parent should prepare consolidated financial statements and an entity with no subsidiaries should prepare individual financial statements. The presentation of separate financial statements for the parent entity or any subsidiary is not required. Separate financial statements are a second set of accounts prepared in addition to any of the following:

- Consolidated financial statements prepared by a parent.
- Financial statements prepared by a parent exempted from preparing consolidated financial statements (see *5.3.2* above).

- Financial statements prepared by an entity that is not a parent but is an investor in an associate or has a venturer's interest in a joint venture.

Note: A parent entity who does not have public accountability may elect to present separate financial statements under this Standard, even if it presents consolidated financial statements under full IFRS, or any other GAAP. For example, a parent who has a listed subsidiary (and therefore would have public accountability on consolidation of the subsidiary) may not apply this Standard and would need to prepare group accounts in accordance with full IFRS. However, the parent's separate accounts could be prepared under this Standard.

5.11.1.2   Definition

Separate financial statements are defined as financial statements presented by a parent, an investor in an associate or a venturer in a jointly controlled entity, in which the investments are accounted for on the basis of the direct equity interest rather than on the basis including the reported results and net assets of the investees. Investors in associates and JVs could therefore also prepare separate financial statements in addition to their individual financial statements.

If separate financial statements are prepared, the following accounting policy election and disclosure must be observed.

5.11.1.3   Accounting policy election

In separate financial statements, investments in subsidiaries, associates, and jointly controlled entities are recorded as either:

- Cost less impairment;
- Fair value with changes in fair value recognised in profit or loss; or
- Using the equity method (refer to *Chapter 9* for details on applying the equity method).

> Accounting policy choice must be made separately for all subsidiaries, associates and jointly controlled entities.

The same accounting policy is applied for all investments in a single class (subsidiaries, associates or jointly controlled entities). For example, all investments in subsidiaries may be accounted for at cost, while all investments in associates may be measured at fair value.

5.11.1.4   Disclosure

The following additional disclosure is required in separate financial statements:

- The fact that the statements are separate financial statements.
- The accounting policy to account for the investments in subsidiaries, jointly controlled entities and associates.
- A reference to the consolidated financial statements or other primary financial statements to which the separate financial statements relate.

5.11.2   Combined financial statements

5.11.2.1   Basic principle

Combined financial statements are a single set of financial statements of two or more entities under common control. The Standard defines common control in the business combinations section (see *Chapter 6*) as a transaction where all of the combining entities or businesses are ultimately controlled by the same party, both before and after the business combination, and that control is not transitory. In *Figure 5-5*, Parent (P) controls A, B and C, and any of A, B or C may be combined. This Standard does not require combined financial statements to be prepared, but when an entity prepares combined financial statements and describes them as conforming to the Standard, those statements must comply with all of the requirements.

Figure 5-5: Combined AFS

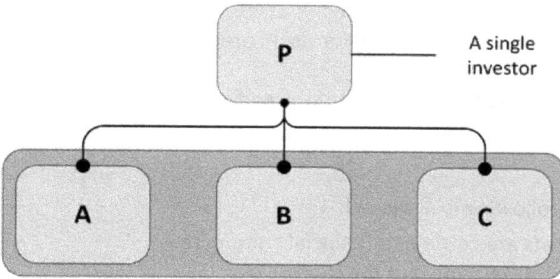

> In combined financial statements share capital of entities may be added together.

Combined financial statements are not necessarily a consolidation. When combined financial statements are provided, all the assets, liabilities, income, expenditure and other comprehensive income, **as well as equity**, of the combined entities are **added together**. This is because the equity is not eliminated against an investment.

Example 5-6: Combined financial statements

Two subsidiaries, namely Rio de Janeiro and Brasília, of the same ultimate parent (ie under common control) are presented in a set of combined financial statements. The abridged information of each subsidiary at 31 December 20X2 are:

	Rio de Janeiro	Brazilia
Assets	4,000,000	3,500,000
Liabilities	3,000,000	2,000,000
Equity	1,000,000	1,500,000

You may assume no inter-subsidiary balances, investments or transactions.

Required

Prepare the abbreviated combined statement of financial position of the two subsidiaries.

Example 5-6: Combined financial statements *(continued)*

Suggested solution

Rio de Janeiro and Brazilia
Combined Statement of Financial Position
at 31 December 20X2

Assets (4 million + 3.5 million)	7,500,000
Liabilities (3 million + 2 million)	5,000,000
Equity (1 million + 1.5 million)	2,500,000
	7,500,000

When combined financial statements are prepared, the following procedures should be applied:

- Intercompany transactions and balances are eliminated.
- Profits or losses on intercompany transactions recognised in assets are eliminated.
- The financial statements included in the combination are prepared on the same reporting date unless it is impracticable to do so.
- Uniform accounting policies are followed for like transactions and other events in similar circumstances.

5.11.2.2   Disclosure

In combined financial statements, the following is disclosed:

- The fact that the financial statements are combined financial statements.
- The reason why combined financial statements are prepared.
- The basis for determining which entities are included in the combined financial statements.
- The basis of preparation of the combined financial statements.
- Normal related party disclosures.

5.12   Summary

- If control exists, a parent company should present consolidated financial statements – control exists when a parent is able to govern the financial and operating policies of an entity. It also requires the consolidation of special purpose entities.
- Any subsidiary acquired with the intention of selling or disposing of it within one year of the acquisition date is excluded from consolidation.
- An intermediate parent need not prepare consolidated financial statements if it is a subsidiary of a group where the ultimate parent produces consolidated financial statements under full IFRS or the Standard.
- For consolidated accounts, normal consolidation rules apply.
- In a parent's separate financial statements, it may account for subsidiaries, associates and JVs that are not held for sale using either cost, fair value through profit or loss, or the equity method.

Chapter 6
Business combinations and goodwill

Contents

6.1   Scope

The guidance applies to all business combinations except:

- Combinations of entities or businesses under common control.
- Formations of a JV.
- Acquisitions of a group of assets that do not constitute a business.

In the Standard, **common control** means that all of the combining entities or businesses are ultimately controlled by the same party or parties, both before and after the business combination, and that control is not transitory. The transfer of a business from one subsidiary to another subsidiary in the same group is a common control transaction. If such a transaction occurs an appropriate accounting policy, if needed, should be developed since the IFRS for SMEs does not provide guidance.

> Full IFRS also provides no guidance regarding business combinations between entities under common control. We recommend that in such a case the accounting treatment follows the contractual arrangement, and complies with the guidance in this chapter as far as possible. The accounting treatment will have to be developed by management based on its best judgement (refer to *Chapter 7*) as to what treatment will result in an accounting policy that achieves relevant and reliable information, and is consistent with the concepts and pervasive principles, and definitions of elements (refer to *Chapter 2*).

6.2   Definitions

A business combination is identified by analysing the definition of a business combination. In the Standard, a **business combination** is defined as the bringing together of separate entities or businesses into one reporting entity. An entity is not defined in the Standard but must normally be created through a formal structure.

A **business** is defined as an integrated set of activities and assets conducted and managed for the purpose of:

- Providing a return to investors; or
- Lowering costs or achieving economic benefits directly and proportionately to shareholders, policyholders or participants.

6.3   Identification of a business combination

Specifically, the Standard presumed that any transferred set of activities that included goodwill, is a business. The Standard clarifies the set of activities included in a business (as set out in *Figure 6-1*) by stating that a business generally consists of inputs, processes applied to those inputs, and resulting outputs that are being used, or capable of being used, to generate revenues or other returns. Therefore, businesses are usually conducted to generate revenue, but in some instances, there may be other objectives such as administrative services.

Figure 6-1: Set of activities included in a business

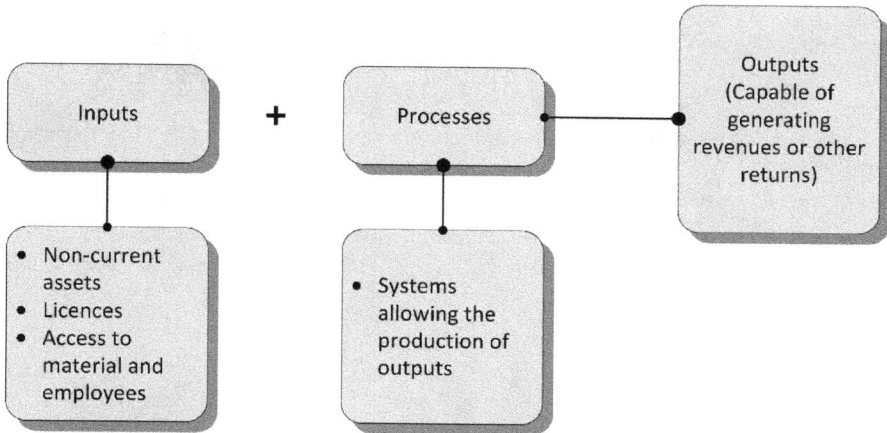

A business combination may be effected directly or indirectly, and structured in a variety of ways for legal, taxation or other reasons. A business combination may be effected directly or indirectly. An **indirect business combination** is achieved through the acquisition of shares or other types of equity in another business, thereby obtaining control of the acquired entity. A **direct business combination** is the purchase of the net assets of another entity, the assumption of the liabilities of another entity, or the purchase of some of the net assets of another entity that represents a business.

If a business is acquired **directly** the accounting for business combinations is applied in the **acquiring entity's** records. Where a business is acquired **indirectly** the accounting for the business combination is only applied in the preparation of the **consolidated financial statements**.

Example 6-1: Direct or indirect purchase of a business

New York is considering acquiring the business of another company, Washington. New York can either buy the assets and liabilities directly or indirectly by purchasing Washington's shares and obtaining control. On the date of purchase, the assets and liabilities of Washington consist of:

	Carrying value	Fair value
Non-current assets	3,800,000	4,300,000
Current assets	2,600,000	2,900,000
Long-term loans	(1,600,000)	(1,600,000)
Current liabilities	(2,100,000)	(2,100,000)
Net value	**2,700,000**	**3,500,000**

The purchase price for Washington is CU4,200,000. If the assets and liabilities are purchased directly you may assume that the revenue authorities will accept the fair value as the purchase price of the acquired assets and liabilities. On the date of purchase, the net equity of Washington consisted of:

Example 6-1: Direct or indirect purchase of a business *(continued)*

Share capital	1,500,000
Retained earnings	1,200,000
	2,700,000

Required

Calculate the amount of goodwill and then determine the journal entries for the following scenarios:

(a) When the assets and liabilities are purchased directly.

(b) The purchase of 100% of the shares of Washington in the consolidated financial statements.

Ignore deferred tax implications.

Suggested solution

Calculation of goodwill:

Purchase price	4,200,000
Fair value of net assets of Washington	3,500,000
Goodwill for direct acquisition	700,000

Direct acquisition (journals in the records of the acquiring company)

Dr	Non-current assets (SFP)	4,300,000	
Dr	Current assets (SFP)	2,900,000	
Dr	Goodwill (SFP)	700,000	
Cr	Long-term loans (SFP)		1,600,000
Cr	Current liabilities (SFP)		2,100,000
Cr	Creditor or cash (purchase price) (SFP)		4,200,000

Direct acquisition of a business.

Under a direct acquisition the assets and liabilities are recognised at fair value in the records of the investor, and the difference between the purchase price and the fair value of the net assets is goodwill.

Indirect acquisition (eliminating journal in the consolidated financial statements)

Dr	Share capital (SFP)	1,500,000	
Dr	Retained earnings (Equity)	1,200,000	
Dr	Non-current assets (SFP)	500,000	
	(4,300,000 - 3,800,000)		
Dr	Current assets (SFP)	300,000	
	(2,900,000 - 2,600,000)		
Dr	Goodwill (SFP)	700,000	
Cr	Investment in subsidiary (SFP)		4,200,000

Eliminating journal entry.

Under an indirect acquisition, goodwill is only reflected in the consolidated financial statements.

6.4 Accounting for business combinations

In a business combination, one entity (the acquirer) obtains control of one or more businesses from another entity (the acquiree). A business combination could also be achieved by creating a new entity to control the combining entities or net assets transferred, or by restructuring one or more of the existing entities that are combined.

Accounting is through the purchase method.

All business combinations are accounted for by applying the purchase method. Application of the purchase method starts from the acquisition date, which is the date on which the acquirer obtains control of the acquiree. In assessing the date on which the acquirer obtains control, all pertinent facts and circumstances surrounding a business combination are considered. Specifically, it is not necessary for a transaction to be closed or finalised at law before the acquirer obtains control.

Applying the purchase method involves the steps identified in *Figure 6-2*:

Figure 6-2: Steps of the purchase method

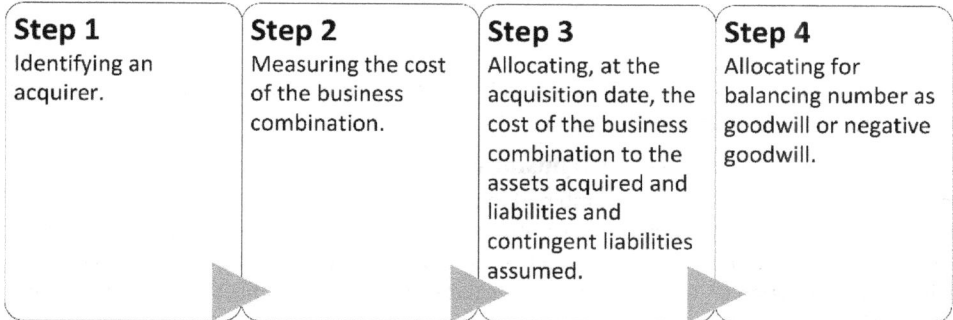

Step 1	Step 2	Step 3	Step 4
Identifying an acquirer.	Measuring the cost of the business combination.	Allocating, at the acquisition date, the cost of the business combination to the assets acquired and liabilities and contingent liabilities assumed.	Allocating for balancing number as goodwill or negative goodwill.

6.4.1 Step 1: Identifying the acquirer

An acquirer must be identified for all business combinations. The acquirer is the entity that obtains control of the other entities or businesses. Control is defined as the power to govern the financial and operating policies of an entity or business so as to obtain benefits from its activities.

The acquirer is the entity that obtains control.

In a direct acquisition of the net assets of another entity, the acquirer is normally apparent. However, if the acquisition is through the indirect method (acquisition of shareholding) it might be more difficult to identify the acquirer. Such an acquisition could be established between the shareholders of two combining entities or between one entity and the shareholders of another entity. The Standard provides the following examples of indicators to identify the acquirer:

- The entity with the greater fair value.
- The entity giving up cash or other assets in exchange for shares.
- The entity whose management is able to dominate the selection of the management team of the combined entity.

These indicators must be applied in conjunction with all the relevant facts and the discussion of the definition of control in *Chapter* 5.

6.4.2   Step 2: Measuring the cost of a business combination

6.4.2.1   Determination of the cost of a business combination

The cost of a business combination is determined at the date of acquisition and is defined as the aggregate of:

- The fair value of assets given by the acquirer, liabilities incurred or assumed by the acquirer, and equity instruments issued by the acquirer, in exchange for control of the acquiree (the consideration).
- Any costs directly attributable to the business combination.

> The cost of a business combination is the purchase consideration plus direct acquisition costs.

The fair value of the consideration needs to be determined on the date of acquisition. The date of acquisition is not defined in the Standard.

6.4.2.2   Uncertainty – cost of a business combination

An adjustment to the cost of the combination contingent on future events may be included in the business combination agreement. An example is an acquisition where the purchase price is linked to future levels of profits, also known as an earn-out. The acquirer must estimate the amount of the contingent consideration as part of the cost of the business combination at the acquisition date, provided the adjustment is probable and can be measured reliably.

When the contingency is not probable or cannot be measured reliably at the acquisition date, it is not included in the cost of a business combination. When a previously uncertain contingent consideration becomes probable and can be measured it is recognised as an adjustment to the cost of the combination, and will affect goodwill **even 12 months after of the acquisition date**.

Example 6-2: Contingent consideration

The purchase price of Paris is contingent on future events. On the date of acquisition the purchase price was estimated to be CU5.6 million, excluding the contingency since it could not be measured reliably. Two years later, the contingent event occurs and the final purchase price is determined to be CU5.8 million.

Required

Provide the journal entry to adjust the purchase price two years after acquisition in the records of the acquirer.

Suggested solution

Journals

Dr	Goodwill (SFP)	200,000	
Cr	Creditor/Bank (SFP)		200,000

Note: The adjustment is created against goodwill since the cost of the business combination is adjusted.

6.4.3 Step 3: Recognition of assets, liabilities and contingent liabilities

Only the identifiable assets of the acquiree, as well as the liabilities and contingent liabilities of the acquiree assumed in terms of the business combination agreement, are recognised as part of the business combination on the date of acquisition. Such identifiable assets, liabilities and contingent liabilities are recognised at fair value, with the exception of deferred tax and employee benefits (refer to *6.4.3.2*), when the applicable recognition criteria are met.

6.4.3.1 Recognition criteria

The recognition criteria for identifiable assets and liabilities (illustrated in *Figure 6-3*) are as follows:

- **Assets other than intangible assets** when it is both:
  - Probable that the assets future economic benefits will flow to the acquirer.
  - The fair value of the assets can be measured reliably.
- **Liabilities other than contingent liabilities** when it is both:
  - Probable that an outflow of resources will be required to settle the obligation.
  - The fair value of the liability can be measured reliably.
- **Intangible assets** when it is both:
  - Probable that future economic benefits will flow to the acquirer.
  - Possible to determine its fair value without undue cost or effort.
- **Contingent liabilities** when:
  - The fair value can be measured reliably.

Figure 6-3: Applicable recognition criteria

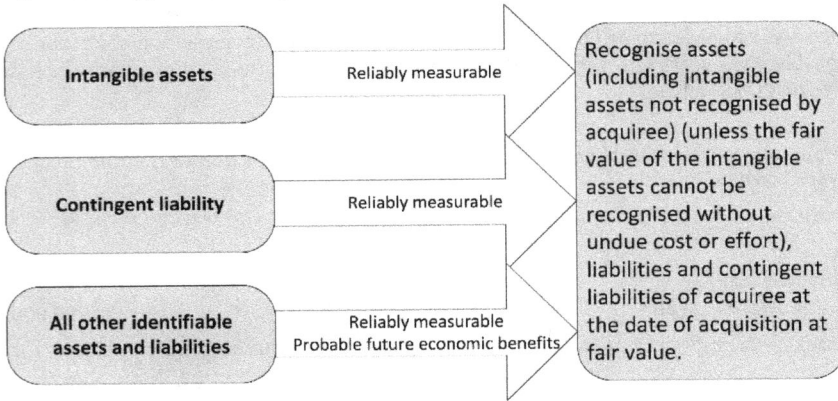

The reliably measurable recognition criterion is applicable to all assets (except intangible assets) and liabilities, but the probable recognition criterion is presumed for intangible assets and contingent liabilities. The following additional guidance is also provided relating to the recognition of identifiable assets and liabilities:

- Assets and liabilities acquired that do not meet the recognition criteria are not recognised on the date of acquisition and are therefore included in the determination of goodwill.
- Liabilities for terminating or reducing the activities of the acquiree are only recognised as part of identifiable assets when the acquiree has, at the acquisition date, an existing liability for restructuring.
- Liabilities for future losses or other costs expected to be incurred as a result of the business combination are specifically not recognised as part of the cost of the combination.

Table 6-1 provides the examples of intangible assets in *IFRS 3 – Business Combinations* that may be recognised as part of identifiable assets acquired in a business combination. Certain of these intangible assets may not have been recognised by the acquiree.

Table 6-1: Identifiable intangible assets

Nature	Examples
Market-related	<ul><li>Trademarks, trade names, service marks, and collective marks</li><li>Trade dress</li><li>Newspaper mastheads</li><li>Internet domain names</li><li>Non-competition agreements</li></ul>
Customer-related	<ul><li>Customer lists</li><li>Order or production backlog</li><li>Customer contracts and related customer relationships</li><li>Non-contractual customer relationships</li></ul>

Table 6-1: Identifiable intangible assets *(continued)*

Nature	Examples
Technology-based	▪ Patented technology ▪ Computer software and mask works ▪ Unpatented technology ▪ Databases, including title plants ▪ Trade secrets, such as secret formulas, processes, and recipes

6.4.3.2   Measurement of identifiable assets or liabilities

The identifiable assets, liabilities and contingent liabilities that satisfy the recognition criteria are recognised at their respective fair values with the exception of:

▪ Deferred tax assets and liabilities acquired in a business combination, which are measured in accordance with measurement principles of Income Tax (refer to *21.4.6*).
▪ An acquiree's employee benefits liability, which is measured in accordance with the requirements of Employee Benefits in *Chapter 20*).

The recognised identifiable assets, liabilities and contingent liabilities represent the net value of the assets, liabilities and contingent liabilities obtained.

6.4.3.3   Uncertainty – fair values of assets, liabilities and contingent liabilities

All other adjustments regarding contingencies (such as adjustments to the provisional amounts, which were determined as the respective values of identified assets, liabilities and contingent liabilities, and accordingly originally recognised) must be regarded as adjustments to the initial accounting (ie only applicable to a period of 12 months after the acquisition date) and treated as discussed in *6.6*.

6.4.4   Step 4: Goodwill and negative goodwill

Goodwill (refer to *Figure 6-4*) is recognised as **an asset in the consolidated financial statements** for an indirect acquisition or in the acquirer's own financial statements for a direct acquisition if the cost of the business combination exceeds the acquirer's share of the net fair value of the identifiable assets, liabilities and contingent liabilities of the acquiree (refer to *6.4.4.1*).

If the acquirer's share of the net fair value of the identifiable assets, liabilities and contingent liabilities of the acquiree exceeds the cost of the business combination, the difference is **recognised in profit or loss as negative goodwill** (refer to *6.4.4.2*).

Figure 6-4: Calculation of goodwill

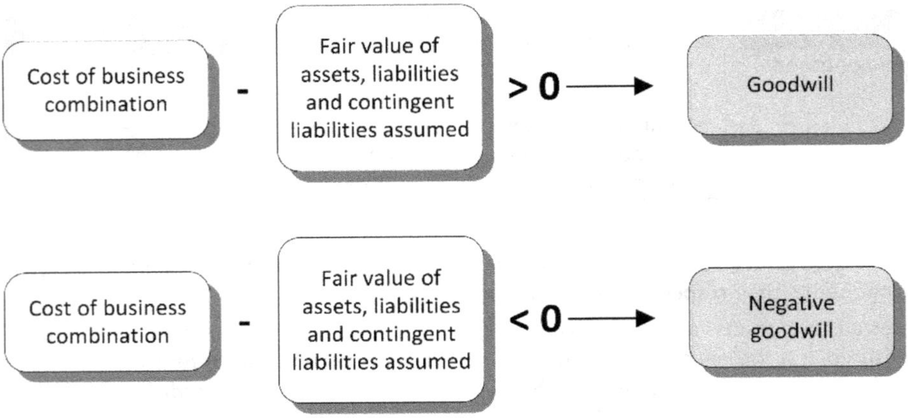

6.4.4.1 Goodwill

6.4.4.1.1 Initial recognition

Goodwill acquired in a business combination is recognised as an asset in the consolidated financial statements and initially measured at cost.

The cost of goodwill is the excess of the cost of the business combination over the acquirer's interest in the net fair value of identifiable assets, liabilities and contingent liabilities, as well as unrecognised intangible assets (refer to *Example 6-1*).

6.4.4.1.2 Subsequent recognition

After initial recognition, goodwill is measured at cost less accumulated amortisation and accumulated impairment losses. The normal principles for the amortisation of other intangible assets are applicable to goodwill (refer to *Chapter 13*). However, if a reliable estimate of the useful life of goodwill cannot be established, the useful life shall be determined using management's best estimate limited to a maximum of 10 years. Impairment is based on the impairment principles included in *Chapter 14*.

6.4.4.2 Negative goodwill

Negative goodwill, also known as a gain on a bargain purchase, occurs when the acquirer's interest in the net fair value of the identifiable assets, liabilities and contingent liabilities recognised exceeds the cost of the business combination (refer to *Example 6-3*). In such a case, the acquirer must apply the following two steps:

- The acquirer must re-assess the identification and measurement of the identifiable net assets included in the cost of the combination.
- If negative goodwill is confirmed, the excess is recognised immediately in profit or loss.

Negative goodwill is recognised in profit or loss.

Example 6-3: Negative goodwill

Lisbon acquired a subsidiary, Barcelona, for CU2.4 million. On the date of purchase, the assets and liabilities of Barcelona consisted of:

	Carrying amount	Fair value
Non-current assets	2,800,000	3,200,000
Current asset	1,600,000	1,800,000
Long-term loan	(1,000,000)	(1,000,000)
Current liabilities	(1,100,000)	(1,100,000)
Net value	2,300,000	2,900,000

Assume a tax rate of 28%.

Required

Calculate the amount of goodwill in Lisbon's consolidated accounts.

Suggested solution

Net fair value of assets	2,900,000
Deferred tax *(28% of 600,000)*	168,000
Net adjusted value	2,732,000
Purchase price	(2,400,000)
Negative goodwill	332,000

Note: *In the consolidated financial statements, the amount of CU332,000 is recognised immediately in profit or loss.*

6.5 Provisional amounts

Provisional amounts may be recognised if the initial accounting for a business combination is incomplete by the reporting date in which the acquisition occurs. Incomplete accounting includes provisional fair value amounts for the initial measurement of identifiable assets, liabilities and contingent liabilities, as well as unrecognised intangibles assets and contingent consideration (in the acquiree's records).

Only within a 12-month period after the acquisition date may the provisional amounts be retrospectively adjusted to reflect the new information obtained. The only exception to the 12 month rule is contingent consideration, which is adjusted when finalised. There is no time limit to the adjustment period of the purchase price. If the contingent consideration differs from the estimated or provisional amount, the purchase price must be updated and the contra-entry will be against the related goodwill.

Beyond the 12 months, adjustments to the initial accounting for a business combination are **only** adjusted if it represents an error, with the required accounting and disclosure as mentioned in *Chapter 7*. The Standard does not describe how to correct adjustments that do not represent errors.

👁 If after 12 months of the acquisition date the contingent consideration is finalised, the purchase price must be updated and the goodwill consequentially amended.

Example 6-4: Change in estimate of provisional amounts

Oslo purchased a subsidiary, Helsinki, on 31 March 20X1. Oslo's reporting date is 30 September. On the acquisition date, 31 March 20X1, goodwill relating to the acquisition of the subsidiary was calculated as follows:

Cost of the business combination	6,700,000
Net fair value of identifiable assets, liabilities, as well as unrecognised intangible assets and contingent liabilities of Helsinki	4,900,000
Goodwill	1,800,000

Included in the cost of the business combination was a provisional amount for the fair value of some property, plant and equipment of Helsinki of CU800,000. The fair value was subsequently finalised, and the effect was that the final fair value estimate is CU300,000 more than the provisional estimate.

The Group policy is to amortise goodwill over 10 years; the goodwill amortised in the 20X1 reporting period amounted to CU90,000 (CU1,800,000/10 x 6/12).

Required
Journalise the adjustment for the fair value of the property, plant and equipment in the consolidated financial statements for the reporting period ended 30 September 20X2 if the fair value was finalised on:

a) 1 November 20X1; and
b) 30 April 20X2.

Suggested solution

a) 1 November 20X1 (less than 12 months after the acquisition date)
The adjustment must be applied retrospectively. The original goodwill of CU1,800,000 is reduced to CU1,500,000 due to the CU300,000 increase in the fair value of the net assets acquired. The adjusted journal entries in Oslo's consolidated financial statements for the year ended 30 September 20X2 are:

Journals

Dr	Property, plant and equipment (SFP)	300,000	
Cr	Goodwill (SFP)		300,000

Recognise reduction in goodwill.

Dr	Accumulated amortisation (SFP)	15,000	
Cr	Retained earnings (Equity)		15,000

Adjust amortisation of the previous year.
(CU300,000/10 x 6/12)

Dr	Amortisation (SCI)	150,000	
Cr	Accumulated amortisation (SFP)		150,000

Amortisation for the year.
(CU1,500,000/10)

b) 30 April 20X2 (more than 12 months after the acquisition date)
No change is made to the carrying amount of the property, plant and equipment or goodwill, except if the initial fair value determination was done erroneously (refer to 7.4).

6.6 Contingent liabilities

6.6.1 Initial recognition

Contingent liabilities are only recognised as part of the business combination if the fair value can be measured reliably. If the fair value cannot be measured reliably the effect is automatically included in goodwill or negative goodwill. The normal disclosures for contingent liabilities are then applicable (refer to *Chapter 15*).

6.6.2 Subsequent measurement

Contingent liabilities are subsequently measured at the higher of the amount that would normally be recognised as a provision (that is when the normal recognition criteria for a provision is met), and the amount initially recognised, less amounts recognised as revenue or income relating to the discharge or expiry of the contingent liability, after the acquisition date (refer to *Example 6-5*).

Example 6-5: Contingent liability

On the date of acquisition of Brussels, the fair value of a contingent liability could not be measured reliably, and so no amount was included in the determination of goodwill. Less than 12 months after the acquisition date, however, experts were able to estimate the fair value of the contingent liability as CU560,000.

Required
Provide the journal entry to record the contingent liability.

Suggested solution

Journals

Dr	Goodwill (SFP)	560,000	
Cr	Provision (SFP)		560,000

Note: Since this adjustment is made within 12 months after the acquisition date, the adjustment is retrospectively made to goodwill. Any related amortisation of goodwill must also be adjusted retrospectively.

6.7 Adjustments in profit or loss

After the acquisition date, the post-acquisition profits or losses of subsidiaries are included in the consolidated financial statements. The profits and losses included are based on the cost of the business combination for the acquirer. Therefore depreciation and amortisation are adjusted in the consolidated financial statements for any fair value adjustments recognised on the acquisition date.

6.8 Disclosure

The following is disclosed for all business combinations effected during the reporting period:

- Names and descriptions of the combining entities or businesses.
- Acquisition date.
- Percentage of voting equity instruments acquired.
- Cost of the combination and its components (cash, shares, or loans).

- Amounts for each class of the acquiree's assets (including goodwill), liabilities and contingent liabilities recognised at the acquisition date.
- A qualitative description of the rationale for goodwill having been recognised.
- Amount of any negative goodwill recognised in profit or loss and the line item in which it was recognised.

The useful lives used to amortise goodwill and a reconciliation of the carrying amount of goodwill (only for the current period) from the opening to closing balance, showing separately:

- New acquisitions.
- Impairment losses.
- Disposals.
- Other changes, such as amortisation.

6.9 Summary

- All business combinations must be accounted for using the purchase method.
- Contingent consideration payable in a business combination must be included in the cost of the business combination at acquisition date if it is probable and can be measured reliably. However, if the potential adjustment is not recognised at acquisition date, but subsequently becomes probable and reliably measurable, the additional consideration must be treated as an adjustment to the cost of the combination (ie an adjustment to goodwill).
- The cost of a business combination must include any costs directly attributable to the business combination.
- The cost of the acquisition needs to be allocated to the fair value of the identifiable assets and liabilities acquired, including a provision for contingent liabilities of the acquiree that can be measured reliably at fair value. Deferred tax assets and liabilities and employee benefit liabilities acquired are measured in accordance with the respective measurement criteria relating to the item. Any difference must be recognised as goodwill/negative goodwill. Goodwill is calculated only for the parent's share in the net assets of the subsidiary.
- Negative goodwill must be recognised immediately in profit or loss.
- Where the accounting for a business combination is incomplete by the reporting date in which the combination occurs, provisional amounts may be used. The entity has 12 months from the acquisition date in which to finalise the provisional accounting, and must make any adjustments required as if they occurred at the acquisition date. After the 12 months, the only changes to be made must be to correct an error as in *Chapter 7*.
- After initial recognition, goodwill must be measured at cost less accumulated amortisation and impairment losses. If an entity cannot determine the period over which the economic benefits are expected, management's best estimate is used to amortise goodwill over the period, but this cannot exceed 10 years.
- An entity must disclose a reconciliation between the carrying amount of goodwill at the beginning and at the end of the reporting period, showing changes arising from business combinations, impairment losses, and disposals of previously acquired businesses.

Chapter 7
Accounting policies, estimates and errors

Contents

7.1   Scope
This chapter applies to all changes in accounting policies, changes in accounting estimates and corrections of material errors in prior periods.

7.2   Accounting policies
7.2.1   Definition
Accounting policies are defined as the specific principles, bases, conventions, rules and practices applied by an entity in preparing and presenting financial statements.

7.2.2   Selection and application of accounting policies
The basic principle is that if the Standard specifically addresses a transaction, other event or condition, the requirements of the Standard are applied. However, the requirements of the Standard need not be applied when the effect of doing so would not be material.

Where the Standard does not specifically address a transaction, other event or condition, **judgement should be used in developing and applying an accounting policy**. Judgement in developing an accounting policy must result in information that is:

- **Relevant** to the economic decision-making needs of users.
- **Reliable**, in that the financial statements:
  - **Represent faithfully** the financial position, financial performance and cash flows of the entity.
  - Reflect the **economic substance** of transactions, other events and conditions, and **not merely the legal form**.
  - Are **neutral** (free from bias).
  - Are **prudent**.
  - Are **complete** in all material respects.

Refer to *Chapter 2* where these qualitative characteristics are discussed in more detail.

In making the judgement based on the qualitative characteristics listed above, the **following sources in descending order** are applied:

- The requirements and guidance in the Standard dealing with similar and related issues.
- The definitions, recognition criteria, and measurement concepts for assets, liabilities, income and expenses and the pervasive principles of the Standard.

The definitions and recognition criteria of assets, liabilities, income and expenses are discussed in detail in *Chapter 2*.

In making any judgements, management **may** also consider the requirements and guidance in full IFRS dealing with similar and related issues.

> No mandatory fall-back to full IFRS is required, ie in developing an accounting policy for transactions and events not covered by the Standard, the entity does not have to refer to the accounting prescribed in full IFRS.

7.2.3 Consistency of accounting policies

Accounting policies are selected and applied consistently for similar transactions, other events and conditions, unless the Standard specifically requires or permits the use of different policies for certain categories of items. In the event that such categorisation is required or permitted, then the accounting policy is selected and applied consistently to each category. Consistency is one of the qualitative characteristics of financial statements in terms of the concepts and principles of the Standard.

7.2.4 Changes in accounting policies

A change in accounting policy is allowed in either of the following situations:

- If it is required by the Standard.
- It results in the financial statements providing reliable and more relevant information about the effects of transactions, other events or conditions on the entity's financial position, financial performance or cash flows.

The basic test for the application of a change in accounting policy is reliable and more relevant information. Such an evaluation is heavily reliant on the judgement of the preparers of the financial statements. It should incorporate an understanding and consideration of the potential users of the financial statements, and the nature of the economic decisions under consideration, whilst remaining unbiased.

Specifically, the following are not changes in accounting policies:

- The application of an accounting policy for transactions, other events or conditions that differ in substance from those previously occurring.
- The application of a new accounting policy for transactions, other events or conditions that did not occur previously or were not material.
- A change to the cost model when a reliable measure of fair value is no longer available (or vice versa) for an asset for which measurement at fair value is required or permitted.

Where a choice of accounting treatment (including the measurement basis) is allowed for a specified transaction or other event or condition, and an entity changes its previous choice – that is a change in accounting policy. Unlike full IFRS, the Standard has a greatly reduced incidence of choices with respect to accounting policies.

7.2.5 Applying changes in accounting policies

A change in accounting policy is accounted for as follows:

- **Resulting from a change in the requirements of the Standard:** In accordance with the transitional provisions, if provided.
- **When an entity elects to follow *IAS 39 – Financial Instruments: Recognition and Measurement*** instead of financial instrument guidance in the Standard and the requirements of IAS 39 change; the entity must account for that change in accordance with the transitional provisions, if any, specified in the revised IAS 39.
- **When an entity elects to follow the revaluation model under *Chapter 17 – Property, Plant and Equipment* where it was previously applying the cost model:** Prospectively.
- **All other changes in accounting policy:** Retrospectively.

7.2.6   Retrospective application

Retrospective application means that the new accounting policy is applied to comparative information as if the new accounting policy had always been applied. An impracticability exemption is provided for retrospective application. Applying a requirement is impracticable when the entity cannot apply it after making every reasonable effort to do so.

When it is impracticable to determine the individual-period effects of a change in accounting policy on comparative information for one or more prior periods presented, the new accounting policy is:

- Applied to the carrying amounts of assets and liabilities at the beginning of the earliest period for which retrospective application is practicable.
- A corresponding adjustment is made to the opening balance of each affected component of equity for that period.

Example 7-1: Change in accounting policy

Dallas is a manufacturing business. During the 20X1 financial year, the directors reviewed Dallas' accounting policies and identified inventories as an area where it could change the current accounting policy with respect to inventory to better reflect the actual economic substance of its business.

The directors decide to change the valuation method used for raw material from the weighted average cost method to the first-in-first-out (FIFO) method.

The value of the inventories is as follow:

	Weighted average	FIFO
31 December 20X0	160,000	140,000
31 December 20X1	190,000	160,000

Required

Prepare the journal entries to account for the change in the accounting policy applied by Dallas.

Suggested solution

The changes in the closing carrying amounts of inventories due to the change in the accounting policy are calculated as follows:

	Weighted average	FIFO	Change
31 December 20X0	160,000	140,000	(20,000)
31 December 20X1	190,000	160,000	(30,000)

Due to the change in the accounting policy, the carrying values of inventories decreased at the beginning of the period with CU20,000 and the end of the period with CU30,000 (ie the period ended 31 December 20X1). The effect of this decrease is an increase in the cost of sales of CU10,000 (CU30,000 - CU20,000) for the period ended 31 December 20X1.

Example 7-1: Change in accounting policy *(continued)*

Journals
31 December 20X1

Dr	Cost of sales (P/L)	10,000	
Dr	Retained earnings – opening balance (Equity)	20,000	
Cr	Inventories (SFP)		30,000

Accounting for the retrospective application of the new accounting policy.

Note: Had the figures for January 20X0 been available then the comparative statement of comprehensive income would also have been restated retrospectively for the change in accounting policy.

7.2.7 Prospective application

Prospective application of a change in accounting policy means that the new accounting policy is applied to transactions, other events and conditions occurring after the date at which the policy is changed. No changes are made to comparative figures.

Example 7-2: Change in accounting policy (cost to revaluation model)

During 20X2 Dallas Co changed its accounting policy from the cost model to the revaluation model.

At the end of 20X1 the cost of the property, plant and equipment was CU25,000 and the accumulated depreciation CU14,000.

Current depreciation for 20X2 is CU1,500.

Management commissioned an engineering survey and the results at the end of 20X2 are:

- Valuation: CU17,000
- Estimated residual value: CU3,000
- Average remaining useful life: 7 years
- Assume a tax rate of 28%.

Required
Prepare the journal entries to account for the change in the accounting policy applied by Dallas for 20X2.

Suggested solution
The change in accounting policy from the cost to the revaluation model for property, plant and equipment constitutes a change in accounting policy and needs to be applied prospectively:

Journals
31 December 20X2

Dr	Depreciation (P/L)	1,500	
Cr	Accumulated depreciation (SFP)		1,500

Recognise current depreciation.

Example 7-2: Change in accounting policy (cost to revaluation model) *(continued)*

31 December 20X2

Dr	Accumulated depreciation (SFP)	15,500	
Cr	Property, plant and equipment (SFP)		8,000
Cr	Revaluation reserve (Equity)		7,500

Recognise revaluation reserve due.

31 December 20X2

Dr	Deferred tax liability (SFP)	2,100	
Cr	Deferred tax expense (P/L)		2,100

Recognise deferred tax on revaluation reserve.

7.2.8 Disclosure of a change in accounting policy

When a change in accounting policy arises as a result of an amendment to the Standard, disclose:

- The nature of the change in accounting policy.
- For the current period and each prior period presented, to the extent practicable, the amount of the adjustment for each financial statement line item affected.
- The amount of the adjustment relating to periods before those presented, to the extent practicable.
- An explanation if it is impracticable to determine the amounts to be disclosed.

Such disclosures need not be repeated in the financial statements of subsequent periods.

Disclosure of a voluntary change in accounting policy (a voluntary change in accounting policy is one that has not been necessitated as a result of a change in the Standard, or IAS 39 if that option has been used, eg a change where the Standard already provides for a choice in accounting policy and an entity alters its choice from one permitted policy to another):

- The nature of the change in accounting policy.
- The reasons for applying the new accounting policy. If it was a voluntary change, the reasons why the change provides reliable and more relevant information should be provided.
- To the extent practicable, the amount of the adjustment for each financial statement line item affected, shown separately:
  - For the current period.
  - For each prior period presented.
  - In the aggregate for periods before those presented.
- An explanation if it is impracticable to determine the amounts to be disclosed.

Such disclosures need not be repeated in the financial statements of subsequent periods.

7.3 Changes in accounting estimates

7.3.1 Definition

A change in accounting estimate is an adjustment to the carrying amount of an asset or a liability, or an amount reflecting the periodic consumption of an asset, that results from the assessment of the present status of, and expected future benefits and obligations associated with, assets and liabilities.

Because changes in accounting estimates result from new information or new developments, they are not regarded as corrections of errors. In practice it may be difficult, under certain circumstances, to distinguish between a change in an accounting policy and a change in an accounting estimate. In such circumstances, the change is treated as a change in an accounting estimate.

7.3.2 Recognition

A change in an accounting estimate is applied prospectively by including the effect of the change in profit or loss in the period of the change (and future periods, if the change affects future periods). The related effect(s) on the carrying amount of assets and liabilities or item of equity are recognised in the period of the change.

Example 7-3: Change in accounting estimate

On 1 January 20X0, Kawasaki purchased a computer server to the value of CU100,000. The estimated useful life of the computer server was assessed as being four years at that stage.

On 1 January 20X1, Kawasaki re-assessed the useful life of the computer server, and realised that only two years were remaining of its useful life.

Ignore the tax effects.

Required

Calculate the impact of the change in the accounting estimate and provide the journal entries to account for the depreciation charge on the machine for the 20X1 financial period.

Suggested solution

Calculations

Previous depreciation charge: CU100,000/4 = CU25,000 pa
Carrying value of asset on 1 January 20X1: CU100 000 - (CU25,000 x 1 year) = CU75,000
New depreciation charge: CU75,000/2 years remaining = CU37,500 pa
Effect on the current period profit due to the change in the accounting estimate:

Previous depreciation charge	20,000
Revised depreciation charge	(37,500)
Gross reduction in profit	(17,000)

Journals
31 December 20X1

Dr	Depreciation (P/L)	37,500	
Cr	Accumulated depreciation (SFP)		37,500

Recognition of depreciation on machine.

As a change in accounting estimate, the increase in depreciation is adjusted prospectively.

7.3.3 Disclosure of a change in estimate

Disclose:

- The nature of any change in an accounting estimate.
- The effect of the change on assets, liabilities, income and expense for the current period.

The effect of the change in one or more future periods is also disclosed if it is practicable for the entity to do so.

7.4 Corrections of prior period errors

7.4.1 Definition

Prior period errors are omissions from, and misstatements in, the entity's financial statements for one or more prior periods arising from a failure to use, or misuse of, reliable information that:

- Was available when financial statements for those periods were authorised for issue.
- Could reasonably be expected to have been obtained and taken into account in the preparation and presentation of those financial statements.

Such errors include the effects of mathematical mistakes in formulas or spreadsheets, or mistakes in applying accounting policies, oversights or misinterpretations of facts, and fraud.

7.4.2 Recognition

A material prior period error is corrected retrospectively in the first financial statements authorised for issue after its discovery, to the extent practicable by:

- Restating the comparative amounts for the prior period(s) presented in which the error occurred.
- If the error occurred before the earliest prior period presented, restating the opening balances of assets, liabilities and equity for the earliest prior period presented.

Materiality and practicability are both required restrictions to the full application of the correction of errors in the Standard. When it is impracticable to determine the period-specific effects of a material error on comparative information for one or more prior periods presented, restate the opening balances of assets, liabilities and equity for the earliest period for which retrospective restatement is practicable.

Example 7-4: Accounting error

During the preparation of Kimberley's 31 December 20X1 annual financial statements, a stock sheet was found by an audit clerk in the prior year's financial statement preparation file, which was omitted from the measurement of inventories on 31 December 20X0. The omission amounted to CU750,000 and is deemed to be material.

Ignore tax effects.

Required
Prepare the journal entry to account for the accounting error by Kimberley.

Example 7-4: Accounting error *(continued)*		
Suggested solution		
Journals		
31 December 20X0		
Dr	Inventories (SFP)	750,000
Cr	Cost of sales (P/L)	750,000

Accounting for the retrospective correction of an error.

Note: This change will be reflected in the comparative amounts in the 31 December 20X1 financial statements, and will flow through to the current period as an increase in the opening retained earnings and the current period's cost of sales.

7.4.3   Disclosure of prior period errors

- The nature of the prior period error.
- For each prior period presented, to the extent practicable, the amount of the correction for each financial statement line item affected.
- To the extent practicable, the amount of the correction at the beginning of the earliest prior period presented.
- An explanation if it is not practicable to determine the amounts to be disclosed.

Disclosure need not be repeated in the financial statements of subsequent periods.

7.5   Summary

- Provides guidance on the selection and application of the accounting policies.
- If the Standard does not address a specific transaction, management should take the following into account when determining an appropriate accounting policy:
  - Requirements and guidance in the Standard dealing with similar or related issues.
  - The definitions, recognition criteria and measurement concepts in the Standard.
- Management may consider the requirements of the full set of IFRS standards in determining an appropriate accounting policy. However, management is not required to do so.
- Accounting policies should be consistent with prior years, unless a change in policy will provide a more reliable outcome or is required by the Standard. Voluntary changes in accounting policies are applied retrospectively unless impracticable.
- Changes in accounting estimates are accounted for prospectively.
- Prior period errors are corrected retrospectively unless impracticable.
- Consequential changes to this section due to the introduction of the revaluation model to the property, plant and equipment section that will result in a change in accounting policy if changed from the cost model.

Chapter 8
Inventories

Contents

8.1   Scope

The inventories section in the Standard is applicable to all inventories, except:

- Work in progress arising under construction contracts, including directly related service contracts (refer to *Chapter 22*).
- Financial instruments, such as shares (refer to *Chapter 17*).
- Biological assets related to agricultural activity and agricultural produce at the point of harvest (refer to *Chapter 29*).

8.2   Definition

Inventories are defined as assets that meet any of the following criteria:

- Held for sale in the ordinary course of business.
- In the process of production for such sale, such as work-in-progress.
- In the form of materials or supplies to be consumed in the production process or in the rendering of services.

Inventories are generally classified into three types based on the definition, namely:

- Inventories are **finished goods** held for sale.
- Inventories that will form part of the final product for sale. For example, **work-in-progress** of products in the production line or items that will form part of the final product for sale will also be classified as inventories.
- **Consumables** used in the production of goods or supply of services are also classified as inventories.

Common types of inventories are goods held for sale, eg vehicles on the showroom floor at a second-hand car dealership, consumables such as oil, nuts and bolts held by a vehicle servicing business, and work-in-progress at a manufacturing company.

Chapter 12 deals with the distinction between spare parts classified as property plant and equipment and those to be classified as inventory.

8.3   Measurement of inventories

Inventories are measured at the lower of cost and the estimated selling price less costs to complete and sell. This measurement principle for inventories does not apply to the following items, which are measured at fair value less costs to complete and sell through profit or loss:

- Certain agricultural produce.
- Certain minerals and mineral products.
- Certain financial assets held by commodity brokers and dealers.

8.4   Cost of inventories

The amount paid or payable to obtain inventories represents their cost. Purchased inventories may require conversion and additional costs to be incurred to get the item(s) into a condition and location for sale or use.

The cost of inventories includes the following:

- Cost of purchase.
- Cost of conversion.
- Additional costs incurred in bringing the inventories to their present location and condition.

8.4.1   Cost of purchase

The cost of purchase comprises the following three elements:

- The purchase price.
- Import duties and other non-refundable taxes.
- Transport, handling, insurance, and other costs directly attributable to bringing the inventories into their present location and condition.

Trade discounts, rebates, and other similar items are deducted in determining the costs of purchase. Inventories may be purchased on terms, whereby payment is deferred for a specified period. Where such terms effectively constitute a financing arrangement (refer to *Chapter 17.7.1*), the cost of inventories represents the present value of all the related payments.

An example of an implicit financing arrangement is where there is a difference between the purchase price for normal credit terms, or cash purchases, and the deferred settlement price. Cash discounts do not, however, always indicate that terms are an implicit financing arrangement. *Figure 8-1* illustrates the different components of the cost of inventories.

Figure 8-1: Components of cost of inventories

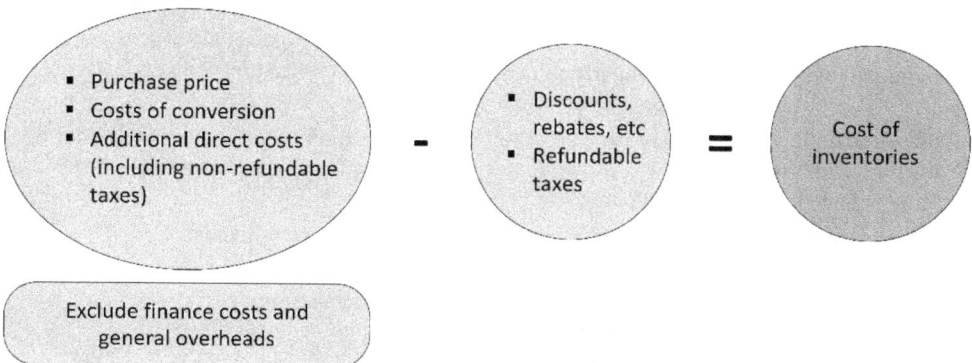

- Purchase price
- Costs of conversion
- Additional direct costs (including non-refundable taxes)

–

- Discounts, rebates, etc
- Refundable taxes

=

Cost of inventories

Exclude finance costs and general overheads

Example 8-1: Cost of inventories

Knysna ordered and received a consignment of retail inventories from a supplier on 15 November 20X1. The purchase price is CU20,000, excluding a cash discount of 5%, which the supplier grants if the payment is made on the date of the order. Knysna's purchase policy is to always pay cash if the discount is 5% or greater, therefore the purchase price was paid in cash on the date of order.

All originally imported retail inventories carry a special non-refundable sales tax of 7%. The shipping and freight amounts to CU15,000 per shipment, and insurance is charged at 0.5% of the purchase price.

Knysna's reporting date is 31 December 20X1; its functional currency is CU.

The CU/USD spot rates were as follows:

| 15 November | 10.0 |
| 31 December | 9.8 |

Required

Determine the cost of the inventories imported in Knysna's functional currency, ie CU.

Suggested solution

	CU
Purchase price (20,000 x 10)	200,000
Cash discount (200,000 x 5%)	(10,000)
Discounted price	190,000
Import duty (200,000 x 7%)	14,000
Shipping and freight	15,000
Insurance (200,000 x 0.5%)	1,000
Additional costs	30,000
Cost of inventories	220,000

8.4.2 Cost of conversion

The costs of conversion of inventories include direct and indirect costs. For example, materials used in the production process and direct labour are considered direct costs. Indirect costs are allocated on a systematic basis and represent fixed and variable production overheads that are incurred in converting materials into finished goods. General administrative costs may not be allocated to inventories.

Fixed production overheads are fixed or determinable overhead costs of production that do not vary significantly in line with the volume of production. Variable production overheads vary in line with the volume of production.

The Standard provides the following two examples of production overheads:

- **Fixed production overheads.** Depreciation and maintenance of factory buildings and equipment, and the cost of factory management and administration.
- **Variable production overheads.** Indirect materials and indirect labour.

8.4.2.1 Allocation of production overheads

Fixed production overheads are allocated to the costs of conversion based on the normal capacity of the production facilities. Normal capacity is the production expected to be achieved on average over a number of periods or seasons under normal circumstances, taking into account the loss of capacity resulting from planned maintenance. Unallocated overheads are recognised as an expense in the period in which incurred.

In the determination of normal capacity, the following are considered:

- The actual level of production may be used if it approximates normal capacity.
- The amount of fixed overheads allocated to each unit of production is not increased as a consequence of low production or idle plant.
- In periods of abnormally high production, the amount of fixed overhead allocated to each unit of production is decreased so that inventories are not measured above cost.

Variable production overheads are allocated to each production unit on the basis of the actual volume of production.

> Although not specifically addressed, excessive or significant unallocated overheads are an indication that the standard costing should be re-assessed.

Example 8-2: Allocation of production overheads

Odessa uses a normal standard costing system to record inventories. The components of the standard cost are:

	CU per unit
Raw material	60
Costs required in converting materials into finished goods	
Direct labour cost	45
Fixed labour cost	15
Other indirect cost (variable)	20
Other indirect cost (fixed)	10
Total standard cost	**150**

Odessa has 3,000 units of finished items in stock at the reporting date. The other indirect costs are directly attributable to the production of inventories.

Required
Determine the carrying amount of inventories on hand at the reporting date.

Suggested solution
Carrying amount of inventories on hand (3,000 x CU150.00) = CU450,000.

8.4.3　Joint products and by-products

More than one product may be produced in the production process. When the purchase costs of raw materials or costs of conversion for different products cannot be separately identified, the costs are allocated between the products on a reasonable and consistent basis. The allocation may be based, for example, on the relative sales price of the final products, or the values when the products become separately identifiable.

The Standard states that most by-products, by their nature, are immaterial. To determine the costs of the main product, the selling price less costs to complete and sell the by-products should be deducted from the production costs.

> 👁 Judgement must be exercised to assess when by-products are deemed to be immaterial.

8.4.4 Additional costs

Additional costs are only included in the cost of inventories to the extent that they are directly attributable in bringing the inventories to their present location and condition.

In terms of hedge accounting rules, certain adjustments to the value of an inventory item are capitalised (refer to *Chapter 17*). For example, when an entity hedges the commodity price risk of inventories held by taking out a futures contract to sell the same commodities.

8.4.5 Costs excluded from inventories

The Standard provides the following examples of costs, excluded from the cost of inventories, that should be expensed:

- Abnormal amounts of wasted materials, labour, or other production costs.
- Storage costs, unless those costs are necessary during the production process before a further production stage.
- Administrative overheads that do not contribute to bringing inventories to their present location and condition.
- Selling costs.

8.4.6 Cost of inventories of a service provider

When an entity provides a service, the related inventories should be measured at the cost of production. Direct costs consist primarily of salaries and wages of staff directly or indirectly involved in delivering the service. Indirect costs may include costs of supervision, and review of the work performed by staff when delivering a service.

Certain indirect costs of a service provider should not be included in the cost of inventories. These would include costs relating to sales, and administrative personnel's salaries and wages.

8.4.7 Cost of agricultural produce harvested from biological assets

The cost of agricultural produce that an entity carries as inventories is measured at the fair value less estimated costs to sell at the point of harvest (refer to *Chapter 29*).

8.4.8 Other techniques

The Standard permits other techniques for allocating costs, where the actual costs cannot be determined. These techniques include the standard cost method, the retail method or the most recent purchase price if they approximate cost. *Figure 8-2* illustrates the relationship between these techniques.

The entity should calculate standard costs by using accepted costing methods, which take into account normal usage levels of materials, supplies and labour. To ensure that the standard costing does not differ significantly from actual costs, the entity should regularly review and revise such costs.

Figure 8-2: Methods to determine cost for recognition and valuation purposes

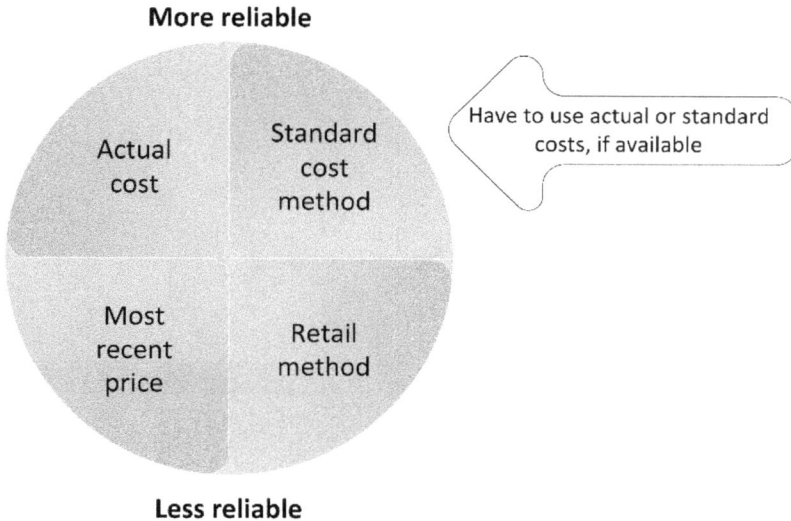

More reliable

Actual cost

Standard cost method

Have to use actual or standard costs, if available

Most recent price

Retail method

Less reliable

The **standard cost** method allocates costs based on an estimated standard cost, which includes the purchase price (refer to *8.4.1*) and costs of conversion (refer to *8.4.2*). The **retail method** calculates the cost of inventories by adjusting the sales price by an appropriate gross margin percentage. The **most recent price** utilises the latest purchase price of the inventory item.

8.5   Cost formulas

The costs of inventories are assigned on the specific identification, first-in-first-out (FIFO), or weighted average method to determine cost of inventories sold or consumed. Specific identification is used for:

- Items not ordinarily interchangeable; and
- Goods or services produced and segregated for specific projects.

Homogenous inventory items that cannot be separately indentified are assigned by using the FIFO or weighted average cost formula. The last-in-first-out method (LIFO) is not permitted by the Standard. A consistent cost formula must be used for all inventories of a similar nature. For inventories with a different nature or use, different cost formulas are justified.

Figure 8-3: Expensing of an item of inventory's carrying amount when sold or derecognised

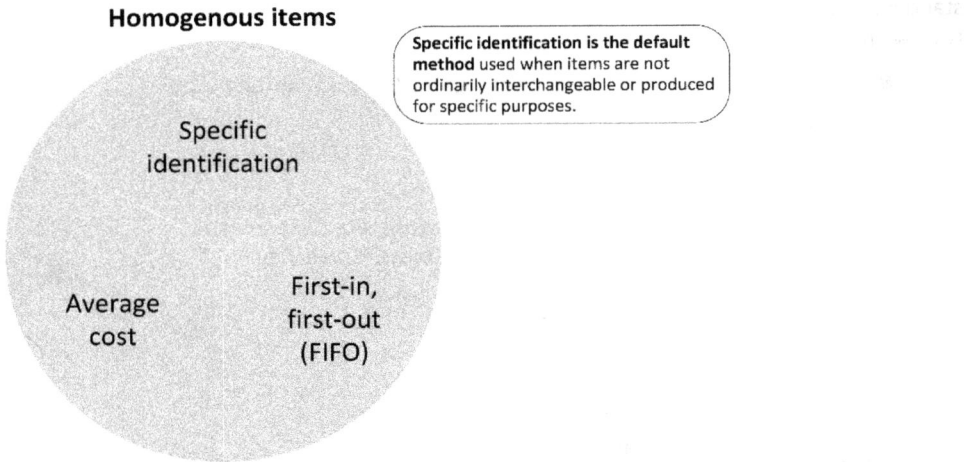

Homogenous items

> Specific identification is the default method used when items are not ordinarily interchangeable or produced for specific purposes.

Specific identification

Average cost

First-in, first-out (FIFO)

Example 8-3: Average cost and FIFO methods

Duisburg purchases four identical units as follows:

- 1st of the month at a cost of CU110.
- 16th of the month at a cost CU115.
- 20th of the month at a cost of CU120.
- 30th of the month at a cost of CU125.

Assume one item is sold on the 31st of the month for CU150.

Required
Determine the costs of goods sold and carrying amount of the remaining inventories on the 31st of the month.

Suggested solution

FIFO method
The cost of goods sold = CU110

The remaining carrying amount of inventories = CU360 (CU115 + CU120 + CU125).

Average cost method
The cost of goods sold = CU117.50 (CU110 + CU115 + CU120 + CU125 / 4)

The remaining carrying amount of inventories = CU352.50 (average cost per unit CU117.50 x 3 remaining units).

8.6 Impairment of inventories

8.6.1 General

At each reporting date the entity must assess whether any inventories are impaired. The assessment is made by comparing the carrying amount of each item of inventory (or group of similar items) with its selling price less costs to complete and sell.

Example 8-4: Estimated selling price less cost to sell

Based on cost, the carrying amount of an inventory item is CU360,000. At the reporting date, it appears that the item may be impaired due to a sudden reduction in customer demand. Upon further investigation, the estimated selling price of the item is established at approximately CU350,000. The estimated cost to sell the item is CU5,000.

Required
Determine the carrying amount of the inventory item at reporting date.

Suggested solution

Selling price	350,000
Approximated costs to sell	(5,000)
Selling price less costs to sell	345,000

Since the selling price less costs to sell is less than the cost, the inventory item should be impaired by CU15,000 (360,000 - 345,000) at the reporting date.

The selling price may have decreased due to damage, obsolescence or deteriorating market conditions. If impaired, the carrying amount is reduced to the selling price less cost to complete and sell, and the resulting impairment loss is recognised in profit or loss.

The selling price less cost to complete and sell is normally determined on an individual basis. In some instances, it may be impracticable to determine the impairment of inventories on an individual basis. In these circumstances, items relating to the same product line, with similar purposes or end uses, and which are produced and marketed in the same geographical area, may be grouped together.

8.6.2 Reversal of impairment

At each subsequent reporting date, the entity should make a new assessment of the selling price less cost to complete and sell. An impairment charge may be reversed when the circumstances that previously caused inventories to be impaired no longer exist, or when there is clear evidence of an increase in selling price because of changed economic circumstances. The reversal is limited to the amount of the original impairment loss.

8.7 Recognition as an expense

When inventories are sold, the carrying amount of those inventories is expensed when the related revenue is recognised.

However, where a section of the Standard requires or permits the capitalisation of the carrying amount of the inventories used in the construction or development of certain assets (such as self-constructed property, plant and equipment), the cost is subsequently expensed through the depreciation or disposal of the capitalised asset.

8.8 Disclosure

The following items must be disclosed where applicable:

- Accounting policies adopted in measuring inventories, including the cost formulae used.
- Total carrying amount of inventories and a breakdown per classifications appropriate to the entity.
- Amount of inventories recognised as an expense during the period.
- Impairment losses recognised or reversed in profit or loss.
- Total carrying amount of inventories pledged as security for liabilities.

Illustrative disclosure 8-1: Inventories		
Inventories		
Finished goods	24,201,345	20,826,049
Provision for obsolescence	(127,434)	(383,677)
	24,073,911	**20,442,372**
Inventories pledged as security		
Inventories pledged as security	24,073,911	20,442,372
Inventories are pledged as security for the overdraft facilities and the loan from the bank detailed in notes 9 and 12.		

8.9 Summary

- Inventories are an asset for sale in the ordinary course of business, being produced for sale or to be consumed in production.
- Measurement is at the lower of cost and selling price, less cost to complete and sell.
- Cost is determined using specific identification, weighted average, or FIFO (LIFO not permitted).
- Included in the cost of inventories are costs to purchase, costs of conversion and costs to bring the asset to its present location and condition.
- Where a production process creates joint products and/or by-products, the costs are allocated on a consistent and rational basis.
- Agricultural produce is measured on initial recognition of inventories at fair value less estimated costs to sell.
- Disclosures include the accounting policies, carrying amounts, amounts expensed during the year, impairments or reversals, and any amounts pledged as security.

Chapter 9
Investments in associates

Contents

9.1 Scope

This guidance applies to the accounting for investments in associates in both of the following financial statements:

- Consolidated financial statements.
- Individual financial statements, ie in the financial statements of a non-parent entity, which does not need to prepare consolidated financial statements.

This guidance is not applicable to separate financial statements that are included in the chapter on consolidated and separate financial statements (refer to *Chapter 5*).

9.2 Definitions

An associate is defined as:

> "An associate is an entity including an unincorporated entity such as a partnership over which the investor has **significant influence** and that is neither a subsidiary nor an interest in a joint venture." *(Emphasis added.)*

Significant influence is the power to participate in the financial and operating policy decisions of the associate, but is not the power to govern or jointly control those policies. Significant influence is presumed to exist if an investor holds, directly or indirectly, **20% or more** of the voting power of the associate, unless it can be clearly demonstrated that this is not the case. Significant influence is presumed not to exist if the investor holds, directly or indirectly, less than 20% of the voting power of the associate, unless such influence can be clearly demonstrated.

Figure 9-1: Levels of ownership

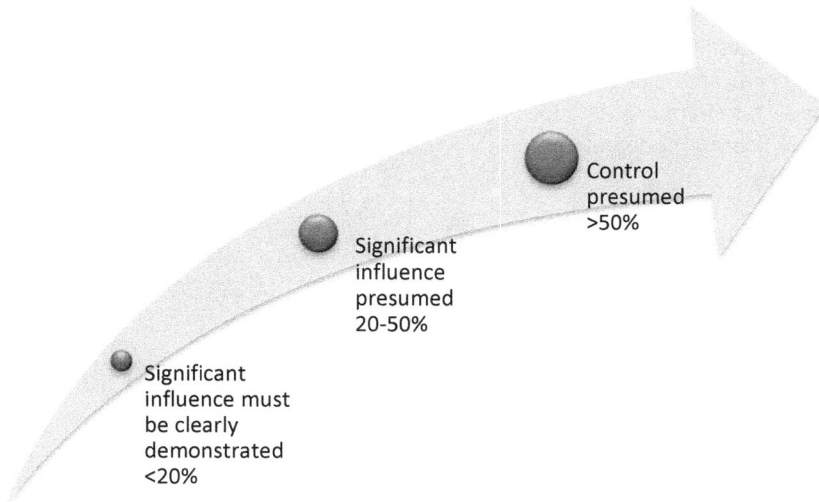

Control presumed >50%

Significant influence presumed 20-50%

Significant influence must be clearly demonstrated <20%

A substantial or majority ownership by another investor does not preclude an investor from having significant influence.

Potential voting rights should be taken into account, in considering significant influence, if they are exercisable at the reporting date. Such potential voting rights may arise from loans and preference shares convertible into ordinary shares at the option of the holder, options held by third parties to purchase equity instruments, as well as options or forwards written by the entity to issue equity instruments. Such convertible instruments held by other parties must be considered by the entity when determining whether it has significant influence.

> Exercisable potential voting rights are considered in determining significant influence.

Example 9-1: Potential voting rights

Florence holds an 18% interest in Venice. Florence also has an option to acquire a further 10% interest in Venice; no other shareholders have such options. The options are exercisable at the reporting date.

Required

Determine whether Florence has significant influence over Venice for accounting purposes.

Suggested solution

Since the options are exercisable at the reporting date they need to be included in determining whether Florence has significant interest with respect to Venice. If the options were exercised, Florence will own a 28% interest in Venice, which would *prima facie* indicate significant influence, unless it could be clearly demonstrated that this would not be the case.

9.3 Accounting policy election

In an entity's consolidated and individual financial statements an entity must choose one of the following as the model applicable to all investments in associates:

Figure 9-2: Accounting policy election for investments in associates

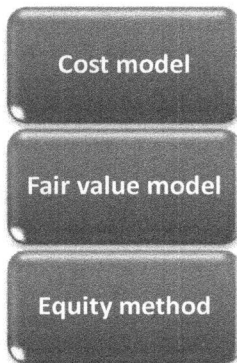

Cost model

Fair value model

Equity method

There are, however, certain limitations in the use of the cost and fair value models.

> ⚠ The accounting policy choice is for all investments in associates and not an investment-by-investment policy choice.

9.4   Cost model

The cost model option is not applicable to investments in associates for which there is a published price quotation available. When published price quotations are available, the fair value (*refer to 9.5*) or IFRS for SMEs' equity method (*refer to 9.6*) must be applied.

Under the cost model, investments in associates are measured at cost less any accumulated impairment losses.

Dividends or other distributions received from the investment are recognised as income. No special treatment is required for pre-acquisition profits of the associate, and therefore the entity does not need to differentiate between dividends received out of post- or pre-acquisition profits

Table 9-1: Cost model

Initial measurement	Subsequent measurement	Limitation
Transaction price including transaction costs.	Cost less accumulated impairment. Dividends treated as income, no adjustment to the carrying amount of the investment.	Under the cost model, associates for which published prices are available must be measured at fair value or by applying the equity method.

Example 9-2: Cost model

On 1 January 20X1, Cape Town purchased a 40% interest in Robben Island for CU2,000,000. On 31 December 20X1 and 31 December 20X2, Robben Island declared dividends of CU200,000 and CU500,000 respectively. Robben Island generated a total profit after tax for the periods ended 31 December 20X1 and 31 December 20X2 of CU600,000 and CU1,200,000 respectively.

Required

Provide the required journal entries to account for the investment in Robben Island, and the dividends received in the financial records of Cape Town for periods ended 31 December 20X1 and 31 December 20X2.

Cape Town elected to account for associates using the cost model.

Example 9-2: Cost model *(continued)*		
Suggested solution		
1 January 20X1		
Dr Investment in associate (SFP)	2,000,000	
Cr Bank (SFP)		2,000,000
Purchase of investment in associate.		
31 December 20X1		
Dr Bank (SFP)	80,000	
Cr Dividends received (P/L)		80,000
Accounting for the dividends received.		
(40% x 200,000)		
31 December 20X2		
Dr Bank (SFP)	200,000	
Cr Dividends received (P/L)		200,000
Accounting for the dividends received.		
(40% x 500,000)		

9.5 Fair value model

Under the fair value model, the investment in an associate is initially measured at the transaction price, excluding transaction costs. At subsequent reporting dates, the investment in the associate is measured at fair value with changes in fair value recognised in profit or loss. The fair valuation guidance under Basic Financial Instruments is used to determine the fair value (*refer to 17.10*).

Table 9-2: Fair value model

Initial measurement	Subsequent measurement	Limitation
Transaction price, excluding transaction costs.	Fair value at each reporting date with adjustments recorded in profit or loss.	When the fair value of an investment in an associate cannot be determined without undue cost or effort, the cost model must be used.

Example 9-3: Fair value model
On 1 January 20X1, Cape Town purchased a 40% interest in Robben Island for CU2,000,000. On 31 December 20X1 and 31 December 20X2, Robben Island declared dividends of CU200,000 and CU500,000 respectively. Robben Island generated a total profit after tax for the periods ended 31 December 20X1 and 31 December 20X2 of CU600,000 and CU1,200,000 respectively.

Example 9-3: Fair value model *(continued)*

The price of a Robben Island share is not publicly quoted, but management obtains the following valuations, deemed to be the fair values, without undue cost and effort:

31 December 20X1	CU2,500,000
31 December 20X2	CU2,400,000

Required

Provide the required journal entries to account for the investment in Robben Island, and the dividends received in the financial records of Cape Town for periods ended 31 December 20X1 and 31 December 20X2. Ignore taxation.

Cape Town elected to account for associates using the fair value model.

Suggested solution

1 January 20X1

Dr	Investment in associate (SFP)	2,000,000	
Cr	Bank (SFP)		2,000,000

Purchase of investment in associate.

31 December 20X1

Dr	Investment in associate (SFP)	500,000	
Cr	Fair value adjustment (P/L)		500,000

Accounting for the CU500,000 increase in the value of the investment.
[2,500,000 (fair value) - 2,000,000 (cost)]

Dr	Bank (SFP)	80,000	
Cr	Dividends received (P/L)		80,000

Accounting for the dividends received.
(40% x 200,000)

31 December 20X2

Dr	Fair value adjustment (P/L)	100,000	
Cr	Investment in associate (SFP)		100,000

Accounting for the CU100,000 decrease in the value of the investment.
[2,400,000 (current fair value) - 2,500,000 (previous fair value)]

Dr	Bank (SFP)	200,000	
Cr	Dividends received (P/L)		200,000

Accounting for the dividends received.
(40% x 500,000)

9.6 IFRS for SMEs' equity method

9.6.1 General

Under the IFRS for SMEs' equity method (hereafter only referred to as the *equity method*), an investment in associate is initially recognised at the transaction price (including transaction costs), and is subsequently adjusted to reflect the investor's share of the profit or loss and other comprehensive income of the associate. On initial recognition, goodwill or negative goodwill must be determined, and goodwill carried as a separate asset.

> ⚠ The IFRS for SMEs' equity method is different to that in full IFRS and is therefore referred to as the *IFRS for SMEs' equity method*.

Table 9-3: Equity method

Initial measurement (cost)	Subsequent measurement	Limitation
Transaction price, including transaction cost. Split between fair values of assets, liabilities, contingent liabilities, with any difference being treated as goodwill.	Cost plus (minus) share of profit or (loss) and/or other comprehensive income/ (loss), less dividends and other distributions received, less accumulated impairment.	None. May be used for associates where published prices are available; however, disclosure of the fair value of such investments is required.

The IFRS for SMEs provides specific principles regarding the application of the equity method. The principles for the equity method of accounting in the IFRS for SMEs are different to that of full IFRS. The full IFRS method should not be confused with the IFRS for SMEs' equity method, and may not be used as a substitute for equity accounting in terms of the IFRS for SMEs.

These principles for the equity method of accounting in terms of IFRS for SMEs are described in more detail in the following paragraphs.

9.6.2   Subsequent measurement

Under the equity method, an investor measures its interest in associates by using the procedures established under the equity method of accounting. Other items of other comprehensive income affecting the equity of the associate should also be considered as they may require adjustments to the investment in associate, for example foreign currency translations of a foreign subsidiary.

9.6.2.1   Profit or loss, other comprehensive income and dividends

The entity's share of the profit or loss and/or the other comprehensive income or loss should be presented separately in the statement of comprehensive income, while dividends and other distributions received are not recognised as profit or loss, or other comprehensive income.

An investor measures its share of profit or loss of the associate and its share of changes in the associate's equity on the basis of present ownership interests. This measurement does not reflect the possible exercise or conversion of potential voting rights. Potential voting rights must only be considered in deciding whether significant influence exists.

> ！ Even though potential voting rights are taken into account in determining significant influence, equity accounting is done in the financial statements at the actual ownership level, ignoring the potential voting rights.

Example 9-4: Equity method

On 1 January 20X1, Cape Town purchased a 40% interest in Robben Island for CU2,000,000. On 31 December 20X1 and 31 December 20X2, Robben Island declared dividends of CU200,000 and CU500,000 respectively. Robben Island generated a total profit after tax for the periods ended 31 December 20X1 and 31 December 20X2 of CU600,000 and CU1,200,000 respectively.

Required
Provide the required journal entries to account for the investment in Robben Island, and the dividends received in the financial records of Cape Town for periods ended 31 December 20X1 and 31 December 20x2.

Cape Town elected to account for associates using the equity method of accounting.

Suggested solution
1 January 20X1

Dr	Investment in associate (SFP)	2,000,000	
Cr	Bank (SFP)		2,000,000

Purchase of investment in associate.

31 December 20X1

Dr	Investment in associate (SFP)	240,000	
Cr	Income from associate (P/L)		240,000

Accounting for the interest in the profit of the associate.
(40% x 600,000)

Dr	Bank (SFP)	80,000	
Cr	Investment in associate (SFP)		80,000

Accounting for the dividends received.
(40% x 200,000)

31 December 20X2

Dr	Investment in associate (SFP)	480,000	
Cr	Income for associate (P/L)		480,000

Accounting for the interest in the profit of the associate.
(40% x 1,200,000)

Dr	Bank (SFP)	200,000	
Cr	Investment in associate (SFP)		200,000

Accounting for the dividends received.
(40% x 500,000)

9.6.2.2   Goodwill and fair value adjustments

An entity should initially apply the same principles as business combinations to the acquisition of an associate. Therefore, the entity should determine the fair value of identifiable assets, liabilities and contingent liabilities on acquisition of the investment in an associate. The difference (whether positive or negative) between the cost of acquisition and the investor's share of the fair values of identifiable assets, liabilities and contingent liabilities of the associate should be accounted for as goodwill or negative goodwill (*refer to Chapter 6*). Goodwill is recognised as a separate asset, which is amortised (presumed not to have a useful life of greater than 10 years). Negative goodwill is recognised in profit or loss.

Figure 9-3: Goodwill

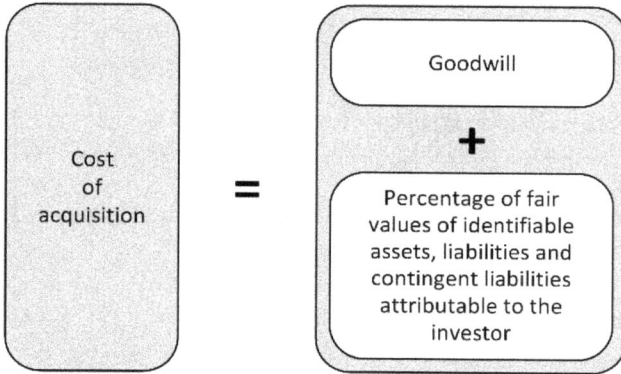

An investor's share of the associate's profits or losses after acquisition is adjusted to account for any additional depreciation or amortisation of the associate's depreciable or amortisable assets (including goodwill). It is based on the calculation of the excess of their fair values determined at acquisition date compared to their carrying amounts in the books of the associate at the acquisition date.

9.6.3 Impairment

When an investor believes there is an indication that the associate may be impaired, the investor should test the entire investment's carrying value for impairment as a single asset. This entire investment's carrying value comprises the carrying amount of the investment in the associate and of the associated goodwill. Goodwill included as part of the carrying amount of the investment in the associate is not tested separately for impairment (refer to *Chapter 14*).

9.6.4 Other equity accounting issues

Under the equity method, an investor measures its interest in associates by using the procedures established under the equity method of accounting. Other items of other comprehensive income affecting the equity of the associate should also be considered as they may require adjustments to the investment in associate, for example foreign currency translations of a foreign subsidiary.

9.6.4.1 Investor's transactions with associates

Under the equity method, an investor eliminates its share of unrealised profits or losses resulting from upstream (associate to investor) and downstream (investor to associate) transactions. Unrealised losses on such transactions may be an indicator of an impairment of the asset transferred.

9.6.4.2   Date of associate's financial information

Financial information of the same reporting date needs to be used unless it is impracticable to do so. If it impracticable, the investor uses the most recent available financial information of the associate with adjustments made for the effects of any significant transactions or events occurring between the accounting period ends.

> 👁 The Standard does not define or explain significant transactions or events further. Significant transactions or events would normally refer to extraordinary transactions, and not necessarily material transactions.
>
> Material routine transactions, even though significant, would naturally cancel out each other if the difference in reporting dates remains constant.

9.6.4.3   Associate's accounting policies

In cases where the associate's accounting policies differ from those of the investor, the associate's financial information should be adjusted to reflect the investor's accounting policies for equity accounting purposes, unless it is impracticable to do so.

> 👁 Uniform accounting policies are required.

9.6.4.4   Losses in excess of investment

The investor discontinues recognising its share of further losses if its share of the losses of an associate equals or exceeds the carrying amount of its investment in the associate. After the investor's interest is reduced to zero, any additional losses are only recognised to the extent that the investor has incurred legal or constructive obligations or has made payments on behalf of the associate. The investor's share in subsequent profits of the associate is only recognised after the share of losses not recognised is eliminated.

> 👁 The Standard does not address other long-term interests. The investment in associate normally includes any other long-term interests that, in substance, form part of the investor's net investment in the associate.
>
> For example, an item for which settlement is neither planned nor likely to occur in the foreseeable future is, in substance, an extension of the entity's investment in that associate. Such items may include preference shares and long-term receivables or loans but do not include trade receivables, trade payables or any long-term receivables for which adequate collateral exists, such as secured loans.

9.7　Loss of significant influence

An investor ceases using the equity method from the date that significant influence ceases. The accounting treatment then depends on the subsequent classification of the investment:

- If the associate becomes a subsidiary or JV, the previously held equity interest is remeasured to fair value and the resulting gain or loss recognised in profit or loss (refer to *Figure 9-4*).

Figure 9-4: Associate becoming a subsidiary or JV

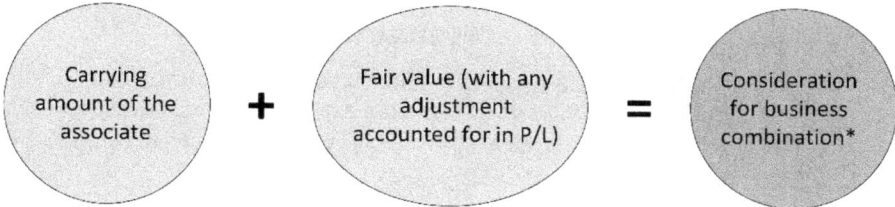

*Refer to Chapter 6.

- If an investor loses significant influence over an associate as a result of a full or partial disposal, the associate is derecognised and a profit or loss is recognised as the difference between:
  - The sum of the proceeds received plus the fair value of any retained interest.
  - The carrying amount of the investment in the associate at the date significant influence is lost.

The investor then accounts for any retained interest as a financial instrument (refer to *Figure 9-5*).

Figure 9-5: Calculating the profit or loss on disposal of associate

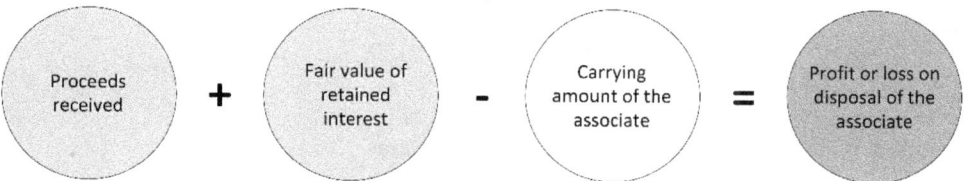

- If an investor loses significant influence for reasons other than a disposal of its investment, the carrying amount of the investment at that date becomes the new cost (refer to *Chapter 17* on Financial Instruments) and is recognised as a financial instrument (refer to *Figure 9-6*).

Figure 9-6: Loss of significant influence for reasons other than a disposal

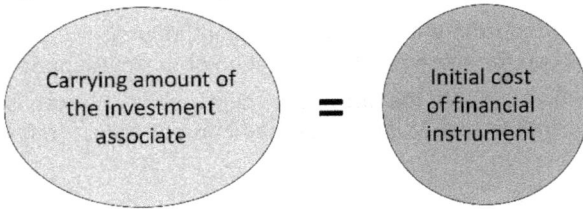

9.8 Financial statement presentation

An investor presents investments in associates as non-current assets on the face of the statement of financial position. Common practice is to detail the percentage held in each associate in the notes to the financial statements. However, this detail is not required in the notes.

9.9 Separate financial statements

In separate financial statements (refer to *Chapter 5*), the investment in the associate may be accounted for at either of the following values:

- Cost less impairment.
- Fair value through profit or loss.

The entity's accounting policy must be consistent for all investments in a single class (ie subsidiaries, associates, or jointly controlled entities). The entity must therefore elect an accounting policy for associates and apply that policy to **all** associates.

9.10 Disclosures

9.10.1 General

- The accounting policy for investments in associates.
- The carrying amount of total investments in associates.

9.10.2 Equity method only

- The fair value of investments in associates accounted for using the equity method for which there is published price quotations.
- The share of the profit or loss of associates.
- The share of any discontinued operations of the associate.

9.10.3 Cost method only

Dividends or other distributions recognised as income for associates accounted for by using the cost model.

9.10.4   Fair value method only

Disclosures for basic financial instruments are applied (refer to *Chapter 17*).

If the fair value for any investment in an associate cannot be determined without undue cost or effort, the investor must disclose that fact as well as the reasons why fair value measurement would involve undue cost or effort, and the carrying amount of investments in associates accounted for using the cost model.

9.11   Summary

- Associates are investments where significant influence exists. Significant influence is defined as the power to participate in the financial and operating policy decisions of the associate but where there is neither control nor joint control over those policies.
- An entity may elect to account for all its associates:
  - At cost less impairment, provided there is no published price for the investment. (Where there is a published price, the equity or fair value method must be used.);
  - Using the equity method; or
  - At fair value with changes in fair value being recognised in profit or loss (fair value method).

Note: The equity method under the IFRS for SMEs is different to that under full IFRS. For example, the Standard requires an acquirer to fair value the underlying assets and liabilities of an acquired associate, and account for the resulting goodwill separately.

Chapter 10
Investments in joint ventures

Contents

10.1   Scope

The guidance on investments in JVs is applicable to:

- Consolidated financial statements (refer to *5.3.2*); and
- Individual financial statements (refer to *5.3.1*).

This guidance is not applicable to separate financial statements (refer to *Chapter 5*).

10.2   Definitions

A **JV** is where two or more parties undertake an economic activity that is subject to a contractual arrangement constituting joint control. **Joint control** is the contractually agreed sharing of control over an economic activity, and exists only when the strategic financial and operating decisions relating to the activity require the unanimous consent of the parties sharing control (the venturers).

Any contractual agreement between venturers where all venturers have to agree to major or strategic operational and financial decisions, or, in other words, where all venturers have veto rights, would constitute **unanimous consent.**

Example 10-1: Joint control

Two entities are building a toll road together. The agreement between the entities stipulates that the toll road must comply with certain standard requirements, agreed with the local government. The agreement further provides a decision-making structure in terms of which the parties must consent on operating and financial decisions.

Required
Determine whether this agreement constitutes joint control.

Suggested solution
This agreement constitutes joint control as unanimous consent of all parties (venturers) is required for major decisions.

JVs may take one of the following three forms:

Figure 10-1: Types of JVs

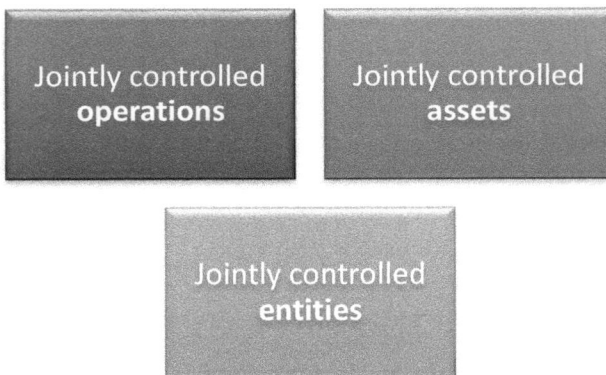

Jointly controlled **operations**

Jointly controlled **assets**

Jointly controlled **entities**

10.3   Jointly controlled operations

10.3.1   Description

This is the first of the two forms of unincorporated JVs. The venturers use their own assets and other resources, rather than the establishment of a company, partnership or other entity that is separate from the venturers. The normal features are:

- Each venturer uses its own property, plant and equipment and carries its own inventories.
- Each venturer incurs its own expenses and liabilities and raises its own finance, which represent its own obligations.
- The venturer's employees carry out the JV activities alongside its other activities.
- The JV agreement usually results in the revenue from the sale of the joint products and any common expenses incurred being shared among the venturers.

For example, two entities agree to market their products as a package, and the revenues from the sale of the combined product will be shared on a pre-determined basis.

10.3.2   Recognition

A venturer recognises in its own financial statements:

- The assets that it controls and the liabilities that it incurs.
- The expenses that it incurs and its share of the income and expenses earned from the sale of goods or services by the JV.

10.4   Jointly controlled assets

10.4.1   Description

This is the second form of unincorporated JV. The venturers jointly control or own assets, which are contributed or acquired for the purpose of the activities of the JV. Similarly to jointly controlled operations, no separate company, close corporation, partnership or other entity, that is separate from the venturers themselves, is established.

For example, unincorporated partnerships of doctors in a medical centre operation where the building and equipment are jointly owned.

10.4.2   Recognition

A venturer recognises in its financial statements:

- Its share of the jointly controlled assets (based on the percentage profit share), classified according to the nature of the assets.
- Any liabilities that it has incurred in its own capacity.
- Its share (based on the percentage profit share) of any liabilities incurred jointly with the other venturers in relation to the JV.
- Any income from the sale or use of its share of the output of the JV together with its share of any expenses incurred by the JV.
- Any expenses that it has incurred in respect of its interest in the JV.

The venturer's share of jointly controlled assets and liabilities, as well as the share of sales, profits or output, will be based on the venturer's percentage profit share.

10.5 Jointly controlled entities

10.5.1 Description

A jointly controlled entity is a JV operating in the form of a company, partnership or other entity in which each venturer has an interest. The distinguishing feature of a jointly controlled entity is that the entity's constitution requires unanimous consent for all strategic decisions.

10.5.2 Measurement – accounting policy election

A venturer accounts for all of its interests in jointly controlled entities using one of the methods indicated in *Figure 10-2*.

Figure 10-2: Methods of accounting for JVs

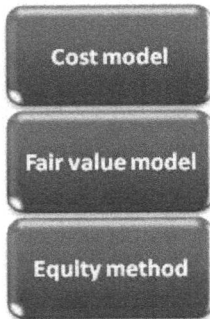

Cost model

Fair value model

Equity method

10.5.3 Cost model

The cost model accounting policy option is not applicable to investments in jointly controlled entities for which there are published prices available. When published price quotations are available, the fair value model or equity method must be applied.

Under the cost model, investments in jointly controlled entities are measured at cost less any accumulated impairment losses.

Dividends or other distributions received from the venture are recognised as income. No special treatment is required for pre-acquisition profits of the jointly controlled entity, and therefore the entity does not need to differentiate between dividends received out of post- or pre-acquisition profits.

Refer to *Example 9-2* for a detailed example of accounting in terms of the cost model.

10.5.4 Fair value model

Under the fair value model, the investment in a JV is initially measured at the transaction price, excluding transaction costs. At subsequent reporting dates, investments in jointly controlled entities are measured at fair value with changes in fair value recognised in profit or loss. The fair valuation guidance under Basic Financial Instruments is used to determine the fair value (refer to *Chapter 17*).

However, under the fair value model, the cost model is used for any JV for which it is impracticable to reliably measure fair value without undue cost or effort.

Refer to *Example 9-3* for a detailed example of accounting in terms of the fair value model.

10.5.5　IFRS for SMEs equity method

Under the equity method, an investment in a jointly controlled entity is initially recognised at the transaction price (including transaction costs), and is subsequently adjusted to reflect the venturer's share of the profit or loss and other comprehensive income of the jointly controlled entity.

The Standard provides specific principles regarding the application of the equity method. These principles are described in detail in *Chapter 9*.

Refer to *Example 9-4* for a detailed example of accounting in terms of the equity method of accounting.

10.5.6　Transactions between a venturer and a JV

The recognition of gains or losses from contributions of assets or assets sold to a JV should reflect the substance of the transaction. If the venturer transferred the significant risks and rewards of ownership of the asset, the venturer should eliminate the portion of a gain or loss that is attributable to its share in the JV, ie only the gains and losses attributable to other venturers are recognised. However, losses are recognised in full when the contribution or sale provides evidence of an impairment loss.

The venturer's share of the profits or losses of the JV from assets purchased from a JV is not recognised until it re-sells these assets to an independent party.　However, losses are recognised immediately when they represent an impairment loss.

10.6　Disclosure

10.6.1　General

- The accounting policy used for recognising interests in jointly controlled entities.
- The carrying amount of investments in jointly controlled entities.
- The aggregate amount of its commitments relating to JVs, including its share in the capital commitments that have been incurred jointly with other venturers, as well as its share of the capital commitments of the JVs themselves.

10.6.2　Cost model only

Only the general disclosure (refer to *10.6.1*) is required.

10.6.3　Fair value method only

Disclosures for basic financial instruments are applied (refer to *Chapter 17*).

If the fair value for any investment in a jointly controlled entity cannot be determined without undue cost or effort, the venturer must disclose that fact as well as the reasons why fair value measurement would involve undue cost or effort, and the carrying amount of investments in jointly controlled entities accounted for using the cost model.

10.6.4   Equity method only

- The fair values of investments in jointly controlled entities accounted for using the equity method for which there are published prices.
- Disclose separately the share of the profit or loss of jointly controlled entities and its share of any discontinued operations.

10.7   Summary

- This is the contractually agreed sharing of control over an entity.
- Three types of JVs occur – jointly controlled operations, jointly controlled assets, and jointly controlled entities.
- For jointly controlled operations, the venturer should recognise assets that it controls and liabilities it incurs as well as its share of income earned and expenses that are incurred.
- For jointly controlled assets, the venturer should recognise its share of the assets and liabilities it incurs as well as income it earns and expenses that are incurred.
- For jointly controlled entities, an entity may elect to account for these investments:
  - At cost less impairment, provided there is no published price for the investment. (Where there is a published price, the fair value method must be used.);
  - Using the equity method as for associates (refer to *Chapter 9*); or
  - At fair value with changes in fair value being recognised in profit or loss (fair value method).

Chapter 11
Investment property

Contents

11.1   Scope

The guidance in this chapter applies to either one of the following assets:

- Land or buildings that meet the definition of investment properties (refer to *11.2*).
- Some property interests held by a lessee under an operating lease that are treated as investment properties (refer to *11.7*).

This chapter applies to an investment property whose fair value can be measured reliably on an ongoing basis, without undue cost or effort. The Standard requires that changes in fair value are recognised in profit or loss.

All other investment property is accounted for as property, plant and equipment using the cost-depreciation-impairment model (refer to *Chapter 12*). If the fair value cannot be obtained without undue cost or effort, then the guidance in this chapter does not apply, and the investment property is accounted for as property, plant and equipment. The decision tree to identify and account for investment properties is illustrated by *Figure 11-1*.

There is no guidance in the Standard or full IFRS as to what is considered *undue cost or effort*. Management will need to apply professional judgment in determining what is considered undue cost or effort. The application of this phrase could differ from entity to entity depending on the management style employed by the directors.

11.2   Definition

The Standard defines investment property as land, buildings, part of a building, or both, that is held by the **owner or by the lessee under a finance lease** to earn rentals or for capital appreciation or both. The following assets are excluded from the scope:

- Assets used in the production or supply of goods or services or for administrative purposes are accounted for as property, plant and equipment (refer to *Chapter 12*).
- Assets held for sale in the ordinary course of business (refer to *Chapter 8*).

Figure 11-1: Investment property decision tree

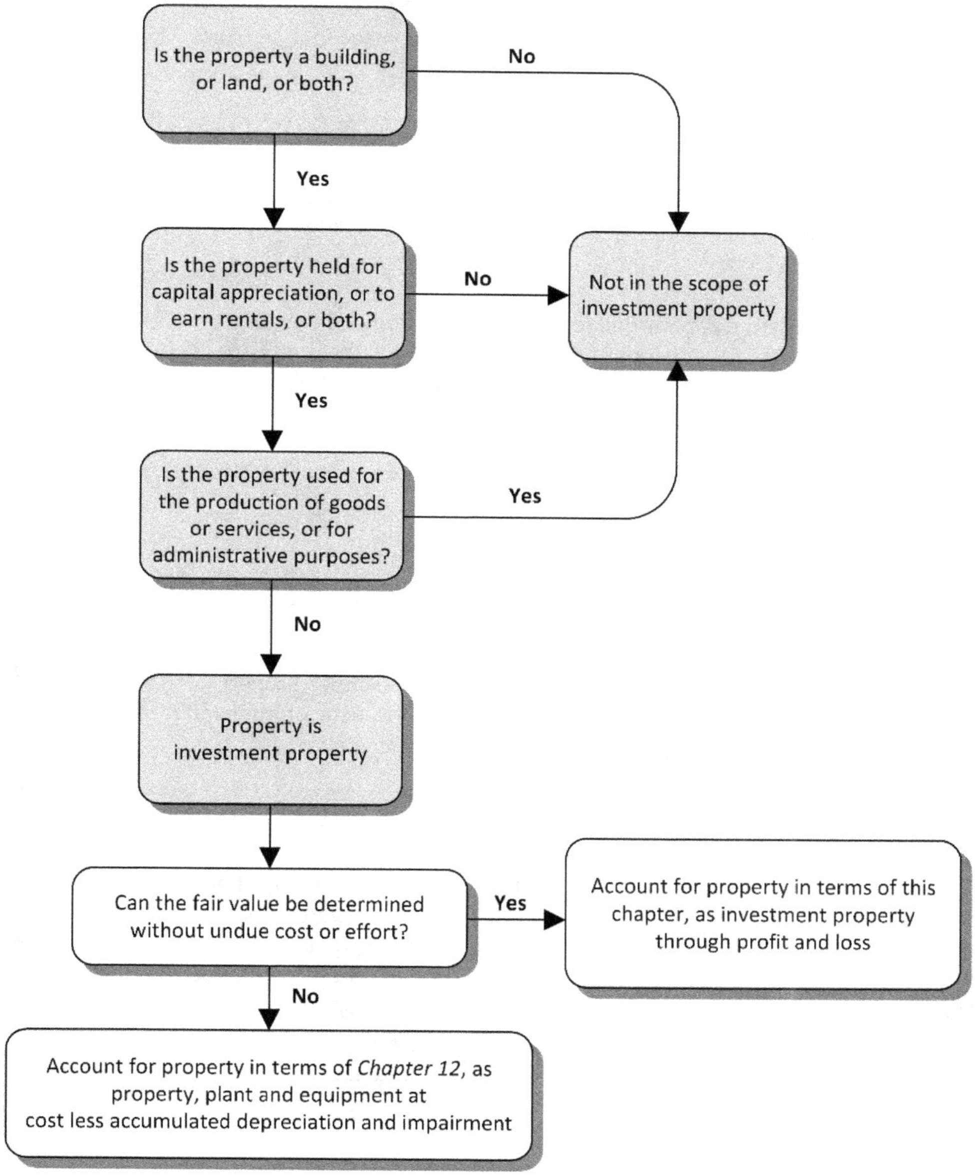

11.3 Measurement at initial recognition

At initial recognition, all investment properties are measured at cost. The cost of a purchased investment property includes the following elements:

- The purchase price.
- Any directly attributable expenditure (for example, legal and brokerage fees, property transfer taxes, and other transaction costs).

Where payment for an investment property is deferred beyond normal credit terms, the cost is the present value of all future payments.

> The Standard does not define normal credit terms. Some argue that this should be assessed based on the nature of the industry in which the entity operates. Others are of the view that this amount should be discounted if the impact of the discounting would be material. This is once again an area where management should set a policy based on its interpretation of the requirement and apply it consistently. *Note: In setting the policy, management should consider the concepts and principles set out in Chapter 2.*

Where an investment property is self-constructed, the guidance of cost under property, plant and equipment (refer to *Chapter 12*) is followed to determine the cost.

> The reference to cost for self-constructed investment property implies that the investment property will only be fair valued from the date of completion of the self-construction, and not at each reporting date prior to completion.

11.4 Subsequent measurement

All investment properties should be accounted for after initial recognition at fair value with changes in fair value recognised in profit or loss. Fair value is determined by applying the fair value guidance under basic financial instruments (refer to *Chapter 17.10*). Investment properties whose fair value cannot be measured reliably without undue cost or effort are accounted for as property, plant and equipment (refer to *Chapter 12*).

Where an entity elects to account for a property interest held under an operating lease as an investment property, the right of use of the property, and not the underlying property itself, is fair valued (refer to *11.7*).

Example 11-1: Accounting for investment property

Sandton, an entity that forms part of the Gauteng Group, identified Stand 347 Gauteng Industrial Park as a good investment due to the central location of the plot and the increasing popularity of Gauteng. On 1 January 20X1 Sandton paid CU3 million to purchase this plot. This piece of land is held for capital appreciation and is not currently being used by Sandton or any entities within the Gauteng Group.

Management annually obtains the services of a property expert, who determines the fair value of the plot as follows:

31 December 20X1	CU6.25 million
31 December 20X2	CU5.4 million

Required

Provide the journal entries to account for the property for the periods ending 31 December 20X1 and 20X2 in Sandton's accounts. In addition, provide journal entries to account for the property in the consolidated financial statements of the Gauteng Group. Assume a statutory usage tax rate of 28% and a capital gains tax rate of 14%.

Assume there are no capital allowances or wear and tear allowances deductible for tax purposes on this property. The tax regime, however, requires capital gains tax (CGT) to be paid on any capital gains realised on the sale of properties.

Suggested solution

Sandton's accounts

The land meets the definition of investment property as it is held for capital appreciation.

Deferred tax should be raised based on the intention of the entity to sell it at its carrying value at the reporting date (refer to *Chapter 21*). There are no capital allowances available for land, and the only future tax consequence is CGT (if the land is sold above its tax cost, which is equal to its cost in this case).

The journal entries to account for the investment property are:

1 January 20X1

Dr	Investment property (SFP)	3,000,000	
Cr	Bank (SFP)		3,000,000

Purchase of investment property.

31 December 20X1

Dr	Investment property (SFP)	3,250,000	
Cr	Fair value adjustment (P/L)		3,250,000

Revaluation from CU3 million up to CU6.25 million.

Dr	Income tax (P/L)	455,000	
Cr	Deferred tax liability (SFP)		455,000

Deferred tax on the revaluation (CU3.25 million at 14%).

Example 11-1: Accounting for investment property *(continued)*		
31 December 20X2		
Dr Fair value adjustment (P/L)	850,000	
Cr Investment property (SFP)		850,000
Revaluation from CU6.25 million down to CU5.4 million.		
Dr Deferred tax liability (SFP)	119,000	
Cr Income tax (P/L)		119,000
Deferred tax on the revaluation (CU850,000 at 14%).		
Consolidation		
The land is not used by any other entity within the Gauteng Group and no additional journal entries are required at Group level.		

11.5   Reclassification of investment properties

If a reliable measure of fair value of an investment property is no longer available, without undue cost or effort, the investment property is accounted for as property, plant and equipment until a reliable measure of fair value becomes available. The carrying value of the investment property on the date that the investment property is reclassified to property, plant and equipment becomes the new cost. *Note: Such a change is a change of circumstance and not a change in accounting policy. As a result, there is no restatement required for comparative figures.*

Example 11-2: Reclassification of an investment property
On 1 January 20X1, the management of Monaco purchased a vacant plot for CU1.5 million. Management believed that the plot would appreciate in value, and that the investment would be sold in 20X4. Management annually obtains the services of a property expert, who determined the fair value of the plot:

31 December 20X1	CU2 million
31 December 20X2	Not determinable

The property expert indicated that the property market has shifted significantly due to a new proposed tax on properties. As this has resulted in a range of possible values, he was unable to reliably determine a fair value.

Required
Provide the journal entries to account for the property for the periods ended 31 December 20X1 and 20X2 in Monaco's accounts. Assume a CGT rate of 14% is applicable.

Suggested solution
This land is held for capital appreciation and is not currently being used by the reporting entity or any of its subsidiaries. The land therefore meets the definition of investment property. If the entity cannot reliably determine the fair value, the investment property should be reclassified to property, plant and equipment.

Example 11-2: Reclassification of an investment property *(continued)*		
The journal entries are as follows:		
1 January 20X1		
Dr Investment property (SFP)	1,500,000	
Cr Bank (SFP)		1,500,000
Purchase of investment property.		
31 December 20X1		
Dr Investment property (SFP)	500,000	
Cr Fair value adjustment (P/L)		500,000
Revaluation from CU1.5 million up to CU2 million.		
Dr Income tax (P/L)	70,000	
Cr Deferred tax (SFP)		70,000
Deferred tax on the revaluation of CU500,000. Deferred tax is calculated by using a rate of 14%, which will be applicable if the asset is sold at its carrying value.		
1 January 20X2		
Dr Property, plant and equipment	2,000,000	
Cr Investment property		2,000,000
Reclassification of investment property to property, plant and equipment.		
The reclassification from investment property to property, plant and equipment does not change the deferred tax consequences based on the intention to sell.		
Note: Land is generally not depreciated but should be assessed for impairment when indicators of impairment exist.		

Other than in the case detailed above, a property is only transferred to or from the investment property category when the property meets, or ceases to meet, the definition of an investment property.

> An investment property that is accounted for as property, plant and equipment (because a reliable measurement of fair value was not available) can later be transferred to investment property when a reliable measurement becomes available.

11.6   Mixed-use property

Mixed-use property is property that is partially used for purposes classified as investment property and partially for other purposes. Properties which are held for mixed-use must be separated between the portion held as an investment property and the portion to be used as property, plant and equipment. However, if the fair value of the investment property component cannot be measured reliably without undue cost or effort, the entire property is accounted for as property, plant and equipment.

> The Standard does not give guidance on how to allocate a mixed-use property between the investment and other portion. However, IAS 40 *Investment Property* gives guidance on this issue stating that an investment property should only be allocated to separate portions when the separate portion is capable of being sold separately, or leased out under a finance lease.
>
> In addition, IAS 40 states that if an entity is providing ancillary services to tenants in a property that it has classified as an investment property, the provision of these ancillary services would not exclude the classification of the building as an investment property, provided these services were insignificant to the lease as a whole. Examples of such services include maintenance or security services.

Example 11-3: Mixed-use property

Dublin purchased a property on 1 January 20X1 for CU15 million (land CU10 million and buildings CU5 million). This included a prime vacant plot in the Doha Industrial Park, a state of the art factory, and newly renovated office facilities. Edinburgh pays Dublin monthly rentals of CU20,000 for the right to use the factory in terms of a short-term lease.

Management annually obtains the services of a property expert who determined the fair value of the property to be:

31 December 20X1	CU20.75 million (land CU10 million and buildings CU10.75 million)
31 December 20X2	CU20.85 million (land CU12 million and buildings CU8.85 million)

On 1 January 20X2, the management of Dublin moved into the unoccupied office facilities. The property expert indicated that the offices constitute a major portion of the fair value.

It is the policy of the Dublin Group to depreciate buildings (production or administrative) over a useful life of 20 years on the straight-line depreciation method. Ignore taxation.

Required

Provide the journal entries to account for the property for the periods ending 31 December 20X1 and 20X2 in the separate accounts of Edinburgh. Also provide the journal entries to account for the property for the period ending 31 December 20X2 in the Dublin Group accounts.

Suggested solution

Edinburgh's separate accounts

During 20X1 the entire production facility was rented by Edinburgh. The production facility therefore meets the definition of investment property in Edinburgh's separate accounts.

The journal entries in the accounting records of Edinburgh are:

1 January 20X1 - 31 December 20X1

Dr	Rentals (SCI)	240,000	
Cr	Bank (SFP)		240,000

Rental of property from Dublin.

Example 11-3: Mixed-use property *(continued)*

1 January 20X2 - 31 December 20X2

Dr	Rentals (SCI)	240,000	
Cr	Bank (SFP)		240,000

Rental of property from Dublin.

Dublin Group Accounts

From inception, the building has been owner-occupied for the group as the subsidiary, Edinburgh, was renting a portion of the building, therefore making it owner-occupied at the consolidation level. The vacant land, however, is not owner-occupied and may be classified as investment property.

The fair value of mixed-use property is to be allocated to the investment property portion and the property, plant and equipment portion. If the fair value of the investment property portion cannot be determined without undue cost or effort, the entire property should be classified as property, plant and equipment.

The journal entries to account for the property in the accounting records of the Dublin Group in 20X1 and 20X2 are:

1 January 20X1

Dr	Property, plant and equipment (SFP)	5,000,000	
Dr	Investment property (SFP)	10,000,000	
Cr	Bank (SFP)		15,000,000

Purchase of land and buildings

31 December 20X1

Dr	Depreciation (SCI)	250,000	
Cr	Accumulated depreciation (SFP)		250,000

Depreciation on buildings (CU5,000,000/20 years).

31 December 20X2

Dr	Investment property (SFP)	2,000,000	
Cr	Fair value gain (SCI)		2,000,000

Fair value adjustment to land classified as investment property

31 December 20X2

Dr	Depreciation (P/L)	250,000	
Cr	Accumulated depreciation (SFP)		250,000

Depreciation on buildings (CU4,750,000/19 years).

Note: In the consolidated financial statements of the Dublin Group, the intercompany rental transactions are eliminated.

11.7   Leased assets

The leasing chapter requires all leases to be classified as either operating or finance leases (refer to *Chapter 18*). The Standard allows an entity to choose to account for a property held under an operating lease as an investment property, where a lessee under an operating lease has a property interest that, if recognised, meets both the following conditions (refer to *Figure 11.2*):

- Meets the definition of an investment property.
- The lessee can measure the fair value of the property interest without undue cost or effort on an ongoing basis.

In the above case, an entity may choose to account for the property interest held under the operating lease as an investment property in its accounts. This choice can be made on a property-by-property basis. Where an entity has chosen to apply the investment property guidance in this chapter to an interest held under an operating lease, the initial cost of the investment property is determined by reference to the guidance for recognition of finance lease assets (refer to *Chapter 18*). The interest held under an operating lease is treated initially as a finance lease asset and recognised at the lower of the following:

- The fair value of the property.
- The present value of the minimum lease payments.

An equivalent amount is recognised as a liability under lease accounting (refer to *Chapter 18*).

Figure 11-2: Identification of an operating lease that may be classified as an investment property

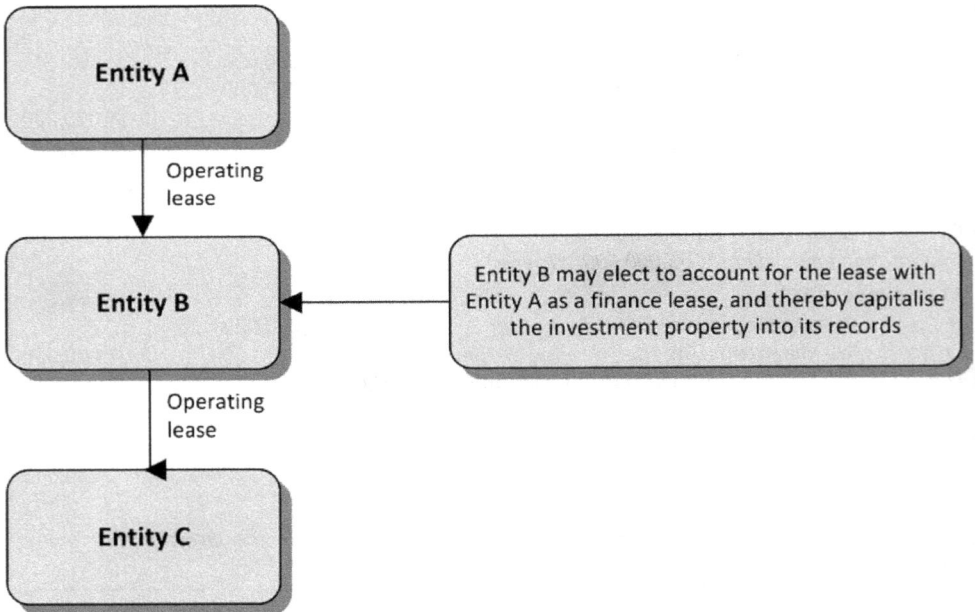

Example 11-4: A lease classified as an investment property

On 1 January 20X1, Wellington sub-lets a building held under an operating lease with Canberra to Stellenbosch. If Wellington was the owner of the building, the lease to Stellenbosch would have resulted in the building being classified as an investment property. Wellington elects to classify the interest held under the lease as an investment property.

An independent valuer determines the fair value of the interest held under the lease to be CU3 million at the beginning of the 20X1 financial period. Management determines the present value of the minimum lease payments to be CU2.9 million.

At the reporting date, an independent valuer determines the fair value of the interest held under the lease to be CU2,600,000.

Required

Provide the journal entries in the books of Stellenbosch to recognise the interest in the lease as investment property and the subsequent fair value movement.

Suggested solution

The initial journal entry to recognise the investment property is:

Dr	Investment property (SFP)	2,900,000	
Cr	Lease liability (SFP)		2,900,000

Recognise the investment property.

The journal entry to recognise the change in fair value at the end of the reporting period is:

Dr	Fair value adjustment (SCI)	300,000	
Cr	Investment property (SFP)		300,000

Recognise the fair value adjustment of the investment property.

11.8 Disclosures

The following disclosures are required for all investment properties:

- The methods and significant assumptions applied in determining the fair value of the investment property.
- The extent to which the fair value of the investment property (measured or disclosed) is based on a valuation by an independent valuer who holds a recognised and relevant professional qualification, and has recent experience in the location and class of the investment property being valued. If there has been no such valuation, that fact should be disclosed.
- Restrictions on the realisability of investment property, or the remittance of income or proceeds of disposal.
- Contractual obligations to purchase, construct or develop investment property, or for repairs, maintenance or enhancements.
- A reconciliation between the carrying amounts of the investment property at the beginning and end of the period (this reconciliation need not be presented for prior periods), showing separately:
  - Additions, disclosing separately those additions resulting from acquisitions through business combinations.
  - Net gains or losses from fair value adjustments.

- Transfers to and from investment property carried at cost less accumulated depreciation and impairment.
- Transfers to and from inventories and owner-occupied property.
- Other changes.

▪ The owner of an investment property held under an operating lease, but who chooses to account for it as investment property (refer to *11.7)*, must also provide the relevant lease disclosure (refer to *Chapter 18*) relating to investment properties held under a lease. The disclosure will differ depending on whether the investment property is held under a finance or operating lease.

11.9   Summary

▪ Investment property is property (land or a building, or part of a building, or both) held by the owner or by the lessee under a finance lease to earn rentals or for capital appreciation or both, rather than for:
- Use in the production or supply of goods or services;
- Administrative purposes; or
- Sale in the ordinary course of business.
▪ Property interests that are held under an operating lease may be classified as an investment property provided the property would otherwise have met the definition of an investment property, and the entity can measure the fair value of its property interest without undue cost or effort.
▪ Measurement is initially at cost and includes costs to bring it into use (except as noted above).
▪ Subsequently, investment properties must be measured at fair value unless a reliable fair value cannot be obtained without undue cost or effort.
▪ Fair value movements are recognised in profit or loss.
▪ If fair value cannot be determined, the investment property will be treated as property, plant and equipment.

Chapter 12
Property, plant and equipment

Contents

12.1 Scope

The guidance in this chapter must be applied when accounting for property, plant and equipment (PPE) and investment property whose fair value cannot be measured reliably without undue cost or effort (refer to *Chapter 11*).

Examples of property are land, buildings, or other items affixed to the land. Such property must be classified as PPE if the land or buildings are occupied (either by itself or another group entity), or used to produce goods (eg a production facility), deliver services (eg a property where assets are repaired), or for administrative purposes (eg an office building).

Examples of plant and equipment include machines, vehicles, computer equipment, office furniture, stand-by equipment, servicing equipment and spare parts (where the latter meets the definition). Excluded from PPE are biological assets, mineral rights and mineral reserves.

The following decision tree is applied to determine the classification of PPE:

Figure 12-1: PPE classification

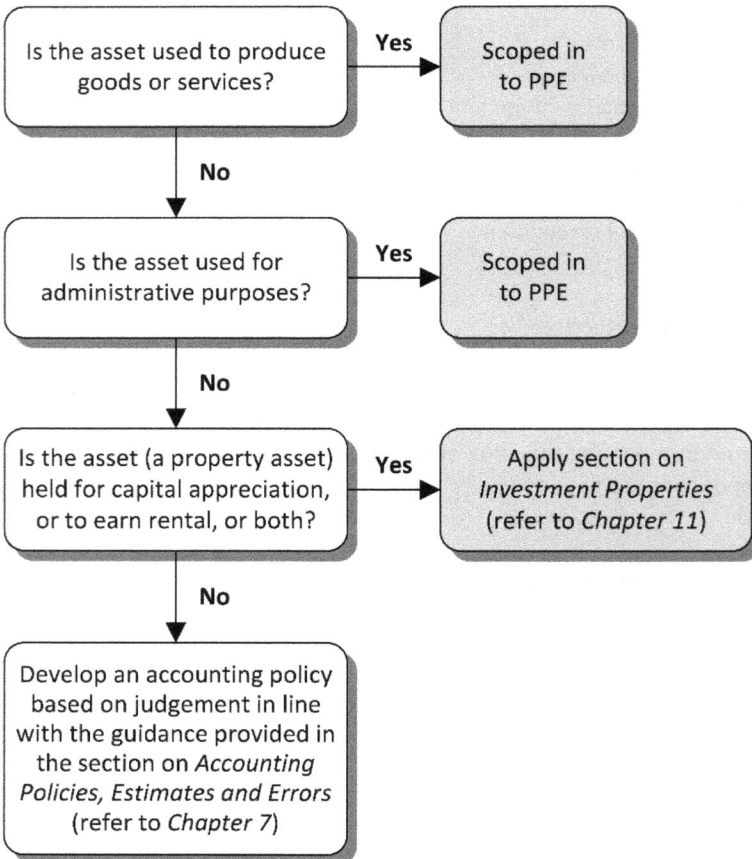

12.2 Definitions

12.2.1 PPE

The Standard defines PPE as:

- Tangible assets held for use in the production or supply of goods or services, for rental to others, or for administrative purposes.
- Tangible assets that are expected to be used over more than one period.

12.2.2 Other definitions relevant to PPE

The Standard also provides the following definitions relating to PPE:

- The **residual value** of an item of PPE is the estimated amount that an entity would currently obtain from disposal of an asset, after deducting the estimated costs of disposal, if the asset were already of the age and in the condition expected at the end of its useful life.
- The **depreciable amount** is the cost of an asset, or other amount substituted for cost (in the financial statements), less its residual value.
- **Depreciation** is the systematic allocation of the depreciable amount of an asset over its useful life.
- The **useful life** of an item of PPE is the period over which an asset is expected to be available for use by an entity, or the number of production or similar units expected to be obtained from the asset by an entity.
- **Fair value** is the amount for which an asset could be exchanged, or a liability settled, between knowledgeable, willing parties in an arm's length transaction.
- The **revalued amount** is the fair value at the date of the revaluation less any subsequent accumulated depreciation and subsequent accumulated impairment losses.

12.3 Recognition

The cost of an item of PPE is recognised as an asset if it meets the recognition criteria for an asset. Accordingly, an item of PPE is recognised if it is probable that future economic benefits associated with the item will flow to the entity, and the cost of the item can be measured reliably.

Further guidance is provided for:

- Major or strategic spare parts, stand-by equipment and servicing equipment (refer to *12.4.3.3*).
- Parts that require regular replacements (refer to *12.4.3.4.*).
- Major parts with significantly different patterns of consumption (refer to *12.5.1.6*).
- Dismantling, removing or restoring obligation (refer to *12.4.1*).
- Major inspections (refer to *12.4.3.5*).
- Separation of land and buildings (refer to *12.4.3.6*).

12.4　　Initial measurement

An item of PPE must be measured at cost at initial recognition.

12.4.1　　Elements of cost

The cost of PPE is the cash price equivalent at the recognition date.

The Standard provides the following elements of the cost of an item of PPE:

- Its purchase price, including legal and brokerage fees, import duties and non-refundable purchase taxes, after deducting trade discounts and rebates.
- Any costs directly attributable to bringing the asset to the location and condition necessary for it to be capable of operating in the manner intended by management. These can include the costs of site preparation, initial delivery and handling, installation and assembly, and testing of functionality.
- The initial estimate of the costs of dismantling and removing the item and restoring the site on which it is located.

> If payment is deferred beyond normal credit terms, the cost is the present value of all future payments. The Standard does not prescribe the discount rate that should be used when discounting the future payments. We believe an appropriate discount rate would be the prevailing market interest rate for a financing arrangement that has some, or all, of the following characteristics:
>
> - Repayment terms, and other terms and conditions, which are similar to the financing transaction.
> - A financed asset which is similar to the item of PPE purchased.
> - For a debtor with a similar credit rating as the reporting entity.

Example 12-1: Initial measurement of PPE

Caracas imported a heavy duty melting oven for an amount of USD1,000,000 from the USA. Caracas' functional currency is the CU (refer to *Chapter 25*). The melting oven was shipped free on board on 1 June 20X1 (exchange rate: USD1 = CU8) and was fully installed and ready for use on 1 July 20X1 (exchange rate: USD1 = CU8.50).

Included in the purchase price was a mandatory training course for the operators and technicians of the oven. The training was included at a cost of USD50,000 and conducted on 1 June 20X1.

Caracas had to obtain the services of an oven specialist to confirm that the oven was in correct working order before production could start. The specialist charged a fee of USD100,000 for this service on 1 July 20X1.

Required

Provide the journal entries required to account for the item of PPE in the financial statements of Caracas for the period ended 31 December 20X1.

Example 12-1: Initial measurement of PPE *(continued)*

Suggested solution

The melting oven was shipped free on board on 1 June 20X1. Therefore, the risks and rewards associated with owning the melting oven transferred to Caracas on this date as Caracas would be responsible for replacing the melting oven if anything had to happen to it after this date. Therefore, Caracas should account for the oven using the spot exchange rate on 1 June 20X1, which was CU8.

The USD100,000 fee paid to the specialist should be included in the cost price of the melting oven as it represents the costs required to ensure that the melting oven operates in the manner intended by Caracas.

The mandatory training course, which was included in the purchase price of the melting oven, should be expensed and not included as part of the cost of the oven.

Journals
1 June 20X1

Dr	PPE (SFP)	7,600,000	
Dr	Training costs (P/L)	400,000	
Cr	Bank (SFP)		8,000,000

Accounting for the purchase of the melting oven and the cost of the training on the transaction date.
(USD (1,000,000 - 50,000) x 8)

1 July 20X1

Dr	PPE (SFP)	850,000	
Cr	Bank (SFP)		850,000

Accounting for the inspection fee of the specialist.
(USD100,000 x 8.5)

12.4.2   Excluded costs

The following costs do not represent costs of an item of PPE, and should be expensed immediately:

- Costs associated with the launching of a completed facility, eg a promotional launch event to unveil a new shopping centre.
- Costs of introducing a new product or service (including costs of advertising and promotional activities).
- Costs of conducting business in a new location or with a new class of customer (including costs of staff training).
- Administration and other general overhead costs.
- Borrowing costs (refer to *Chapter 24*).

Any income and related expenses if those operations were only incidental and not essential to bring the item to its intended location and operating condition, during construction or development of an item of PPE, must be recognised in profit or loss. For example, income earned by using a building site as a parking area or as a movie set.

12.4.3   Special situations

12.4.3.1   Exchanges of assets

PPE may be exchanged for other non-monetary assets, or a combination of monetary and non-monetary assets. The cost of the acquired asset in an exchange of assets is measured at the fair value of the item of PPE acquired. There are two exceptions to this guidance, namely if either of the following conditions exists:

- The exchange transaction lacks commercial substance.
- The fair value of the asset received is not reliably measurable.

In case of these exceptions, the new asset's acquired cost is measured at the carrying amount of the item of PPE given up.

Example 12-2: Exchange of assets for combination of monetary and non-monetary assets

Bucharest, which sells second-hand vehicles, was approached by an unrelated company, Damascus. The parties agreed that Bucharest will exchange a delivery truck with a sales price of CU120,000 (carrying amount of CU80,000), in exchange for eight laptops with a sales price of CU15,000 each (carrying amount of CU9,500 each), as well as CU20,000 in cash.

Damascus urgently needed a delivery truck for its laptop distribution division. It does not have the cash flow to purchase a vehicle, and several financial institutions have indicated that they would not finance the purchase.

All the related exchanges and the payment were made in December 20X1. Bucharest plans to use the laptops for administrative purposes.

Required
Provide the journal entries to account for the exchange transaction in the financial statements of Bucharest for the financial period ended 31 December 20X1.

Suggested solution
The items exchanged are dissimilar and the cost of the laptops acquired must be accounted for at their fair value, since the cost of the acquired asset is measured at the fair value of the item of PPE acquired. The fair value is equivalent to the selling price of the laptops, which is CU15,000 each.

The revenue received from the disposal of the truck is recorded at the fair value of the consideration received, which is equivalent to the fair value of the laptops acquired and the cash received (refer to *Chapter 22*).

Journals
December 20X1

Dr	PPE (SFP)	120,000	
(8 X CU15,000)			
Dr	Bank (SFP)	20,000	
Cr	Revenue (P/L)		140,000

Record the sale of the truck, the acquisition of the laptops and cash received.

Dr	Cost of sales (P/L)	80,000	
Cr	Inventories (SFP)		80,000

Accounting for the cost of sales of the truck exchanged.

12.4.3.2   Commercial substance

For the purpose of determining whether an exchange transaction has **commercial substance**, the entity-specific value of the portion of the entity's operations affected by the transaction shall reflect post-tax cash flows. The result of these analyses may be clear without an entity having to perform detailed calculations.

> 👁 The Standard does not define an exchange transaction that lacks commercial substance. Full IFRS addresses this issue and the guidance provided is included below. This guidance should be used in determining whether an exchange transaction lacks commercial substance.
>
> In full IFRS an entity determines whether an exchange transaction has commercial substance by considering the extent to which its future cash flows are expected to change as a result of the transaction. An exchange transaction has commercial substance if:
>
> - The configuration (risk, timing and amount) of the cash flows of the asset received differs from the configuration of the cash flows of the asset transferred.
> - The entity-specific value of the portion of the entity's operations affected by the transaction changes as a result of the exchange.
>
> The difference in any of the previous two items is significant relative to the fair value of the assets exchanged.

12.4.3.3   Spare parts, stand-by equipment and servicing equipment

Spare parts, stand-by equipment and servicing equipment must be classified as PPE when they meet the definition of PPE, and when it is expected to be used during more than one period. If the spare parts, stand-by equipment and servicing equipment can be used only in connection with another item of PPE, they are considered to be PPE.

> 👁 Major spare parts and stand-by equipment are not defined. Management must use its judgement to determine which items are of such a nature and assess if this guidance applies.
>
> As this Standard requires PPE to be depreciated once it is available for use, the major spare parts and stand-by equipment classified as PPE should be depreciated, even if it is not yet in use.

Example 12-3: Recognition and depreciation of spare parts

Dakar purchases spare parts at its refinery plants; the spare parts relate to critical items and no significant downtime can be afforded. These parts are kept ready for installation. The installation process can be performed quickly and without much cost or effort.

The spare parts were purchased on 1 January 20X1 for CU1,200,000 and classified as PPE by Dakar. They have a total estimated average remaining useful life of five years at 1 January 20X1.

Example 12-3: Recognition and depreciation of spare parts *(continued)*

Required

Provide the journal entries to account for the spare parts in the financial statements of Dakar for the period ending 31 December 20X1.

Suggested solution

Even though the spare parts are not yet being used, they are available for use. In addition, they are not items held for sale in the ordinary course of business or for consumption in the production of items of inventory. As a result, they must be classified as PPE and depreciated.

Journals

1 January 20X1

Dr	PPE (SFP)	1,200,000	
Cr	Accounts payable/bank		1,200,000

Reclassification of strategic parts to PPE.

31 December 20X1

Dr	Depreciation (P/L)	240,000	
Cr	Accumulated depreciation (SFP)		240,000

Accounting for depreciation of strategic spare parts.
(1,200,000/5)

12.4.3.4   Regular replacement

Special guidance is also provided for parts of PPE that may require replacement at regular intervals. Examples of such items are the roof of a building and major components of manufacturing machines. The cost of the replacement part is only capitalised when the replacement part is expected to increase the future benefits produced by the asset. The carrying amount of those parts that are replaced must be derecognised regardless of whether the replaced parts had been depreciated separately. If it is not practicable for an entity to determine the carrying amount of the replaced part, the entity may use the cost of the replacement as an indication of what the cost of the replaced part was at the time it was acquired or constructed.

12.4.3.5   Major inspections

Major inspections are treated similarly to replacements. When each major inspection is performed, the cost is recognised in the carrying amount of the item of PPE as a replacement provided the recognition criteria are satisfied. Any remaining carrying amount of the previous major inspection must be derecognised. This derecognition must take place regardless of whether the cost of the initial major inspection was separately identified. The estimated cost of a future similar inspection may be used as an indication of what the cost of the initial inspection component was when the item was acquired or constructed.

> 👁 Major inspections are not defined. Management must use its judgement to determine when inspections are major. The entity may also need to estimate whether the previous inspection still has a carrying value, distinct from the physical components, if the entity did not account for the previous inspection separately.

12.4.3.6   Land and buildings

Land and buildings must be accounted for separately even when they are acquired together. The entity must allocate the purchase price between the land and buildings on a systematic basis.

👁 Management must use its judgement to determine the relative fair values. The value of land can usually be obtained with reference to the market price for land in the surrounding area. Deducting this deemed cost of land from the purchase price will provide a basis for determining the value of the building(s).

Example 12-4: Separation and depreciation of land and buildings

Vienna acquired a property for CU25,000,000. The property transfer and payment took place on 1 July 20X1, which is also the date the risks and rewards of ownership transferred. The company estimated that the building has a useful life of 30 years from 1 January 20X1 and the land has an indefinite useful life.

A specialist property valuator determined that the value of the land is CU15,000,000 and the balance of CU10,000,000 can be attributed to the building.

The directors have estimated the residual value of the building as CU6,000,000.

Required

Provide the journal entries to account for the item of PPE in the financial statements of Vienna for the period ending 31 December 20X1.

Suggested solution

Vienna should start depreciating the depreciable amount of the building once the building is available for use.

Vienna should depreciate the building on a straight-line basis over 30 years. The depreciable amount of the building is CU4,000,000 (value of CU10,000,000 less residual value of CU6,000,000).

No depreciation for the land is required since it is generally assumed to have an indefinite useful life unless circumstances suggest otherwise.

Journals
1 July 20X1

Dr	PPE – Land (SFP)	15,000,000	
Dr	PPE – Buildings (SFP)	10,000,000	
Cr	Bank (SFP)		25,000,000

Accounting for the purchase of the property.

31 December 20X1

Dr	Depreciation (P/L)	133,333	
Cr	Accumulated depreciation (SFP)		133,333

Accounting for the depreciation charge for the period.
(CU4,000,000 / 30 years)

12.5 Measurement after initial recognition

An entity shall choose either the cost or the revaluation model as its accounting policy and shall apply that policy to an entire class of PPE. An entity shall apply the cost model to investment property whose fair value cannot be measured reliably without undue cost or effort (refer to *Chapter 11*).

12.5.1 Cost model

After initial recognition, items of PPE must be measured at cost less accumulated depreciation and accumulated impairment losses.

12.5.1.1 Depreciation

12.5.1.2 Depreciation method

The Standard refers to three types of depreciation methods. The depreciation method selected should reflect the pattern in which an entity expects to consume the asset's future economic benefits. The methods provided are:

- Straight-line method.
- Diminishing balance method.
- A method based on usage (eg the units of production method).

> The methods provided by the Standard are not deemed to be an exhaustive list, and if another method provides for a better basis to expense the cost of an item of PPE in relation to the pattern in which an entity expects to consume the asset's future economic benefits, this other method may be used.

If there is an indication that there has been a significant change since the last reporting date in the pattern by which an entity expects to consume an asset's future economic benefits, the depreciation method must be reviewed. If the entity determines that the depreciation method needs to be changed, such changes are treated as changes in accounting estimates (refer to *Chapter 7*).

12.5.1.3 Useful life

The following factors must be considered in determining the useful life of an item of PPE:

- The expected usage of the asset. Usage is assessed by reference to the asset's expected capacity or physical output.
- Expected physical wear and tear, which depends on operational factors such as the number of shifts for which the asset is to be used, the repair and maintenance programme, and the care and maintenance of the asset while idle.
- Technical or commercial obsolescence arising from changes or improvements in production methods, or from a change in the demand for the product or service output of the asset.
- Legal or similar limits on the use of the asset, such as the expiry dates of related leases.

Example 12-5: Calculating depreciation

Belgrade and Mogadishu use identical vehicles for transporting clients, which were brought into use on 1 January 20X1. The total original cost of the vehicles for each entity is CU5,000,000.

Belgrade uses its vehicles until they no longer function properly, assuming appropriate maintenance and services are performed as required. It has determined that, on average, its vehicles need replacement every seven years, based on historical records. The residual value of the vehicle after seven years is determined to be R500,000 on 31 December 20X1.

Mogadishu has a company policy to replace its vehicles when the vehicle reaches the age of four years irrespective of the condition of the vehicles, while maintaining and servicing the vehicles as required. The residual value of the vehicles at 31 December 20X1 is deemed to be CU1,000,000 based on the policy that the vehicles are replaced after four years.

Required

Provide the journal entries to account for the vehicles in the financial statements of Belgrade and Mogadishu for the period ending 31 December 20X1.

Suggested solution

Belgrade

Belgrade should depreciate its vehicles on a straight-line basis over the expected useful life of seven years.

Journals

31 December 20X1

Dr	Depreciation (P/L)	642,857	
Cr	Accumulated depreciation (SFP)		642,857

Accounting for the depreciation charge for the year.
((5,000,000 - 500,000) / 7 years)

Mogadishu

Mogadishu should depreciate its vehicles on a straight-line basis over the expected useful life of four years.

31 December 20X1

Dr	Depreciation (P/L)	1,000,000	
Cr	Accumulated depreciation (SFP)		1,000,000

Accounting for the depreciation charge for the year.
((5,000,000 - 1,000,000) / 4 years)

12.5.1.4   Residual value

The residual value is not a subjective estimate of a future value but rather an objective estimate, based on current prices of the asset as if it was of the age and condition at the end of its expected useful life.

Example 12-6: Determining the residual value and calculating depreciation

Ottawa acquired a truck for CU2,000,000 on 1 January 20X1. The truck is expected to have a useful life of five years. The expected value that the company will recover from the sale of the truck in five years' time is CU300,000. The current second-hand value of the same truck that is five years old is CU250,000.

Required

Provide the journal entries to account for the truck in the financial statements of Ottawa for the period ending 31 December 20X1.

Suggested solution

Ottawa should determine the residual value based on the current value of the truck that is of the same age and condition as management expects the truck will be at the end of its useful life. The residual value is therefore measured at CU250,000.

Journals

31 December 20X1

| Dr | Depreciation (P/L) | 350,000 | |
| Cr | Accumulated depreciation (SFP) | | 350,000 |

Accounting for the depreciation charge for the year.

((2,000,000 - 250,000) / 5 years)

12.5.1.5   Re-assessment of useful life, residual value and depreciation method

The useful life, residual value and depreciation method of the item of PPE must be reviewed only when there is an indication of changes.

A significant change in the pattern by which an entity expects to consume an asset's future economic benefits might indicate a change in depreciation method. A change in the useful life of an asset could be indicated by factors such as:

- Changing the manner in which the asset is used.
- Significant unforeseen wear and tear.
- Technological advancement.
- Changes in the market value of the item of PPE.

Such changes in estimates are accounted for as changes in accounting estimates (refer to *Chapter 7*).

> Only re-assess the residual value, depreciation method or useful life if an **indicator** of change has been identified.

Example 12-7: Change in useful life and calculating the revised depreciation

Jerusalem purchased a machine for an amount of CU20,000,000, that was delivered on 1 March 20X1. At this date, Jerusalem estimated the useful life to be 10 years.

At 31 December 20X2, management estimated that the total useful life would be only seven years, after which date it would no longer be cost effective to keep the machine in operation.

For the purposes of this example assume a residual value of zero.

Required

Provide the journal entries to account for the machine by Jerusalem for the period ending 31 December 20X2.

Suggested solution

In 20X1, the machine would have been depreciated over a useful life of 10 years, and a depreciation charge of CU1,666,667 would have been recorded for the 10 months that the machine was in use (CU20,000,000 / 10 years x 10 / 12). The opening net book value at 1 January 20X2 would therefore be CU18,333,333 (CU20,000,000 - CU1,666,667).

The change in estimate of the useful life is adjusted prospectively, and no adjustment is made to the depreciation charge recorded for the financial period ended 31 December 20X1. At 1 January 20X2, the beginning of the current financial period, the remaining useful life of the machine, based on the revised total useful life of seven years, is 74 months [(7 years x 12 months) - 10 months].

The remaining carrying amount at 1 January 20X1 of CU18,333,333 is therefore depreciated over the remaining useful life of 74 months.

Journals

31 December 20X1

Dr	Depreciation (P/L)	2,972,973	
Cr	Accumulated depreciation (SFP)		2,972,973

Accounting for the depreciation charge based on the new estimated total useful life.
(CU18,333,333 / 74 x 12 = 2,972,973)

12.5.1.6   Commencement and cessation of depreciation

Depreciation begins when an asset is available for use. An asset is available for use when the asset is in the location and condition necessary for it to be capable of operating in the manner intended by management.

Depreciation ceases when the asset is derecognised (refer to *12.7*). Depreciation, however, does not cease when the asset becomes idle or is retired from active use and there is no actual production, unless the asset is fully depreciated. Depreciation could be zero under the usage methods of depreciation.

> Depreciation (for all depreciation methods other that the usage method) on an item of PPE is not discontinued due to an asset becoming idle or being retired from active use.

Example 12-8: Calculating depreciation when the machine is no longer in use

Pretoria has a manufacturing machine with a total useful life of five years, purchased for CU800,000 and used from 1 January 20X1. On 1 January 20X2, management decided to withdraw the machine from active use as the market for the product it produces has significantly decreased but is expected to rebound in the near future. The remaining estimated useful life from 1 January 20X2, due to the withdrawal, is estimated to be six years. Assume a residual value of zero for this example.

Pretoria has provided sufficient evidence to assure itself that the machine's recoverable amount exceeds its carrying value at the reporting date.

Required
Provide the journal entries to account for the machine by Pretoria for the period ending 31 December 20X2.

Suggested solution
In 20X1, the machine would have been depreciated over a useful life of five years. The depreciation charge recorded for the period ended 31 December 20X1 was CU160,000 (CU800,000/5 years) and carrying amount of the machine at this date was CU640,000 (CU800,000 - CU160,000).

Although the machine was not used during 20X2, the machine must still be depreciated for the full year. Furthermore, the estimated useful life has changed. The change in useful life is adjusted prospectively as this is a change in estimate.

The net book value of the machine at the beginning of the current financial period, 1 January 20X2, is depreciated over the remaining useful life of six years.

Journals
31 December 20X2

Dr	Depreciation (P/L)	106,667	
Cr	Accumulated depreciation (SFP)		106,667

Accounting for the depreciation charge for the year.
(CU640,000 / 6 years)

12.5.1.7 Componentisation

If the major parts of an item of PPE have significantly different patterns of consumption of economic benefits, the initial cost of the asset is allocated to the major parts and depreciated separately over their useful lives.

> **👁 Both full IFRS and IFRS for SMEs require componentisation.**
>
> As stated in full IFRS, only 'major' parts, compared to items with 'a significant cost in relation to the item as a whole', should be interpreted as such: only where parts are truly major, rather than only significant, a component depreciation approach should be followed. In addition, these major parts must have significantly different patterns of consumption of economic benefits.
>
> The requirement to apply the componentisation appears to be less stringent in the IFRS for SMEs.

Example 12-9: Recognition of different components of an item of PPE, and calculating depreciation on the different components

Kathmandu purchased a melting oven for CU8,000,000. It arrived at the factory on 1 May 20X1 and was installed and ready for use on 1 July 20X1. The company estimated that the oven can be used to produce 20 million units, and therefore decided to depreciate the oven based on the amount of units produced. It is expected to take 20 years to produce the 20 million units.

The lining of the oven needs to be replaced every two years and CU2,000,000 of the purchase price can be attributed to the lining based on advice from engineers. On 1 July 20X1 the company also had a major inspection done by a specialist that cost CU200,000. These inspections are required (by law) initially and every five years thereafter.

The oven started operating on the 1 September 20X1. By 31 December 20X1, Kathmandu has produced 100,000 units.

Required

Provide the journal entries to account for the melting oven by Kathmandu for the period ended 31 December 20X1.

Suggested solution

Kathmandu should start depreciating the melting oven from the date that it was available for use, which was 1 July 20X1.

Kathmandu should depreciate the melting oven, the lining and the major inspection separately as they have completely different patterns of consumption and the items are deemed to be major. The melting oven should be depreciated based on usage; the oven lining and major inspection should be depreciated on a straight-line basis over the appropriate period.

Once the lining is repaired or the new major inspection is conducted, Kathmandu should derecognise the carrying amounts of the previous lining and major inspection components. The new costs incurred should then be capitalised and depreciated over the remaining useful lives.

Example 12-9: Recognition of different components of an item of PPE, and calculating depreciation on the different components *(continued)*

Journals

1 June 20X1

| Dr | PPE (SFP) | 8,200,000 | |
| Cr | Bank (SFP) | | 8,200,000 |

Accounting for the purchase of the melting oven on the transaction date including the inspection.

The PPE must be split between three components:

- Melting oven – CU6,000,000.
- Lining – CU2,000,000.
- Major inspection – CU200,000.

31 December 20X1

Melting oven

| Dr | Depreciation (P/L) | 30,000 | |
| Cr | Accumulated depreciation (SFP) | | 30,000 |

Depreciation of melting oven.
(6,000,000 / 20 million x 100,000)

Oven lining

| Dr | Depreciation (P/L) | 500,000 | |
| Cr | Accumulated depreciation (SFP) | | 500,000 |

Accounting for the depreciation charge for the oven lining for six months in the 20X1 financial period.
(CU2,000,000 / 2 years x (6/12 months))

Major inspection

| Dr | Depreciation (P/L) | 30,000 | |
| Cr | Accumulated depreciation (SFP) | | 30,000 |

Accounting for the depreciation charge for the major inspection for six months in the 20X1 financial period.
(200,000 / 5 years x (9/12 months))

12.5.1.8 Land

Land and buildings must be separated for depreciation purposes (refer to *12.4.4*). Land generally has an unlimited useful life and therefore is not depreciated. Exceptions include land that is depleted through use such as quarries and sites used for landfill.

Example 12-10: Separation of land and buildings and calculating depreciation thereon

Kingston, a platinum mining company, purchased land to the value of CU200,000,000, on 1 July 20X0, with the intention of operating an open cast mine. Kingston spent CU100,000,000 building roads and erecting various buildings and operating plants on the property for the purposes of the mining operations. The mining operations could only commence once all of the roads, buildings and operating plants were completed. On 1 April 20X1, all of the required construction was completed and the facilities were ready for use.

Management estimated that the mine will be able to produce platinum for 30 years. At the end of the life of the mine, the roads, buildings and operating plants will be abandoned while the land may be sold for an estimated value of CU200,000 as it will be suitable only for limited activities, and it is remotely located. The current value of similar land that has been mined in a similar manner for 30 years is CU140,000.

Required

Provide the journal entries required to account for the land and buildings in the financial statements of Kingston for the financial periods ended 31 December 20X0 and 31 December 20X1.

Suggested solution

The land must be depreciated since the value of the land at the end of the life of the mine is significantly lower than the price paid for the land. The land is only depreciated from 1 April 20X1, as this is the date that the land was in the location and condition necessary for it to be capable of operating in the manner intended by management.

The residual value of the land is CU140,000. There is no residual value for the roads, buildings and operating plants as these will be abandoned.

Journals

1 July 20X0

Dr	PPE – Land (SFP)	200,000,000	
Cr	Bank (SFP)		200,000,000

Accounting for the purchase of the land on the transaction date.

1 April 20X1

Dr	PPE – buildings and plant (SFP)	100,000,000	
Cr	Bank (SFP)		100,000,000

Accounting for the construction of the buildings and operating plants on the transaction date.

31 December 20X1

Dr	Depreciation (P/L)	2,500,000	
Cr	Accumulated depreciation (SFP)		2,500,000

Accounting for the depreciation of the buildings and operating plants for the financial period.
(CU100,000,000 / 30 years x 9/12 months)

Dr	Depreciation (P/L)	4,996,500	
Cr	Accumulated depreciation (SFP)		4,996,500

Accounting for the depreciation of the land for the financial period.
((CU200,000,000 - CU140,000) / 30 years x 9/12 months)

| ∮ Land is normally not depreciated. |

12.5.2 Impairment

12.5.2.1 Recognition and measurement of impairment

The guidance on impairment of assets needs to be applied only when there is an indication of impairment for an item of PPE (refer to *Chapter 14*).

Example 12-11: Impairment of machinery and calculating depreciation after impairment

On 1 January 20X0, Las Vegas purchased a machine for CU700,000 to be used in manufacturing television parts. At the time of purchase, it was expected that the machine would have a total useful life of seven years.

At 1 January 20X2, due to technological advancements, management realised that over the last year, the demand for the television parts manufactured by the machine had decreased dramatically. The fair value less cost to sell the machine was estimated to be CU100,000, while the value-in-use was estimated to be CU200,000.

Management decided to continue manufacturing the television parts. Management reconsidered the total useful life and residual value of the machine, and concluded that these were the same as originally anticipated. Assume a residual value of zero for this example.

Required

Provide the journal entries to account for the machine of Las Vegas for the period ended 31 December 20X2.

Suggested solution

At 1 January 20X2, the beginning of the current financial period, the carrying amount of the machine was CU500,000 [CU700,000 - ((CU700,000/7 years) x 2 years)]. The machine must be written down to the higher of the recoverable amount or the value in use. In this case, the value-in-use was higher with a value of CU200,000.

Once the machine has been impaired, the net book value after the impairment must be depreciated over the remaining useful life. In this case, the remaining useful life at 1 January 20X1 was five years.

Journals

1 January 20X2

Dr	Impairment (P/L)	300,000	
Cr	Accumulated impairment (SFP)		300,000

Accounting for the impairment of the machine.
(CU500,000 - CU200,000)

31 December 20X2

Dr	Depreciation (P/L)	40,000	
Cr	Accumulated depreciation (SFP)		40,C00

Accounting for the depreciation of the machine for the financial period.
(CU700,000 – CU200,000 – CU300,000) = (CU200,000 / 5 years)

12.5.2.2 Compensation for impairment

Compensation from third parties for PPE that is impaired, lost or given up is included in profit or loss when the compensation becomes receivable.

12.5.3 Revaluation method

After initial recognition at cost, an entity may measure PPE at a revalued amount provided the fair value can be measured reliably. The difference between the cost model and the revaluation model is that the revaluation model allows both downward and upward adjustment in value of an asset, while the cost model allows only downward adjustment due to impairment loss. Revaluations shall be made with sufficient regularity to ensure that the carrying amount does not differ materially from that which would be determined using fair value at the end of the reporting period (refer to *Chapter 17* for fair value guidance). If an item of property, plant and equipment is revalued, the entire class of property, plant and equipment to which that asset belongs shall be revalued.

12.5.3.1 Revaluation

If an asset's carrying amount is increased as a result of a revaluation, the increase shall be recognised in other comprehensive income and accumulated in equity under the heading 'revaluation surplus'. However, the increase shall be recognised in profit or loss to the extent that it reverses a revaluation decrease of the same asset previously recognised in profit or loss.

If an asset's carrying amount is decreased as a result of a revaluation, the decrease shall be recognised in profit or loss. However, the decrease shall be recognised in other comprehensive income to the extent of any previous revaluation surplus recognised in respect of that asset. The decrease recognised in other comprehensive income reduces the amount accumulated in equity under the heading 'revaluation surplus'.

Example 12-12: Revaluation of PPE

Assume on 31 December 20X2, Haifa intends to switch to the revaluation model and carries out a valuation, which estimates the fair value of its building to be CU190,000. The building's cost was CU200,000 with an expected useful life of 20 years and was bought three years ago, thus the carrying amount at the date is CU170,000. The remaining useful life of the building has not changed.

Required

Provide the journal entries to effect the revaluation of the building to fair value for the year 20X2 as well as the entries for the depreciation of the building.

Suggested solution

The revalued amount is CU190,000 so an upward adjustment of CU20,000 is required to the carrying amount of the building. It is recorded through the following journal entry:

Journals

Dr	Building (PPE)	20,000	
Cr	Revaluation surplus		20,000

Revaluation surplus on building recognised (CU190,000 – CU170,000)

A revaluation surplus is not considered a normal gain and is recognised in Other Comprehensive Income and accumulated in equity under the heading 'revaluation surplus'. Revaluation surplus accumulates all the upward revaluations of a company's assets until those assets are disposed of.

The depreciation in periods after revaluation is based on the revalued amount, and the depreciation for the year shall be the new carrying amount divided by the remaining useful life.

Dr	Depreciation	11,176	
Cr	Accumulated depreciation		11,176

Depreciation of building (CU190,000 / 17)

12.5.3.2 Reversal of revaluation

If a revalued asset is subsequently valued down due to impairment, the loss is first written off against any balance available in the revaluation surplus and if the loss exceeds the revaluation surplus of the same asset, the difference is charged to profit or loss as an impairment loss.

Example 12-13: Reversal of revaluation

Two years after an initial surplus valuation of a building of CU20,000, Sefat's building is devalued to CU140,000. The carrying amount as at that date after depreciating the building is CU167,648.

Required

Provide the journal entries to reflect the reversal of the revaluation for Sefat for the year.

Suggested solution

The revaluation surplus is calculated (CU167,648 – CU140,000) as CU27,648. As CU20,000 of the revaluation is reflected in equity as a revaluation surplus, the balance of the devaluation of CU7,648 (CU27,648 – CU20,000) is reflected in profit or loss.

Journals

Dr	Revaluation surplus	20,000	
Dr	Impairment losses (P/L)	7,648	
Cr	Building		20,000
Cr	Accumulated impairment losses		7,648

Accounting for devaluation of buildings (CU 167,648 – CU 140,000)

12.6 Binding sale agreements

A plan to dispose of any asset, including PPE, before the expected end of its estimated useful life, could be an indicator of impairment that triggers the application of the impairment guidance.

The financial statement presentation chapter prescribes certain disclosure requirements for assets with binding sale agreements in place (refer to *Chapter 3*), but no other presentation, recognition or measurement guidance is given for PPE held for sale, or with binding sale agreements (refer to *Example 3-5* in *Chapter 3*).

> A plan to dispose of an item of PPE is an indicator of impairment.

12.7 Derecognition

PPE must be derecognised when it is no longer controlled (ie disposed of) or does not meet the recognition criterion of probable future economic benefits.

An entity shall derecognise an item of PPE when either of the following occurs:

- On disposal.
- When no future economic benefits are expected from its use or disposal.

The date of disposal is determined by applying the criteria for the recognition of revenue from the sale of goods (refer to *Chapter 22*).

A gain or loss on derecognition of PPE is recognised in profit or loss. Such a gain or loss must not be classified as revenue, but separately. If the amount is material, it may be necessary to disclose the amount separately in the notes or presented separately on the face of the statement of comprehensive income. The gain or loss on derecognition of PPE is the difference between the net disposal proceeds and the carrying amount of the item.

Note: Certain profits or losses on sale and lease-back transactions are not recorded in profit or loss (refer to Chapter 18).

Example 12-12: Derecognition and sale of PPE

Helsinki purchased a machine on 1 January 20X0 for CU700,000 to be used in manufacturing television parts. At the time of purchase, it was expected that the machine would have a total useful life of seven years.

At 1 August 20X1 Helsinki received an offer from a competitor, Malmö, who were willing to purchase the machine for CU60,000. The value of the machine had declined dramatically due to technological advancements and Helsinki had decided it was no longer viable to continue in this line of business. Helsinki accepted the offer on that date and delivered the machine to Malmö.

Required
Provide the journal entries to account for the machine in the financial statements of Helsinki for the period ending 31 December 20X1.

Suggested solution
At 1 August 20X1, the date that the risks and rewards of ownership transferred to Malmö, the carrying amount of the machine was CU541,667 (CU700,000 - ((CU700,000 / 84 (12 x 7) months) x 19 months). The machine was sold for CU60,000, therefore the loss on the disposal of the machine is CU481,667 (CU541,667 - CU60,000).

Journals
1 August 20X1

Dr	Depreciation (P/L)	58,333	
Cr	Accumulated depreciation (SFP)		58,333

Accounting for the depreciation of the machine up until the date of derecognition.
(CU700,000 / 7 x 7/12 months)

Dr	Bank (SFP)	60,000	
Dr	Loss on disposal of asset (P/L)	481,667	
Dr	Accumulated depreciation (SFP)	158,333	
Cr	PPE (SFP)		700,000

Accounting for the disposal of the machine.
Accumulated depreciation: (CU100,000 in respect of 20X0 and CU58,333 in respect of 20X1).

12.8   Disclosure

Disclose for each class of PPE:

- The measurement bases used for determining the gross carrying amount.
- The depreciation methods used.
- The useful lives or the depreciation rates used.
- The gross carrying amount and the accumulated depreciation (aggregated with accumulated impairment losses) at the beginning and end of the reporting period.
- The existence and carrying amounts of PPE to which the entity has restricted title, or that is pledged as security for liabilities.
- The amount of contractual commitments for the acquisition of PPE.

- A reconciliation of the carrying amount at the beginning and end of the reporting period (this reconciliation need not be presented for prior periods), showing separately:
  - Additions.
  - Disposals.
  - Acquisitions through business combinations.
  - Transfers to investment property if a reliable measure of fair value becomes available.
  - Impairment losses recognised or reversed in profit or loss.
  - Depreciation.
  - Other changes.
- The reason why the fair value of an investment property cannot be determined without undue cost or effort.
- Where the revalued model is used:
  - The effective date of the revaluation.
  - The independence of the valuer.
  - Methods and significant assumptions in determining fair value.
  - The carrying amount that would have been recognised for each class of property plant and equipment that has been revalued.
  - The revaluation surplus reflecting the changes for the period and any restriction on distribution relating thereto.

12.9   Summary

- At recognition, PPE is measured at cost, which includes the purchase price and other costs to bring the asset to the location and condition necessary, as well as any future dismantling costs and site restoration costs, less any discounts or rebates. If payment is to occur over a period of time, cost is the present value of all future payments.
- The following costs are excluded and should be expensed when incurred – new facility opening costs, new product or services launches, and administration and overhead expenditure.
- Borrowing costs must not be capitalised into the carrying amount of PPE.
- Spare parts and stand-by equipment are included as part of PPE when an entity expects to use them for more than one period.
- If parts are replaced, the cost will be added to the carrying value of the asset if it is expected to provide incremental economic benefit. If not, then the repairs should be expensed.
- Subsequent to acquisition, the entity shall measure PPE at cost or fair value less accumulated depreciation and accumulated impairment losses.
- Assets shall be depreciated over the anticipated useful life after taking into consideration the residual value at the end of the asset's life. The method of depreciation shall be the method that best demonstrates the life of the asset.   Clearly identified significant components should be depreciated separately.
- Significant unexpected wear and tear, technological advancement, and changes in market prices may indicate that the residual value or useful life of an asset has changed since the most recent annual reporting period. If such indicators are present, an entity

must review its previous estimates and amend the residual values, depreciation methods and useful lives as required. Such changes must be accounted for as changes in an accounting estimate. Impairment must be assessed at each reporting date and recognised as a current period expense.

- Indicators of impairment must be considered at each reporting date and, if they exist, the recoverable amount should be determined. Any impairment is recognised in profit or loss.
- Plans to dispose of an asset before the previously expected date are an indicator of impairment; an impairment test must be performed to determine the extent, if any, of impairment.
- Derecognition must occur on disposal or when no future economic benefits are expected from the assets – this may result in gains or losses to be recognised in profit or loss for that period.
- The measurement basis, depreciation methods, useful lives, gross carrying amounts and accumulated depreciation, reconciliation showing additions, disposals, acquisitions, impairments, depreciation, any foreign exchange differences and other changes shall all be disclosed.

Chapter 13
Intangible assets other than goodwill

Contents

13.1   Scope

Guidance is provided for all intangible assets other than goodwill and intangible assets that represent inventories, because they are held by an entity for sale in the ordinary course of business. The amortisation guidance provided also applies to goodwill.

Specifically, intangible assets do not include:

- Financial assets.
- Mineral rights and mineral reserves, such as oil, natural gas and similar non-regenerative resources.

13.2   Definition and recognition criteria

An intangible asset is defined as an identifiable non-monetary asset without physical substance.

> An intangible asset must be identifiable to be recognised.

13.2.1   Identifiability

Intangible assets are identifiable when they meet either of the following criteria:

- Assets that are separable, ie capable of being separated or divided from the entity and sold, transferred, licensed, rented or exchanged, either individually or together with a related contract, asset or liability.
- Assets that arise from contractual or other legal rights, regardless of whether those rights are transferable or separable from the entity or from other rights and obligations.

> No further guidance is given in IFRS for SMEs. Full IFRS states that the capacity of an entity to control the future economic benefits of an intangible asset would normally stem from enforceable legal rights although this is not conclusive, since control might be created through other means.

Example 13-1: Purchase of an intangible asset

Marseille produces and sells various types of products. During the 20X1 financial year, Marseille acquired rights to advertise at international rugby tournaments. The proposal to acquire the rights was approved by Marseille's board of directors on 1 March 20X1. Marseille incurred the following costs from 1 June 20X1 up to 31 July 20X1 regarding the rights:

Research into different rugby tournaments	CU125,000
Attendance at exhibits	CU195,000
Meetings with various rugby unions	CU170,000

Example 13-1: Purchase of an intangible asset *(continued)*

On 31 August 20X1, Marseille signed a contract with the Rugby Committee. The terms are:

- Marseille will acquire the rights to advertise ('advertisement rights') until 31 August 20X5.
- Marseille will pay the Rugby Committee CU1,200,000 in total for these rights, which are payable in three equal annual instalments commencing 31 August 20X2. A reasonable discount rate for a similar asset on similar payment terms is determined to be 12%.
- Marseille can begin to utilise the rights on 1 September 20X1.

On 31 December 20X1 the directors estimate the fair value of the advertisement rights to be CU2,000,000, and wish to record the advertisement rights at this amount.

Required

Discuss the appropriate recognition and measurement of the advertisement rights in the accounting records of Marseille. Also provide journal entries for the financial period ended 31 December 20X1.

Suggested solution

Recognition

The advertisement rights should be recognised as an intangible asset because:

- It is separately identifiable as it arises from a contractual and legal right. The legal right additionally ensures that Marseille will control the advertisement rights for at least a period of four years.
- It is a non-monetary asset without physical substance, which will result in future economical benefits to flow to Marseille as the advertisement rights will most probably be sold for consideration.

The cost of the purchased rights is clearly stipulated in the purchase contract and can therefore be measured reliably.

Measurement

Cost incurred from 1 June 20X1 – 31 July 20X1

The total expenses of CU490,000 incurred between 1 June 20X1 and 31 July 20X1 are internally generated and should be expensed. It should not form part of the purchase price of the purchased intangible asset.

Cost incurred on 1 August 20X1

The advertisement rights purchased should initially be measured at **cost**. The fair value may not be used.

Because payment is deferred, the sponsorship rights must be recorded at the present value of the future payments on 1 September 20X1. This value is calculated as CU960,733.

Subsequent measurement

The difference between the present value of the three instalments and the nominal amount is interest, and this will be recognised as an expense on a time proportion basis.

The advertisement rights will have to be amortised over its useful life of four years.

The amortisation period and method should be reviewed by Marseille, only if there is an indication that the original estimates made by Marseille have changed.

Example 13-1: Purchase of an intangible asset *(continued)*

Journal entries

31 August 20X1

Dr	Intangible asset (SFP)	960,733	
Cr	Instalment sale (SFP)		960,733

Recognition of intangible asset.

31 December 20X1

Dr	Interest expense (P/L)	38,429	
Cr	Instalment sale (SFP)		38,429

Accrual of interest on instalment sale.
(12% x 960,733 x 4/12 months)

Dr	Amortisation(P/L)	80,061	
Cr	Accumulated amortisation		80,061

Amortisation of intangible asset.
(960,733/4 years x 4/12 months)

13.2.2 Legal enforceable rights

Legal enforceable rights are the first test to determine whether an intangible asset could be capitalised. In the absence of such legal rights it is much more difficult to demonstrate control, a prerequisite for the capitalisation of an asset. Full IFRS also states that the future benefits that flow from an intangible asset might include revenue, cost savings and other benefits.

> **Separation and contractual-legal requirements**
>
> *IFRS 3 – Business Combinations*, provides the following examples of the separation and contractual-legal requirements:
>
> - Customer and subscriber lists are purchased and thus meet the separation criterion, except if confidentiality or other agreements prohibit the transfer.
> - An operator has a licence to operate a power plant. Even though the operator may not transfer the licence, the licence meets the contractual-legal requirement.
> - An entity owns a patent that is licensed to others for their exclusive use.
> - An assembled workforce is not regarded to be an identifiable asset as it cannot meet the control criteria.

13.3 Methods of acquisition and initial measurement

An intangible asset is **initially measured at cost.** Specific guidance is provided for what constitutes cost for separate purchase, business combinations, government grants and exchange transactions as illustrated in *Table 13-1*. In some instances cost represents the fair value on the acquisition date.

Table 13-1: Methods of acquisition of intangible assets

Method of acquisition	Measurement (cost)
Separate purchase	Cost
Business combination	Fair value (unless fair value cannot be measured without undue cost or effort at the acquisition date, future economic benefits do not have to be proved)
Government grant	Fair value
Exchange of assets	Fair value unless: ■ Lacks commercial substance ■ Fair value of neither asset is reliably measurable
Internally generated	Expense All research and development costs are expensed

13.3.1 Separate purchase

Intangible assets must be acquired from a third party to be recognised. The probability recognition criterion is always considered satisfied for separately purchased intangible assets.

13.3.1.1 Cost separate purchase

The cost of a separately purchased intangible asset is the purchase price plus any directly attributable costs of preparing the intangible for its intended use. The purchase price includes import duties and non-refundable purchase taxes, and is reduced by any trade discounts and rebates.

The IFRS for SMEs does not provide examples of **directly attributable costs**.

However, full IFRS provides the following examples of costs, which are deemed to be directly attributable:

- Salaries.
- Professional fees.
- Testing costs.

Full IFRS also provides the following examples of costs which are *not* deemed to be directly attributable, and are expensed:

- Costs of introducing a new product or service.
- Costs of conducting a business in a new location or with a new customer.
- Staff training costs.
- Advertising and promotion costs.
- Other general administration costs.

Example 13-2: Determining the cost of an intangible asset acquired through separate purchase

Oklahoma purchases a trademark from an overseas company to manufacture items under the trademark. Oklahoma incurs the following expenses in purchasing the trademark:

Amount paid for trademark	8,000,000
Import duties	80,000
Legal fees (negotiating the deal and ensuring the terms of the trademark are fair)	100,000
Training costs (required by overseas company before the trademark can be used)	20,000
Advertising new product	30,000
Cost of registering the trademark in the USA (required in terms of agreement with supplier)	90,000

Required

Determine the cost of the intangible asset purchased by Oklahoma.

Suggested solution

In terms of the Standard, the cost of the intangible is the purchase price plus any directly attributable costs of preparing the intangible asset for its intended use. The following costs are therefore included:

- The amount paid for the trademark, ie the purchase price.
- Import duties, since this is a directly attributable cost. If this cost had not been paid, the trademark could not have been used by the company in the USA, and is therefore incurred in preparing the asset for its intended use.
- Legal fees, since these were incurred in negotiating the terms of the trademark. Such costs were necessary in preparing the asset for its intended use since the manner in which the trademark can be used is influenced by the terms negotiated.
- Cost of registering the trademark in the USA since this cost must be incurred to comply with the agreement, and the trademark may only be used if this term has been met. Therefore the cost was necessarily incurred to be able to use the asset as intended.

The following costs are not included in the cost of the intangible:

- Advertising costs of the new product, since these are not costs incurred to be able to use the asset. The asset can be used regardless of whether the advertising costs are incurred.
- Training costs, since it does not satisfy the control criterion of an asset.

The calculation of the cost of the trademark purchased is as follows:

Amount paic for trademark	8,000,000
Import duties	80,000
Legal fees	100,000
Cost of registration of trademark	90,000
Total	8,270,000

13.3.2   Acquisition as part of a business combination

The probability recognition criterion is presumed to be met for intangible assets acquired in a business combination. Intangible assets acquired in a business combination must be recognised at fair value unless the fair value cannot be reliably measured without incurring undue cost or effort at the date of acquisition. The assessment to apply the exemption to recognising such intangible assets should be applied when weighing the benefit to the users of the financial statements of having this information against the cost or effort of obtaining this information for each acquisition.

> ⚠ Once identified in a business combination, recognition is based on measurability.

An intangible asset acquired in a business combination is measured at its fair value at the acquisition date, provided the fair value can be measured reliably, and the undue cost or effort exemption is not applied.

Example 13-3: Determining whether an item acquired in a business combination qualifies as an intangible asset

Inverness purchased a company, Glencoe. Glencoe is an ice-cream manufacturer, and its brand has become extremely popular and well known. At the date of purchase, the fair value of the ice-cream brand manufactured by Glencoe was considered to be CU1,000,000. This fair value was based on amounts paid by other ice-cream manufacturers to purchase brands of similar popularity. Inverness was willing to pay for the valuation of the Glencoe brand.

Required
Determine whether the ice cream brand acquired in the purchase of Glencoe can be recognised as an intangible asset.

Suggested solution
In terms of the Standard, an intangible asset is an identifiable non-monetary asset without physical substance that is capable of being separated from the entity.

There appears to be a market for the purchase of ice-cream brands, as the example states that other ice-cream manufacturers have purchased brands of similar popularity. As a result, the requirement that the asset is capable of being separated from the entity is met.

The asset is identifiable since the ice-cream brand is well known and popular, and this would have affected the price paid for Glencoe. If another manufacturer with a less popular brand was purchased, the purchase price would not be the same. It could also be a reason for the purchase of Glencoe as opposed to another ice-cream manufacturer.

The Standard is also clear that to recognise the intangible asset, the fair value must be reliably measurable. Since there has been recent market activity in the purchase of ice-cream brands, a reliable fair value is determinable.

Note: If Inverness decided that it would involve undue cost or effort to determine the separate value of the Glencoe ice-cream brand, it could have applied the exemption and the above mentioned value would have formed part of the Goodwill at acquisition and have been subsequently amortised as part of the Goodwill.

13.3.3 Government grants

Intangible assets may be obtained by way of a government grant. The entity may obtain the intangible asset for nil or nominal consideration, and in some cases, include other directly attributable costs such as legal and due diligence costs.

An intangible asset acquired by way of a government grant is measured at its fair value at the date the grant is received or receivable. Refer to *Chapter 23* for details on the treatment of the contra-entry, ie the credit or income entry.

Example 13-4: Accounting treatment of intangible asset arising from a government grant

On 1 December 20X1, the government grants Brighton the contractual right to operate a nuclear power plant. The estimated fair value of the right is CU15 million. However, in terms of the grant, Brighton must build free housing for the local community within two years. It is estimated that the housing will cost CU10 million.

On 30 November 20X2, the housing project is completed for CU10.5 million (housing cost incurred for 20X1 amounted to CU4 million).

Required

Discuss the accounting treatment of the above transaction for the periods ending 31 December 20X1 and 31 December 20X2, including the journal entries.

Suggested solution

Brighton must recognise the right as an intangible asset since it meets the contractual-legal condition for recognition. The right needs to be recognised at its fair value, CU15 million. However, there is a government grant and an obligation to build houses. The initial journal is:

1 December 20X1

Dr	Intangible asset (SFP)	15,000,000	
Cr	Housing liability (SFP)		10,000,000
Cr	Deferred government grant (SFP)		5,000,000

Recognition of intangible asset.

The deferred government grant of CU5,000,000 will be recognised as income when the future performance conditions are met (refer to *Chapter 23.3*). As 40% of the housing obligation is met at 31 December 20X1, 40% of the grant could be recognised as income.

31 December 20X1

Dr	Housing liability (SFP)	4,000,000	
Cr	Bank (SFP)		4,000,000

Recognition of costs incurred.

Dr	Deferred government grant (SFP)	2,000,000	
Cr	Government grant (SCI)		2,000,000

Recognition of 40% of the grant.

By 31 December 20X2 all the performance conditions have been met.

31 December 20X2

Dr	Housing liability (SFP)	6,000,000	
Dr	Additional costs (SCI)	500,000	
Cr	Bank (SFP)		6,500,000

Recognition of cost incurred.

Dr	Deferred government grant (SFP)	3,000,000	
Cr	Government grant (SCI)		3,000,000

Recognition of remaining 60% of the grand.

13.3.4   Exchange of assets

An intangible asset may be acquired in exchange for another non-monetary asset.

An intangible asset acquired in an exchange transaction is measured at its fair value at the date of the acquisition, unless either of the following circumstances exist:

- The exchange transaction lacks commercial substance.
- The fair value of neither the asset received nor the asset given up is reliably measurable.

In the case of the exceptions mentioned above, the asset is measured at the **carrying amount** of the asset given up.

The Standard does not define commercial substance, but full IFRS defines it as follows:

> **Full IFRS extract (IAS 38.46):**
>
> An entity determines whether an exchange transaction has commercial substance by considering the extent to which its future cash flows are expected to change as a result of the transaction. An exchange transaction has commercial substance if:
>
> a) The configuration (ie risk, timing and amount) of the cash flows of the asset received differs from the configuration of the cash flows of the asset transferred; or
> b) The entity-specific value of the portion of the entity's operations affected by the transaction changes as a result of the exchange; and
> c) The difference in (a) or (b) is significant relative to the fair value of the assets exchanged.
>
> For the purpose of determining whether an exchange transaction has commercial substance, the entity-specific value of the portion of the entity's operations affected by the transaction shall reflect post-tax cash flows. The result of these analyses may be clear without an entity having to perform detailed calculations.

Example 13-5: Determining accounting treatment of intangible assets acquired through an exchange of assets

Long Island exchanged its property, with a carrying value of CU1,000,000 and fair value of CU1,500,000, for the right to use a patent, on 31 December 20X1. The estimated fair value of the patent acquired is CU1,600,000. The acquisition of the patent will expand the range of products currently offered by Long Island.

Required

Discuss the accounting treatment of the above transaction by Long Island for the period ending 31 December 20X1, including the journal entries.

Suggested solution

Long Island has acquired a patent that will expand its product range, and therefore increase sales. The above transaction does not lack commercial substance since the company has exchanged dissimilar assets, and the asset acquired was valued more than the asset given up. The risks associated with the patent are dissimilar to the risks associated with the property.

The patent should be recognised, at 31 December 20X1, at its fair value, CU1,600,000.

Example 13-5: Determining accounting treatment of intangible assets acquired through an exchange of assets *(continued)*		
Journals		
1 December 20X1		
Dr Intangible asset (SFP)	1,600,000	
Cr Property, plant and equipment		1,000,000
Cr Gain on exchange of intangible asset (P/L)		600,000
Recognition of intangible asset.		
Note: *If no fair value was determinable for the patent, it would be recognised at CU1,500,000 being the fair value of the asset given up.*		

13.4 Internally generated intangible assets

All expenditure incurred on internally generated intangible assets (including research and development costs) is expensed immediately unless the cost could be capitalised in the cost of another asset.

> All research and development costs are expensed.

Specifically, the Standard provides the following examples of intangible assets that should be expensed:

- Internally generated brands.
- Mastheads.
- Publishing titles.
- Customer lists.
- Start-up activities (establishing, opening, and starting costs).
- Training activities.
- Advertising and promotional activities.
- Relocating or re-organising activities.
- Internally generated goodwill.

This is not a comprehensive list.

However, pre-payments made in advance of the delivery of goods or the rendering of services may still be recognised as assets, but not under this section of the Standard.

13.5 Items previously expensed

Any expenditure on intangible assets that was previously expensed cannot be capitalised at a later date.

13.6 Measurement after initial recognition

After initial recognition, intangible assets are measured at cost less any accumulated amortisation and any accumulated impairment losses.

13.7   Amortisation

> ♫ All intangible assets must be amortised, including goodwill.

13.7.1   Useful life

All intangible assets are considered to have a finite useful life and the useful life must be estimated. If the useful life of an intangible asset cannot be reliably determined, the life must be determined based on management's best estimate but cannot exceed 10 years.

> ♫ A maximum of 10 years useful life is presumed for intangible assets without a contractual period of use.

When the useful life of an intangible asset arises from contractual or other legal rights, the useful life is limited to the period of the contractual or other legal rights, but may be reduced if the period of expected usage is shorter. Renewal periods, in such contracts or legal rights, are only considered if there is supporting evidence that the renewal is available without significant cost.

> 👁 Because a renewal period is only considered if there is supporting evidence that the renewal is available without significant cost, an intangible asset still in use during the renewal period, may be carried at a zero value – unless there is a cost of renewal which will need to be capitalised or the useful life was re-assessed in light of the renewal period prior to the asset being fully amortised.

13.7.2   Amortisation period and amortisation method

The depreciable amount of intangible assets is allocated on a systematic basis over the useful life. The amortisation method must reflect the expected pattern in which the asset's future economic benefits are consumed, for example the unit of production method when the intangible asset is linked to a specific production process. If a pattern cannot be determined reliably, the straight-line method should be used.

> ♫ Amortisation reflects the pattern of the consumption of economic benefits.

Example 13-6: Calculating amortisation of intangible asset using the straight-line method

Pisa acquires a fishing licence on 1 January 20X1 for the amount of CU100,000.

Required

Account for the fishing licence by Pisa for the period ending 31 December 20X1, if the fishing licence is valid from 1 March 20X1 for:

- A three-year period.
- An undeterminable period.
- A three-year period with another three-year renewal option at a nominal cost.

Suggested solution

The fishing licence qualifies as an intangible asset since the contractual-legal requirement is met. The initial journal is:

1 January 20X1

Dr	Intangible asset (SFP)	100,000	
Cr	Bank/Cash (SFP)		100,000

Account for the purchase of the licence.

For a three-year period

The entity must amortise the licence over three years on the straight-line basis from 1 March 20X1, as this is the date that it is available for use; Pisa cannot use it before this date.

Journal

31 December 20X1

Dr	Amortisation expense (P/L)	27,778	
Cr	Intangible asset – accumulated amortisation (SFP)		27,778

Account for the purchase of the licence.
(CU100,000/3 years x 10/12 months)

Undeterminable period

When there is no contractual period, the licence may be amortised over a maximum period of 10 years. Pisa's management should assess over what period the economic benefits will be available to the entity. If this is determined for at least 10 years then the maximum 10-year period may be used. If not, the shorter period determined should be applied as in the above example.

The journal below is based on the assumption that the fishing licence will provide economic benefits for at least 10 years.

Journal

31 December 20X1

Dr	Amortisation expense (P/L)	8,333	
Cr	Intangible asset – accumulated amortisation (SFP)		8,333

Account for the amortisation of the licence.
(CU100,000 10 years x 10/12 months)

For a three-year period with a renewal option

Renewal periods are only considered if there is supporting evidence that the renewal is available without significant cost. In this case, the renewal option for a further three years appears to be available without any significant cost, therefore the licence will be amortised over six years.

Example 13-6: Calculating amortisation of intangible asset using the straight-line method *(continued)*

Journal

31 December 20X1

Dr	Amortisation expense (P/L)	13,889	
Cr	Intangible asset – accumulated amortisation (SFP)		13,889

Account for the amortisation of the licence.

(CU100,000/6 years x 10/12 months)

The amortisation charge for each period is expensed in profit or loss, unless it can be capitalised into the cost of another asset. Amortisation commences when the intangible asset is available for use. An intangible asset is available for use when it is at the location, and in a condition necessary for use in the manner intended by management. Amortisation ceases when the asset is derecognised.

Example 13-7: Calculation of amortisation of intangible asset using the unit of production method

Oceania acquires a fishing licence on 1 January 20X1 for the amount of CU100,000. The licence is valid from 1 March 20X1 and is limited to 1 million units of fish per period, running 1 March to 28 February annually. Due to seasonality, by 31 December 20X1, the company has almost utilised its quota for the year and has already consumed 950,000 units.

Required

Account for the fishing licence by Oceania for the period ending 31 December 20X1.

Suggested solution

The fishing licence qualifies as an intangible asset since the contractual-legal requirement is met.

A straight-line method of depreciation is not suitable, since the consumption of units changes depending on the seasons. Therefore a unit of production method is more appropriate. In total, the entity is permitted to fish three million units over the three-year period.

Journals

1 January 20X1

Dr	Intangible asset (SFP)	100,000	
Cr	Bank (SFP)		100,000

Account for the purchase of the licence.

31 December 20X1

Dr	Amortisation expense (P/L)	31,667	
Cr	Intangible asset – accumulated amortisation (SFP)		31,667

Account for the amortisation of the licence.

(CU100,000 / 3 million units x 950,000 units)

13.7.3 Residual value

In most cases, the residual value of an intangible asset is presumed to be zero.

The default residual value of an intangible asset is zero. However, there are two exceptions:

- When there is a commitment by a third party to purchase the intangible at the end of its useful life; or
- When there is an active market for the intangible asset.

In the last instance, the residual value must be determinable by reference to such a market, and it must be probable that the market will exist at the end of the intangible's useful life.

> 👁 It is highly unlikely that an active market will exist for intangible assets as it requires homogenous products.

13.7.4 Review of amortisation period and amortisation method

> 📖 A review is triggered by indicators.

A change in the residual value or useful life of an intangible asset could be indicated by factors such as a change in how an asset is used, technological advancement, and changes in market prices. If such indicators are present, previous estimates are reviewed, and the residual value, amortisation method or useful life appropriately amended. Such changes represent changes in accounting estimates and are accounted for prospectively (refer to *Chapter 7*).

Example 13-8: Calculation of amortisation when useful life changes

Luxembourg purchased a patent, on 1 January 20X0, for the amount of CU2,000,000 to manufacture computer parts. At 1 January 20X0, management considered the useful life to be 10 years.

However, by 31 December 20X1 a competitor had released a new product that is significantly better than Luxembourg's product, and Luxembourg had noticed a large decline in the demand for its products. Management reconsidered the useful life of the patent, and considers that it will only be useful for another two years from 31 December 20X1.

Required

Account for the patent by Luxembourg for the period ending 31 December 20X1.

Suggested solution

The patent qualifies as an intangible asset as it was not internally generated and was a separate purchase.

At 1 January 20X1, the carrying amount of the patent would have been CU1,800,000 (CU2,000,000 less accumulated amortisation of CU200,000 (CU2,000,000/10 x 1 year). At 1 January 20X1, the carrying value of CU1,800,000 is amortised over the remaining revised useful life of three years (management estimated a remaining useful life of two years from 31 December 20X1).

Example 13-8: Calculation of amortisation when useful life changes *(continued)*		
Journal		
31 December 20X1		
Dr Amortisation expense (P/L)	600,000	
Cr Intangible asset – accumulated amortisation (SFP)		600,000
(CU1,800,000/3 years x 1 year)		
Account for the amortisation of the patent.		

13.8   Impairment

Impairment of intangible assets is based on the normal impairment guidance of assets (refer to *Chapter 14*).

13.9   Retirements and disposals

An intangible asset is derecognised and a gain or loss recognised in profit or loss on disposal. A loss is also recognised when no future economic benefits are expected from the intangible asset.

Refer to *Chapter 12* as the calculation of the gain or loss on disposal of an asset is the same as for property, plant and equipment.

13.10   Disclosures

Disclose the following for each class of intangible asset:

- The useful lives or the amortisation rates.
- The amortisation methods.
- The gross carrying amount and any accumulated amortisation (aggregated with accumulated impairment losses) at the beginning and end of the reporting period.
- The line item(s) in the statement of comprehensive income in which any amortisation charge is included.
- A reconciliation of the carrying amount at the beginning and end of the reporting period, showing separately:
  - Additions.
  - Disposals.
  - Acquisitions through business combinations.
  - Amortisation.
- Impairment losses.
- Other changes.

This reconciliation is only required for the current year.

13.10.1   Additional disclosures

- A description of the carrying amount and the remaining amortisation periods of any individual intangible assets that are material to the entity's financial statements.

- For intangible assets acquired by way of a government grant initially recognised at fair value:
  - Their fair values initially recognised.
  - Their carrying amounts at the reporting date.
- The existence and carrying amounts of intangible assets to which the entity has restricted title or that are pledged as security for liabilities.
- The amount of contractual commitments for the acquisition of intangible assets.
- The aggregate amount of research and development expenditure recognised as an expense during the period; this excludes items capitalised in other assets.

13.11   Summary

- An identifiable non-monetary asset without physical substance is recognised as an asset when it is probable that future economic benefits will result, and the cost can be measured reliably.
- Measurement at initial recognition:
  - Generally measured at cost, which may include its actual cost, costs to bring it to use, less any discounts.
  - Measured at fair value in the event of an exchange of assets, as a result of a government grant in certain instances, or as part of a business combination if the undue cost or effort exemption is not applied.
- All research and development expenditure must be recognised as an expense when it is incurred unless it forms part of the cost of another asset that meets the recognition criteria in terms of the Standard.
- Items that are always recognised as expenses include internally generated brands/mastheads and others, start-up costs, training costs, advertising, and relocating a division or entity.
- After initial recognition, an entity must measure intangible assets at cost less any accumulated amortisation and any accumulated impairment losses.
- All intangibles are considered to have a finite useful life. For intangible assets arising from contractual or other legal rights, the useful life must not exceed the period of the contractual or legal rights, but may be shorter depending on the period over which the entity expects to use the assets. If the useful life of an intangible asset cannot be reliably determined, the life must be determined based on management's best estimate but cannot exceed 10 years.
- Factors such as a change in how an intangible asset is used, technological advancement, and changes in market prices may indicate that the residual value or useful life of an intangible asset has changed since the most recent annual reporting date. If such indicators are present, an entity must review its previous estimates, and amend the residual value, amortisation method or useful life, as appropriate. The entity must account for any such changes as changes in accounting estimate.
- The measurement basis, amortisation methods, useful lives, gross carrying amounts and accumulated amortisation, reconciliation showing additions, disposals, acquisitions, impairments, amortisation, and other changes must all be disclosed.

Chapter 14
Impairment of assets

Contents

14.1   Scope

The impairment guidance in this chapter relates to the accounting of all assets other than:

- Inventories (refer to *Chapter 8*).
- Deferred tax assets (refer to *Chapter 21*).
- Assets arising from employee benefits (refer to *Chapter 20*).
- Financial assets (refer to *Chapter 17*).
- Investment property measured at fair value (refer to *Chapter 11*).
- Biological assets related to agricultural activity measured at fair value less estimated cost to sell (refer to *Chapter 29*).
- Assets arising from construction contracts (refer to *Chapter 22*).

The guidance under this chapter is therefore applicable to all other assets, such as property, plant and equipment (including investment property not recognised at fair value), intangible assets, goodwill, investments in associates, and investments in JVs. For investments in associates and JVs, the impairment should be done on the investment as a single asset. *Table 14-1* is a summary of the impairment guidance applicable to different assets.

Table 14-1: Impairment guidance

Asset	Impairment guidance
Inventories	Estimated selling price less costs to complete and sell (refer to *Chapter 8.6*)
Deferred tax assets	Undiscounted amount based on deductible temporary differences and unutilised tax losses with a valuation allowance to ensure the carrying amount is the highest amount that is more likely than not to be recovered based on current and/or future taxable profit (refer to *Chapter 21.4*).
Employee benefits	Fair value (refer to *Chapter 20.9*).
Financial assets	Financial assets held at fair value are not impaired (refer to *Chapter 17*). Impairment of a financial asset measured at amortised cost is the difference between the asset's carrying amount and the present value of estimated cash flows discounted at the asset's original effective interest rate. If such a financial instrument has a variable interest rate, the discount rate for measuring any impairment loss is the current effective interest rate determined under the contract (refer to *Chapter 17.9*). Impairment of a financial asset measured at cost less impairment is the difference between the asset's carrying amount and the best estimate of the amount that the entity would receive for the asset, if the asset were sold at the reporting date (refer to *Chapter 17.9*). Refer to *Figure 17-6* for a graphical illustration of the impairment model for financial instruments.

Table 14-1: Impairment guidance *(continued)*

Asset	Impairment guidance
Investment properties	Investment properties held at fair value are not impaired (refer to *Chapter 11*). If the investment property is not measured at fair value, the property is treated as property, plant and equipment. Therefore, it is subject to the impairment guidance in this chapter.
Biological assets and agricultural produced harvest	Biological assets held at fair value are not impaired. If certain biological assets are not measured at fair value, they are subject to the impairment guidance in this chapter. Agricultural produce harvest is treated as inventories. For further guidance on the accounting for biological assets and agricultural produce, refer to *Chapter 29.2*.
All other assets, not excluded above	The higher of fair value less cost to sell and value-in-use.

14.2 Definitions

The impairment of other assets is based on the following definitions:

- An **impairment loss** is the amount by which the carrying amount of an asset exceeds its recoverable amount.
- The **recoverable amount** is the higher of an asset's (or cash-generating unit's) fair value less cost to sell and its value-in-use.
- A **cash-generating unit (CGU)** is the smallest identifiable group of assets that generates cash inflows that are largely independent of the cash inflows from other assets or groups of assets.
- **Fair value less cost to sell** is the amount obtainable from the sale of an asset or CGU in an arm's length transaction between knowledgeable, willing parties, less the costs of disposal.
- **Value-in-use** is the present value of the future cash flows expected to be derived from an asset or CGU.

14.3 Impairment principles

The carrying amount of the asset is only reduced to its recoverable amount when the recoverable amount is less than the carrying amount. An impairment loss is then recognised in profit or loss unless the asset is carried at a revalued amount. An impairment loss on a revalued asset is treated as a revaluation decrease to the extent that the impairment loss equates to or is less than the amount of the revaluation that stands to the credit of the related assets. Where the impairment exceeds the amount of the credit in the revaluation reserve, then such amount is recognised in profit or loss. *Figure 14-1* indicates how the impairment principles are applied in this chapter by including the different options that are available to determine the recoverable amount.

Figure 14-1: Impairment principle

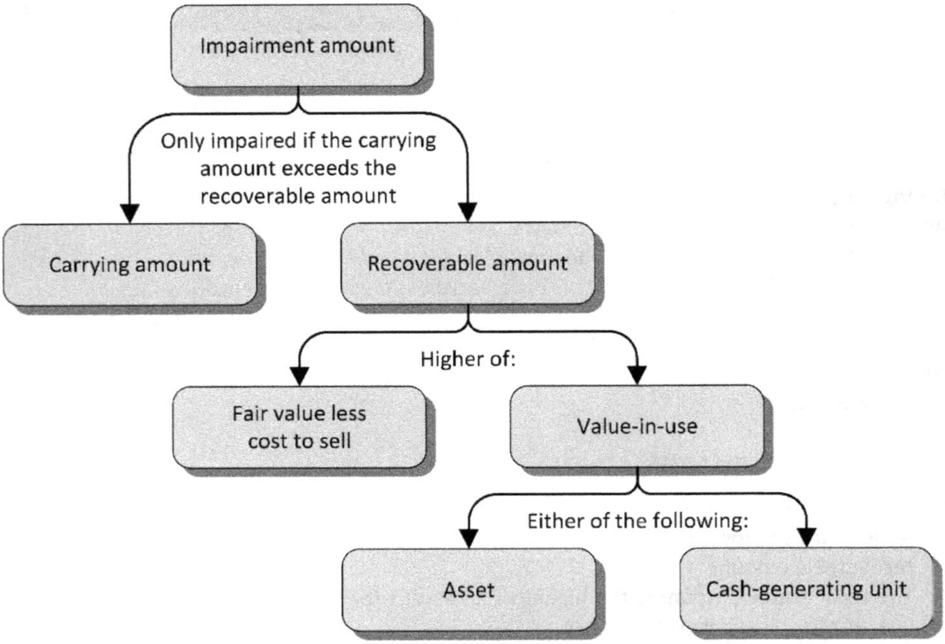

14.3.1 Indicators of impairment

Assets only need to be impaired when there is an indicator of impairment (refer to *Table 14-2* and *Table 14-3* for the indicators of impairment, included in the Standard). At the reporting date, entities must therefore assess whether there are indicators of impairment. If there are such indicators, the recoverable amount of an asset is estimated. If the recoverable amount of an individual asset cannot be estimated, the recoverable amount of the CGU to which the asset belongs is estimated. Impairment guidance is thus provided for single assets and CGUs.

> An impairment test is only carried out when there are indicators of impairment.

Table 14-2: External indicators of impairment

External sources of information
An asset's market value has declined significantly more than would be expected as a result of the passage of time or normal use.
Significant changes with an adverse effect on the entity have taken place, or will take place in the near future, in the technological, market, economic or legal environment in which the entity operates, or in the market to which an asset is dedicated.

Table 14-2: External indicators of impairment *(continued)*

Market interest rates or other market rates of return on investments have increased, and those increases are likely to materially affect the discount rate used in calculating an asset's value-in-use, and decrease the asset's fair value less cost to sell.
The carrying amount of the net assets of the entity is more than the estimated fair value of the entity as a whole.

Table 14-3: Internal indicators of impairment

Internal sources of information
Evidence is available of obsolescence or physical damage of an asset.
Significant changes with an adverse effect on the entity have taken place, or are expected to take place in the near future, the extent to which, or manner in which, an asset is used or is expected to be used. These changes include the asset becoming idle, plans to discontinue or restructure the operation to which an asset belongs, plans to dispose of an asset before the previously expected date, and re-assessing the useful life of an asset as finite rather than indefinite.
Evidence is available from internal reporting indicating that the economic performance of an asset is, or will be, worse than expected. In this context, economic performance includes operating results and cash flows.

Example 14-1: Impairment indicator
An indicator exists that the carrying amount of a server may be impaired since the item will be replaced by new technology in one year's time. An impairment calculation is prepared and the value-in-use (taking into consideration the possible replacement technology) is above the carrying amount.
No impairment is required, but the server must be depreciated over the remaining period to the estimated residual value at the date of anticipated disposal or retirement.

An indicator of impairment may also trigger a review of the remaining useful life, the depreciation (amortisation) method, or the residual value of an asset. These items might need to be adjusted when no impairment loss is recognised.

14.3.2   Recoverable amount

Impairment is based on the higher of the fair value less cost to sell and the value-in-use.

The recoverable amount of an asset or a CGU is the higher of its fair value less cost to sell and its value-in-use. Normally, if an impairment test is applicable, both an asset's fair value less cost to sell and its value-in-use should be determined. However, it is not necessary to determine both in either one of the following situations:

- The value determined first (ie its fair value less cost to sell or its value-in-use) exceeds the asset's carrying amount.
- There is no reason to believe that the asset's value-in-use may materially exceed the assets fair value less cost to sell. This might be the case when an entity is going to dispose of an asset in the near future.

14.3.3   Fair value less cost to sell

Fair value less cost to sell is the amount obtainable from the sale of an asset in an arm's length transaction between knowledgeable, willing parties, less the costs of disposal. Fair value is determined in terms of the fair value guidance in *Chapter 17*.

14.3.4   Value-in-use

Value-in-use is the present value of the future cash flows expected to be derived from an asset. *Figure 14-2* provides the elements considered in determining value-in-use. Value-in-use is a normal present value calculation determined by estimating the future cash flows and applying the appropriate discount rate to the future cash flows, ie a financial calculator or spreadsheet program may be used to calculate the value.

The cash flows include **cash flows from the continuing use of the asset and from its ultimate disposal**. The discount rate is the current market risk-free rate of return.

Figure 14-2: Elements to consider in a value-in-use calculation

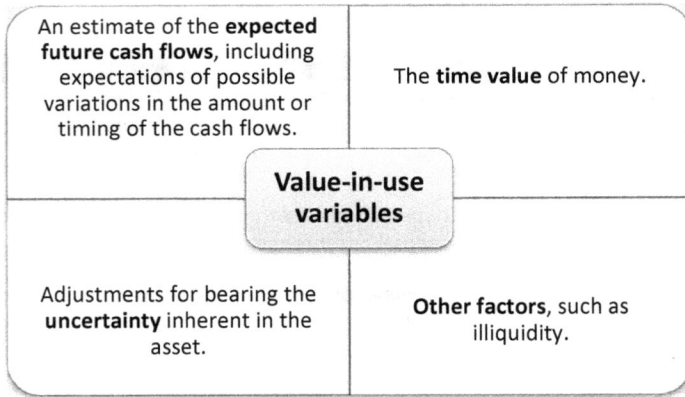

An estimate of the **expected future cash flows**, including expectations of possible variations in the amount or timing of the cash flows.	The **time value** of money.
Value-in-use variables	
Adjustments for bearing the **uncertainty** inherent in the asset.	**Other factors**, such as illiquidity.

14.3.4.1   Estimation of future cash flows

$$\text{Future cash flows} = \text{inflows} - \text{attributable outflows} + \text{net proceeds on disposal.}$$

Estimates of future cash flows include inflows from continuing usage; cash outflows that are necessarily incurred to generate the cash inflows and net cash flows on the disposal of the asset at the end of the useful life. The cash outflows include outflows to prepare the asset for use and cash flows that are directly related or allocated on a reasonable and consistent basis to the asset. The estimation of the net cash flow on disposal must be based on an arm's length transaction. Specifically, the estimation of future cash flows does not include expected cash flows from the following:

- Cash inflows or outflows from financing activities.
- Income tax receipts or payments.

To assist in the projection of the cash flows, recent financial budgets or forecasts may be used to estimate the cash flows. An extrapolation of the projections based on the budgets or forecasts may be applied to estimate future cash flows beyond those budgeted or forecast. This may be done by using a steady or declining growth rate for subsequent years, unless an increasing rate can be justified.

Example 14-2: Calculating value-in-use of a CGU

An indicator exists that the assets of a division of Canberra are impaired. The indicator is the decision to sell the division at the end of the next period (31 December 20X2). The cash flows of the division for 20X2 are as follows:

Revenue	560,000
Cost to produce the revenue	420,000
Estimated selling price less cost to sell at 31 December 20X2	250,000

The estimated selling price less cost to sell is estimated to be CU310,000 at 31 December 20X1.

Required

Determine the recoverable amount at 31 December 20X1.

Assumptions

- An appropriate discount rate for this division is 12%.
- Cash flows from revenue and costs are earned and incurred evenly throughout the year.

Suggested solution

The value-in-use is the present value of the future cash flows, calculated as follows:

Discounted revenue	529,150
Discounted cost to produce the revenue	(396,863)
Operating cash flow	132,287

Note: Amounts are discounted at 12% for a half-year period to reflect the average discount rate for the next year.

Fair value less costs to sell (CU250,000 discounted at 12%)	223,214
The value in use is the present value of the future operating cash flow (CU132,287) plus the present value of the estimated fair value less cost to sell at 31 December 20X2 (CU223, 214) = CU355,501.	355,501

The recoverable amount is the higher of the value-in-use (CU355,501) and fair value less cost to sell at 31 December 20X1 (CU310,00), in this case, the value in use.

Future cash flows are estimated for the asset in its current condition. Therefore a future restructuring to which an entity is not yet committed is excluded, and so are any future activities for improving or enhancing the asset's performance.

Example 14-3: Future restructuring

There is an indicator that the assets of a certain division of an entity might be impaired. The management of the entity believes that if the division is restructured, it will be profitable again. Since the entity is not currently committed to the restructuring of the division, an impairment assessment of the assets of the division must be carried out, without considering the effect of any restructuring.

14.3.4.2   Discount rate

The discount rate (or rates) used in the present value calculation is a pre-tax rate. The rate reflects current market assessments of the time value of money, which is normally the current market risk-free rate of return. The rate must, however, be adjusted for any risk specific to the asset for which the future cash flow estimates have not been adjusted.

> The discount rate must be based on the risk-free market rate, adjusted for inherent risks.

To eliminate any duplication, the discount rate is not adjusted for any risks incorporated in the cash flows.

> In estimating the future cash flows of an asset considered for impairment, uncertainty regarding the outcome is factored into the cash flows. These uncertainties may not be considered again in the determination of the discount rate.

14.4   Impairment of a CGU

An impairment test for a CGU is based on an assessment of the total unit. An impairment loss is recognised when the recoverable amount of the CGU is less than the carrying amount of all the assets of the CGU. The Standard prescribes five steps as the impairment methodology for a CGU (*refer to Figure 14.3*):

Figure 14-3: Five steps for the impairment of a CGU

Step 1: Identify the CGU

Step 2: Calculate the recoverable amount

Step 3: Calculate the amount of the impairment loss

Step 4: Allocate the impairment loss to the assets

Step 5: Adjust future amortisation and depreciation

14.4.1   Step 1: Determine/identify CGUs (if applicable)

The first step in the impairment of a CGU is to identify the unit. The unit is identified by applying the definition of a CGU. A CGU is the smallest identifiable group of assets that generates cash inflows that are largely independent of the cash inflows from other assets or group of assets. The independent generation of cash flows is the decisive factor.

Example 14-4: Identification of a CGU

A company uses coal to create heat in its production process. It also mines the coal on the same property and owns a conveyer belt that transports the coal from the mine to the factory.

Required
Determine whether or not the activities constitute different CGUs.

Suggested solution
To determine whether the mining activities and the production process are two different CGUs the entity must consider whether the mine and the factory could generate cash flows that are largely independent. 1) It must assess whether the coal could be sold independently to third parties by taking the location of the mine and the possible market into consideration. 2) It must assess whether coal could be obtained from third parties by considering the location of the factory.

If any of these assessments result in losses, but the overall performance results in a profit, this points to co-dependence of the various units – the mine and the factory must be regarded as one CGU.

14.4.2   Step 2: Calculate recoverable amount

The next step is to calculate the recoverable amount for the CGU by calculating the fair value less cost to sell (refer to *14.3.3*) and value-in-use (refer to *14.3.4*) for the CGU.

The best evidence of the fair value is a binding sale agreement or an active market. If neither is available, the entity should determine the fair value less cost to sell based on the best information available to reflect the amount that the entity would obtain on the disposal of the CGU in an arm's length transaction (refer to *Chapter 2.8.3*).

If the recoverable amount is less than the carrying amount of the total net assets allocated to the CGU, an impairment loss is recognised. The impairment loss is the difference between the carrying amount of total net assets allocated to the CGU and the recoverable amount.

Figure 14-4: Determining the impairment loss

14.4.3 Steps 3 and 4: Calculation and allocation of impairment loss

The impairment loss must be allocated to all the assets of the CGU to determine the carrying value of each asset after the recognition of the impairment. The impairment loss is allocated to the carrying amount of each asset in the following order:

- Reduce the carrying amount of any goodwill included (this is applicable to subsidiaries and JVs or associates accounted for using the equity method).
- Allocate the balance pro-rata on the basis of the carrying amount of each asset.

However, a restriction is provided, in that the carrying amount of all assets in the CGU (excluding goodwill) is not reduced below the highest of:

- Its fair value less cost to sell (if determinable).
- Its value-in-use (if determinable).
- Zero.

Any excess amount of the impairment loss that cannot be allocated to an asset because of the restriction is allocated to the other assets of the CGU pro-rata, on the basis of the carrying amount of those other assets.

Example 14-5: Allocation of impairment loss

The following information is provided for the impairment of a CGU as at the reporting date:

	Carrying value	Fair value less cost to sell
Goodwill	10,000	-
Machinery	20,000	14,000
Computer equipment	4,000	3,500
	34,000	**17,500**

Example 14-5: Allocation of impairment loss *(continued)*

Based on the discounted cash flow method, the recoverable amount of the CGU was determined to be CU18,000.

Required

Allocate the impairment loss among the assets of the CGU.

Suggested solution

The steps to determine the impairment loss and allocate the loss to the different assets of the CGU are:

- The impairment loss is CU16,000 (CU34,000 - CU18,000) based on the difference between the carrying amount and recoverable amount of the CGU.
- CU10,000 is first allocated to goodwill.
- The balance of CU6,000 is allocated pro-rata to the machinery and the computer equipment in relation to the carrying amounts (CU20,000:CU4,000), ie (5:1). The allocation must, therefore, be allocated CU5,000 (5/6 x 6,000) to the machinery and CU1,000 to the computer equipment (1/6 x 6,000).
- However, the fair value less cost to sell of the computer equipment is CU3,500. Therefore the impairment of the computer equipment is limited to CU500 (CU4,000 - CU3,500).
- The amount not impaired regarding the computer equipment of CU500 is re-allocated to the machinery. The impairment of the machinery is thus CU5,500 (CU5,000 + CU500).

The overall effect of the impairment at the reporting date is:

Asset	Carrying value	Impairment	Adjusted carrying value
Goodwill	10,000	10,000	-
Machinery	20,000	5,500	14,500
Computer equipment	4,000	500	3,500
	34,000	**16,000**	**18,000**

14.4.4   Step 5: Adjust future amortisation and depreciation

After assets are impaired, amortisation or depreciation of each asset must be appropriately adjusted in the future periods to reflect the effect of the impairment.

Example 14-6: Adjustment of depreciation and amortisation

A machine's remaining useful life is five years at the reporting date. At this date the carrying value of the machine is impaired from CU20,000 to CU15,000. The balance of CU15,000 is now depreciated over the remaining useful life of five years, thus CU3,000 per year.

14.5   Reversal of an impairment loss

An impairment loss for goodwill can never be reversed. Reversals of impairment of other assets begin with an assessment of an indicator(s) whether an impairment loss no longer exists or may have decreased. Reversal indicators are generally the opposite of the indicators for impairment listed above.

When an indicator of a reversal of impairment exists, an assessment is made whether or not a reversal is required. The reversal determination depends on whether the prior impairment loss on the asset was based on the impairment of an individual asset or a CGU.

14.5.1 Reversal of individual impaired asset

The new recoverable amount is estimated at the reporting date for the individual asset that was impaired. If the recoverable amount exceeds the carrying amount a reversal is recognised.

The amount of the reversal is determined by deducting the carrying amount from the recoverable amount, if the recoverable amount is higher than the carrying amount. However, the reversal of an impairment loss is limited to the carrying amount that would have been determined (net of amortisation or depreciation) had no impairment loss been recognised previously. If such limitation is applicable, the reversal is restricted to the amount the asset would have been carried. If not, the reversal is limited to the recoverable amount.

The amount of the reversal is recognised in profit or loss unless the asset is carried at a revalued amount. An impairment reversal on a revalued asset is treated as a revaluation increase. After a reversal of an impairment loss, the depreciation or amortisation of the future periods must also be adjusted appropriately.

Example 14-7: Calculation of a reversal of an individual asset

Two years ago an asset was impaired. The current carrying value of the asset is CU15,000. If the asset was not impaired, the current carrying value would be CU18,000. An indicator exists that the reasons for the impairment have reversed. The new recoverable amount of the asset is estimated to be CU20,000.

Required
Determine the amount of an impairment reversal, if applicable.

Suggested solution
The amount of the reversal is limited to what would have been the carrying amount had there been no initial impairment, ie.CU18,000. The reversal recognised in profit or loss is thus CU3,000 (18,000 - 15,000). The new carrying value of CU18,000 must be depreciated over the remaining estimated useful life to the estimated residual value.

Note: The original impairment indicator does not have to be reversed.

14.5.2 Reversal for a CGU

When the original impairment loss was based on a CGU, the reversal steps are based on a combination of the steps followed for an impairment of a CGU, and the limitations of reversal of an individual asset. These steps are illustrated in *Figure 14-5* and explained in *Example 14.8*. Impairment reversals of revalued assets are also treated as revaluation increases.

Figure 14-5: Steps in the reversal of a previously recognised CGU impairment

Step 1: Estimate the recoverable amount of the CGU at the current reporting date.

Step 2: Determine the total amount of the reversal: the amount by which the recoverable amount of the CGU exceeds the carrying amount.

Step 3: Allocate the reversal to all the assets (except goodwill) of the CGU pro rata to the carrying amounts of each asset.

Step 4: Limit the reversal of each asset to the lower of:
- Recoverable amount.
- Carrying amount that would have been determined had no impairment loss been recognised previously.

Step 5: Any excess amount not allocated to individual assets is re-allocated pro rata to the other assets not limited.

Step 6: After all excesses are allocated, the balance of the reversal is recognised in profit and loss.

Step 7: The depreciation or amortisation of each asset is adjusted appropriately.

Example 14-8: Allocation of a reversal

The following items are regarded as one CGU:

	Carrying value	Carrying value if no previous impairment	Individual recoverable amount
Goodwill	-	10,000	-
Boiler machine	20,000	24,000	25,000
Strainer machine	4,000	5,000	4,800
Total	**24,000**	**39,000**	**29,800**

There is an indicator of a reversal; the new total recoverable amount of the CGU is determined to be CU33,000.

Required

Determine the amount of the reversal and allocate it between the different assets of the CGU.

Suggested solution

The steps to allocate the reversal to the different assets of the CGU are:
- The total possible reversal is CU9,000 (CU33,000 - CU24,000).
- Goodwill may not be reversed, thus the reversal of CU9,000 must be allocated to the boiler machine and strainer machine in relation to their carrying values (CU20,000:CU4,000), ie 5:1. The allocation is CU7,500 for the boiler machine and CU1,500 for the strainer machine.
- However, the reversal of each asset is limited to the lower of each asset's individual recoverable amount or the carrying amount had no impairment been applicable. The reversal of the boiler machine is thus limited to CU4,000 (CU24,000 - CU20,000); the strainer machine to CU800 (CU4,800 - CU4,000). The reversal is thus limited for each machine.

Example 14-8: Allocation of a reversal *(continued)*

The overall effect of the reversal:

	Carrying value	Reversal	Adjusted carrying value
Goodwill	-	-	-
Boiler machine	20,000	4,000	24,000
Strainer machine	4,000	800	4,800
	24,000	**4,800**	**28,800**

14.6　Additional requirements for impairment of goodwill

The Standard stipulates additional guidance for the following:

- Allocation of goodwill on the date of acquisition.
- Unrecognised goodwill relating to non-controlling interest.
- When goodwill cannot be allocated to CGUs.

Goodwill acquired in a business combination should be allocated to the appropriate CGUs, which may be part of the existing or acquired business, on the date of acquisition. Goodwill is allocated to each CGU that is expected to benefit from the synergies of the combination. This allocation is made irrespective of whether or not some of the assets or liabilities of the acquiree are assigned to such CGUs.

The recoverable amount of a CGU includes the non-controlling interest in goodwill that is not recognised in the financial statements. Only the parent's share of goodwill is recognised in the consolidated financial statements. The Standard requires that the amount of goodwill included in the carrying amount of a CGU must be notionally adjusted. This is done by grossing up the carrying amount of goodwill allocated to the CGU to include the goodwill attributable to the non-controlling interest. This notionally adjusted carrying amount is then compared with the recoverable amount of the unit to determine whether the CGU is impaired.

Example 14-9: Adjustment to non-controlling interest

The Vatican City has an 80% interest in Brussels. Goodwill of CU22,000 was recognised on the acquisition of Brussels, which has been amortised to CU16,000 at the reporting date.

The investments in Brussels are considered for impairment. Brussels as an entity is regarded to be a CGU.

In the consolidated financial statements of the Vatican City Group, the consolidated values of the Brussels' assets must be considered for impairment. The consolidated impairment loss will be the difference between the consolidated carrying amounts of Brussels' assets (including goodwill) and its recoverable amounts. The amount of goodwill will be adjusted to CU20,000 (CU16,000 x 100/80) to include the non-controlling interest share.

If goodwill cannot be allocated on a non-arbitrary basis to CGUs after a business combination, special guidance is provided. The impairment of goodwill in such instances depends on whether the acquired business is integrated or not. Integrated means the acquired business has been restructured or dissolved into the reporting entity or other subsidiaries.

For an acquired business that is **not integrated**, the impairment assessment will be made for the acquired business. When the acquired business is **integrated** in the group, impairment will be assessed for the entire group of entities, excluding any entities or businesses that have not been integrated.

14.7   Disclosure

Disclose the following for each class of assets:

- The amount of impairment losses recognised in profit or loss and the line item(s) in the statement of comprehensive income (or income statement) in which those impairment losses are included.
- The amount of reversals of impairment losses recognised in profit or loss during the period and the line item(s) in the statement of comprehensive income (or income statement) in which those impairment losses are reversed.

The information required above is disclosed for each of the following classes of asset:

- Inventories.
- Property, plant and equipment (including investment property accounted for using the cost method).
- Goodwill.
- Intangible assets other than goodwill.
- Investments in associates.
- Investments in JVs.

14.8   Summary

- **Inventories**
  - At each reporting date, the carrying amount of the inventories should be compared to the selling price less costs to complete and sell. If the item is impaired, the amount must immediately be recognised in profit or loss for the period.
  - When the circumstances that led to the impairment no longer exist, the impairment may be reversed.
- **Other non-financial assets**
  - An entity must assess, at each reporting date, whether there is an indicator of impairment. If there is, the carrying amount of the assets should be compared to the recoverable amount, and any resulting impairment recognised.
  - The recoverable amount is the higher of the fair value less cost to sell and the value-in-use.
  - If an impairment indicator exists, the entity should review the useful life and the depreciation methods even though an impairment loss may not be recognised.
  - When the circumstances that led to the impairment no longer exist, the impairment may be reversed.

- If it is not possible to estimate the recoverable amount of an individual asset, the CGU to which the asset belongs needs to be identified and tested for impairment.

- **Goodwill**
  - An entity must assess at each reporting date whether there is an indicator of impairment of goodwill.
  - If there is an indicator of impairment, the entity should:
    - Allocate the goodwill to components of the entity that benefit from the goodwill;
    - Measure the fair value of the components;
    - Compare the fair value to the carrying amount of the component; and
    - Recognise any resulting impairment firstly against the goodwill and then against the non-current assets of the component.
  - No reversal of goodwill impairments is permitted.

Chapter 15
Provisions and contingencies

Contents

15.1   Scope

This chapter applies to all provisions, contingent liabilities and assets except:

- Construction contracts, other than onerous construction contracts (refer to *Chapter 22*).
- Employee benefit obligations (refer to *Chapter 20*).
- Income tax (refer to *Chapter 21*).
- Leases, other than onerous operating leases (refer to *Chapter 18*).

The guidance does not apply to executory contracts unless they are onerous contracts (refer to *15.2* and *15.7*). Executory contracts are defined as contracts under which neither party has performed any of its obligations, or both parties have partially performed their obligations to an equal extent.

Provisions for depreciation, doubtful receivables and slow moving or obsolete inventories are impairments to the carrying amounts of the assets, and are not liabilities, and therefore are not covered by the guidance on provisions.

15.2   Definitions

A **provision** is a liability of uncertain timing or amount.

A **constructive obligation** is defined as an obligation that derives from an entity's actions where:

- By an established pattern of past practice, published policies or a sufficiently specific current statement, the entity has indicated to other parties that it will accept certain responsibilities; and
- As a result, the entity has created a valid expectation on the part of those other parties that it will discharge those responsibilities.

An **onerous contract** is a contract in which the unavoidable costs of meeting the obligations under the contract exceed the economic benefits expected to be received from it.

A **contingent asset** is defined as a possible asset that arises from past events and whose existence will be confirmed only by the occurrence or non-occurrence of one or more uncertain future events not wholly within the control of the entity.

A **contingent liability** is:

- A possible obligation that arises from past events and whose existence will be confirmed only by the occurrence or non-occurrence of one or more uncertain future events not wholly within the control of the entity; or
- A present obligation that arises from past events but is not recognised because either:
  - It is not probable that an outflow of resources embodying economic benefits will be required to settle the obligation; or
  - The amount of the obligation cannot be measured with sufficient reliability.

Figure 15-1: Determining whether a provision must be recognised or a contingent liability must be disclosed

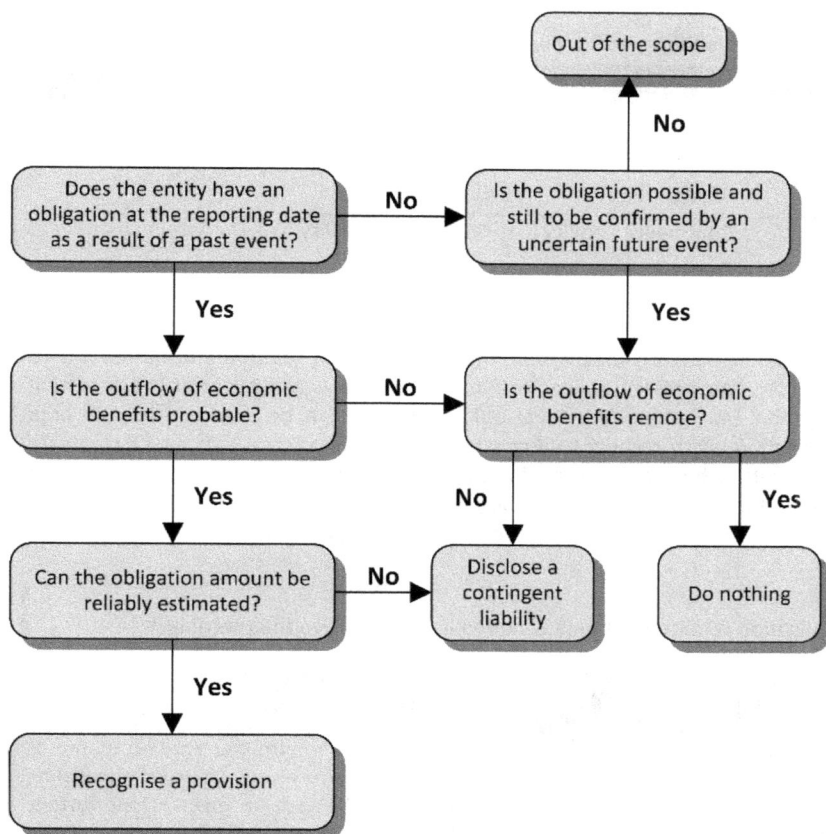

15.3   Initial recognition

A provision is recognised when all three of the following criteria are met:

- The entity must have an obligation at the reporting date as a result of a past event.
- It is probable that the entity will be required to transfer economic benefits in settlement of the obligation.
- The amount of the obligation can be estimated reliably.

All three criteria must be met before a provision is recognised.

If the three criteria are met, a provision is recognised on the statement of financial position and the related expense is recognised, unless capitalised as part of another asset (refer to *Figure 15-1*).

Table 15-1 provides a summary of the recognition criteria and respective impact on disclosure of provisions and contingent liabilities.

Table 15-1: Contingent liabilities and provisions

	Outflow of economic benefits		
Liabilities	**Probable**	**Possible**	**Remote**
Reliable estimate	Liability *Recognised*	Contingent liability *Disclose*	*Do nothing*
No reliable estimate	Contingent liability *Disclose*	Contingent liability *Disclose*	*Do nothing*

15.3.1   Present obligation criterion

The present obligation criterion means that the entity has no realistic alternative but to settle the obligation. This present obligation must arise from a past event at the reporting date. The obligation can either be a legal obligation that can be enforced by law or a constructive obligation. With respect to a constructive obligation, the past event creates a valid expectation with other parties that the entity will discharge the obligation. The past event may be a pattern of past practice, published policies or a sufficiently specific current statement by which the entity has indicated to other parties that it will accept certain responsibilities.

> Present obligation requirement means no realistic alternative than settling.

Example 15-1: Determining whether an event qualifies as a provision due to a constructive obligation

Portland, a car manufacturer, offers a three-year or 100,000 kilometre warranty on its motor vehicles (whichever is reached sooner). During 20X4, Portland receives numerous complaints regarding the turbos on the 20X0 models, which cost CU10,000 each to repair. Upon further investigation, it is identified that the problem with the turbos is a factory fault. Since all of the 20X0 models are older than three years, there is no legal obligation for Portland to repair the turbos at its expense. However, Portland realises that its reputation may be tainted, and therefore makes a public announcement that it is willing to replace the turbos on the 20X0 models when there are problems, at no cost to the customer.

Based on the information available, management has estimated that the cost to replace the turbos on the 20X0 models will be CU2,000,000. Furthermore, management is concerned that there will be claims from customers who have already paid for the replacement of their turbos, and estimate that it will have to refund ±CU750,000 to these customers.

Required
Determine whether the above qualifies as a provision at 31 December 20X4.

Example 15-1: Determining whether an event qualifies as a provision due to a constructive obligation *(continued)*

Suggested solution

Although Portland has no legal obligation to repair the vehicles, it has created an expectation that the vehicles will be repaired, because it has made a public announcement. Portland has a present obligation as a result of a constructive obligation.

There will be an outflow of economic benefits since it is anticipated that Portland will spend CU2,750,000 to rectify the turbos, and refund customers who have already paid for the repairs.

The provision is of uncertain timing and amount as it is not certain that all 20X0 vehicles will need to be repaired; the turbo will only be repaired when the vehicle has a problem. The amount is measurable and probable, and a provision for CU2,750,000 must be recognised.

15.3.2   Future actions

Obligations that will arise from the entity's future actions do not satisfy the present obligation criterion because no past event yet exists. This is even if the future actions are certain to occur or are contractually binding. The reason is that the future outflow can be avoided by future actions, such as cancelling the contract or the contract remains an executory contract until one of the parties performs its obligations under the contract.

Example 15-2: Determining whether expected future losses on a contract qualify for recognition as a provision

Cancun, a can manufacturer, supplies cans to a major soft drink manufacturer. On 1 November 20X1, Cancun concludes an agreement with the customer to supply 10 million cans a month for the next four months at a price of CU0.50 each. The agreement can be cancelled at any time by Cancun with no legal implications. At 31 December 20X1, Cancun realises that the cost of manufacturing the cans is CU0.60 each. Due to excessive price increases in the cost of materials, Cancun is now making a loss on the contract. However, management decides to uphold the contract to maintain good relations with the customer.

Required

Determine whether Cancun can raise a provision for the future losses to be incurred on the contract at 31 December 20X1.

Suggested solution

Cancun does not have a present obligation as a result of a past event. The loss will only be incurred when Cancun delivers the products in the future. As the contract can be cancelled, and Cancun elects not to cancel the contract, it is not deemed to be an onerous contract as the costs are not unavoidable and could be mitigated if management reconsiders its decision and cancels the contract at a future date. As a result, Cancun cannot raise a provision at 31 December 20X1.

15.3.3   Probability criterion

The recognition criteria, probability, is interpreted to mean *more likely than not*.

> 👁 The term *more likely than not* is not explained further in the IFRS for SMEs. In full IFRS it means that the probability that an event will occur is greater than the probability that it will not occur. This is an area of judgement and all available evidence, including the opinion of experts, needs to be considered.

15.3.4   Measurability criterion

No information is provided to explain the measurability criterion.

> 👁 The measurability criterion is not explained further in the IFRS for SMEs. Full IFRS states that only in rare circumstances will an entity not be able determine a range of possibilities and not be able to measure a provision.

15.3.5   Examples

The Standard provides examples in the Appendix to *Section 21 Provisions and Contingencies* on how the above principles should be applied. The outcome of the different examples could be summarised as follows:

Table 15-2: Examples of provisions and contingencies

Example	Present obligation	Probability	Nature
Future operating losses	No past event	Not applicable	Not applicable
Onerous contract	Contractually required	Probable	Provision
Restructuring	Only if legal or constructive obligation	Then probable	Provision
Warranties included in a contract	Sales contract (legal obligation)	For warranties as a whole	Provision
Known policy to refund purchases	Sales contract (constructive obligation)	Portion of sale will be returned	Provision
Closure of division (not implemented)	No obligating event	Not applicable	Not applicable
Closure of division (communicated and implemented)	Constructive obligation	Probable	Provision
Future staff training resulting from changes in income tax system	No present obligation	Not applicable	Not applicable
Court case: lawyers advice not probable	No present obligation	Not probable	Possible contingent liability

Table 15-2: Examples of provisions and contingencies *(continued)*

Example	Present obligation	Probability	Nature
Court case: lawyers advice probable	Present obligation	Probable	Provision
Fitting of smoke filters required by law or commercial pressure	No past event: Can avoid future expenditure	Not applicable	Not applicable

15.4 Initial measurement

Measurement is based on best estimate.

A provision is measured at the best estimate of the amount required to settle the obligation at the reporting date.

The IFRS for SMEs does not describe the best estimate. Full IFRS describes it as the amount that an entity would rationally pay to settle an obligation at the end of the reporting period or to transfer it to a third party at that date.

The Standard provides two methods to measure provisions. Firstly, when the provision consists of a single obligation, the best estimate is normally the most likely outcome.

However, when the most likely outcome is used, other possible outcomes must be considered. If the other possible outcomes are mostly higher or mostly lower than the most likely outcome, the best estimate may be a higher or lower amount than the most likely outcome.

Figure 15-2: Measurement of provisions

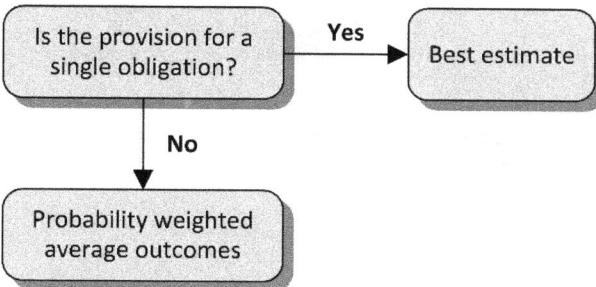

Example 15-3: Calculating provision using most likely outcome method

Nottingham is a property developer that is currently developing an exclusive golf estate. Recently, the company received a legal claim from four residents regarding continuous damage to their properties caused by golf balls. The residents are claiming together in one case. The residents claim that their houses were built too close to the golf course, and this was Nottingham's as it had advised them on the position of their homes.

Nottingham has sought legal advice on the matter, and the following information is available:

Claimant	Amount claimed by claimant	Out of court settlement – attorney's estimate
Els – Stand 10	25,000	15,000
Price – Stand 7	42,000	25,000
Woods – Stand 5	55,000	25,000
Player – Stand 13	15,000	7,000
Total	**137,000**	**72,000**

The attorney's opinion is that if Nottingham wants to avoid legal costs it will have to offer a settlement to the residents (as estimated above). However, if Nottingham does not offer the settlement, the attorney's opinion is that there is a 30% chance that Nottingham will win each of the cases.

At 31 December 20X1, management is not certain whether it will defend the claim. There is a 50% chance that it will offer a settlement to the residents.

Required
Calculate the amount of the provision at 31 December 20X1.

Suggested solution
When using the most likely outcome method, it must be determined which outcome is most likely to happen. The amount of the claims and outcomes are summarised as follows:

Discharge of obligation	Amount of claim/settlement (CU)
Settlement is offered	72,000
Residents win the case	137,000
Nottingham wins the case	-

As can be seen above, the most likely outcome is that Nottingham will offer a settlement to the residents. Therefore, the provision should be CU72,000.

Secondly, when the provision involves a large population of items, the best estimate reflects the weighting of all possible outcomes by their respective probabilities.

Example 15-4: Calculation of provision using weighted average of possibilities

Jerusalem recently received separate legal claims from four residents regarding continuous damage to their properties caused by golf balls. The residents claim that their houses were built too close to the golf course, and this was Jerusalem's fault as it had advised them on the position of their homes.

The situation is identical to the previous example with Nottingham, except that the claim is lodged by the four residents collectively with damages to be assessed individually once proven. The lawyers assess that there is a 60% chance all claims will be proven and that the average final cost per claim will be CU30,000 based on past experience.

Required
Calculate the amount of the provision at 31 December 20X1.

Suggested solution
When using the weighted amount of all possibilities method, the probability of each outcome needs to be multiplied by the quantitative amount of the outcome.

These are the possible outcomes:

- Jerusalem wins the case (40% chance of success in which case no claims will be paid).
- Jerusalem loses the case (60% chance of being unsuccessful, in which case an average of CU30,000 will be paid to each claimant).

The calculation of the provision is as follows:

Claimant	Amount of claim/settlement (CU)	Probability ratio (%)	Quantified amount of outcome (CU)
Claims are successful	120,000	60	72,000
Claims are unsuccessful	0	40	0
Total			**72,000**

Based on the weighted-average possible outcomes, Jerusalem must raise a provision of CU72,000.

The effect of the time value of money is considered when it is material. If material, the amount of a provision is measured as the present value of the expected future amounts required to settle the obligation. The discount rate (or rates) is a pre-tax rate that reflects current market assessments of the time value of money. Any risks related to the liability could either be incorporated in the discount rate, or in the estimation of the expected future amounts, but not both.

Specifically, gains from the expected disposal of assets are excluded from the measurement of provisions.

15.5 Reimbursement assets

A reimbursement asset is recognised when it is virtually certain that the reimbursement will be received. A reimbursement arises when another party may refund an amount relating to a provision. The full provision is recognised as a liability. The amount recognised for the reimbursement asset may not exceed the amount of the related provision. The reimbursement asset may not be offset against the provision; the credit may be offset against the related expense in profit or loss.

> Reimbursement assets are recognised only when their receipt is virtually certain.

Example 15-5: Accounting for the recognition of a reimbursement asset

Georgetown had a claim against it amounting to CU550,000 at 31 December 20X1. The company is virtually certain that its insurance company will refund 80% of the claim.

Required
Provide the journal entries required to account for the transaction in the financial statements of Georgetown for the financial period ended 31 December 20X1.

Suggested solution
As described above, the reimbursement asset and the provision must be recognised separately and cannot be offset. However, the net debit of CU110,000 to profit or loss can be offset.

Journals

Dr	Reimbursement asset (SFP)	440,000	
Dr	Expense (P/L)	110,000	
Cr	Provision for claim (SFP)		550,000

Recognise provision to settle claim and reimbursement right.

15.6 Subsequent measurement

The Standard confirms that a provision may subsequently only be used for the purpose for which it was created. A provision is reviewed at each reporting date. The amount of the provision is adjusted to reflect the current best estimate of the amount that would be required to settle the obligation at the new reporting date. All such adjustments are recognised in profit or loss unless the provision was originally capitalised as part of the cost of an asset. The unwinding of the discount relating to the provision is recognised as a finance cost in profit or loss.

Example 15-6: Provision for restoration, dismantling or removing of items of PPE

Bavaria has an obligation to restore land at the end of its ground-moving activities. The provision is increased every year by the portion of the land that has been damaged. At 31 December 20X1, the value of the expected future amounts required to restore the portion of the land damaged to date is estimated. The following information is provided:

Balance at 1 January 20X1	
(Present value of the estimated future reconstructing cost) (CU)	300,000
Applicable discount rate (%)	9
Value of estimated future reconstructing cost at 31 December 20X1 for damages incurred to date (CU)	367,000

Example 15-6: Provision for restoration, dismantling or removing of items of PPE *(continued)*

Required

Account for the movement in the provision for the period ended 31 December 20X1, assuming that the discount rate has not changed year-on-year.

Suggested solution

The provision is measured at the present value of the expected future amounts required to settle the obligation. As a result, the carrying amount of the provision must be increased as a result of the unwinding of the discount. This is calculated as CU300,000 x 9% (the discount factor).

The provision, after adjusting for the discount rate, must then be compared to the estimated restoration costs at 31 December 20X1. In this case, the CU327,000 must be compared to the full provision required at 31 December 20X1 of CU367,000. An additional CU40,000 must be raised to provide for the restoration costs.

Balance at 1 January 20X1	300,000
Unwinding factor (finance charge) (CU300,000 x 9%)	27,000
Additional provision for the year	40,000
Provision required at 31 December 20X1	367,000

Journals
31 December 20X1

Dr	Restoration costs (P/L)	40,000	
Dr	Finance charges (P/L)	27,000	
Cr	Provision for restoration (SFP)		67,000

Account for the increase in the provision for restoration.

15.7 Onerous contract

An onerous contract is defined as a contract in which the unavoidable costs of meeting the obligations under the contract exceeds the economic benefits expected to be received from the contract. The unavoidable costs are the lowest net cost to exit the contract. The unavoidable cost is therefore the lower of the cost to complete the contact, or any compensation or penalties payable from failure to complete the contract.

Example 15-7: Identifying an onerous contract and determining the amount of the provision required

Abuja recently moved its operations to new premises. The non-cancellable lease contract for the old premises still has another three years remaining, and Abuja is not allowed to sub-lease the vacant building in terms of its rental contract. At 31 December 20X1, the present value of future rental payments still due for the old premises is CU908,000; the cost to cancel the contract is estimated to be CU775,000.

Required

Determine the nature of any provision that should be created and provide the required journal entry to account for the transaction in the financial statements of Abuja for the financial period ended 31 December 20X1.

Example 15-7: Identifying an onerous contract and determining the amount of the provision required *(continued)*

Suggested solution

The contract is onerous – Abuja is not going to receive any economic benefits from the rental of the property as it is unable to recover the rentals by sub-leasing the property, and it is no longer earning income from the use of the property.

The unavoidable cost is the lowest net cost to exit the contract. Abuja can either continue paying the rentals with a present value of CU908,000 or it can pay penalties of CU775,000 for cancelling the contract. Since CU775,000 is the lowest cost, this represents the unavoidable costs, and hence the amount to be recognised as a provision. The journal to recognise the transaction is:

Journals

Dr	Onerous rental expense (P/L)	775,000	
Cr	Provision for onerous contract (SFP)		775,000

Recognise provision for onerous contract.

15.8   Restructuring

A restructuring is defined as a programme that is planned and controlled by management, and materially changes either the scope of a business undertaken by an entity, or the manner in which that business is conducted. A provision for restructuring costs is recognised similar to other provisions when the entity has a legal or constructive obligation to restructure. A constructive obligation to restructure only arises when an entity has a detailed formal plan for the restructuring, which identifies at least the following:

- The business or part of a business concerned.
- The principal locations affected.
- The location, function and approximate number of employees who will be compensated for terminating their services.
- The expenditures that will be undertaken.
- When the plan will be implemented.

The entity must also have raised a valid expectation that it will carry out the restructuring by starting to implement the plan or by announcing the main features to those affected.

Example 15-8: Provision in respect of a restructuring

Hebron has, in terms of a restructuring programme, decided to sell its construction division. A formal detailed plan of the restructuring, containing the following details, has been approved by the directors on 3 December 20X1:

- The construction divisions, located in Lebanon and Israel, will be sold.
- Of the 300 employees, 100 have been identified that can be placed in other divisions of the company, while the remaining 200 employees will have the option of taking a retrenchment package or negotiating a new package with the new owners. It is estimated that half of these employees will choose to take the retrenchment package.

Example 15-8: Provision in respect of a restructuring *(continued)*

- An announcement will be made to the company (including to all employees) on 1 February 20X2. On 2 February 20X2, a public announcement will be made to find a potential buyer for the business.
- The expected costs, which include legal fees for negotiating the sale, relocation costs for certain employees, the expected retrenchment packages that will be paid and various consulting fees, are anticipated to be CU1,000,000.

At 31 December 20X1, the entity has not identified a potential buyer for the business.

Required

Discuss the appropriate accounting treatment in the financial statements of Hebron for the financial period ended 31 December 20X1.

Suggested solution

At 31 December 20X1, no valid expectation has been created to those affected or the public that Hebron will carry out the restructuring. As a result, a provision may not be raised at 31 December 20X1.

Since no contract has been concluded at 31 December 20X1 to transfer the assets and liabilities of the construction division, the related assets and liabilities must continue to be recognised. If a binding sales agreement had been signed, this would need to be disclosed in the financial statements.

It should be considered whether there is a possible impairment of any assets relating to the construction division at 31 December 20X1. When considering the impairment, the expected sales proceeds must be considered as well as the expenses to be incurred in the disposal of the division.

Assuming that the restructuring was announced to the employees on 1 February 2010, this would be the date that a provision could be raised in respect of the restructuring since this is the date that the main features were announced to those affected.

15.9 Disclosure related to provisions

For each class of provision, the following should be disclosed:

- A reconciliation for the current period, ie not comparative period, showing:
  - The carrying amount at the beginning and end of the period.
  - The effect of discounting.
  - New amounts charged against the provision.
  - Unused amounts reversed during the period.
- A brief description of the nature of the obligation, and the expected amount and timing of any payments.
- An indication of the uncertainties about the amount or timing.
- The amount of any expected reimbursement, stating the amount of any asset that has been recognised for the expected reimbursement.
- The amount of any expected reimbursement, stating the amount of any asset recognised.

15.10   Contingent liabilities

A contingent liability is defined as either a possible but uncertain obligation to be confirmed by uncertain future events, or a present obligation that is not recognised because the outflow of economic resources is not probable or reliably measurable. Therefore, there are two distinct types of contingent liabilities (refer to *Figure 15-3*).

Figure 15-3: Type of contingent liabilities

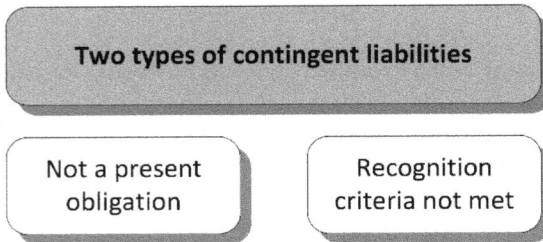

A contingent liability is not recognised as a liability but disclosed as detailed below. The only exception is contingent liabilities recognised in a business combination. In instances where an entity is jointly and severally liable for an obligation together with other parties, the part of the obligation that is expected to be met by other parties is also treated as a contingent liability (refer to *Figure 15-1*).

15.10.1   Disclosure

Contingent liabilities must be disclosed unless the possibility of an outflow of resources is remote. A brief description of the nature of the contingent liability must be disclosed, and when practicable:

- An estimate of its financial effect.
- An indication of the uncertainties relating to the amount or timing.
- The possibility of any reimbursement.

The fact must be disclosed when it is impracticable to make one or more of these disclosures.

Illustrative disclosure 15-1: Contingent liabilities in the notes to the financial statements

Litigation is in process relating to a dispute with a customer who alleges that several products were defective that resulted in damages to the customer's reputation. The claim is for an amount of CU1,000,000 and the expected legal costs to be incurred in defending the claim are CU200,000. The entity's lawyers and management consider that the claim is unlikely to be successful, and the case should be resolved within the next two years.

Should the action be successful, insurance cover exists for litigation costs and claims. The insurance policy is sufficient to cover the claim although only 80% will be payable as there is a 20% excess.

15.11 Contingent assets

A contingent asset is defined as a possible asset that arises from past events and whose existence will be confirmed only by the occurrence or non-occurrence of one or more uncertain future events not wholly within the control of the entity.

A contingent asset is never recognised as an asset. However, when the flow of future economic benefits is virtually certain, it recognises the asset in the statement of financial position.

Disclosure of a contingent asset is required when an inflow of economic benefits is probable but not virtually certain. In this case, probability also means more likely than not. A description of the nature of the contingent assets is disclosed and an estimate of the financial effect unless this would involve undue cost or effort. If such an estimate would involve undue cost or effort, the entity shall disclose the reasons why estimating the effect would involve undue cost or effort.

Table 15-3 provides a summary of the recognition criteria and their impact on recognition or disclosure of assets and contingent assets, respectively.

Table 15-3: Contingent assets and assets

Assets	Inflow of economic benefits		
Virtually certain	**Probable**	**Possible**	**Remote**
Asset as per definition	Contingent asset *Disclose*	*Do nothing*	Do *nothing*

15.12 Prejudicial disclosures

Only in extremely rare cases, disclosure required for provisions, contingent liabilities or contingent assets can be expected to seriously prejudice the position of the entity in a dispute with other parties. Such prejudicial information need not be disclosed but the following should, however, be disclosed:

- The general nature of the dispute.
- The fact that, and reason why, the information has not been disclosed.

15.13 Summary

- **Provisions**
  - Provisions are recognised when there is a present obligation as a result of a past event – it is probable that the entity will be required to transfer economic benefits and the amount can be estimated reliably.
  - The obligation may arise from a contract or from law or when there is a constructive obligation due to valid expectations having been created from past events. However, these do not include any future actions. Expected future losses cannot be recognised as provisions.

- These are initially recognised at the best possible estimate at the reporting date. This value should take into account the time value of money, if material. When the provision has a reimbursive condition from a third party, the reimbursement asset is to be recognised separately only when it is virtually certain payment will be received.
- Subsequently, provisions are to be reviewed at each reporting date and adjusted to meet the best current estimate. Any adjustments are recognised in profit or loss, while any unwinding of discounting must be treated as a finance cost.

- **Contingent liabilities**
  - These are not recognised as liabilities in the statement of financial position.
  - Unless remote, disclose an estimate of the financial effect, indications of the uncertainties relating to timing or amount, and the possibility of reimbursement.
- **Contingent assets**
  - These are not recognised as assets in statement of financial position.
  - Disclosure requires a description of the nature and the financial effect.
- **Prejudicial disclosure**
  - In extremely rare cases, where the disclosure of information required for provisions, contingent liabilities or contingent assets can be expected to seriously prejudice the position of the entity in a dispute with other parties, the Standard allows an exception. In such cases, an entity need not disclose the information, but must disclose the general nature of the dispute, together with the fact that, and reason why, the information has not been disclosed.

Chapter 16
Liabilities and equity

Contents

16.1   Scope

The guidance in the Standard establishes the principle that financial instruments issued to investors in their capacity as owners should normally be regarded as equity. Thereafter guidance is provided for the classification of financial instruments as either liabilities or equity, and for addressing the accounting for equity instruments.

The guidance is applicable to the classification of all types of financial instruments except the following, which is provided elsewhere:

- Interests in subsidiaries, associates and JVs (refer to *Chapters 5, 9* and *10*).
- Employers' rights and obligations under employee benefit plans (refer to *Chapter 20*).
- Contracts for contingent consideration in a business combination (refer to *Chapter 6*).
- Financial instruments, contracts and obligations under share-based payments to which share-based payment applies (refer to *Chapter 19*).

Accounting for equity instruments issued to employees and other vendors acting in their capacity as vendors of goods and services are therefore included in *Chapter 19* which deals with share-based payments. This guidance, however, applies to treasury shares to the extent that these are utilised in fulfilling employee share option plans, employee share purchase plans, and in other share-based payment arrangements.

Figure 16-1 creates the structure in the Standard to distinguish equity from liabilities.

Figure 16-1: Classification of an instrument as a financial liability or equity

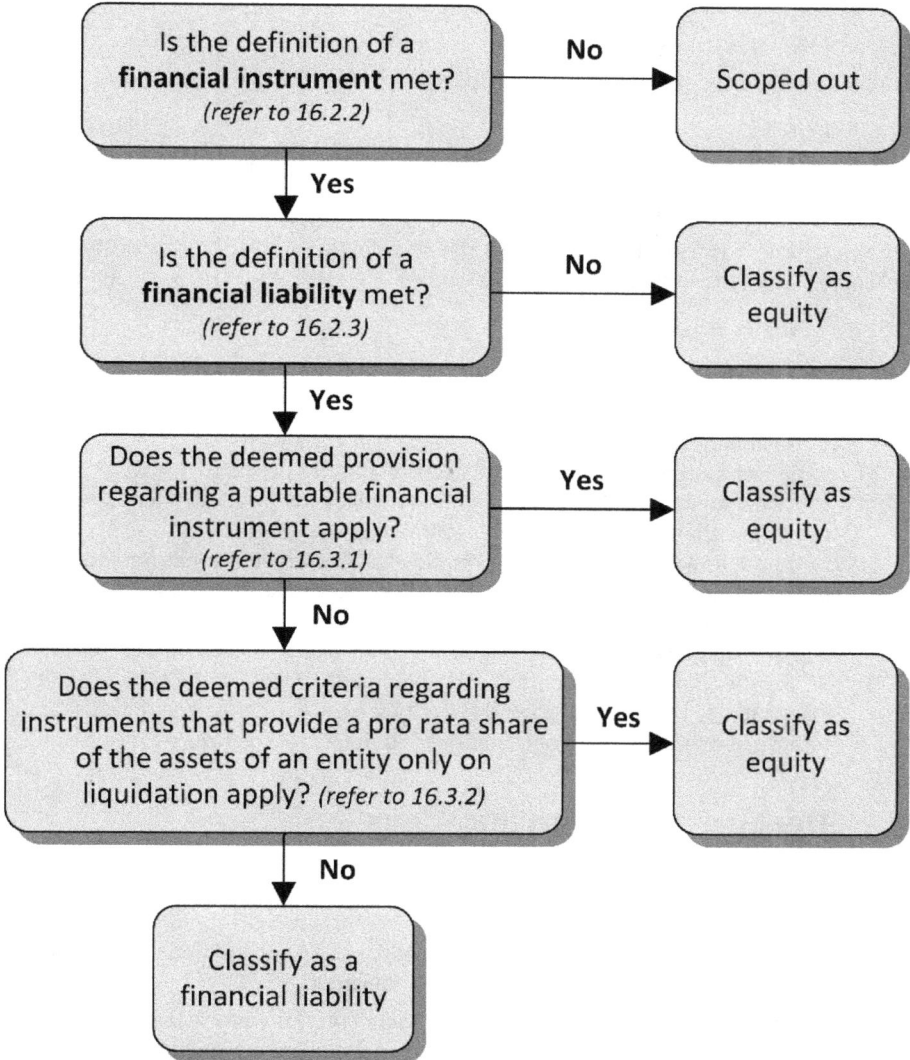

```
┌──────────────────────────────┐
│ Is the definition of a       │   No    ┌──────────────┐
│ financial instrument met?    │────────►│ Scoped out   │
│ (refer to 16.2.2)            │         └──────────────┘
└──────────────────────────────┘
             │ Yes
             ▼
┌──────────────────────────────┐
│ Is the definition of a       │   No    ┌──────────────┐
│ financial liability met?     │────────►│ Classify as  │
│ (refer to 16.2.3)            │         │ equity       │
└──────────────────────────────┘         └──────────────┘
             │ Yes
             ▼
┌──────────────────────────────┐
│ Does the deemed provision    │   Yes   ┌──────────────┐
│ regarding a puttable financial│───────►│ Classify as  │
│ instrument apply?            │         │ equity       │
│ (refer to 16.3.1)            │         └──────────────┘
└──────────────────────────────┘
             │ No
             ▼
┌─────────────────────────────────────┐
│ Does the deemed criteria regarding  │  Yes  ┌──────────────┐
│ instruments that provide a pro rata │──────►│ Classify as  │
│ share of the assets of an entity    │       │ equity       │
│ only on liquidation apply?          │       └──────────────┘
│ (refer to 16.3.2)                   │
└─────────────────────────────────────┘
             │ No
             ▼
┌──────────────────────────────┐
│ Classify as a                │
│ financial liability          │
└──────────────────────────────┘
```

16.2   Definitions

The Standard provides the following definitions:

16.2.1   Equity

Equity is the residual interest in the assets of the entity after deducting all its liabilities.

16.2.2   Financial instrument

A financial instrument is a contract that gives rise to a financial asset of one entity, and a financial liability or equity instrument of another entity.

16.2.3   Financial liability

Any liability that is:

a) a contractual obligation:
   i.   to deliver cash or another financial asset to another entity, or
   ii. to exchange financial assets or financial liabilities with another entity under conditions that are potentially unfavourable to the entity; or
b) a contract that will or may be settled in the entity's own equity instruments and:
   i.   under which the entity is or may be obliged to deliver a variable number of the entity's own equity instruments; or
   ii. will or may be settled other than by the exchange of a fixed amount of cash or another financial asset for a fixed number of the entity's own equity instruments. For this purpose the entity's own equity instruments do not include instruments that are themselves contracts for the future receipt.

16.3   Deemed equity classifications

Financial instruments must be classified as financial liabilities or as equity in accordance with the substance of the contractual agreement, not merely its legal form, and in accordance with the definitions of financial liabilities and equity. A contractual obligation would usually meet the definition of a financial liability unless the entity has an unconditional right to avoid delivering cash or another financial asset to settle the obligation.

The deemed equity classification criteria (*deemed equity criteria*) state that some financial instruments that meet the definition of a liability are classified as equity because they represent a residual interest in the net assets of the entity. The deemed equity criteria override the definition of a liability and the instruments are therefore classified as equity. The first criterion relates to puttable instruments, and the second relates to instruments that provide the holder with a pro rata share of the net assets of an entity only upon liquidation (refer to *Figure 16-2*).

Figure 16-2: Deemed equity criteria

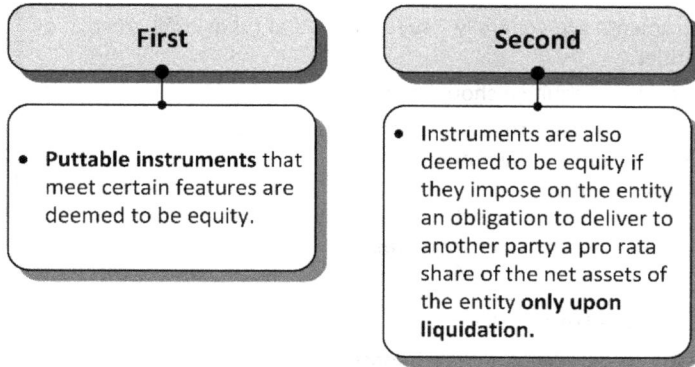

First	Second
• **Puttable instruments** that meet certain features are deemed to be equity.	• Instruments are also deemed to be equity if they impose on the entity an obligation to deliver to another party a pro rata share of the net assets of the entity **only upon liquidation.**

16.3.1   Puttable instruments

A puttable instrument is defined as a financial instrument that gives the holder the right to sell that instrument back to the issuer for cash or another financial asset, or is automatically redeemed or repurchased by the issuer on the occurrence of an uncertain future event or the death or retirement of the instrument holder.

Only puttable instruments that have **all** of the following five features are classified as equity:

- The holder is entitled to a pro rata share of the entity's net assets in the event of the equity's liquidation.
- The instrument is the most subordinate class of instrument, ie it is in the class of instruments that is repaid after all other obligations are settled.
- All financial instruments in the most subordinate class have identical features.
- Apart from the puttable feature the instrument includes no other financial instrument features. So except for the contractual obligation for the issuer to repurchase or redeem the instrument for cash or another financial asset, the instrument does not include any contractual obligation to deliver cash or another financial asset to another entity. There is also no contractual obligation to exchange financial assets or financial liabilities with another entity under conditions that are potentially unfavourable to the entity. It is also not a contract that will or may be settled in the entity's own equity instruments.
- The total expected cash flows attributable to the instrument over the life of the instrument are based substantially on the change in the value of the entity, excluding any effects of the instrument. For example, the expected cash flows could be based on either profit or loss, the change in the recognised net assets, or the change in the fair value of the recognised and unrecognised net assets of the entity.

All other puttable instruments are classified as liabilities.

> Possible puttable instruments are generally issued by mutual funds, unit trusts, co-operatives and similar entities.
>
> To classify membership interest as equity it should have all of the following features:
> - Each member is pro-rata entitled to the net value of the co-operative on liquidation.
> - Members' interest is subordinate to any other claims.
> - All members have the same rights.
> - The puttable feature is the only financial instrument feature.
> - Cash flows are only based on dividends and repayment of the share of the net assets.

16.3.2   Entitlement upon liquidation

Instruments are also deemed to be equity if they impose on the entity an obligation to deliver to another party a pro rata share of the net assets of the entity **only** upon liquidation. Any entitlement before that date will render such an instrument a liability. To qualify, the instruments must also be subordinate to all other classes of instruments. A portion of an instrument may also be classified as equity under these provisions. Ordinary shares and other non-puttable equity instruments will normally fall under this provision.

Example 16-1: Entitlement upon liquidation

New Delhi issues non-redeemable preference shares with a fixed dividend rate of 10% per year. Upon liquidation the non-redeemable preference shares are only entitled to the face value of the instruments.

Required
Determine whether the non-redeemable preference shares will be classified as equity.

Suggested solution
The preference shares are only redeemable upon liquidation. However, the amount of the redemption is limited to the face value. The preference shares are not entitled to a pro-rata share of New Delhi's net assets.

The non-redeemable preference shares are therefore classified as liabilities and not equity.

16.4   Instruments classified as liabilities

Based on the definition and deemed equity criteria, the Standard provides the following four examples of instruments that should be classified as liabilities:

- An instrument that entitles the holder to a distribution of net assets upon liquidation subject to a maximum amount (a ceiling).
- The holder of an instrument which is entitled to an amount of the pro rata share of the net assets of the entity measured on some other accounting basis, such as local GAAP.
- The instrument obliges the entity to make payments to the holder before liquidation, eg a mandatory dividend feature.

- A preference share that provides for mandatory redemption by the issuer for a fixed or determinable amount at a fixed or determinable future date, or gives the holder the right to require the issuer to redeem the instrument at or after a particular date for a fixed or determinable amount.

16.5   Members' share in co-operative entities

Members' shares in co-operative entities and similar instruments (eg interests in partnerships and farming co-operations) are only classified as equity if, either:

- The entity has an unconditional right to refuse redemption of the members' shares.
- The redemption of the instrument is unconditionally prohibited by local law, regulation, or the entity's constitution.

If the entity could not refuse redemption, the members' shares are classified as liabilities.

Classification of members' interests in co-operative entities, as either equity or liabilities, are determined as illustrated in *Figure 16-3*:

Figure 16-3: Co-operative entities' classification of liabilities and equity

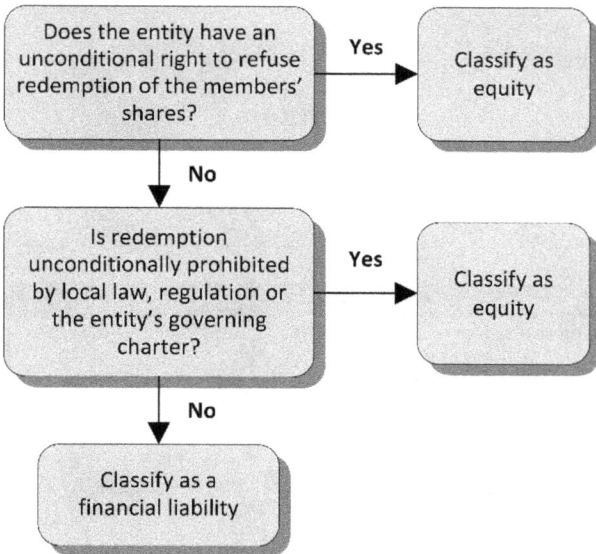

16.6   Original issue of shares or other equity instruments

Ordinary shares or other equity instruments are recognised as equity when the instruments are issued and another party is obliged to provide cash or other resources in exchange for the instruments.

16.6.1 Issuance of shares

The Standard provides guidance on how to account for different types of share issue situations, including:

- When the shares are issued before the cash or other resources are received, the amount receivable is presented as an offset to equity in the statement of financial position and not as an asset (effectively no additional equity is recognised until the consideration is received) (refer to *Example 16-2*).
- When cash or other resources are received before the shares are issued, and the entity has no obligation to repay the cash or other resources already received, the cash or resources received are recognised as an increase in equity (refer to *Example 16-3*).
- Any shares subscribed for, before the shares are issued, for which no cash has been received cannot be recognised as equity.

Example 16-2: Shares issued before cash or other resources are received

Pyongyang issued 4,000 shares before the reporting date, with a par value of CU1 per share. The issued amount of CU4 million is payable within one month after the reporting date.

Required
Provide the journals at the date of the transaction.

Suggested solution

Dr	Unpaid shares (Equity)	4,000,000	
Cr	Share premium (Equity)		3,996,000
Cr	Share capital (Equity)		4,000

Shares issued.
(CU1,000 per share at par value = CU1 x 4,000)

Example 16-3: Cash or other resources are received before the shares are issued

An investor paid CU1 million upfront for 4,000 shares in Hong Kong. At the reporting date, the shares have not been issued.

Required
Provide the journals for this transaction.

Suggested solution
The nature of the credit depends on whether or not the amount received is repayable by the entity to the investor.

If repayable
If the contributions are repayable, based on some contingent event, the journal would be:

Dr	Bank/Cash (SFP)	1,000,000	
Cr	Capital received in advance – liability (SFP)		1,000,000

If not repayable
If not repayable, the journal entry would be:

Dr	Bank/Cash (SFP)	1,000,000	
Cr	Unissued shares (Equity)		1,000,000

16.6.2   Measurement of equity instruments

Equity instruments (other than those issued as part of a business combination, or those issued to extinguish financial liabilities – refer to *16.9*) are initially measured at the fair value of the cash or other resources received or receivable after deducting transaction costs. When payment is deferred and the time value of money is material, the initial measurement is the present value of consideration receivable. Any income relating to the transaction costs deducted from equity is accounted for in accordance with the section on Income Tax (refer to *Chapter 21*).

Example 16-4: Transaction costs associated with the issuing of shares		
Beijing issued 10,000 shares with a par value of CU1.00 each at CU3.00 per share. Beijing received the cash, which is not refundable. Transaction costs incurred with the issue of the shares are CU0.05 per share.		
Required		
Provide the journal entries to account for the transaction.		
Suggested solution		
Dr Bank/Cash (SFP)	30,000	
Cr Share premium (Equity)		20,000
Cr Share capital (Equity)		10,000
Recognition of the share issue.		
Dr Share premium (Equity)	500	
Cr Bank (SFP)		500
Recognition of transaction cost.		
(CU0.05 x 10,000)		

> Initial measurement is at the fair value of the consideration less transaction costs.

Example 16-5: Non-cash contributions for equity		
Taipei issued 10,000 shares with a par value of CU1.00 each in exchange for a building. The fair value of the building is CU15,000.		
Required		
Provide the journal entry to account for the transaction.		
Suggested solution		
Dr Property, plant and equipment (SFP)	15,000	
Cr Share premium (Equity)		5,000
Cr Share capital (Equity)		10,000
Recognition of the shares issue.		

16.6.3   Presentation of shares or other equity instruments

The presentation of the issued shares, share options, rights and warrants in the statement of financial position is determined by applicable local laws. Share premium may be presented separately from the par value of shares if required in a particular jurisdiction.

Illustrative disclosure 16-1: Share capital

Authorised

20,000 ordinary shares of CU1 each	20,000

900 unissued ordinary shares are under the control of the director in terms of a resolution of members passed at the last annual general meeting. This authority remains in force until the next annual general meeting.

Issued

10,000 ordinary shares of CU1 each issued and fully paid	10,000
Share premium	5,000
	15,000

1,000 shares are held by the company's subsidiary, Tainan and 2,000 shares are held by the company's associate, Jilong.

16.6.4   Issue of share options, rights, and warrants

The above recognition and measurement principles for equity instruments are also applicable to share options, rights, warrants, and similar equity instruments.

Example 16-6: Options to purchase shares in an entity

Shanghai issues 10,000 options to purchase shares in Shanghai at CU0.20 per option. The options entitle the holder to buy par value shares of CU1.00 each at a fixed price of CU3.00 per share on a specified future date. On the specified date, only 8,000 options were exercised.

Required

Provide the journal entries to account for the transaction by Shanghai.

Suggested solution

Date of issuing of options

Dr	Bank/Cash,(SFP)	2,000	
Cr	Options issued (Equity)		2,000

Recognition of options issued.
(10,000 x CU0.20)

Date of exercise of options

Dr	Bank/Cash (SFP)	24,000	

(8,000 x CU3)

Dr	Options issued (Equity)	2,000	
Cr	Share premium (Equity)		18,000
Cr	Share capital (Equity)		8,000

Recognition of issue of shares and cancellation of options.

Total equity recognised =		
Initial options issued	10,000 x CU0.20	2,000
Subsequent exercise of options	8,000 x CU3.00	24,000
		26,000

(18,000 + 8,000 = 26,000)

Example 16-7: Forward contracts

Chennai enter into a contract to issues 10,000 shares at a par value of CU1.00 at a specified future date for CU3.00 per share. An initial amount of CU0.50 per share is payable on signing the contract and the balance is payable on the issue date.

Required

Provide the journal entries to account for the initial contract and subsequent issue of the shares by Chennai.

Suggested solution

Date of entering into the contract

Dr	Bank (SFP)	5,000	
Cr	Unissued shares (Equity)		5,000

Accounting for the initial amount.
(10,000 x CU0.5)

Date of issuing the shares

Recognition of the contract.

Dr	Bank (SFP)	25,000	
	(10,000 x CU2.50)		
Dr	Unissued shares (Equity)	5,000	
Cr	Share premium (Equity)		20,000
Cr	Share capital (Equity)		10,000

Recognition of issue of shares.

16.7 Capitalisation and bonus share issues, and share splits

A capitalisation or bonus issue is the issue of new shares to shareholders in proportion to their existing holdings without additional consideration. A share split is the dividing of an entity's existing shares into multiple shares. Previous outstanding shares may be replaced by new shares.

> Total equity is not adjusted as a result of capitalisation and bonus share issues, and share splits.

Total equity is not changed due to capitalisation, bonus issues and share splits. The amounts recognised in equity are reclassified as required by applicable laws with no overall change in total equity.

Example 16-8: Bonus share issue

Kolkata issued one bonus share to existing shareholders for each five shares owned.

Required

Provide the journal entries if necessary.

Suggested solution

No journal entries are required. The equity amount stays the same, but the disclosure of share capital must be updated accordingly to show the new number of shares in issue.

16.8 Convertible debt and similar compound financial instruments

A convertible debt or similar compound financial instrument that contains both a liability and an equity component must be split between the liability and equity component on initial recognition. The Standard requires that the fair value of the liability component be determined first. The amount of the liability component is determined as the fair value of a similar liability that does not have a conversion feature or similar associated equity component. The balance of the proceeds is the equity component (refer to *Figure 16-4*). Transaction costs are allocated based on each component's relative fair value.

The initial allocation is not revised in later periods. Interest on repayments of the liability component is recognised by using the effective interest method.

Figure 16-4: Compound financial instrument initial measurement

The Standard requires that the fair value of the liability component be remeasured at each reporting date. The amount of the equity component is never remeasured.

The subsequent measurement of the liability component is measured in accordance with *Chapter 11* if the liability component fulfils all four of the basic conditions of a debt instrument under *Chapter 11* (refer to *17.4.2*), otherwise it is measured at fair value through profit or loss under *Chapter 12*.

Example 16-9: Compound financial instruments

On 1 January 20X1 Colombo issued 500 convertible bonds at face value of CU100 per bond, ie a total amount of CU50,000 is received. The bonds are issued for a five-year period. Interest is payable annually in arrears at 4%. On conversion, 25 ordinary shares will be received for each bond. The market interest rate for similar bonds without any conversion option is 6%, Colombo has a 31 December reporting date.

Required
Determine the liability and equity portion, and provide the journals on 1 January 20X1 and 31 December 20X1.

- If the net amount of the liability is recognised, with no related separate bond discount asset recognised.
- If the gross amount of the liability is recognised, with a separate bond discount asset recognised separately.

Example 16-9: Compound financial instruments *(continued)*

Suggested solution

Value of liability portion

Present value of capital repayable in five years, discounted at 6%	37,363
Present value of interest at 4% for five years, discounted at 6%	8,425
Fair value of liability portion	45,788

Value of equity portion

Total issue price	50,000
Liability portion	45,788
Value of equity portion (balancing figure)	4,212

The Standard provides two options to record the initial transaction depending on whether a separate discount on issue of the bonds is applied.

Journals on date of issue – 1 January 20X1

1. No separate discount recognised

If no discount is applied the journal is:

Dr	Bank/Cash (SFP)	50,000	
Cr	Convertible bond – financial liability (SFP)		45,788
Cr	Equity portion of convertible bond (Equity)		4,212

Initial recognition of bond issue.

2. Discount recognised separately

If a discount is applied, the initial journal will be:

Dr	Bank/Cash (SFP)	50,000	
Dr	Bond discount (SFP)	4,212	
Cr	Convertible bond – financial liability (SFP)		50,000
Cr	Equity portion of convertible bond (Equity)		4,212

Initial recognition of a bond issue.

Journals at the reporting date – 31 December 20X1

1. No separate discount recognised

Dr	Interest (SCI)	2,747	
	(6% of CU45,788)		
Cr	Convertible bond - financial liability (SFP)		747
Cr	Bank (SFP)		2,000

Recognition of interest for the year and interest paid.

2. Discount recognised separately

Dr	Interest (SCI)	2,747	
	(6% x CU45,788)		
Cr	Bond discount (SFP)		747
Cr	Bank (SFP)		2,000

Recognition of interest paid and interest accrued for the year.

16.9 Extinguishing financial liabilities with equity instruments

An entity may renegotiate terms of a financial liability with its creditor in a way that its obligation is extinguished fully or partially by issuing equity instruments of the entity to its creditor. The fair value of the equity instruments issued is deemed to be the consideration paid for the purposes of measuring a profit or loss on derecognition of a liability (refer to *17.11.5*). However, if the fair value of the equity instruments issued cannot be determined reliably without undue cost or effort, the fair value of the equity instruments issued is measured indirectly at the fair value of the liability that has been extinguished. The difference between the fair value of the equity instruments issued and the carrying amount of the extinguished liability is recognised in profit or loss.

If part of the consideration paid relates to a modification of the terms of the remaining part of the liability, the consideration paid must be allocated on a reasonable basis between the part of the extinguished liability and the remaining liability outstanding. If the remaining liability has been substantially modified, the modification should be accounted for as the extinguishment of the original liability and the recognition of a new liability (refer to *17.11.5*).

The above principles do not apply if the creditor is also a direct or indirect shareholder of the entity and is acting in its capacity as direct or indirect shareholder, or where the creditor and the entity are part of the same group and the substance of the transaction includes an equity distribution by, or contribution to, the entity.

The above principles are also not applicable if the issue of the equity instruments to extinguish the financial liability is in accordance with the original terms of the contract, in which case the instrument would be accounted for as a convertible debt or similar compound instrument (refer to *16.8*).

16.10 Withholding tax on dividends

An entity must account for any withholding tax on dividends as a liability owing to the relevant tax authority. The amount owing to shareholders is reduced accordingly.

Example 16-10: Withholding tax on dividends

Islamabad declared and approved dividends of CU1 million on 31 December 20X1. The local tax regulations require an entity to pay 10% of dividends declared to the tax authority, on behalf of shareholders, as a withholding tax on dividends.

Required
Provide the journal entry on 31 December 20X1.

Suggested solution

Dr	Dividends declared (Equity – may be allocated to (ie reduce) retained earnings)	1,000,000	
Cr	Dividends payable to shareholders (SFP)		900,000
Cr	Withholding tax payable to tax authorities (SFP)		100,000

16.11   Treasury shares

Treasury shares are defined as the equity instruments of an entity that have been issued and subsequently re-acquired by the entity.

The fair value (including cash) of the consideration given for treasury shares is deducted from equity. No gain or loss may be recognised in profit or loss on the purchase, sale, re-issue or cancellation of treasury shares because this represents transactions in an entity's own equity.

Example 16-11: Repurchase of treasury shares

Karachi repurchased 1,000 of its own shares, with a par value of CU1,000, at CU3,000 per share on 31 December 20X1. The payment was made on the same date.

Karachi re-issued the shares at CU5,000 per share on 31 December 20X2. The payment was received on the same date.

Required

Provide the journal entries on 31 December 20X1 and 31 December 20X2.

Suggested solution

31 December 20X1

Dr	Treasury shares (Equity)	1,000,000	
Dr	Share premium (Equity)	2,000,000	
Cr	Bank (SFP)		3,000,000

Repurchase of Karachi's own shares.

31 December 20X1

Dr	Bank (SFP)	5,000,000	
Cr	Treasury shares (Equity)		1,000,000
Cr	Share premium (Equity)		4,000,000

Re-issue of Karachi's own shares.

> No profit or loss may be recognised on the repurchase, resale, re-issue, or cancellation of treasury shares.

16.12   Distributions to owners

Equity is reduced with the amount of distributions to owners. Any income tax consequences for the entity, resulting from the distribution to owners, are accounted for in accordance with the section on Income Taxes (refer to *Chapter 21*). Withholding tax payable on behalf of shareholders forms part of the dividend charged to equity.

> Distributions to owners, such as dividends, are deducted in equity.

16.12.1   Distribution of non-cash assets to owners

Dividends can also be paid in a non-cash distribution of assets to shareholders. Such distributions are recognised when the entity has an obligation to distribute the non-cash assets. The dividend liability is measured at the fair value of the assets to be distributed except where the fair value of the assets cannot be measured reliably without undue cost or effort, in which case the liability is measured at the carrying amount of the assets to be distributed. The amount recognised must subsequently be remeasured at each reporting date and at the date of settlement to reflect changes in the fair value of the assets to be distributed. This would also apply if the liability was measured initially at the carrying amount of the assets to be distributed because the fair value could not be reliably measured without undue cost or effort at the declaration date, and prior to settlement of the liability, the fair value can be measured reliably without undue cost or effort. Such changes are recognised as adjustments to the liability amount of the distribution and the contra-entry to equity.

When the dividend payable is settled, any difference between the carrying amount of the assets distributed and the carrying amount of the dividend payable is recognised in profit or loss.

The principles discussed above do not apply to distributions of non-cash assets where the assets are ultimately controlled by the same party or parties before and after the distribution (eg where a subsidiary distributes a non-cash asset to its parent). This exclusion applies to the separate, individual and consolidated financial statements of the entity making the distribution.

Example 16-12: Non-cash distributions to owners

Kabul decides to distribute a vehicle it owns to its sole shareholder. The dividend is approved by the shareholder on 30 November 20X1. The vehicle is delivered to the shareholder on 31 January 20X2. The company's policy on vehicles is to account for them at amortised cost. Kabul has a 31 December reporting date.

The values of the vehicles are as follows:

Date	Carrying amount of the vehicle (CU)	Fair value (CU)
30 November 20X1	100	150
31 December 20X1	100	145
31 January 20X2	100	125

Required

Record the journals that Kabul should pass in relation to the asset and the dividend at:

1. 30 November 20X1
2. 31 December 20X1
3. 31 January 20X2

Suggested solution

1. 30 November 20X1

Dr	Retained earnings – dividend payable (Equity)	150	
Cr	Shareholder for dividend – liability (SFP)		150

Record the dividend payable at fair value.

2. 31 December 20X1

Dr	Shareholder for dividend – liability (SFP)	5	
Cr	Retained earnings – dividend payable (Equity)		5

Adjust dividend for movement in fair value of assets.

3. 31 January 20X2

Dr	Shareholder for dividend – liability (SFP)	20	
Cr	Retained earnings – dividend payable (Equity)		20

Adjust dividend for movement in fair value of assets.

Dr	Shareholders for dividends – liability (SFP)	125	
Cr	Property, plant and equipment (SFP)		100
Cr	Profit or loss on sale of PPE (P/L)*		25

Record disposal of asset and settlement of liability.

16.13 Non-controlling interest

Previously referred to as minority interests, non-controlling interest in the net assets of a subsidiary forms part of equity in the consolidated financial statements. Changes in a parent's equity interest that do not result in a loss of control are regarded as transactions with equity holders in their capacity as equity holders, and are therefore recognised in equity. The carrying amount of the non-controlling interest is adjusted to reflect the change in the parent's interest in the subsidiary's equity. Any difference between the amount of such adjustment and the fair value of the consideration paid or received is recognised directly in equity as attributable to shareholders of the parent. The carrying amounts of any assets (including goodwill) or liabilities may not be adjusted as a result of such transactions.

Refer to *Example 5-3* in *Chapter 5*.

[🕯 Transactions are only recognised in profit or loss if control is lost.]

16.14   Disclosure

Disclosure of equity is included in the chapter on financial statement presentation (refer to *Chapter 3*).

If the fair value of a non-cash asset distributed to the entity's owners could not be measured reliably without undue cost or effort, the entity must disclose that fact together with reasons why a reliable fair value measurement would involve undue cost or effort.

16.15   Summary

- Shares are only recognised as equity when another party is obliged to provide cash or other resources in exchange for the instruments. The instruments are measured at the fair value of cash or resources received, net of direct costs of issuing the equity instruments, unless the time value of money is significant, in which case initial measurement is at the present value of the amount.
- The principles outlined above should also be applied to equity issued by means of options, rights or similar equity instruments.
- Members' shares in co-operative entities and similar instruments are only classified as equity if 1) the entity has an unconditional right to refuse redemption of the members' shares, or 2) the redemption is unconditionally prohibited by local law, regulation or the entity's governing charter. If the entity cannot refuse redemption, the members' shares are classified as liabilities.
- A puttable financial instrument is only recognised as equity if it has **all** of the following features:
  - The holder is entitled to a pro rata share of the entity's net assets in the event of liquidation.
  - The instrument is the most subordinate class of instrument.
  - All financial instruments in the most subordinate class have identical features.
  - Apart from the puttable features, the instrument includes no other financial instrument features.
  - The total expected cash flows attributable to the instrument over the life of the instrument are based substantially on the change in the value of the entity.
- Instruments are deemed to be equity if they impose on the entity an obligation to deliver to another party a pro rata share of the net assets of the entity only on liquidation.
- Capitalisation and bonus issues and share splits do not result in changes to total equity. An entity must reclassify amounts within equity as required.

- When shares are issued before the cash or other resources are received, the amount receivable is presented as an offset to equity in the statement of financial position and not as an asset.
- When cash or other resources are received before shares are issued, and the entity cannot be forced to repay the cash or other resources received, the cash or resources are recognised as an increase in equity.
- Any shares subscribed for which no cash is received cannot be recognised as equity before the shares are issued.
- Compound financial instruments, ie those that contain both liability and equity components, should be split by the entity at issuance. The liability is measured at fair value with the difference being the equity component. The liability is subsequently measured using the effective interest rate method.
- Treasury shares are an entities' own shares that are acquired or re-acquired. The fair value of the consideration received must be deducted from equity. No gain or loss must be recognised in profit or loss on the subsequent resale of treasury shares.
- Changes in the non-controlling interest that do not affect control, must not result in a gain or loss being recognised in profit or loss. These are equity transactions between the entity and its owners.
- Dividends paid in the form of distribution of assets, other than cash, are recognised when the entity has an obligation to distribute the non-cash assets. The dividend liability is measured at the fair value of the assets to be distributed except where the fair value of the assets cannot be measured reliably without undue cost or effort, in which case the liability is measured at the carrying amount of the assets to be distributed.

Chapter 17
Financial instruments

Contents

17.1 Scope

The IFRS of SMEs deals with financial instruments in two sections: Section 11, *Basic Financial Instruments* and Section 12, *Other Financial Instruments Issues*. **Basic financial instruments** are the less complex financial instruments, and apply to all entities. **Other financial instruments** are more complex financial instruments and transactions. Each entity needs to assess whether its financial instruments fall under the scope of basic financial instruments or other financial instruments, or both. This chapter deals with both basic and other financial instruments.

17.1.1 Specific exclusions

The following instruments are **excluded** from the scope of **all financial instruments** (both basic and other) because they are dealt with in other sections of the IFRS for SMEs:

- Investments in **subsidiaries, associates** and **JVs** (refer to *Chapters 5, 9* and *10*).
- Instruments representing the reporting entity's **own equity** (refer to *Chapter 16*).
- **Leases** (refer to *Chapter 18*), **except** that the **derecognition requirements** (refer to *17.11*) apply to lease receivables held by a lessor and lease payables owing by a lessee, **and** leases with **contractual provisions** (unrelated to changes in the price of the leased asset, foreign exchange rates or default by one of the counterparties), which may result in a **loss to either party**, are included in the scope of other financial instruments. The **impairment** requirements (refer to *17.9*) apply to lease receivables.

> Lease contracts which may result in a loss from factors other than eg price, foreign exchange rates or default, as described above, are included in the scope of other financial instruments.

- Employers' rights and obligations under **employee benefit plans** (refer to *Chapter 20*) and financial instruments, contracts and obligations in terms of **share-based payments** (refer *Chapter 19*).
- Reimbursement assets that are accounted for in terms of **provisions and contingencies** *(Chapter 15)*.

The following contracts are additionally **excluded** from the scope of **other financial instruments**:

- Most contractual rights related to insurance contracts. However, an insurance contract with certain contractual provisions (unrelated to changes in the insured risk, foreign exchange rates or default by either party), which may result in a loss to either party, are included in the scope.

> Insurance contracts with risks (other than the three risks identified above) are included in the scope of other financial instruments.

- A contract providing for contingent consideration in a business acquisition (this exemption only applies to the acquirer) (refer to *Chapter 6*).
- A contract that was entered into to buy or sell a non-financial item, except for the two specific inclusions discussed under *17.1.2.1* and *17.1.2.2*.

17.1.2   Contracts for non-financial items

Contracts to purchase or sell non-financial items are **excluded** from the scope of financial instruments, in terms of the last exclusion referred to above, only if the contract meets the expected purchase, sale or usage requirements of the entity.

> The exclusion applies to contracts such as options, forwards and other similar contracts, to buy or sell non-financial items.

Most contracts to buy or sell non-financial or tangible items (eg a commodity, inventories or biological assets) are not financial instruments, and are therefore excluded from the sections on financial instruments.

> An entity does not have to account for a derivative at fair value when the derivative is a contract to buy or sell non-financial items for its expected purchase, sale or usage requirements.

Example 17-1: Contracts excluded from the scope

Waterloo is an entity that grows and sells maize. It enters into contracts to sell its maize and purchase fertiliser at pre-determined prices after the reporting date. These contracts are exclusively for its usage and sale requirements. The entity has never speculated with such contracts and has no intention of doing so.

On 31 December 20X1, Waterloo's reporting date, it has purchase contract assets valued at CU100,000 and sale contract liabilities valued at CU50,000, which will be exercised early in the following year.

Required

Determine the accounting treatment of the contracts held by Waterloo on 31 December 20X1.

Suggested solution

As Waterloo entered into the contracts for its purchase and sale requirements no asset of CU100,000 or a liability of CU50,000 should be raised. The contracts are outside the scope of financial instruments.

However, two instances exist where non-financial contracts are included in the scope of other financial instruments.

17.1.2.1   First inclusion: Other risks

When the contracts impose risks on either party which are *not typical* of contracts to buy or sell *tangible assets*, the contracts are included within the scope of *other financial instruments*. The following three types of risk are deemed to be typical of contracts to buy or sell tangible assets:

- Risks related to changes in the price of the non-financial item.
- Risks related to changes in the foreign currency exchange rates.
- Risks related to default by one of the counterparties.

All non-financial contracts with imposed risks other than the three above must be accounted for as other financial instruments.

> **Example 17-2: Other risks in a non-financial contract**
>
> Dubai entered into a contract to purchase coal after the reporting date. The purchase price is linked to the crude oil price in United States Dollars.
>
> **Required**
> Determine whether or not the contract entered into by Dubai should be treated as a financial instrument.
>
> **Suggested solution**
> The crude oil price risk is unrelated to the price of coal. Therefore, the total contract is included within the scope of other financial instruments.

17.1.2.2   Second inclusion: Net settlement

Included in the scope are contracts to buy or sell non-financial items, *not* entered into for the purposes of meeting the entity's expected purchase, sale or usage requirements, and that meet any of the following conditions:

- Capable of being settled net in cash or another financial instrument.
- Capable of being exchanged with another financial instrument in a manner so that, in substance, the contract can be regarded as a financial instrument.

> **Example 17-3: Net settlement**
>
> Beira entered into a purchase contract to purchase a specific commodity. The terms of the contract specify that if the seller is unable to deliver the commodity, a penalty of the difference between the contract price and the market value, if higher, is payable by the seller.
>
> **Required**
> Determine whether or not the contract entered into by Beira should be treated as a financial instrument.
>
> **Suggested solution**
> Since the contract could be settled net in cash at the counterparty's option, the contract is included in the scope of other financial instruments, unless the contract is entered into for meeting Beira's expected purchase, sale or usage requirements.

17.2   Definitions

A **financial instrument** is defined as a contract that gives rise to a financial asset of one entity, and a financial liability or equity instrument of another entity.

A **financial asset** is defined as an asset that is any one of the following instruments:

- Cash.
- Equity instrument of another entity.
- A contractual right to:
  - Receive cash or another financial asset from another entity; or
  - Exchange financial assets or financial liabilities with another entity under conditions potentially favourable to the entity.
- A contract that will or may be settled in the entity's own equity instruments and that:
  - The entity is or may be obliged to receive a variable number of the entity's own equity instruments; or
  - Will or may be settled other than by the exchange of a fixed amount of cash or another financial asset for a fixed number of the entity's own equity instruments.

A **financial liability** is defined as a liability that is either of the following instruments:

- A contractual obligation to:
  - Deliver cash or another financial asset to another entity; or
  - Exchange financial assets or financial liabilities with another entity under conditions potentially unfavourable to the entity.
- A contract that will or may be settled in the entity's own equity instruments, and:
  - Under which the entity is or may be obliged to deliver a variable number of the entity's own equity instruments; or
  - Will or may be settled other than by the exchange of a fixed amount of cash or another financial asset for a fixed number of the entity's own equity instruments.

Effective interest rate is defined as the rate that exactly discounts estimated future cash payments or receipts over the expected life of the financial instrument or, when appropriate, a shorter period to the net carrying amount of the financial asset or financial liability.

Amortised cost is defined as the amount at which the financial asset or financial liability is measured at initial recognition minus principal repayments, plus or minus the cumulative amortisation using the effective interest rate method of any difference between that initial amount and the maturity amount, and minus any reduction (directly or through the use of an allowance account) for impairment or expected default.

17.3   Accounting policy choice

In terms of the Standard an entity may choose to apply the above sections with respect to financial instruments, or apply the recognition and measurement provisions of IAS 39 *Financial Instruments: Recognition and Measurement* and the disclosure requirements of the above sections to account for all of its financial instruments (an entity does not have to apply IFRS 7: *Financial Instruments: Disclosures* under any circumstances, refer to *Figure 17-1*).

This choice is an accounting policy choice, and is subject to the normal guidance in the Standard regarding changes in accounting policies (refer to *Chapter 7*).

Until IAS 39 is superseded by IFRS 9 Financial Instruments, an entity shall apply the version of IAS 39 that is effective at the entity's reporting date. When IAS 39 is superseded by IAS 39 that version of IAS 39 that is applied immediately prior to that shall by applied thereafter. A copy of that 'last' IAS 39 shall be maintained on the IASB website for reference purposes. An entity applying the IFRS for SMEs Standard may not apply IFRS 9 as an accounting policy for financial instruments

Figure 17-1: Accounting policy choice and measurement, and disclosure impact

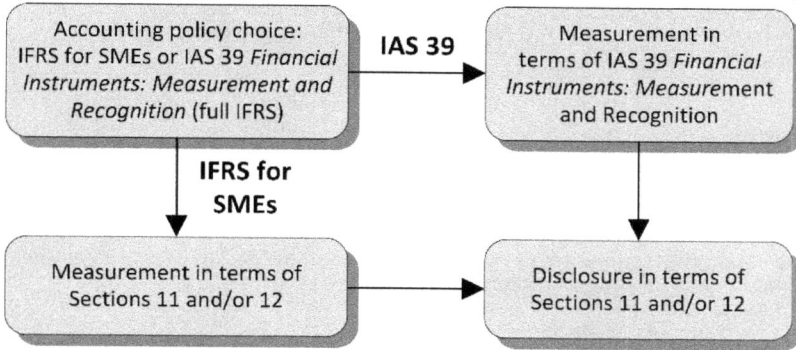

> 👁️ When the significant amendments that are currently considered for IAS 39 are implemented, the amendments will also be applicable to SMEs that have chosen the IAS 39 option.

17.4 Distinction between basic and other financial instruments

An entity first determines whether a financial instrument is a basic financial instrument. Any financial instrument not meeting the basic financial instrument definition is by default another financial instrument.

17.4.1 Definition of basic financial instruments

The Standard identifies four types of financial instruments (refer to *Table 17-1*) that are regarded as basic financial instruments.

Table 17-1: Types of basic financial instruments

Cash.
Debt instruments that meet certain conditions (refer to *Table 17-2*).
Commitments to receive a loan: • That cannot be settled net in cash; and • When executed, the loan is expected to meet the conditions for debt instruments (refer to *Table 17-2*).
Investment in non-convertible and non-puttable preference shares, and non-puttable ordinary shares of another entity.

> ☝ A puttable instrument gives the holder (purchaser) the option to sell the instrument back to the company at a pre-determined price.

17.4.2   Special conditions for debt instruments

Debt instruments (and loan commitments when exercised) need to fulfil all four of the conditions set out in *Table 17-2* to be regarded as basic financial instruments.

Table 17-2: Basic conditions of debt instruments

Condition 1
Returns to the holder, assessed in the currency in which the debt instrument is denominated, comprise any of the following: • A fixed amount of capital and, for example, a fixed amount of interest per month. • A fixed rate of return over the life of the instrument. • A variable return that, over the life of the instrument, is equal to a single stated, quoted or observable interest rate (such as the LIBOR). A combination of fixed and variable rates (such as the JIBAR plus 300 basis points), provided that both the fixed and variable rates are positive.

Condition 2
There is no contractual provision that could result in the holder (lender/creditor) losing the principal amount or any interest attributable to the current period or prior periods. A contractual subordination agreement is not an example of this condition.

Condition 3
Contractual provisions that permit or require the issuer (debtor/borrower) to prepay the debt instrument or permit or require the creditor to demand repayment before maturity are not contingent on future events **other than** to protect the holder against a change in credit risk of the issuer or instrument (eg a credit downgrade or loan covenant violation) or a change in control of the issuer, or protect the holder or issuer from changes relevant to taxation or law.

Condition 4
There are no conditional returns or repayment provisions except for the variable rate of return and pre-payment provisions described in Condition 3.

Example 17-4: Basic conditions of debt instruments

Manchester extended a loan to Birmingham of CU1 million, repayable over five years at a fixed interest rate of 8% pa. Birmingham supplies the main raw material for the manufacturing process of Manchester. The following four scenarios are provided:

- **Scenario 1.** The terms are stated above, except that the interest rate is LIBOR plus 1% pa.
- **Scenario 2.** The terms are stated above, except that Birmingham does not have to pay interest in any year that it supplies 100,000 tons of the raw product during the year.
- **Scenario 3.** The terms are stated above, except that Birmingham must repay the total loan outstanding if interest rates rise above 15%.
- **Scenario 4.** The terms are stated above, except that Birmingham must pay a penalty of 10% of the outstanding balance on the loan if it does not supply 100,000 tons of raw material during the year.

Required

Determine how the loan should be classified in terms of the financial instrument criteria.

Suggested solution

- **Scenario 1.** As the loan returns to the holder a fixed amount of capital and a combination of a variable return based on a published interest rate (LIBOR) and a fixed rate (plus 1%) throughout the life of the instrument, it is deemed to be a basic financial instrument.
- **Scenario 2.** As there is a contractual provision that could result in Manchester losing the interest (ie Birmingham does not have to pay any interest in any year that it supplies 100,000 tons of the raw material during the year), the loan will be classified as another financial instrument.
- **Scenario 3.** As there is a contractual condition that is subject to a future event that could result in Birmingham having to repay the total loan as a result of a contingency (the interest rate rising above 15%), the loan must be classified as an other financial instrument.
- **Scenario 4.** As there is a contractual provision that could result in Manchester receiving a return other than the interest as stated in the contract (Birmingham having to pay a penalty of 10% of the outstanding balance on the loan, if it does not meet the condition to supply 100,000 tons of the raw material during the year), the loan will be classified as an other financial instrument.

17.4.3   Examples of basic and other financial instruments

All financial instruments that are not included in the four types of basic financial instruments (being debt instruments, not fulfilling the conditions above) are classified as other financial instruments. *Table 17-3* provides examples of financial instruments and their classification.

Table 17-3: Examples of basic and other financial instruments

Basic financial instruments	Other financial instruments
Trade accounts, notes and loans receivable and the principle amount payable (fixed term deposits, bonds and commercial paper, or bills).	Such instruments not meeting the conditions of debt instruments above (refer to *17.4.2*).
Accounts payable in a foreign currency.	Loans payable that include other risks such as a link to an inflation index or a share price (Condition 1).
Loan commitments where the commitments cannot be net settled in cash (refer to *17.4.1*).	Forward commitments to purchase commodities or financial instruments that are capable of being net cash-settled that could result in positive or negative cash flows (refer to *17.1.2.2*).
Loans to or from subsidiaries or associates that are due on demand.	Loans to or from subsidiaries or associates that are repayable if certain targets are met (Condition 4).
Debt instruments becoming receivable when the issuer defaults on interest or the principal amounts payable (Condition 3).	Loans receivable becomes repayable when certain future conditions are met such as a change in specified market conditions (Condition 3).
Subordinated debt instruments and loans secured by a specific asset (Condition 2).	Asset-backed securities, such as collateralised mortgage obligations, repurchase agreements and securities packages of receivables.
Investments in non-convertible and non-puttable preference shares.	Investments in the puttable and convertible preference shares.
Investments in non-puttable ordinary shares (refer to *17.4.1*).	Investments in puttable ordinary shares.
A bank loan that has a fixed rate for an initial period then reverts to a variable rate after that period.	Options and forward contracts because the return to the holder is not fixed (Condition 1).
A bank loan that permits the borrower to terminate the arrangement early even though the borrower may be required to pay a penalty for early termination.	Interest rate swaps that return a variable cash flow (Condition 1).

17.5 Initial recognition of financial assets and liabilities

All financial assets and liabilities (identified in terms of the definitions and scope inclusions) are initially recognised when the entity becomes a party to the contractual provisions of the instrument. The important criterion is to establish whether the entity is contractually committed, or has a contractual right, which creates a financial liability or financial asset for the entity in terms of the definitions in the Standard.

> Recognise a financial instrument when the entity becomes a party to the contractual provisions of the instrument.

17.6 Measurement models

The default measurement model for basic financial instruments is amortised cost. The default measurement model for other financial instruments is fair value (refer to *Figure 17-2*). However, certain exceptions and exemptions are applicable in both sections. The initial measurement of basic and other financial instruments also differs.

Figure 17-2: Basic measurement models, including initial measurement

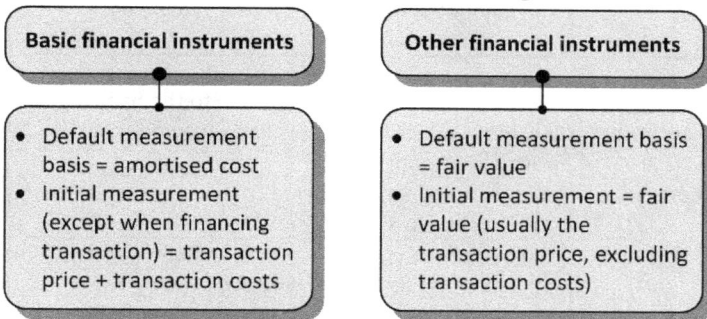

Basic financial instruments

- Default measurement basis = amortised cost
- Initial measurement (except when financing transaction) = transaction price + transaction costs

Other financial instruments

- Default measurement basis = fair value
- Initial measurement = fair value (usually the transaction price, excluding transaction costs)

17.7 Initial measurement

Financial instruments, which are not measured at fair value (eg cost and amortised cost), are initially measured at the **transaction price (including transaction costs)** unless the arrangement constitutes, in substance, a financing transaction (refer to *17.7.1*) for either entity or a counterparty to the arrangement.

Financial instruments, which are measured at fair value, are initially measured at fair value. Transaction costs are not included in the initial measurement of financial assets and liabilities at fair value and are expensed as incurred. The fair value is the amount that a willing, knowledgeable buyer would agree to pay in an arm's length transaction, and therefore the transaction price is normally the best evidence of the fair value.

> Transaction price is normally the best evidence of the fair value.

Table 17-4 indicates how this recognition principle is applicable to certain financial assets and liabilities.

Table 17-4: Initial measurement of basic financial instruments

Type of transaction	Initial measurement
Financial assets	
A long-term loan made to another entity at below market related rates (refer to *17.7.1.*).	The present value of the cash receivable (eg including interest payments and repayment of the principal amount).
A long-term loan made to another entity at market related rates.	Transaction price, including transaction costs.
Goods sold on short-term credit.	The undiscounted cash receivable, which is normally the invoice price.
Items sold on longer-term credit, including interest-free credit.	The current cash sale price for that item. If the current cash sale price is unknown, the measurement is estimated as the present value of the cash receivable, discounted using the prevailing market rate(s) of interest for a similar receivable.
Purchase of ordinary shares.	The amount of consideration paid, excluding transaction costs.
Financial liabilities	
Loan received from a bank at a below market rate of interest (refer to *17.7.1.*).	The present value of cash payable to the bank (eg including interest payments and repayment of the principal amount).
For goods purchased on short-term credit.	Undiscounted amount owed to the supplier, which is normally the invoice price.
For goods purchased on longer term credit.	The current cash sale price for that item. If the current cash sale price is unknown, the measurement is estimated as the present value of the cash receivable, discounted using the prevailing market rate(s) of interest for a similar receivable.

17.7.1   Financing transactions

The initial measurement of transactions, which constitute financing transactions, are accounted for at the present value of the future cash flows.

Indicators of a financing transaction are either of the following:

- Payment terms are deferred over a period that is deemed to be beyond normal business terms.
- Providing interest-free credit to buyers of goods or services.
- A transaction is financed at non-market interest rates.
- An interest-free or non-market interest rate for an employee loan.

Example 17-5: Long-term loan below market related interest rate

Tripoli obtains a loan of CU200,000 from another entity at 8%, which is 2% below the market related interest rate of 10%, on 1 January 20X1. The term of the loan is five years and equal instalments of CU49,417 are payable at each reporting date (31 December).

Required

Determine the initial measurement of the loan payable by Tripoli, and provide the journals related to the loan in the financial records of Tripoli for the period ended 31 December 20X1.

Suggested solution

The loan is deemed to be a finance transaction since the loan is granted below the market related interest rate. Therefore, the loan must initially be recognised at the present value of the future cash flows.

The present value of five instalments of CU49,417 discounted at 10% is CU190,399. Therefore, a financial liability of CU190,399 must be recognised on 1 January 20X1.

1 January 20X1

Dr	Bank (SFP)	200,000	
Cr	Profit on recognition of loan (P/L)		9,601
Cr	Loan (SFP)		190,399

Recognise the loan at the present value of 10%.

Note: The Standard does not determine where the day-one profit or loss should be recognised. In this example the day-one profit is recognised in profit or loss.

31 December 20X1

Dr	Interest expense (P/L)	19,040	
Cr	Loan (SFP)		19,040

Recognise interest charge for the period at 10% pa.
(10% x CU190,339)

Dr	Loan (SFP)	49,417	
Cr	Bank (SFP)		49,417

Payment of instalment.

Example 17-6: Long-term loan with no interest from holding company

Gibraltar obtains a loan of CU500,000 from its holding company at 0% interest on 1 January 20X1. The term of the loan is five years and equal instalments of CU100,000 are payable at each reporting date (31 December). The market related interest rate for a similar loan is deemed to be 8% on 1 January 20X1.

Required

Determine the initial measurement of the loan payable by Gibraltar, and provide the journals related to the loan in the financial records of Gibraltar for the period ended 31 December 20X1.

Suggested solution

The loan is deemed to be a finance transaction since the loan is granted below the market related interest rate. Therefore, the loan must initially be recognised at the present value of the future cash flows.

Example 17-6: Long-term loan with no interest from holding company *(continued)*

The present value of five instalments of CU100,000 discounted at 8% is CU399,271. Therefore, a financial liability of CU399,271 must be recognised on 1 January 20X1.

1 January 20X1

Dr	Bank (SFP)	500,000	
Cr	Additional capital contribution (Equity)		100,729
Cr	Loan (SFP)		399,271

Recognise the loan at the present value of 10%.

Note: The Standard does not determine where the day-one profit or loss should be recognised. In this example the day-one profit is recognised in equity as it is deemed to be an equity contribution from the owner.

31 December 20X1

Dr	Interest expense (P/L)	31,942	
Cr	Loan (SFP)		31,942

Recognise interest charge for the period at 8% pa.
(8% x 399,271)

Dr	Loan (SFP)	100,000	
Cr	Bank (SFP)		100,000

Payment of instalment.

17.8 Subsequent measurement

Basic financial instruments are subsequently measured differently as illustrated in *Figure 17-3*.

Figure 17-3: Subsequent measurement of basic financial instruments (measurement bases)

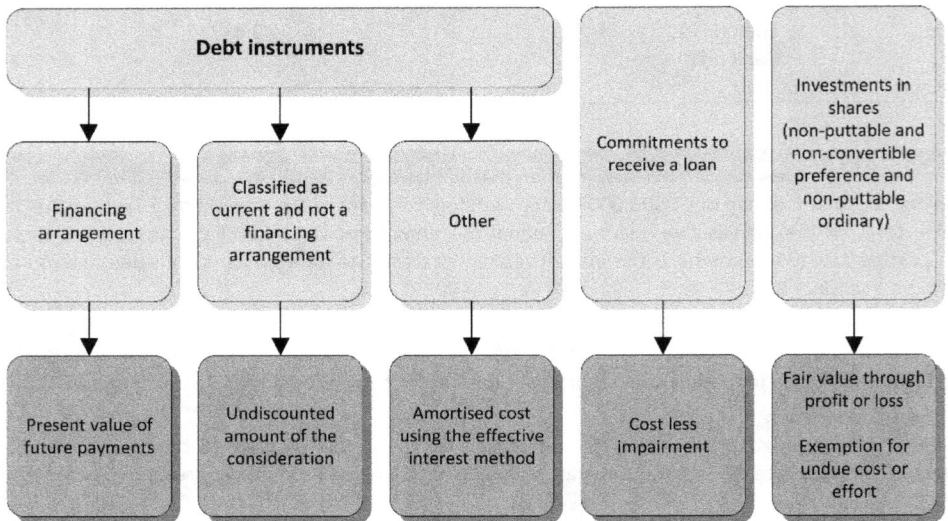

17.8.1   Basic financial instruments

Basic financial instruments are measured at each subsequent reporting date as follows, without any deduction for transaction costs that may be incurred on sale or other disposal:

17.8.1.1   Debt instruments

The default measurement of debt instruments is amortised cost using the effective interest rate method. An exception exists for debt instruments classified as current. Debt instruments that are classified as current assets or current liabilities, and which do not relate to a financing arrangement are measured at the undiscounted amount of the cash or other consideration expected to be paid or received (ie net of impairment) at each reporting date, unless the arrangement constitutes, in effect, a financing transaction. However, if such arrangement constitutes a financing transaction, the entity must measure the debt instrument at the present value of the future payments discounted at a market rate of interest for a similar debt instrument at each reporting date (refer to *Figure 17-4*).

Only current financial instruments that constitute a financing transaction are measured at the present value of payments. All other non-current financial instruments are measured at amortised cost. Current financial instruments are measured at the undiscounted amount of the cash or other consideration expected to be paid or received.

Figure 17-4: Subsequent measurement of debt instruments

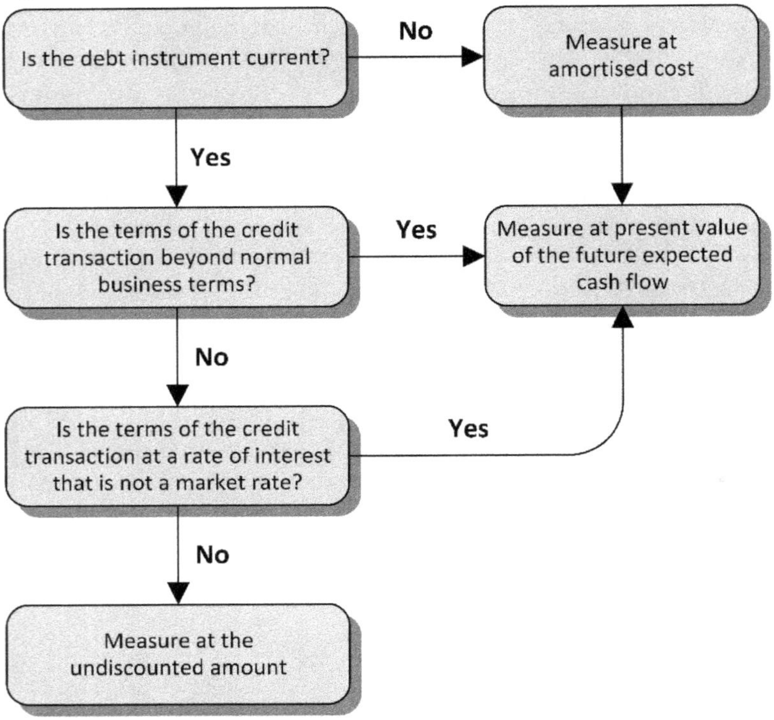

- Debtors within normal business terms are subsequently measured at the outstanding value (invoice value less any repayments), less any impairment (refer to *17.9*), at each reporting date.
- Debtors at market related rates are subsequently measured at amortised cost, which requires interest to be accrued at the internal interest rate, and subtracting any payments received, at each reporting date. However, since no initial adjustment is made to the original invoice price and the instalments are based on the agreed interest rate, the agreed interest is equal to the internal interest rate.
- Therefore, the balance of trade debtors at each reporting date will be the original amount plus interest accumulated (when due) less any payments received, and less any impairment (refer to *17.9*).

The following examples illustrate how different types of basic financial instruments are subsequently measured. An example of calculating the effective interest rate is included under *17.8.3*.

Example 17-7: Trade debtors that are not regarded as financing transactions

1. Within normal business terms

Sofia has trade debtors of CU3 million outstanding, at the reporting date, before any impairments. Debtors are granted three months to pay without any interest being charged. Three months is considered to be the normal credit term provided to buyers in Sofia's jurisdiction.

Required

Determine the trade debtors' balance of Sofia at the reporting date.

Suggested solution

The debtor transactions are not regarded as financing transactions because the three-month term is regarded to be within normal business terms. Therefore, the debtors are recognised at their invoice values of CU3 million. The outstanding balances at the reporting date should be tested for impairment if there are indicators of impairment.

2. Market related interest

Adelaide is a retailer that allows customers to pay the balance of any sales, after deducting the deposit, in equal instalments over two years. The interest charged on the extended terms is market related. Adelaide has trade debtors of CU250,000 outstanding at the reporting date, after taking into account interest accrued and all payments received during the period, before any impairment.

Required

Determine the accounting treatment of the sales made by Adelaide with regards to the initial measurement of trade debtors and the trade debtors' balance at the reporting date.

Suggested solution

The debtor transactions are not regarded as financing transactions as Adelaide is charging its customers market related interest. Therefore, no initial adjustment is required on the dates of sales. The trade debtors' balance will therefore be CU250,000. The outstanding balances at the reporting date should be tested for impairment if there are indicators of impairment.

> The only adjustment that needs to be made to the carrying amount of trade debtors at reporting dates that are not regarded as financing transactions is impairment (refer to *17.9*).

Example 17-8: Trade debtors that are regarded as financing transactions

Mombasa is a retailer that allows customer to pay the balance of any sales within six months, without charging interest. After the six-month period, a market related interest rate is charged. Mombasa has trade debtors with a face value (nominal invoice value) of CU250,000 outstanding at the reporting date. There were no debtors with balances outstanding for more than six months, at the reporting date.

Assume that sales on six-month interest-free terms are usually charged interest at 12% pa, and this rate was applicable for the whole period. The normal credit terms provided to buyers in Mombasa's jurisdiction is three months.

Example 17-8: Trade debtors that are regarded as financing transactions *(continued)*

Required
Determine the accounting treatment of the sales made by Mombasa with regards to the initial measurement of trade debtors and the trade debtors' balance at the reporting date.

Suggested solution
The debtor transactions are regarded as financing transactions as the six-month term is regarded not to be within normal credit terms. Therefore, the debtors must initially be recognised at their present value of future payments, discounted at a market rate of interest for a debtor, ie 12% pa or 1% per month.

The trade debtors' balance will therefore be the original amount recognised for the debtors of CU235,511 (present value of CU250,000, discounted for six months at 12%). As the average debtor is three months old, interest for three months of CU7,136 must be accrued. Therefore, the debtors' balance will be CU242,647, at the reporting date (CU235,511 + CU7,136).

The outstanding balances at the reporting date should be tested for impairment, if there are indicators of impairment. In practice, this calculation should be done for each debtor's balance separately for which there is an indication of impairment.

17.8.1.2   Commitments to receive a loan

Commitments to receive a loan must be measured at cost, including transaction costs, (which is sometimes nil), less impairment at each reporting date.

Example 17-9: Commitment to receive a loan

Liverpool enters into an agreement to grant a loan of CU1 million to a subsidiary, Yorkshire, for no consideration. The cash flow to grant the loan only takes place after the reporting date. Yorkshire incurs costs, including legal fees, directly related to the loan of CU450 before the reporting date.

Required
Determine the initial measurement, and the measurement at the reporting date of the commitment to receive a loan, in the separate financial statements of Yorkshire.

Suggested solution
The agreement represents a commitment to receive a loan at the reporting date and should be recognised at cost, including transaction costs, less impairment, in the individual financial statements of Yorkshire. The legal fees of CU450 must be capitalised as the cost of the commitment to receive a loan, and will represent the amount of the initial measurement of the commitment to receive a loan.

Therefore, Liverpool will show an asset of CU450 on initial recognition, and at each reporting date, subject to impairment.

Note: The legal fees of CU450 should also be included in the initial measurement of the debt instrument, ie loan payable, when the cash related to the loan is transferred to Yorkshire.

17.8.1.3   Investments in equity of another entity

The default measurement basis for preference and ordinary shares classified as basic financial instruments is fair value through profit or loss, unless the preference share is classified as a financial liability (refer to *Chapter 16*). If the fair value cannot be measured reliably without undue cost or effort, the investments are measured at cost less impairment.

Example 17-10: Investment in unlisted shares

Zagreb purchased an investment in the shares of Bishkek for CU500,000 on 1 January 20X1. This amount includes direct costs of CU12,000. Bishkek's shares are not listed. Management asked an expert to determine the fair value of this investment as at 31 December 20X1, the reporting date. *Note: The investment does not result in a subsidiary, associate or JV.*

The expert determined a value of CU480,000 at this date by using an accepted valuation model. The expert charged a fee of CU35,000 to perform this valuation. Although the cost of the valuation is significant, it is deemed to be a reasonable cost by management.

Required

Prepare the journal entries for the purchase of the investment in the accounting records of Zagreb for the period ending 31 December 20X1.

Suggested solution

In this case, the fair value can be determined without undue cost or effort, as determined by management.

Journal entries to account for the investment in the unlisted shares are as follows:

1 January 20X1

Dr	Investment in unlisted shares (SFP)	488,000	
Dr	Share purchase costs (P/L)	12,000	
Cr	Bank (SFP)		500,000

Purchase of shares and expense of the direct transaction costs.

31 December 20X1

Dr	Valuation cost (P/L)	35,000	
Cr	Bank (SFP)		35,000

Expense the valuation cost.

Dr	Fair value adjustment (P/L)	8,000	
Cr	Investment in unlisted shares (SFP)		8,000

Accounting for the fair value adjustment.

Impairment or recoverability must be assessed for financial instruments that are not recognised at fair value.

> 👁 No undue cost or effort exception is applicable to the determination of the fair value of equity instruments. The only exception is that the fair value cannot be determined reliably.

17.8.2   Other financial instruments

Other financial instruments are measured at fair value through profit or loss at the end of each reporting period. Shares which do not have published prices or whose fair value cannot be measured reliably without undue cost or effort must be measured at cost less impairment. In addition, contracts linked to such shares (eg derivatives based on such shares) that, if exercised, will result in delivery of such shares, must also be measured at cost less impairment.

If the fair value of an equity instrument that does not have a published price, but is measured at fair value through profit or loss, can no longer be measured reliably without undue cost or effort, its last reliably determined fair value becomes the deemed cost of the instrument. The entity must measure the instrument at this cost amount, less accumulated impairment, until the fair value becomes reliably measurable without undue cost or effort.

The exemption for undue cost or effort is only applicable to equity instruments. Therefore, other financial liabilities and financial assets that are not classified as equity investments must be measured at fair value.

17.8.3   Amortised cost and effective interest rate method

17.8.3.1   Amortised cost

The **amortised cost** of a financial asset (liability) is the present value of future cash receipts (payments) discounted at the effective interest rate. The Standard states that the amortised cost of a financial asset or liability, at each reporting date, is calculated as follows:

- The amount at which the financial asset or liability is measured at initial recognition.
- Plus or minus the cumulative amortisation using the effective interest rate method of any difference between the amount at initial recognition and the maturity amount.
- Less any repayment of the principal.
- Less, in the case of a financial asset, any reduction (directly or through the use of an allowance account) for impairment or uncollectibility.

Financial assets and liabilities, classified as current, that have no stated interest rate are measured at an undiscounted amount. Therefore the amortised cost of financial assets and liabilities that are classified as current, are measured without considering the effect of interest on the amount outstanding, unless the arrangement constitutes a financing transaction.

17.8.3.2   Effective interest rate method

The effective interest rate method is a financial calculation that is used to determine the amortised cost of an individual or group of financial assets and liabilities. The method also prescribes the allocation of interest income or interest expense to the relevant period.

The Standard defines the **effective interest rate** as the rate that exactly discounts estimated future cash payments or receipts over the expected life of the financial instrument, or when appropriate, a shorter period, to the carrying amount of the financial asset or liability.

Under the effective interest rate method:

- The amortised cost of a financial asset (liability) is the present value of future cash receipts (payments) discounted at the effective interest rate.
- The interest expense (income) in a period equals the carrying amount of the financial liability (asset) at the beginning of a period multiplied by the effective interest rate for the period (or a combination of interest expenses when there is more than one payment in the period).

The effective interest rate is determined based on the carrying amount of the financial asset or liability at initial recognition, and is not subsequently remeasured for changes in market rates of interest.

When calculating the effective interest rate, the entity must estimate cash flows considering all contractual terms of the financial instrument, such as pre-payment, call and similar options, as well as known credit losses that have been incurred. The entity must not consider expected future credit losses, which have not yet been incurred.

Example 17-11: Effective interest rate method

Indianapolis purchased a government bond for CU5 million on 1 January 20X1. The bonds pay no interest, but CU7.5 million is repayable at maturity on 31 December 20X8. The risk-free rate of return for similar five-year instruments is 6% pa.

Required
Prepare the journal entries for the purchase of the investment in the accounting records of Indianapolis for the period ending 31 December 20X1.

Suggested solution
The internal rate of return (IRR) of an amount purchased of CU5 million and repayable at CU7.5 million in five years time, with no interest payments is 8.45%.

1 January 20X1

Dr	Investment in government bonds (SFP)	5,000,000	
Cr	Bank (SFP)		5,000,000

Purchase of bonds recognised at the present value.

31 December 20X1

Dr	Investment in government bonds (SFP)	422,359	
Cr	Accrued interest on government bonds		422,359

Accrued interest income.
(5,000,000 x 8.45%)

17.8.3.3   Ancillary costs

The calculation of the effective interest rate includes any related ancillary costs or income, which should initially be capitalised. Examples include fees related to the raising of finance, finance charges, transaction costs, and premiums or discounts.

A shorter period must be used if the ancillary costs or income relate to a period shorter than the expected life of the instrument. This will apply, for example, where the ancillary costs or income relates to the re-pricing to market rates, before the expected maturity of the instrument. In such cases, the ancillary costs or income must be amortised until the next re-pricing date.

17.8.3.4   Variable rate instruments

In the case of a variable rate financial instrument, the cash flows are periodically re-estimated to reflect changes in market rates. This will result in a change in the effective interest rate.

However, when the cash flows are re-estimated, for reasons other than a change in the variable interest rate, the carrying amount of the financial instrument is adjusted to reflect the revised estimates. The new carrying amount of the financial instrument (or group of financial instruments) must then be based on the original effective interest rate.

Therefore, the carrying amount is re-calculated by computing the present value of the future cash flows based on the new effective interest rate. The adjustment to the carrying amount is recognised in profit or loss.

If the variable rate financial instrument is initially recognised equal to the settlement amount at maturity, any re-estimation of future interest payments will have no effect on the carrying amount of the financial instrument. The carrying amount of the financial instrument is not re-calculated if the interest rate changes.

17.9   Impairment

Financial assets recognised at fair value are not impaired. Impairment is only applicable to financial assets recognised at cost or amortised cost.

> Financial assets measured at fair value are not subject to the impairment rules.

17.9.1   Indicators

Financial assets recognised at cost or amortised cost need to be tested for impairment if there is an indicator of impairment. The assessment to determine whether there are such indicators must be done at each reporting date. The following table provides examples of objective evidence that a financial asset or group of assets may be impaired.

Table 17-5: Objective indicators of evidence of impairment

Significant financial difficulty of the issuer.
A breach of contract, such as a default or delinquency in interest or principal payments.
Granting a debtor a concession that would normally not be considered.
Probability that the debtor will enter bankruptcy or similar financial re-organisation.
Observable data indicating that there has been a measurable decrease in the estimated future cash flows from a group of financial assets since the initial recognition of those assets. Such observable data includes adverse national or local economic conditions, or adverse changes in industry conditions.

Other factors that may be evidence of impairment include significant adverse changes in the technological, market, economic or legal environment in which the issuer operates.

> An assessment for indicators of impairment of eligible financial assets must be done annually, but an impairment test is only performed when an indicator of impairment exists.

17.9.2 Individual or group assessment

When an indicator of impairment exists, the following financial assets are assessed **individually** for impairment:

- **All** equity instruments **(regardless of significance)**.
- Non-equity instruments **individually significant**.

All other financial assets may be assessed individually or **in groups of financial assets with similar credit risk characteristics**. *Figure 17-5* provides a diagrammatical illustration of the decision to determine whether financial assets should be impaired individually or not.

> The Standard does not define similar credit risk characteristics.
>
> Full IFRS defines credit risk as the risk that one party to a financial instrument will cause a financial loss for the other party by failing to discharge an obligation.

Figure 17-5: Individual or group assessment

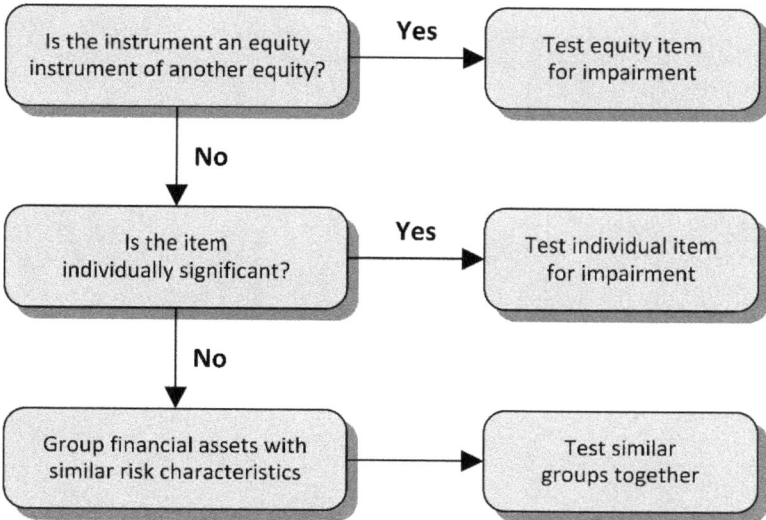

17.9.3 Recognition

An impairment loss may be recognised directly against the asset or through an allowance account (for example, a provision for doubtful debts). The debit is recognised directly in profit or loss, ie charged as an expense.

17.9.4 Measurement

An impairment loss for an instrument, measured at **amortised cost,** is measured as the difference between the financial asset's carrying amount and the present value of the estimated cash flows, discounted at the asset's original effective interest rate.

The impairment loss for an instrument, measured at **cost,** is the difference between the financial asset's carrying amount and the best estimate of the amount that the entity could realise the asset at the reporting date. This amount will be an approximation, and may be zero.

Figure 17-6 describes the different guidance applicable to calculate the impairment loss on instruments measured at amortised cost and cost.

Figure 17-6: Determining the impairment value

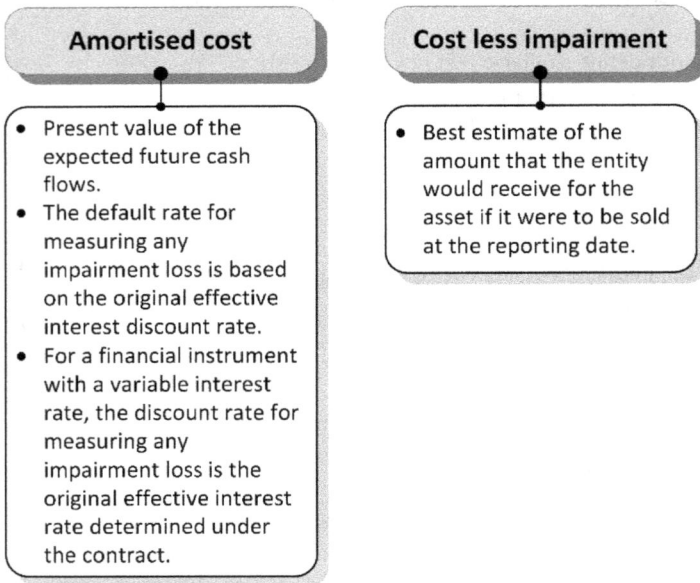

Amortised cost	Cost less impairment
• Present value of the expected future cash flows. • The default rate for measuring any impairment loss is based on the original effective interest discount rate. • For a financial instrument with a variable interest rate, the discount rate for measuring any impairment loss is the original effective interest rate determined under the contract.	• Best estimate of the amount that the entity would receive for the asset if it were to be sold at the reporting date.

Example 17-12: Impairment of assets

Here are the details of financial assets recorded in San Diego's statement of financial position.

Investment in listed shares

San Diego has an investment in the listed shares of Tel Aviv. At the last reporting date, the fair value was CU3 million. The quoted price is now CU2 million.

Debtors

San Diego has debtors of CU100 million at year-end. The following details are available:

- The Hague has been declared bankrupt. Its balance was CU10 million.
- Antananarivo has had problems with paying on time over the last six months. Its balance was CU5 million. Management believes that it will recover CU2 million of the outstanding balance.
- Reykjavík is the biggest debtor of the company. Its balance is R35 million. There are no indicators of impairment.
- Port-Au-Prince has been placed under judicial management. The balance is CU7 million, and management believes it will all be recovered.

Of the remaining debtors, the company believes that 8% will go bad in the next year due to the financial crisis.

From experience, management believes that 6% of debtors have become unrecoverable over the last year. It has not been able to identify which debtors make up the 6%.

Required

Assess the financial assets for impairment and, if applicable, quantify the impairment loss to be recognised.

Suggested solution

Investment in the listed shares

As the shares of Tel Aviv are traded in an active market, they will be accounted for at fair value through profit or loss. San Diego should therefore account for the CU1 million as a fair value adjustment, not an impairment.

Debtors

The debtors impairment should be recognised on the following:

- The Hague – Full impairment.
- Antananarivo – CU3m impairment.
- Reykjavík – No individual provision required.
- Port-Au-Prince – No provision required; there is an indicator of impairment but management has assessed that it expects a full recovery.

Example 17-12: Impairment of assets *(continued)*

Portfolio provision – Additional provision after the impairment of specific items

Balance	100,000,000
Less: Specific impairments	
The Hague	(10,000,000)
Antananarivo	(5,000,000)
Balance after items already impaired	85,000,000
Total impairment:	
Individual assessment	15,000,000
Group assessment (CU85 million x 6%)	5,100,000
	20,100,000

17.9.5 Reversal of impairment losses

An impairment of a financial asset may be reversed in certain instances. If an entity determines that an impairment loss recognised has reversed in a subsequent period, the cause of the reversal must be determined. If the reversal can be attributed to an event occurring after the impairment was recognised (such as the re-establishment of an active market for a financial asset), the entity must reverse the previously recognised impairment through profit or loss.

A reversal may not result in the carrying amount of a financial asset exceeding the amount that the carrying amount would have been, had the asset not previously been impaired.

17.10 Fair value guidance

17.10.1 Fair value hierarchy

Figure 17-7 describes the hierarchy that should be followed to estimate the fair value of financial instruments. This guidance is applicable to all fair value calculations required in the Standard, unless otherwise stated.

Figure 17-7: Hierarchy of fair value

Most reliable

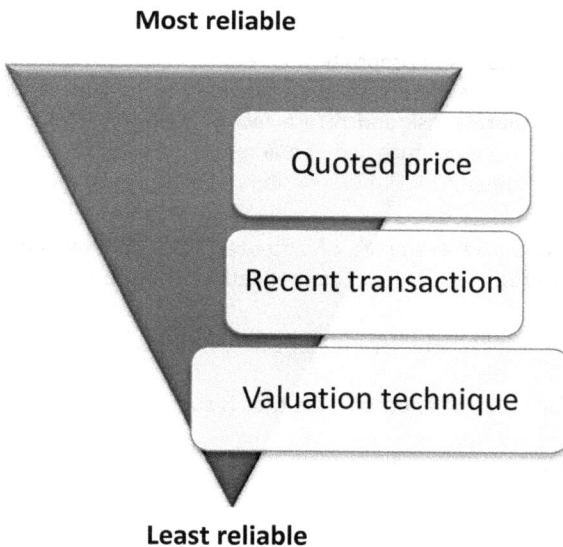

Quoted price

Recent transaction

Valuation technique

Least reliable

A **quoted price** in an **active market** is the best evidence of fair value. Usually, the current bid price is used.

When quoted prices are unavailable, the price of a **recent transaction** for an identical asset is used to determine fair value. The price of a recent transaction is regarded as a reliable estimate when there has not been a significant change in economic circumstances or a significant lapse of time since the occurrence of the transaction. To determine a reliable estimate, the recent price should be adjusted for any such economic changes or the effect of time.

Forced transactions, involuntary liquidation or distress sales normally do not provide a reliable estimate, and should also be adjusted if the fact that the last transaction price is not a good indicator of fair value can be demonstrated.

If quoted prices are not available and recent prices do not provide a reliable estimate, fair value is estimated using a **valuation technique**. The objective of using a valuation technique is to estimate what the transaction price would be on the measurement date in an arm's length exchange, motivated by normal business considerations.

Refer to *2.8.3* for a detailed definition of fair value as stated in the section on *Concepts and Pervasive Principles*.

17.10.2 Valuation techniques

A valuation technique should attempt to determine what the transaction price would have been on the measurement date in an arm's length transaction based on normal business considerations. A valuation technique is appropriate if it reflects how the market could be expected to price the asset, and the inputs to the valuation technique represent the market's expectations, and incorporate risk and return factors inherent in the asset. The valuation technique used should make as much use of market inputs as possible, and should rely as little as possible on entity-specific inputs or inputs determined by the entity's management.

The Standard refers to the following examples of accepted valuation techniques. Even though this is not an exhaustive list, it is highly recommended that they be used if available. The examples provided are:

- Recent arm's length market transactions for an identical asset between knowledgeable, willing parties.
- Reference to the current fair value of another asset that is substantially the same as the asset being measured.
- Discounted cash flow analysis.
- Option pricing models.

> 👁 Valuation techniques such as net asset value, dividend yield and earnings yield (or dividend yield and earnings yield potential) may also be used to value financial instruments, if applicable and appropriate to the circumstances.

A generally accepted valuation technique that has been demonstrated to provide reliable estimates of prices actually obtained in market transactions should be used to determine fair value.

17.10.3 Reliability of fair value estimate

Fair value of assets determined using a valuation technique is **reliable** if either of the following conditions exist:

- The variability in the range of reasonable fair value estimates is not significant for that asset; and
- The probabilities of the various estimates within the range can be reasonably assessed and used in estimating fair value.

Generally, the fair value of an asset, not traded in an active market, can be determined reliably. An asset purchased from an external party is evidence of a market, and therefore a fair value of the asset can be determined. An entity is not allowed to measure the asset at fair value where the range of fair value estimates is significant, or the probabilities of the various estimates are not reliably determinable. In this case, the entity should account for the asset at cost less accumulated impairments.

If the fair value of an asset can no longer be estimated reliably or without undue cost or effort, its carrying amount at the last date the asset was reliably measurable becomes its new cost. The asset must then be measured at this deemed cost amount less impairment until a reliable measure of fair value becomes available without undue cost or effort whereupon the asset will again be measured at fair value.

> ♩ There is **no undue cost or effort exemption** for measuring the fair value of financial assets, including investments in unlisted shares.
>
> An undue cost or effort exemption is applicable to investment properties (refer to *Chapter 11*) and biological assets (refer to *Chapter 29*) for which the fair value of the asset cannot be reliably determined without undue cost or effort.

17.11   Derecognition

17.11.1   Derecognition of a financial asset

This guidance is applicable to **basic and other financial instruments**. *Table 17-6* provides the three conditions under which financial assets should be derecognised and *Figure 17-8* sets out the decision tree to apply the three conditions of derecognition.

Table 17-6: Instances when financial assets need to be derecognised

Condition 1
The contractual rights to the cash flows from the financial asset expire or are settled.

Condition 2
The entity transfers to another party substantially all of the risks and rewards of ownership of the financial asset.

Condition 3
Despite having retained some significant risks and rewards of ownership, the entity has transferred control of the asset to another party. The other party has the practical ability to sell the asset in its entirety to an unrelated third party, and is able to exercise that ability unilaterally and without needing to impose additional restrictions on the transfer. In this case, the entity must derecognise the asset and recognise separately any rights and/or obligations due to the transfer.

Figure 17-8: Derecognition decision tree

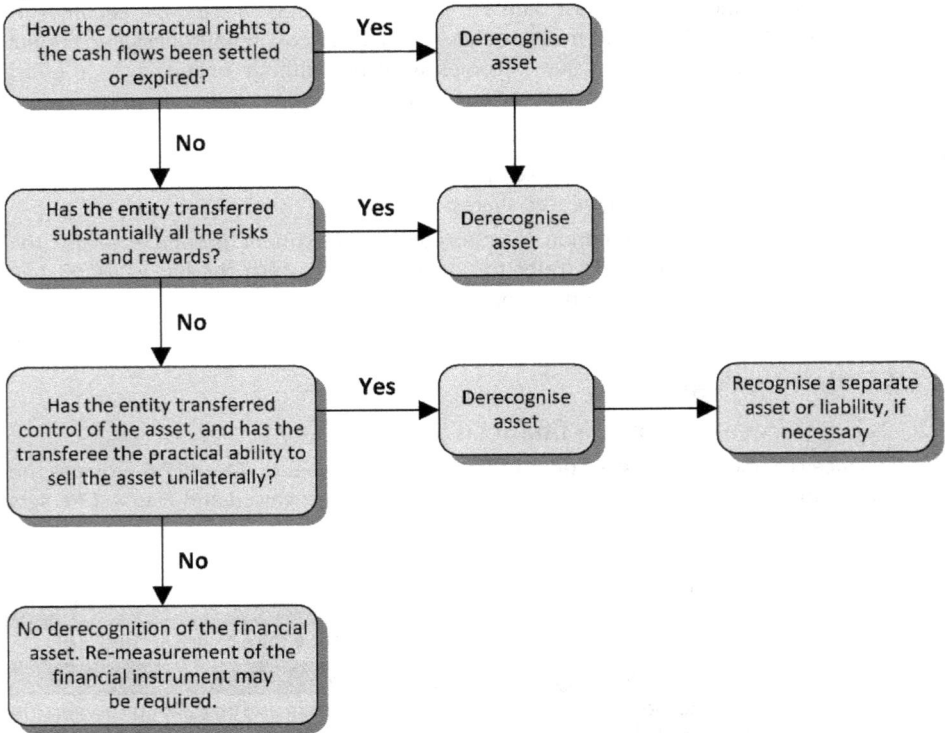

Example 17-13: Transfer that qualifies for derecognition

Manila sells a portion of its debtors, with a carrying amount of CU5.2 million, to Nagoya for CU4.5 million on 1 January 20X1. Manila continues to handle collections from the debtors on behalf of Nagoya, including sending monthly statements. Nagoya pays Manila an annual service fee for these services. Manila must pay any and all amounts collected from the debtors sold to Nagoya immediately. Manila has no obligation to Nagoya for slow payment or non-payment by the debtors.

Manila received an amount of CU5,000,000 from these debtors, and a service fee of CU50,000 was received from Nagoya during the year ended 31 December 20X1. All amounts were paid to Nagoya as per the agreement.

Required
Determine whether Manila may derecognise the sold debtors, and if so, what journal entries are required.

Suggested solution
In this case, Manila has transferred to Nagoya substantially all of the risks and rewards of ownership of the receivables.

Example 17-13: Transfer that qualifies for derecognition *(continued)*

The debtors are thus derecognised and the loss on derecognition is calculated as follows:

Consideration received	4,500,000
Carrying value of debtors	5,200,000
Loss on derecognition	**700,000**

1 January 20X1

Dr	Bank/Cash (SFP)	4,500,000	
Dr	Loss on sale of trade debtors (P/L)	700,000	
Cr	Trade debtors (SFP)		5,200,000

Recognition of sale of trade debtors.

On the respective transaction dates during the period ended **31 December 20X1**:

When the proceeds are received from the debtors sold, the journal is:

Dr	Bank (SFP)	5,000,000	
Cr	Liability payable to Nagoya (SFP)		5,000,000

Amounts received on behalf of Nagoya.

Service fees are accrued over the year, the accumulated journal is:

Dr	Bank (SFP)	50,000	
Cr	Service fee for managing debtors (SFP)		50,000

Recognition of service fee for managing debtors.

17.11.2 Retaining some of the risks or rewards of ownership

If a transfer results in the transferor retaining some of the risks and rewards of ownership (refer to *Table 17-6: Conditions 2 or 3*), the asset is derecognised, and any rights or obligations retained or created in the transfer is recognised separately. The carrying amount of the transferred asset is allocated between the rights or obligations retained and those transferred, based on their relative fair values, at the transfer date. Any new rights and obligations created must be measured at fair value, at the transfer date. Any difference between consideration received and amounts recognised and derecognised must be recognised in profit or loss in the period the transfer takes place.

17.11.3 Transfers that do not result in derecognition

When a transfer does not result in the derecognition of a financial asset, the financial asset continues to be recognised in its entirety and a separate financial liability is recognised for the consideration received. The asset and liability may **not** be offset in the statement of financial position.

Example 17-14: Transfer that does not qualify for derecognition

On 1 January 20X1, Atlanta transferred a group of debtors with a carrying amount of CU3.5 million to a financial institution, Detroit, for CU3.15 million (90% of the value). Atlanta continues to handle collections from the debtors including sending monthly statements. Detroit pays Atlanta an annual service fee of CU30,000 for these services. Atlanta has agreed to buy back from Detroit any receivables for which the debtor is in arrears for more than 90 days. Atlanta incurred the following transactions for the period ended 31 December 20X1:

- Atlanta received an amount of CU3,000,000 from transferred debtors.
- The balance of debtors of CU500,000 was not refunded; Atlanta had to buy back these debtors.

Required

Determine whether Atlanta may derecognise the transferred debtors, and if so, what journal entries are required.

Suggested solution

Atlanta retains a significant amount of risk, namely the risk of slow payment or non-payment by the debtors. Atlanta is thus not regarded to have transferred the debtors to Detroit, and does not derecognise the debtors.

1 January 20X1

Dr	Bank (SFP)	3,150,000	
Cr	Liability payable to Detroit (SFP)		3,150,000

Recognise the proceeds received.

The liability payable to Detroit is a loan secured by the receivables.

On the respective transaction dates during the period ended **31 December 20X1:**

Journal for cash received from debtors:

Dr	Bank (SFP)	3,000,000	
Cr	Debtor (SFP)		3,000,000

Repayment received from a debtor.

When the **proceeds are transferred** to Detroit, the journal is:

Dr	Liability payable to Detroit (SFP) (90%)	2,700,000	
Dr	Loss on settlement of debtors (10%)	300,000	
Cr	Bank (SFP)		3,000,000

Transfer of cash to Detroit.

Service fees are accrued over the year, the accumulated journal is:

Dr	Bank / Cash (SFP)	30,000	
Cr	Service fee for managing debtors (SFP)		30,000

Recognition of service fee for managing debtors.

When the **debtors are bought back** from Detroit, the journal is:

Dr	Liability payable to Detroit (SFP) (90%)	450,000	
Dr	Loss on settlement of debtors (10%)	50,000	
Cr	Bank (SFP)		500,000

Recognition of debtors bought back.

Note: The CU500,000 debtors retained with no cash received need to be tested for impairment as the long-outstanding status is an indicator of impairment.

17.11.4   Collateral

If a financial asset is transferred, the transferor (ie transferring party) may provide non-cash collateral (eg debt or shares) to the transferee (ie receiving party). The accounting for the collateral by the transferor and the transferee depends on whether the transferee has the right to sell or re-pledge the collateral, and on whether the transferor has defaulted. As long as the transferor has not defaulted, the asset will continue to be recognised by the transferor. The accounting treatment of the transferor and transferee is set out in *Figure 17-9*.

Figure 17-9: Accounting for collateral

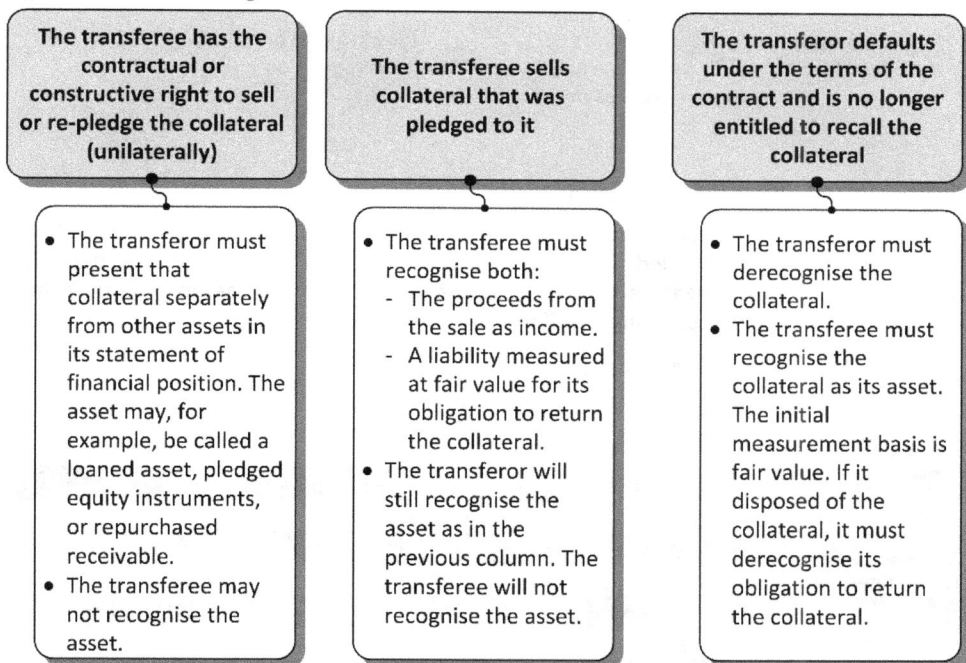

The transferee has the contractual or constructive right to sell or re-pledge the collateral (unilaterally)

The transferee sells collateral that was pledged to it

The transferor defaults under the terms of the contract and is no longer entitled to recall the collateral

- The transferor must present that collateral separately from other assets in its statement of financial position. The asset may, for example, be called a loaned asset, pledged equity instruments, or repurchased receivable.
- The transferee may not recognise the asset.

- The transferee must recognise both:
  - The proceeds from the sale as income.
  - A liability measured at fair value for its obligation to return the collateral.
- The transferor will still recognise the asset as in the previous column. The transferee will not recognise the asset.

- The transferor must derecognise the collateral.
- The transferee must recognise the collateral as its asset. The initial measurement basis is fair value. If it disposed of the collateral, it must derecognise its obligation to return the collateral.

17.11.5   Derecognition of a financial liability

A financial liability (or a part thereof) is derecognised only when the obligation in the contract is extinguished. An obligation is extinguished if the contractual obligations are discharged, cancelled or expired.

A financial liability is also derecognised when the financial liability is exchanged or modified.

- If the financial liability is **exchanged** for a financial liability with terms that are substantially different, the borrower must derecognise the original financial liability and recognise a new financial liability.
- If the terms of a financial liability are **modified** substantially, the borrower must also derecognise the original financial liability and recognise a new financial liability. This

would be the case even if the renegotiation of terms was due to the financial difficulty of the borrower.

Any difference (as illustrated in *Figure 17-10*) between the carrying amount of the financial liability derecognised and the consideration paid, including any non-cash assets transferred or liabilities assumed, must be recognised in profit or loss.

Figure 17-10: Profit or loss on derecognition of a liability

Consideration paid − Carrying amount of financial liability derecognised = Profit/(loss) on derecognition

17.12 Hedge accounting

The Standard allows hedge accounting for certain specified risks and under certain conditions. When the specified **conditions** are met, the entity may **designate** a **hedging relationship** between a **hedging instrument** and a **hedged item** for the **allowed risks**. An entity may apply hedge accounting only if the entity makes such a designation.

17.12.1 Hedging conditions

To apply hedge accounting, all of the conditions set out in *Table 17-7* must apply.

Table 17-7: Conditions for hedge accounting

Condition 1
The hedging relationship is designated and documented.
Condition 2
The hedged item and the related risk qualify.
Condition 3
The hedging instrument qualifies.
Condition 4
The entity expects that the hedging instrument will be highly effective in offsetting the designated hedged risk.

17.12.1.1 The hedging relationship is designated and documented

The entity must designate and document the hedging relationship so that the risk being hedged, the hedged item, and the hedging instrument are clearly identified. The risk in the hedged item must be the risk that is hedged with the hedging instrument.

> 👁 Condition 1 is a formal condition for which documented evidence must be kept.

17.12.1.2 The hedged item and the related risk qualify

Table 17-8 identifies the items that qualify as hedged items and the related risks that may be hedged by the hedging instruments. Only the hedged items and related risk illustrated in *Table 17-8* and *Figure 17-11* qualify for hedge accounting.

Table 17-8: Qualifying hedge items and related risks

Qualifying hedged item	Related risk that may be hedged
Debt instrument measured at amortised cost.	Interest rate risk.
Firm commitment or a highly probable forecasted transaction.	Foreign exchange or interest rate risk.
Commodity held, firm commitment or highly probable forecast transaction to purchase or sell a commodity.	Price risk.
Net investment in a foreign operation.	Foreign exchange risk.

The Standard states that foreign exchange risk of a debt instrument measured at amortised cost is not included in qualifying hedge items because hedge accounting would not have any significant effect.

Figure 17-11: Qualifying hedging risks

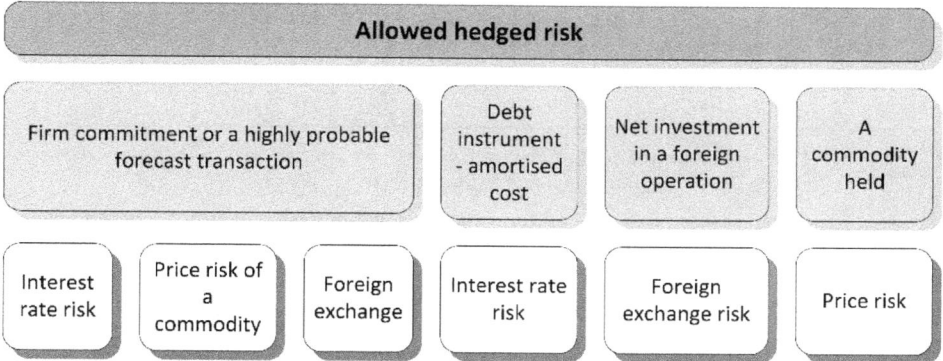

17.12.1.3 The hedging instrument qualifies

The Standard's definition of a hedging instrument limits the types of financial instruments that may be used as hedging instruments to those listed in *Table 17-9*.

Table 17-9: Allowed hedging instruments

Interest rate swap.
Foreign currency swap.
Foreign currency forward exchange contract.
Commodity forward exchange contract.

The definition of a hedge instrument also specifies that the above allowed hedging instruments must adhere to all the features in *Table 17-10* before hedge accounting may be applied.

Table 17-10: Feature of a qualifying hedging instrument

The hedging instrument is expected to be highly effective in offsetting a permitted risk that is designated as the hedged risk (refer to Condition 4).
The hedge must involve a party external to the reporting entity (ie external to the group, segment or individual entity being reported on).
The hedge instrument's notional amount must be equal to the designated amount of the principal or notional amount of the hedged item.
The hedge instrument must have a specified maturity date not later than: ▪ The maturity of the financial instrument being hedged.   ▪ The expected settlement of the commodity purchase or sale commitment.   ▪ The occurrence of the highly probable forecast foreign currency or commodity transaction being hedged.
The hedge instrument may not have any pre-payment, early termination or extension features.

17.12.1.4 The entity expects that the hedging instrument will be highly effective in offsetting the designated hedged risk

The last condition states that the entity expects the hedging instrument to be highly effective in offsetting the designated hedged risk. The effectiveness of a hedge is the degree to which changes in the fair value or cash flows of the hedged item that are attributable to the hedged risk are offset by changes in the fair value or cash flows of the hedging instrument.

The Standard does not specify the degree of effectiveness that will be considered *highly effective*. As a minimum, the entity needs only to demonstrate that they expect the hedge to be highly effective when designating the hedge. Meeting all of the features of a hedge instrument (refer to *Table 17-7*) would normally result in effectiveness.

17.12.2 Hedges of fixed interest rate risk of a recognised financial instrument or commodity price risk of a commodity held

Hedge accounting is treated similarly for the following two hedging relationships:

- Fixed interest rate risk of a debt instrument measured at amortised cost.
- The commodity price risk of a commodity held.

If the above two hedge relationships are designated in a qualifying hedge relationship, the hedge instrument and hedge item are treated as follows (refer to *Figure 17-12*):

- The change in the fair value of the hedging instrument for the period of the hedge is recognised in profit or loss.
- The change in the fair value of the hedged item is also recognised in profit or loss and as an adjustment to the carrying amount of the hedged item.

Figure 17-12: Hedges of existing transactions or balances

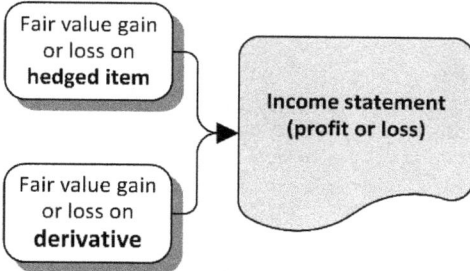

Example 17-15: Hedge of an inventory item held

A jewellery company holds gold as inventories that it uses in its manufacturing process. As management was concerned that the gold price would decrease, it decided to enter into a gold futures contract as a seller (put option) to hedge any possible decrease in the gold price.

On 1 September 20X1, the company decided to hedge 1,000 ounces of gold held. The future contracts are only available in 10 ounce units, therefore the company entered into 100 future contracts as the seller. The contracts mature on 31 December 20X1, and the value was settled in cash. The hedging relationship was appropriately designated and documented.

The normal selling price of one ounce gold was as follows:

1 September 20X1	CU1,167
31 December 20X1	CU1,024

The market value of the December futures contracts were as follows:

1 September 20X1	CU11,526
31 December 20X1	CU10,212

The carrying value of the inventories of 1,000 ounces of gold at cost was CU600,000 on 1 September 20X1.

Example 17-15: Hedge of an inventory item held *(continued)*

Required

Provide the journal entries to journalise the hedging transaction during the period ended 31 December 20X1.

Suggested solution

Since the hedge is appropriately documented and designated, and meets the features of a hedging instrument, the hedge accounting for the price risk of the commodity held is:

Dr	Loss on value of inventories (P/L)	143,000	
Cr	Inventories (SFP)		143,000
	(1,000 x (CU1,167 - 1,024))		

Recognise the loss in the value of inventories for the four months.

Dr	Bank (SFP)	131,500	
Cr	Profit on gold futures (P/L)		131,500
	((100 x (CU11,526 - CU10,211)		

Recognise the profit on the gold futures contracts.

Note: No effectiveness test is done when the hedge is recognised. Management only needs to demonstrate initially that it expects that the hedge will be highly effective. Changes in the fair value of the gold futures are recognised in profit or loss. Hedge accounting results in the recognition of the changes in the fair value of the inventories of gold in profit or loss for the duration of the hedge.

If an interest rate swap is used to hedge the fixed interest rate of a debt instrument, the periodic net cash settlements on the interest rate swap must be recognised in profit or loss, in the period in which the net settlement accrues.

Hedge accounting is discontinued prospectively if any of the following occurs:

- The hedging instrument expires, is sold or terminated.
- The hedge no longer meets the conditions for hedge accounting.
- The entity revokes its designation.

In a hedge relationship of an asset or liability carried at amortised cost, fair value gains or losses are recognised as adjustments to the carrying amount of the hedged item. If hedge accounting is discontinued, such fair value gains or losses, recognised as adjustments to the carrying amount of the hedged item, are amortised into profit or loss using the effective interest rate method over the remaining life of the hedged item.

17.12.3 Hedges of variable interest rate risk of a recognised financial instrument, foreign exchange risk or commodity price risk in a firm commitment or highly probable forecast transaction, or net investment in a foreign operation

These hedges include:

- Hedges of a variable interest rate risk of a **debt instrument measured at amortised cost**.
- Foreign exchange or commodity price risk on a firm commitment or a highly probable forecast transaction, also known as a **cash flow hedge**.
- Foreign exchange risk in a **net investment in a foreign operation**, ie a subsidiary, branch, associate or JV (refer to *Figure 17-13*).

> A net investment in a foreign operation includes investments in shares or loans receivable from a foreign operation where the loan is deemed to be an integral part of the investment in the foreign operation.

In these hedge relationships, the entity must recognise the effective portion of the change in the fair value of the hedging instrument in other comprehensive income, and defer it in equity until the hedged item occurs, is realised, or is settled. The cumulative amounts related to a hedge of a net investment in a foreign operation recognised in other comprehensive income shall not be reclassified to profit or loss on disposal, or partial disposal, of the foreign operation. The entity must determine the effectiveness of the hedge with reference to the extent in which the change in the fair value of the hedging instrument offsets the change in the fair value or expected cash flows of the hedged item.

Figure 17-13: Example of a net investment in a foreign operation hedge

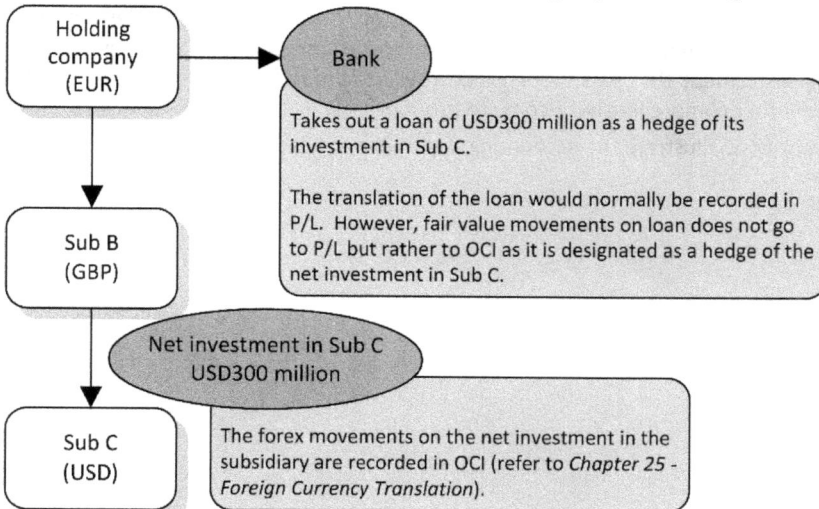

> In these hedge relationships, an effectiveness test must be done to split the effective and ineffective portion. The effective portion is recognised in OCI and the ineffective portion in profit or loss.

The Standard determines that the ineffective portion is the excess of the fair value change of the hedging instrument over the change in the fair value of the hedging item or the expected cash flows.

Example 17-16: Determining the ineffective portion

Kiev hedges the commodity price risk in a firm commitment of a highly probable forecast transaction with a commodity future, and complies with all hedge accounting requirements. The fair value movement on the commodity future for the current reporting period was CU240,000. The increase in the price of the commodity for the same period was CU211,000.

Required

Determine the ineffective portion, if any, and the related accounting treatment by Kiev.

Suggested solution

The ineffective portion is the amount CU29,000 by which the fair value change in the commodity future CU240,000 exceeds the increase in the fair value of the commodity CU211,000.

Commodity future movement (CU240,000) - Commodity movement (CU211,000) = Ineffective portion (CU29,000).

The effective portion of CU211,000 is recognised in other comprehensive income and the ineffective portion of CU29,000 in profit or loss.

The gain or loss deferred in equity, and recognised in other comprehensive income, must be reclassified to profit or loss when the hedged item is recognised in profit or loss, or when the hedging relationship ceases. If the forecast transaction is no longer expected to take place or if the hedged debt instrument measured at amortised cost is derecognised, any gain or loss on the hedging instrument that was recognised in other comprehensive income must be reclassified from other comprehensive income to profit or loss.

Figures 17-14 and *17-15* illustrate the accounting treatment of a cash flow hedge.

Figure 17-14: Other hedges – Before forecast transactions or firm commitments occur

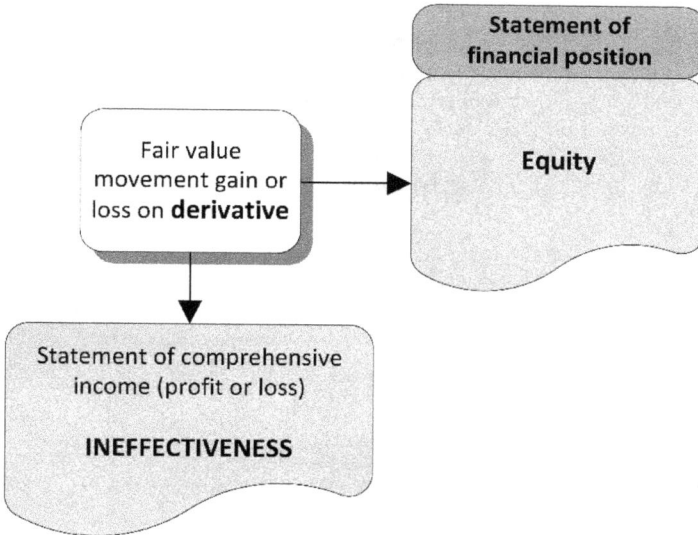

Figure 17-15: Other hedges – When forecast transactions or firm commitments occur

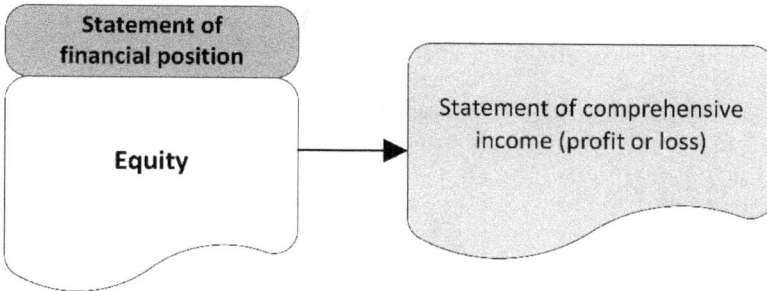

Example 17-17: Hedge of a foreign transaction

Hanoi entered into a legal agreement to **purchase** raw material to the value of USD100,000 on 1 January 20X1, and entered into a nine-month forward exchange contract for the same amount on the same date to hedge the creditor payable. The raw material was shipped on 30 June 20X1 on which date all risks and rewards of ownership passed to Hanoi. The raw material was received in the Durban harbour on 15 July 20X1. The amount is payable on 30 September 20X1. Hanoi's reporting date is 30 April 20X1.

The relevant exchange rates were:

Date	Spot rate USD1 =	Forward rate USD1 =
1 January 20x1	CU6,80	CU6,90 (9 months)
30 April 20X1	CU6,85	CU6,94 (5 months)
30 April 20X1	CU6,85	CU6,98 (9 months)
30 June 20X1	CU6,90	CU6,96 (3 months)
15 July 20X1	CU6,92	
30 September 20X1	CU7,00	

Hanoi complied with all the requirements of hedge accounting and documented the hedging relationship as required.

Required
Provide the journal entries to account for the purchase of the raw materials within the 20X1 and 20X2 financial reporting periods.

Suggested solution

1 January 20X1
No journal entry required at the inception of the foreign exchange contract as the forward rate provided on the FEC is available to all market participants and therefore reflects no fair value at this date.

30 April 20X1 (reporting date)
Calculate the ineffective portion:

Loss on firm commitment	CU5,000
(USD100,000 x (CU6,85 - CU6,80))	
Profit on FEC	CU4,000
(USD100,000 x (CU6,94 - CU6,90))	
	CU1,000

The profit on the FEC is less than the loss on the firm commitment. Therefore the total profit on the FEC is recognised in other comprehensive income.

Dr	FEC financial asset (SFP)	4,000	
Cr	Hedging reserve (OCI)		4,000
	(USD100,000 x (CU6,94 - CU6,90))		

Accounting for the fair value movement of the FEC.

Example 17-17: Hedge of a foreign transaction *(continued)*

30 June 20X1 (transaction date as risks and rewards pass)

Calculation of ineffective portion (cumulative):

Loss on firm commitment (USD100,000 x (CU6,90 - CU6,80))	CU10,000
Profit on fair value FEC (USD100,000 x (CU6,96 - CU6,90))	CU6,000

Again the profit on the FEC is less than the loss on the firm commitment, and therefore the total amount (CU6,000) less the amount previously recognised (CU4,000) is recognised in other comprehensive income.

Dr	FEC debtor (SFP)	2,000	
Cr	Hedging gain (OCI)		2,000

Accounting for the fair value movement of the FEC.
(USD100,000 x (CU6,96 - CU6,94))

On the transaction date, the inventories are recognised. The journal will be as follows:

Dr	Inventories at cost price (SFP)	690,000	
Cr	Trade creditor (SFP)		690,000

Accounting for the transaction at transaction date.
(USD100,000 x CU6.90 at spot rate)

Note: The balance in the hedging reserve may not be capitalised in the value of inventories.

30 September 20X1 (maturity date of the FEC and settlement date of creditor)

Dr	FEC debtor (SFP)	4,000	
Cr	Hedging gain (P/L)		4,000
	(USD100,000 x (CU7.00 - CU6.96)		

Accounting for the fair value movement of the FEC.

Dr	Trade creditor (SFP)	700,000	
Cr	Bank (SFP)		700,000

Settle creditor at spot rate on maturity date. (USD100,000 x CU)

Dr	Bank (SFP)	10,000	
Cr	FEC debtor (SFP)		10,000
	(CU4,000 + CU2,000 + CU4,000)		

The hedging gain recognised in other comprehensive income is reclassified to profit or loss when the inventories are sold or when the hedging relationship ends, whichever is earlier. In this case, the reclassification is done when the hedging relationship ends on 30 September 20X1.

Dr	Hedging reserve (OCI)	6,000	
Cr	Hedging gain (P/L)		6,000

Reclassification of amount in other comprehensive income.

If an interest rate swap is used to hedge the variable interest rate of a debt instrument, the periodic net cash settlements on an interest rate swap must be recognised in profit or loss in the period in which the net settlement accrues.

The entity must discontinue hedge accounting prospectively if any of the following occurs:

- The hedging instrument expires or is sold or terminated.
- The hedge no longer meets the conditions for hedge accounting.
- In a hedge of a forecast transaction, the forecast transaction is no longer highly probable.
- The entity revokes the designation.

17.13 Disclosure

17.13.1 Disclosure of accounting policies for financial instruments

In the summary of significant accounting policies, disclose the measurement basis (or bases) used for financial instruments and the other accounting policies used for financial instruments that are relevant to an understanding of the financial statements.

17.13.2 Statement of financial position

Disclose the carrying amounts of each of the following categories of financial assets and liabilities at the reporting date, in total, either in the statement of financial position or in the notes:

- Financial assets measured at fair value through profit or loss.
- Financial assets measured at amortised cost.
- Equity instruments measured at cost less impairment.
- Loan commitments measured at cost less impairment.
- Financial liabilities measured at fair value through profit or loss.
- Financial liabilities measured at amortised cost.

Disclose information that enables users of the financial statements to evaluate the significance of financial instruments for its financial position and performance. This disclosure may include information such as interest rate, maturity, repayment schedule, and restrictions.

For all financial assets and liabilities measured at fair value, disclose the basis for determining fair value, eg quoted market price in an active market or a valuation technique. When a valuation technique is used, the entity must disclose **the assumptions applied in determining fair value** for each class of financial assets or liabilities. For example, if applicable, an entity discloses information about the assumptions relating to pre-payment rates, rates of **estimated credit losses**, and **interest rates** or **discount rates**.

If a reliable measure of fair value is no longer available, or is not available without undue cost or effort, when such exemption is provided for an equity instrument that would otherwise be measured at fair value through profit or loss, the carrying amounts of such assets, and if the undue cost or effort exemption was applied, the reasons why determining a reliable fair value would involve undue cost or effort must be disclosed.

17.13.3   Derecognition

If a financial asset is transferred to another party in a transaction that does not qualify for derecognition, disclose for each class of such financial assets all of the following information:

- The nature of the assets.
- The nature of the risks and rewards of ownership to which the entity remains exposed.
- The carrying amounts of the assets and of any associated liabilities that the entity continues to recognise.

17.13.4   Collateral

When financial assets are pledged as collateral for liabilities or contingent liabilities, the following must be disclosed:

- The carrying amount of the financial assets pledged as collateral.
- The terms and conditions relating to its pledge.

17.13.5   Defaults and breaches on loans payable

For loans payable (recognised at the reporting date) for which there is a breach of terms or default of principal, interest, sinking fund, or redemption terms that has not been remedied by the reporting date, disclose:

- Details of that breach or default.
- The carrying amount of the related loans payable at the reporting date.
- Whether the breach or default was remedied, or the terms of the loans payable were re-negotiated, before the financial statements were authorised for issue.

17.13.6   Items of income, expense, gains or losses

Disclose all the following items of income, expense, gains or losses, where applicable:

- Income, expense, gains or losses, including changes in fair value, recognised on:
  - Financial assets measured at fair value through profit or loss.
  - Financial liabilities measured at fair value through profit or loss.
  - Financial assets measured at amortised cost.
  - Financial liabilities measured at amortised cost.
- Total interest income and total interest expense (calculated using the effective interest rate method) for financial assets or liabilities that are not measured at fair value through profit or loss.
- The amount of any impairment loss for each class of financial asset.

17.13.7   Hedge accounting

Disclose all the following information separately for hedges of each type of risk:

- A description of the hedge.
- A description of the financial instruments designated as hedging instruments and their fair values at the reporting date.
- The nature of the risks being hedged, including a description of the hedged item.

Relating to the hedge accounting for a hedge of fixed interest rate risk or commodity price risk of a commodity held, the following must be disclosed:

- The amount of the change in fair value of the hedging instrument recognised in profit or loss.
- The amount of the change in fair value of the hedged item recognised in profit or loss.

Relating to the hedge accounting for a hedge of variable interest rate risk, foreign exchange risk, commodity price risk in a firm commitment or highly probable forecast transaction, or a net investment in a foreign operation, the following must be disclosed:

- The periods when the cash flows are expected to occur, and when they are expected to affect profit or loss.
- A description of any forecast transaction for which hedge accounting had previously been used, but which is no longer expected to occur.
- The amount of the change in fair value of the hedging instrument that was recognised in other comprehensive income during the period.
- The amount that was reclassified to profit or loss for the period.
- The amount of any excess of the cumulative change in fair value of the hedging instrument over the cumulative change in the fair value of the expected cash flows that was recognised in profit or loss for the period.

17.14   Summary

- **Basic and other financial instruments**
  - A financial instrument is a contract that creates a financial asset for one entity and a financial liability or equity instrument for another.
  - These two sections deal with the recognition, derecognition, measurement and disclosure of all financial instruments. Each entity needs to assess whether its financial instruments fall under the scope of basic financial instruments only, or include other financial instruments.
  - A policy choice exists in which an entity may either apply the provisions of these sections or apply IAS 39, *Financial Instruments: Recognition and Measurement*. If IAS 39 is adopted by an SME, it **does not** have to comply with the disclosure requirements of IFRS 7, *Financial Instruments: Disclosure*, but the disclosure required by sections 11 and 12 of this Standard must be followed.
  - *Note: As this is an accounting policy choice, it is subject to the normal guidance in the IFRS for SMEs regarding changes in accounting policies.*
  - Interests in subsidiaries, associates and JV, employers' rights, insurance contracts, part of an entity's own equity leases, and most contracts involving non-financial items are all excluded from this section because they are covered in other sections of the Standard.
  - Financial assets and liabilities are recognised when the parties become bound by the contractual provisions of the instrument.
  - Derecognition of an asset occurs when:
    - The contractual rights to the cash flows from the financial asset expire or are settled;

- The entity transfers to another party all of the significant risks and rewards relating to the financial asset; or
- The entity, despite having retained some significant risks and rewards relating to the financial asset, has transferred the ability to sell the asset in its entirety to an unrelated third party who is able to exercise that ability unilaterally and without needing to impose additional restrictions on the transfer.
  - A liability is derecognised when the obligation is settled.
- **Basic financial instrument issues**
  - Basic financial instruments comprise of the less complex financial instruments that entities carry, and therefore this section applies to all entities. Examples of basic financial instruments are long-term loans, cash, demand and fixed-term deposits, trade debtors and trade creditors. Other more complex financial instruments and transactions are dealt with in the next section.
  - The recognition model for basic financial instruments is the amortised cost model.
  - Basic financial assets and liabilities are initially measured at the transaction price (including transaction costs except in the initial measurement of financial assets and liabilities that are measured at fair value through profit or loss) unless the arrangement constitutes, in effect, a financing transaction. A financing transaction may be indicated in relation to the sale of goods or services, for example, if payment is deferred beyond normal business terms or is financed at a rate of interest that is not a market rate. If the arrangement constitutes a financing transaction, the entity must measure the financial asset or liability at the present value of the future payments, discounted at a market rate of interest for a similar debt instrument as determined at initial recognition.
  - Subsequent measurement is as follows:
    - Debt instruments at amortised cost using the effective interest method.
    - Debt instruments that are classified as current assets or liabilities must be measured at the undiscounted amount of the cash or other consideration expected to be paid or received (ie net of impairment) unless the arrangement constitutes, in effect, a financing transaction. If the arrangement constitutes a financing transaction, the entity must measure the debt instrument at the present value of the future payments discounted at a market rate of interest for a similar debt instrument as determined at initial recognition.
    - Investments in non-convertible preference shares and non-puttable ordinary or preference shares:
      - If the shares are **publicly traded** or their fair value can otherwise be measured reliably without undue cost or effort, the investment shall be measured at fair value with changes in fair value recognised in profit or loss.
      - All other such investments shall be measured at cost less impairment.
  - At each reporting date, an entity shall assess financial assets for objective evidence of impairment, if they are not recognised at fair value. If an impairment indicator exists, an impairment test must be done. Reversals of impairments are required if they arise as a result of an event after the impairment was recognised.

- **Other financial instrument issues**
    - This section deals with other financial instrument issues, and applies to all financial instruments that are not basic financial instruments, for example derivatives, shares and instruments with highly variable or uncertain cash flows.
    - The recognition model for other financial instruments is the fair value model, which is normally the transaction price. This is exclusive of transaction costs.
    - Subsequent measurement:
        - Other financial instruments are measured at the end of each reporting period at fair value, and changes in fair value are recognised in profit or loss. There is an exception for equity instruments that are not publicly traded, and whose fair value cannot otherwise be measured reliably, and contracts linked to such instruments that, if exercised, will result in delivery of such instruments. These instruments must be measured at cost less impairment.
        - If a reliable measure of fair value is no longer available for an equity instrument that is not publicly traded, but is measured at fair value through profit or loss, its fair value at the last date the instrument was reliably measurable is treated as the cost of the instrument. Going forward, the entity must measure the instrument at this cost amount less impairment until a reliable measure of fair value becomes available.
    - A hierarchy for the fair value calculation is provided. The most reliable evidence is a quoted price in an active market; this is usually the current bid price at reporting date. When a quoted price is not available, the price in a binding sale agreement or the most recent transaction price between willing and knowledgeable parties provides evidence of fair value. However, this price may not be a good estimate of fair value if (1) there has been a significant change in economic circumstances or (2) a significant period of time between the date of the binding sale agreement or transaction. If there is no active market, binding sale agreement or recent market transactions, another valuation technique should be used.
    - Hedge accounting (matching the gains and losses on a hedging instrument and hedged item) is only permitted for specific types of risks (eg interest rate risk, foreign exchange risk and foreign exchange risk on a foreign operation), and only if certain specified hedging instruments are used. Comprehensive hedge documentation and a simplified measurement of hedge effectiveness are still required.

Chapter 18
Leases

Contents

18.1 Scope

18.1.1 Scope exclusions

This guidance applies to all leases other than the following:

- Leases to explore and exploit minerals, oil, natural gas, and similar non-regenerative resources (refer to *Chapter 29.3*).
- Licencing agreements that give rise to intangible assets including motion picture films, video recordings, plays, manuscripts, patents, and copyrights (refer to *Chapter 13*).
- Onerous operating leases which occur when the lessee's economic benefits received under the lease are less than the lessee's obligations under the lease. An entity is required to recognise a provision for the onerous lease under the chapter on provisions (refer to *Chapter 15*).
- Leases that are regarded as financial instruments. For example, leases where payments are linked to underlying indices that are not linked to the price of the leased asset, changes in lease payments resulting from variable interest rates or foreign exchange prices (refer to *Chapter 17*).
- Leases where their measurement criteria are set out in other chapters. These include:
  - Measurement of property held by lessees is accounted for as investment property, and measurement of investment property provided by lessors under operating leases (refer to *Chapter 11*).
  - Measurement of biological assets held by lessees under finance leases and biological assets provided by lessors under operating leases (refer to *Chapter 29*).

18.1.2 Arrangements containing a lease

This chapter also applies to arrangements that transfer the right of use of assets but excludes arrangements that are contracts for services, which only convey the right to use assets without effecting transfer of an asset from one contracting party to the other.

An arrangement may convey the right to use an asset in return for a series of payments. Contracts that convey the right to use an asset are accounted for as leases in this chapter. Examples of such arrangements may include:

- Outsourcing arrangements, such as some information technology services or catering services.
- Take-or-pay contracts, eg contracts in terms of which a customer agrees to utilise all of an agreed amount of output from a supplier, or pay for output that they fail to utilise.

👁 As the Standard gives no detailed guidance on the application of lease accounting to arrangements containing a lease, an entity may choose to look at the principles in full IFRS. IFRIC 4, *Determining Whether an Arrangement Contains a Lease* in full IFRS provides detailed guidance on whether an arrangement contains a lease element.

The guidance requires that all the following three criteria be met:

- The 'purchaser' has the ability or right to operate the asset or direct others to operate the asset in a manner it determines while obtaining or controlling more than an insignificant amount of the output or other utility of the asset.
- The 'purchaser' has the ability or right to control physical access to the underlying asset while obtaining or controlling more than an insignificant amount of the output or other utility of the asset.
- Facts and circumstances indicate that it is remote that one or more parties other than the 'purchaser' will take more than an insignificant amount of the output or other utility that will be produced or generated by the asset during the term of the arrangement, and the price that the 'purchaser' will pay for the output is neither contractually fixed per unit of output nor equal to the current market price per unit of output as of the time of delivery of the output.

18.2   Definition of a lease

🖐 A lease is an agreement whereby the lessor conveys to the lessee in return for a payment or series of payments the right to use an asset for an agreed period of time.

18.3   Classification of leases

Leases are classified as either finance or operating leases. The key difference is that with a finance lease, the lease substantially transfers all the risks and rewards incidental to ownership of the asset from the lessor to the lessee. Should the contract not substantially transfer all the risks and rewards incidental to ownership, then the lease is accounted for as an operating lease.

The difference in accounting for an operating versus a finance lease is that with a finance lease, the asset is derecognised from the lessor's statement of financial position. For an operating lease, the asset remains on the lessor's statement of financial position. This accounting is discussed in greater detail further in the chapter. *Figures 18-1* and *18-2* provide an illustrative overview of the accounting of an operating and finance lease, respectively, by a lessor and lessee.

Figure 18-1: Accounting treatment of an operating lease

Lessor	Lessee
• The leased asset remains on the statement of financial position. • Depreciate the asset. • Recognise lease income in the statement of comprehensive income.	• Don't recognise the asset on the statement of financial position. • Recognise an expense in the statement of comprehensive income.

Figure 18-2: Accounting treatment of a finance lease

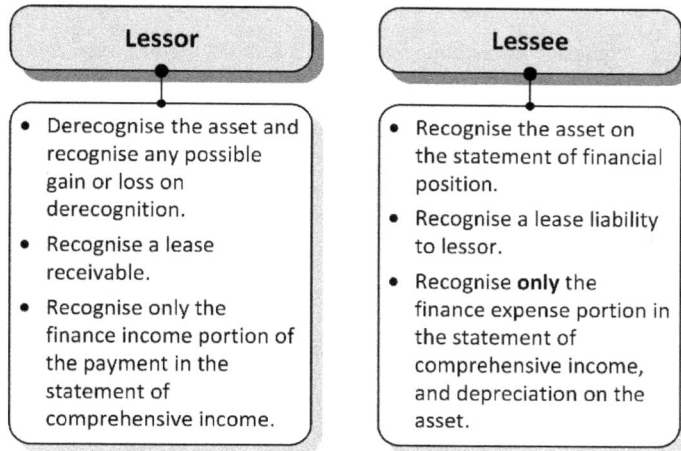

Lessor	Lessee
• Derecognise the asset and recognise any possible gain or loss on derecognition. • Recognise a lease receivable. • Recognise only the finance income portion of the payment in the statement of comprehensive income.	• Recognise the asset on the statement of financial position. • Recognise a lease liability to lessor. • Recognise **only** the finance expense portion in the statement of comprehensive income, and depreciation on the asset.

18.3.1 Primary lease indicators

Primary indicators provided by the Standard that individually or in combination would normally lead to a lease being classified as a finance lease are set out in *Table 18-1*.

Table 18-1: Primary indicators of a finance lease

The lease transfers ownership of the asset to the lessee by the end of the lease term (refer to *Example 18-1*).
The lessee has the option to purchase the asset at a price that is expected to be sufficiently lower than the fair value at the date the option becomes exercisable. And, it is reasonably certain, at the inception of the lease, that the option will be exercised (refer to *Example 18-2*).
The lease term is for the major part of the economic useful life of the asset even if title is not transferred (refer to *Example 18-3*).

Table 18-1: Primary indicators of a finance lease *(continued)*

At the inception of the lease, the present value of the minimum lease payments amounts to at least substantially all of the fair value of the leased asset (refer to *Example 18-4*).
The leased assets are of such a specialised nature that only the lessee can use them without major modifications (refer to *Example 18-5*).

18.3.1.1   Transfer of ownership

Example 18-1: Ownership of the asset transferred at the end of the lease

Sydney enters into a 10 year lease with Perth, the owner of the lease building. Perth is wholly owned by Melbourne. Sydney has a separate agreement with Melbourne, which states that at the conclusion of the lease, Sydney may purchase all the shares in Perth for zero consideration.

As this in substance transfers ownership of the asset at the end of the lease term, it would be an indicator of a finance lease.

> All contracts should be evaluated in determining whether this indicator has been met. This includes agreements, which in substance, result in the transfer of the asset to the lessee on non-market terms.

18.3.1.2   Bargain purchase price option

Example 18-2: An option to purchase the asset at a bargain price

Darwin leases a car from Auckland for three years on market terms. Darwin has the option to purchase the car for CU100,000 at the end of the lease. At inception, the CU100,000 does not represent a bargain purchase option as this is the expected market value of the car in three years time. One year into the lease, the prices of second-hand cars increase, and it is now expected that the value of the car at the end of the lease will be CU150,000.

Even though the purchase option is now a bargain purchase option, it was not a bargain option at the inception of the lease, and therefore there is no indicator of a finance lease.

> The existence of an option to purchase the asset at the end of the lease is not evidence in itself of a finance lease. Both the existence of a bargain purchase price and the assessment must be evaluated only once at the inception of the lease. When a bargain purchase arises at a later date due to market movements in the prices of the underlying asset, the lease would not be re-evaluated.

18.3.1.3 Lease term is a major part of the economic useful life of the asset

Example 18-3: Lease term is a major part of the economic useful life of the asset

Lima leases a truck for seven years. The economic life of this model of truck is estimated to be eight years. As a result, the lease represents 87.5% of the useful life of the asset. As this can be judged to represent the major part of the asset's economic useful life, it would be an indicator of a finance lease.

> The Standard does not define *major part*. As a result, judgement is required in determining whether the lease term is for the major part of the economic life of the asset. Under previous versions of *IAS 17 – Leases*, the major part was defined as greater than 75% of the economic useful life of the asset. Whereas the current *IAS 17 – Leases* and the IFRS for SMEs do not use this indicator, it may be a useful guide.

18.3.1.4 Present value of the minimum lease payments

Example 18-4: Present value of the minimum lease payments vs the fair value of the leased asset

Prague enters into a five-year lease agreement with Bratislava over office equipment on 31 December 20X0. The equipment is expected to have a useful life of seven years and is not specialised.

The payments provided in the lease agreement are:

- Prague will pay CU35,000 pa for the equipment commencing in December 20X1. This amount includes CU10,000 pa for a maintenance contract.
- Prague will have the option to purchase the equipment at the end of the five-year period for CU10,000. If Prague does not purchase it, it must return the equipment to Bratislava.
- There is no secondary rental period.
- The interest rate implicit in the lease is 11%. At inception, the fair value of the equipment is CU100,000 with an estimated residual value of CU10,000.

As inflation rises dramatically over the first three years of the contract, the fair value of the equipment at the end of five years is CU25,000.

Required

Determine the lease classification of the lease in terms of the Standard.

Example 18-4: Present value of the minimum lease payments vs the fair value of the leased asset *(continued)*

Suggested solution

As the present value of the minimum lease payments is 92.4% (refer to calculation below) of the equipment's fair value at inception, this indicates that the lease may be a finance lease.

Calculation of the present value of the minimum lease payments

Fair value		100,000		
Discount rate (%)		11.00		
First-year discount variable		1.11		

	Years	Amounts	Discount variable	Discounted amounts
Minimum lease payments	20X1	25,000	1.11	22,523
	20X2	25,000	1.23	20,291
	20X3	25,000	1.37	18,280
	20X4	25,000	1.52	16,468
	20X5	25,000	1.69	14,836
Present value of minimum lease payments				92,397
Percentage of fair value				92.4

An indicator of a finance lease has been identified.

> ♪ This is a quantitative test to determine whether the lessee has substantially paid for the asset over the lease term. As per the previous indicator, there is no definition of *substantially all* in the Standard. Previous versions of *IAS 17 – Leases* used 90% as the indicator of having met this requirement, ie if the present value of the minimum lease payments amounted to more than 90% of the asset's fair value at inception of the lease, it indicated a finance lease. Whereas these quantitative guidelines no longer appear in the Standard, it can be a useful guideline in applying judgement.

18.3.1.5 Leased assets of a specialised nature

Example 18-5: Specialised assets

A piece of machinery is delivered to a paper manufacturer, Accra. It is installed at its factory, and requires concrete foundations with custom-made components that only Accra uses in its production line. The piece of machinery will require significant modifications to be leased to another entity.

As the machinery is specialised in nature, this would be an indicator of a finance lease.

> ♪ A lessor should assess whether the asset would need to undergo major modifications to be used by another lessee. The interpretation of *major* is once again a matter of judgement.

18.3.2   Secondary lease indicators

The Standard then gives us secondary indicators of a finance lease. Only when the primary indicators are inconclusive, should these secondary indicators be considered in determining whether a lease is classified as a finance lease.

Secondary indicators provided by the Standard, that individually or in combination could possibly lead to a lease being classified as a finance lease, in conjunction with one or more primary indicators, are set out in *Table 18-2*. Significant judgement is required in this regard.

Table 18-2: Secondary indicators of a finance lease

If the lessee can cancel the lease, the lessor's losses associated with the cancellation are borne by the lessee (refer to *Example 18-6*).
Gains or losses from the fluctuation in the residual value of the leased asset accrue to the lessee (refer to *Example 18-7*).
The lessee has the ability to continue the lease for a secondary period at a rental that is substantially lower than market rentals (refer to *Example 18-8*).

18.3.2.1   Cancellation losses are borne by the lessee

Example 18-6: Losses of cancellation of the lease are borne by the lessee

Halifax rents an office building from Quebec. The contract states that should Halifax cancel the lease before the termination date stipulated in the agreement, Halifax will continue to pay Quebec rental until the earlier of the date the agreement terminates, or until Quebec finds an alternative tenant.

This is an indicator of a finance lease because the loss of cancelling the leases is borne by Halifax.

If a lease includes a clause which penalises the lessee for cancelling the lease, and this penalty is significant, this is an indicator of a finance lease.

18.3.2.2   Residual value movements accrue to the lessee

Example 18-7: Residual value of the asset accrue to the lessee

Canberra rents a piece of land from Wellington. The agreement states that Canberra will pay the difference between the actual value of the piece of land at the end of the lease and the residual amount indicated in the lease if the difference is positive, but will receive the difference if the difference is negative.

As the movements in the residual value accrue to Canberra, this is an indication of a finance lease.

Where the lessee bears the risk of changes in the residual value of the asset, this indicates a finance lease.

18.3.2.3   A secondary period at a bargain rental

Example 18-8: Ability to continue the lease for a secondary period at a bargain rental

Maputo rents land to Milan to run its operations for five years at a market related rental of CU1,000 per month. The agreement stipulates that Milan has the option to renew the lease for CU200 per month for an additional three years. At inception, the market expectation of rentals for this land in five years time is CU1,200 per month. The secondary period rental therefore represents a substantial discount on the market rate, and would be an indicator of a finance lease.

⹗ The existence of the option to extend a lease for a secondary period is not in itself an indicator of a finance lease. When assessed at inception of the lease, the rental payable in the secondary period would have to be substantially lower than the expected market rental that would be payable in this period. There is no definition of *substantial*, judgement is required.

The lease evaluation above must be done at the inception of the lease. Once the lease is classified as operating or finance, this classification is not revisited unless the terms of the lease are amended. This excludes renewing the lease on new terms or terms that existed at inception of the lease that would have been taken into account when completing the initial lease evaluation.

⹗ The application of the above factors requires a significant amount of professional judgement on the part of the entity's management.

18.4   Financial statements of lessees: finance leases

18.4.1   Initial recognition and measurement

The acquisition of an asset under a finance lease is initially recognised at amounts equal to the fair value of the leased asset or, if lower, the present value of the minimum lease payments, determined at the inception of the lease. The direct costs incurred in negotiating and arranging the lease are included in the carrying amount of the asset. These costs may include legal fees, stamp duty, and any other directly attributable costs.

The present value of the minimum lease payments should be calculated using the interest rate implicit in the lease. If this rate cannot be determined, the lessee's incremental borrowing rate must be used.

The interest rate implicit in the lease is determined at inception of the lease by calculating the rate that causes the minimum lease payments and the unguaranteed residual value to be equal to the sum of the fair value of the leased asset and any initial direct costs of the lessor.

Example 18.9: Initial recognition of a finance lease

Islamabad (the lessee) enters into a five-year lease agreement with Mumbai (the lessor) over computer equipment on 31 December 20X0.

The payment provisions in the lease are as follows.

- Islamabad will pay CU25,000 pa commencing 31 December 20X1 for the equipment.
- Islamabad will have the option to purchase the equipment at the end of the five-year period for CU10,000. If Islamabad does not purchase the equipment, it must be returned to Mumbai.
- The fair value of the equipment is CU80,000 at the inception of the lease.

Assume the lease is classified as a finance lease (refer to 18.3).

Required

Provide the journal entries to record the lease in Islamabad's accounts on 31 December 20X1.

Suggested solution

The fair value of the asset is CU80,000, the annual rental is CU25,000 and the unguaranteed residual value is CU10,000. Based on these variables, the **implicit rate of lease** can be calculated as shown below. This rate must be used to discount the minimum lease payments (refer to calculation of the present value of the minimum lease payments below).

Calculation of implicit rate of the lease

20X0	Initial investment (asset received)	(80,000)
20X1	Payment at 31 December 20X1	25,000
20X2	Payment at 31 December 20X2	25,000
20X3	Payment at 31 December 20X3	25,000
20X4	Payment at 31 December 20X4	25,000
20X5	Payment at 31 December (25,000) PLUS unguaranteed residual value of asset (10,000) at 31 December 20X5	35,000

This gives an IRR (or implicit rate) of 19.34%.

Discount rate (%)	19.34
First year discount variable	1.1934

	Year	Amount	Discount variable	Discounted amount
Lease payment	20X1	25,000	1.1934	20,949
Lease payment	20X2	25,000	1.4242	17,554
Lease payment	20X3	25,000	1.7000	14,706
Lease payment	20X4	25,000	2.0284	12,325
Lease payment	20X5	25,000	2.4206	10,328
Present value of minimum lease payments discounted at the implicit rate of the lease				75,862

Example 18.9: Initial recognition of a finance lease *(continued)*

Because the present value of the minimum lease payments, discounted at the implicit rate of the lease, is lower than the fair value of the leased equipment, both the computer equipment and finance lease liability must be accounted for at the lower value of CU75,862.

31 December 20X1

Dr	Property, plant and equipment (SFP)	75,862	
Cr	Finance lease obligation – liability (SFP)		75,862

18.4.2 Subsequent measurement

18.4.2.1 Leased asset

Subsequent to initial recognition, the lessee accounts for a leased asset under the appropriate section of the Standard, for example property, plant and equipment (refer to *Chapter 12*).

If there is no reasonable certainty that the lessee will obtain ownership by the end of the lease term, the asset must be fully depreciated, ie not to its residual value, over the shorter of the lease term and its useful life. An assessment of impairment must be performed on leased assets at each reporting date.

The guidance on impairment of assets needs to be applied only when there is an indication of impairment for the leased asset (refer to *Chapter 14*).

> ⓘ The leased asset's depreciation method is limited by the lease term if there is no reasonable certainty that ownership will pass at the end of the lease term.

18.4.2.2 Lease obligation

Subsequent to initial recognition, the lessee apportions the minimum lease payments between the finance charges and the reduction of the outstanding liability of the lessee (ie lease obligation) using the effective interest rate method. This is achieved by the lessee allocating the finance charge to each period over the lease term so as to produce a constant periodic rate of interest on the remaining balance of the liability.

Contingent rentals are not included in the calculation above but are expensed in the period in which they are incurred. An example of contingent rental is a turnover rental where a tenant of a retail shop may have to pay a percentage of their turnover to the lessor. These charges would be calculated in terms of the lease agreement and expensed as they fall due.

> ⓘ All leased assets must be tested for impairment at each reporting date, ie annually.

18.4.3 Disclosures

The following disclosures are required for finance leases in the financial statements of the lessee:

- For each asset class, the net carrying amount at the reporting date.

- The total future minimum lease payments at the reporting date, for each of the following periods:
  - Not later than one year.
  - Later than one year and not later than five years.
  - Later than five years.
- A general description of the significant terms of a lessee's significant lease contract and other deemed leasing arrangements, including:
  - Information about contingent rentals.
  - Renewal or purchase options.
  - Escalation clauses.
  - Sub-leases.
  - Restrictions imposed by lease arrangements.

In addition, the normal disclosures for assets under the appropriate chapter of assets must be provided.

Illustrative disclosure 18-1: Finance lease obligation		
Minimum lease payments due		
Within one year	699,286	240,238
In second to fifth year inclusive	1,556,366	960,952
	2,255,652	1,201,190
Less: future finance charges	(318,267)	(340,131)
Present value of minimum lease payments	1,937,385	861,059
Present value of minimum lease payments due		
Within one year	1,369,419	734,884
In second to fifth year inclusive	567,966	126,175
	1,937,385	861,059
Non-current liabilities	1,369,419	734,884
Current liabilities	567,966	126,175
	1,937,385	861,059

It is company policy to finance certain furniture and fixtures under finance leases. The lease terms are five years and the average effective borrowing rate is 15% (20X1: 16%). Interest rates are linked to prime, at the contract date. All leases have fixed repayments and no arrangements have been entered for the payment of contingent rent.

The company's obligations under finance leases are secured by the lessor's charge over the leased assets. Refer to note 2.

18.5 Financial statements of lessees: operating leases

18.5.1 Recognition and measurement

Operating lease payments are recognised as an expense in the statement of comprehensive income.

18.5.1.1   Escalation clauses

The Standard requires that leases with fixed rate escalations built into the lease contract must be accounted for on a straight-line basis. This requirement excludes leases where:

- Another systematic basis may be used, which is more representative of the benefit pattern to the user, even if the payments are not structured on that basis.
- The payments to the lessor are structured to increase in line with expected general inflation (based on published indexes or statistics) to compensate for the lessor's expected inflationary cost increases.

Example 18-10: Recognition of an operating lease by a lessee

Rome entered into a lease of property, plant and equipment, on 1 January 20X1. The terms of the lease are:

- Duration of lease is three years.
- Lease payment CU100 pa escalating at a fixed rate of 6% pa.
- The general inflation index is forecast to be 6% for the next three years.

Required

Prepare the journal entries for years 20X1 to 20X3 in Rome's accounts. Ignore deferred tax implications.

Suggested solution

The effect of the escalation reflects the expected general inflation. Therefore, the lease expense should not be spread, ie accounted for as the amounts actually paid.

20X1

Dr	Lease expense (SCI)	100	
Cr	Bank (SFP)		100

Recognition of lease payment and expense.

20X2

Dr	Lease expense (SCI)	106	
Cr	Bank (SFP)		106

Recognition of lease payment and expense.

20X3

Dr	Lease expense (SCI)	112	
Cr	Bank (SFP)		112

Recognition of lease payment and expense.

The second exemption is not met if payments vary because of factors other than general inflation (eg foreign exchange rates or interest rates).

In addition, the costs for services such as insurance and maintenance are not included in the straight-lining of a lease expense.

Example 18-11: Straight-lining of an operating lease by a lessee

Venice entered into a lease of land on 1 January 20X1. The terms of the lease are:

- Lease duration is three years.
- Lease payment CU100 pa escalating at a fixed rate of 10% pa.
- The general inflation index is forecast to be 6% for the next three years.

Required

Prepare the journal entries for years 20X1 to 20X3 in Venice's accounts. Ignore deferred tax implications.

Suggested solution

The effect of the escalation does not reflect the expected general inflation. Therefore, the lease expense must be spread over three years.

The effect of the escalation results in the following lease payments:

20X1 – lease payment	100
20X2 – lease payment	110
20X 3 – lease payment	121
Total	**331**

The average annual charge must be 110 (331/3 years).

The journals will be as follows over the three years:

20X1

Dr	Lease expense (SCI)	110	
Cr	Bank (SFP)		100
Cr	Lease smoothing provision (SFP)		10

20X2

Dr	Lease expense (SCI)	110	
Cr	Bank (SFP)		110

20X3

Dr	Lease expense (SCI)	111	
Dr	Lease smoothing provision (SFP))	10	
Cr	Bank (SFP)		121

Note: There would also be deferred tax implications on the smoothing of the lease payments; this has not been illustrated above.

18.5.2   Disclosures

The following disclosures are required for operating leases in the lessee's accounts:

- The total of future minimum lease payments under non-cancellable operating leases for each of the following periods:
  - Not later than one year.
  - Later than one year and not later than five years.
  - Later than five years.
- Lease payments recognised as an expense.

- A general description of the lessee's significant leasing arrangements including, for example, information about contingent rental, renewal or purchase options and escalation clauses, sub-leases, and restrictions imposed by lease arrangements.

18.6 Financial statements of lessors: finance leases

18.6.1 Initial recognition and measurement

For a finance lease, a lessor derecognises the leased asset from its statement of financial position, and recognises a finance lease receivable in its place. The lease receivable is recognised at an amount that is equal to the net investment in the lease. The net investment in a lease is the lessor's gross investment in the lease, discounted at the interest rate implicit in the lease (refer to calculation in *Example 18-9*). The gross investment in the lease is the aggregate of:

- The minimum lease payments receivable by the lessor under a finance lease.
- Any unguaranteed residual value accruing to the lessor.

The direct costs incurred in negotiating and arranging the lease agreement are included in the carrying amount of the finance lease receivable, and amortised as part of the financial asset over the term of the lease. These costs include legal fees, stamp duties, and any other directly attributable costs.

18.6.2 Subsequent measurement

The lessor recognises the finance income on the lease in its statement of comprehensive income as its return on the lease. The recognition of finance income is based on a pattern reflecting a constant periodic rate of return on the lessor's net investment in the finance lease. The lease payments received must be split between the finance component that is recognised as revenue, and applied against the gross investment in the lease to reduce both the principal and the unearned finance income of the lease receivable. If there is an indication that the estimated unguaranteed residual value used in computing the lessor's gross investment in the lease has changed significantly, the income allocation over the lease term is revised, and any reduction in respect of amounts accrued is recognised immediately in profit or loss.

18.6.3 Manufacturer or dealer lessors

Manufacturers or dealers often offer customers the choice of either buying or leasing an asset. For example, a motor car manufacturer could offer a customer the option of paying cash for a car or entering into a finance lease agreement. These are referred to by many names, but in substance are all leases and therefore accounted for under the guidance in this chapter.

Where a manufacturer or dealer enters into a finance lease, two types of income arise:

- Profit or loss equivalent to the profit or loss resulting from an outright sale of the asset being leased, at normal selling prices, reflecting any applicable volume or trade discounts.
- Finance income over the lease term.

The sales profit is calculated as the difference between the sales revenue and the cost of the sale of the asset. This is calculated as follows:

- The sales revenue recognised at the commencement of the lease term by a manufacturer or dealer lessor is the lower of:
  - The asset's fair value.
  - The present value of the minimum lease payments accruing to the lessor, computed at a market rate of interest.
- The amount of the cost of sale recognised is the cost, or carrying amount if different, of the leased asset less the present value of the unguaranteed residual value.

Where low interest rates are offered by a manufacturer or dealer, the above must be based on market interest rates. This is very common – customers are offered low interest rates as an enticement to purchase the asset.

Directly attributable costs incurred by a manufacturer or dealer are expensed when the selling profit is recognised as detailed above.

18.6.4   Disclosures

The following disclosures are required for finance leases in the financial statements of the lessor:

- A reconciliation between the gross investment in the lease at the reporting date and the present value of minimum lease payments receivable at the reporting date. In addition, an entity must disclose the gross investment in the lease and the present value of minimum lease payments receivable at the reporting date, for each of the following periods:
  - Not later than one year.
  - Later than one year and not later than five years.
  - Later than five years.
- Unearned finance income.
- The unguaranteed residual values accruing to the benefit of the lessor.
- The accumulated allowance for uncollectible minimum lease payments receivable.
- Contingent rentals recognised as income in the period. A general description of the lessor's significant leasing arrangements, including, for example, information about contingent rental, renewal or purchase options and escalation clauses, sub-leases, and restrictions imposed by lease arrangements.

18.7   Financial statements of lessors: operating leases

18.7.1   Recognition and measurement

Lessors who enter into an operating lease must continue to recognise the leased asset on their statement of financial position. The asset is accounted for under the relevant chapter relating to that type of asset.

Operating lease receipts are recognised as income in the statement of comprehensive income.

18.7.1.1 Escalation clauses

The Standard requires that leases with fixed rate escalations built into the lease contract be accounted for on a straight-line basis. This requirement excludes leases where:

- Another systematic basis may be used, which is more representative of the benefit pattern to the user even if the payments are not on that basis.
- The payments to the lessor are structured to increase in line with expected general inflation (based on published indexes or statistics) to compensate for the lessor's expected inflationary cost increases.

Example 18-12: Accounting treatment of an operating lease by a lessor

Mexico City leases out an item of property, plant and equipment under an operating lease. The terms of the lease are:

- Lease duration is three years.
- Lease payment CU100 pa escalating at inflation.
- Inflation rates were:
  Year 1   8%
  Year 2   6%

The effect of the escalation is not fixed, and therefore not determinable at the inception of the lease. And so the lease expense should not be spread, ie accounted for as the amounts actually paid.

The journals will be as follows over the three years:

Year 1

| Dr | Bank (SFP) | 100 | |
| Cr | Lease income (SCI) | | 100 |

Year 2

| Dr | Bank (SFP) | 108 | |
| Cr | Revenue (SCI) | | 108 |

Year 3

| Dr | Bank (SFP) | 114 | |
| Cr | Lease income (SCI) | | 114 |

The second exemption is not met if receipts vary because of factors other than general inflation (for example, foreign exchange rates or interest rates).

In addition, the costs for services such as insurance and maintenance are not included in the straight-lining of lease income.

Example 18-13: Accounting treatment of an operating lease by a lessor

Moscow leases property, plant and equipment under an operating lease. The terms of the lease are:

- Lease duration is three years.
- Lease payment CU100 pa escalating at a fixed rate of 10% pa.
- For this lease, the general inflation index is forecast to be 15% for the next three years.

The effect of the escalation does not reflect the expected general inflation. Therefore, the lease expense must be spread over three years.

The effect of the escalation results in the following lease payments:

20X1 – lease payment	100
20X2 – lease payment	110
20X 3 – lease payment	121
Total	**331**

The average annual charge must be 110 (331/3 years).

The journals will be as follows over the three years:

Year 1

Dr	Bank (SFP)	100	
Dr	Lease smoothing receivable (SFP)	10	
Cr	Revenue (SCI)		110

Year 2

Dr	Bank (SFP)	110	
Cr	Revenue (SCI)		110

Year 3

Dr	Bank (SFP)	121	
Cr	Revenue (SCI)		111
Cr	Lease smoothing receivable (SFP)		10

Note: There would also be deferred tax implications on the smoothing; this has not been illustrated above.

A manufacturer or dealer lessor does not recognise any profit on sale when entering into an operating lease because it is not the equivalent of a sale.

18.8   Disclosure

The following discloses are required for operating leases in the lessor's financial statements:

- The future minimum lease payments under non-cancellable operating leases for each of the following periods:
  - Not later than one year.
  - Later than one year and not later than five years.
  - Later than five years.
- Total contingent rentals recognised as income.
- A general description of the lessor's significant leasing arrangements, including, for example, information about contingent rentals, renewal or purchase options and escalation clauses, and restrictions imposed by lease arrangements.

In addition, the normal disclosures for assets under the appropriate chapter of assets must be provided.

18.9 Sale and lease-back transactions

A sale and lease-back transaction occurs when an entity sells an asset to another entity, and then leases it back. These transactions are common where an entity is looking to raise finance. The lease terms and the sale price are usually interdependent because they are negotiated as a package.

The accounting for sale and lease-back transactions depends on whether the lease is a finance or operating lease. The lease should be evaluated in terms of the criteria set out above for determining whether substantially all the risks and rewards incidental to ownership of the leased asset pass to the lessee or remain with the lessor. Once this has been determined, the accounting for such transactions is detailed below.

18.9.1 Sale and lease-back transaction resulting in a finance lease

If a sale and lease-back transaction results in a finance lease, the seller that becomes the lessee does not recognise any profit made on the sale of the building to the lessor. Any profit (being the excess of the proceeds over the carrying value of the asset) is deferred and amortised over the lease term.

Example 18-14: Sale and lease-back transaction (finance lease)

Manufacturing firm, Port Louis, is looking to raise finance to fund expansion. It has a factory building that is fully paid off, with a carrying amount of CU4,000,000 and remaining useful life of 25 years at 1 January 20X1.

To raise funding, it approaches St Petersburg Bank, who agrees to enter into a sale and lease-back agreement. As a result, Port Louis sells the building to St Petersburg Bank for CU10 million on 1 January 20X1, and receives the cash proceeds from the sale. The fair value of the building is determined to be CU10 million on the date of sale.

Port Louis still requires the factory building for its operations. It immediately enters into a lease with St Petersburg Bank over 20 years for CU2 million per year. In this way, it can continue using the building as it did before, and have 20 years to repay St Petersburg Bank. This lease is determined to be a finance lease (refer to *Example 18-3*). The estimated residual value of the factory building is deemed to be CU2 million.

Required
Provide the journal entries to account for the transaction in 20X1.

Example 18-14: Sale and lease-back transaction (finance lease) *(continued)*

Suggested solution

Calculation of implicit rate of the lease

20X1	Initial cash receipt	(10,000,000)
Years 20X2 to 20X19	Lease payments	2,000,000
20X20	Payment at 31 December 20X20 (2,000,000) PLUS unguaranteed residual value of asset (2,000,000) at 31 December 20X20	4,000,000

This gives an IRR of 19.55%.

Discount rate (%) 19.55

	Year	Amount	Discount variable	Discounted amount
Lease payment	20X1	2,000,000	1.196	1 672 977
Lease payments	20X2 to 20X19	36,000,000	Various	8,214,494
Lease payment	20X2	2,000,000	35.55	56,264
Total discounted minimum lease payments				**9,943,735**

Because the present value of the minimum lease payments, discounted at the implicit rate of the lease (CU9,943,735), is lower than the fair value (10,000,000) of the leased building, the finance lease obligation must be accounted for at the lower value of CU9,943,735.

1 January 20X1

Dr	Bank/Cash (SFP)	10,000,000	
Cr	Deferred profit on sale of fixed property (SFP)		6,000,000
Cr	Factory building (SFP)		4,000,000

Sale of factory building.

Dr	Leased factory building (SCI)	9,943,735	
Cr	Finance lease obligation (SFP)		9,943,735

Recognition of finance lease.

31 December 20X1

Dr	Interest on finance lease (SCI)	1,944,000	
Dr	Finance lease obligation – liability (SFP)	56,000	
Cr	Bank/Cash (SFP)		2,000,000

*Recognition of lease payment and interest incurred on finance lease (9,943,735 * 19.55%).*

Dr	Deferred profit on sale of fixed property (SFP)	300,000	
Cr	Gain on sale of fixed property (I/S)		300,000

Amortisation of the profit on sale of the asset.
(6,000,000/20)

Dr	Depreciation (P/L)	397,749	
Cr	Accumulated depreciation(9,943,735 / 25)		397,749

Depreciation of the asset over its useful life.

18.9.2 Sale and lease-back transaction results in an operating lease

If a sale and lease-back transaction results in an operating lease, *Table 18-3* applies:

Table 18-3: Operating sale and lease-back transactions

Sale was at fair value	Recognise any profit or loss immediately.
Sale is below fair value	Recognise any profit or loss immediately unless the loss is compensated for by future lease payments at below market price. If this is the case, the seller must defer and amortise the loss in proportion to the lease payments over the period for which the asset is expected to be used.
Sale is above fair value	The seller that becomes the lessee must defer the excess over fair value and amortise it over the period for which the asset is expected to be used.

Example 18-15: Sale and lease-back transaction (operating lease)

Antananarivo sells its administration building to Havana Bank for CU100 million cash on 1 January 20X1. The carrying amount of the asset at the time of the sale is CU80 million and the fair value CU90 million. Antananarivo immediately enters into a 10-year lease with Havana Bank over the administration building at CU10 million per year. This lease is determined to be an operating lease *(refer to Example 18-3).*

Required
Determine the initial and subsequent accounting treatment, as well as the journal entries relating to the lease by Antananarivo for the year ending 31 December 20X1.

Suggested solution
On inception of the agreement, Antananarivo will defer the CU20 million profit (CU100 million proceeds less CU80 million carrying amount) in the statement of financial position. This will be recognised over the lease term by releasing CU2 million (CU20 million/10-year lease).

Journals

1 January 20X1

Dr	Bank (SFP)	100,000,000	
Cr	Property, plant and equipment (SFP)		80,000,000
Cr	Profit on sale to fair value (P/L)		10,000,000
Cr	Deferred profit on sale of fixed asset (SFP)		10,000,000

Recognise the sale of the asset.

31 December 20X1

Dr	Deferred profit on sale of fixed asset (SFP)	1,000,000	
Cr	Amortisation of deferred profit (P/L))		1,000,000

Recognition of deferred profit on sale of fixed property.
(CU10 million/10)

Dr	Lease expense (SCI)	10,000,000	
Cr	Bank (SFP)		10,000,000

Recognition of lease payment.

18.9.3   Disclosure

The disclosure requirements under a sale and lease-back transaction are as per the disclosure requirements detailed above for lessors and lessees under operating and finance leases. *Note: The only additional disclosure required is the terms of the sale and lease-back transaction.*

18.10   Summary

- **Leases**
  - Leases are split between finance and operating leases. The key difference between the two is that finance leases result in substantially all the risks and rewards incidental to ownership being transferred to the lessee, whilst operating leases do not.
  - Indicators of a finance lease include: ownership transferring to the lessee; bargain purchase option; lease duration for the major part of the economic life of the asset; leased assets are of a specialised nature; the present value of the minimum lease payments amounts to substantially all of the fair value of the asset; the lessee bears the lessor's losses if cancelled; a secondary rental period at below market rates; and the residual value risk being borne by the lessee.
- **Lessees – finance leases**
  - The rights and obligations are recognised as assets and liabilities at fair value or, if lower, the present value of the minimum lease payments. Any direct costs of the lessee are added to the value of the asset recognised. Subsequently, payments are to be split between a finance charge and a reduction of the liability. The asset should be depreciated either over the useful life or the lease term.
- **Lessees – operating leases**
  - Payments are recognised as an expense on a straight-line basis, unless payments are structured to increase in line with expected general inflation, or another systematic basis is better representative of the time pattern of the user's benefit.
- **Lessors – finance leases**
  - The rights are recognised as an asset, ie as a receivable, at an amount equal to the net investment in the lease. The net investment in a lease is the lessor's gross investment in the lease (including any unguaranteed residual value), discounted at the interest rate implicit in the lease.
  - For finance leases other than those involving manufacturer or dealer lessors, initial direct costs are included in the initial measurement of the finance lease receivable and reduce the amount of income recognised over the lease term.
  - If there is an indication that the estimated unguaranteed residual value used in computing the lessor's gross investment in the lease has changed significantly, the income allocation over the lease term is revised, and any reduction in respect of amounts accrued is recognised immediately in profit or loss.

- **Lessors (manufacturer or dealer) – finance leases**
  - A finance lease of an asset by a manufacturer or dealer lessor gives rise to two types of income:
    - Profit or loss equivalent to the profit or loss resulting from an outright sale of the asset being leased, at normal selling prices, reflecting any applicable volume or trade discounts; and
    - Finance income over the lease term.
  - The sales revenue recognised at the commencement of the lease term by a manufacturer or dealer lessor is the fair value of the asset or, if lower, the present value of the minimum lease payments accruing to the lessor, computed at a market rate of interest.
  - The cost of sale recognised at the commencement of the lease term is the cost or carrying amount, if different, of the leased property less the present value of the unguaranteed residual value. The difference between the sales revenue and the cost of sale is the selling profit, which is recognised in accordance with the entity's policy for outright sales.
  - If artificially low rates of interest are quoted, selling profit must be restricted to that which would apply if a market rate of interest were charged. Costs incurred by manufacturer or dealer lessors in connection with negotiating and arranging a lease must be recognised as an expense when the selling profit is recognised.
- **Lessors – operating leases**
  - Lessors retain the assets on their statement of financial position, and receipt of the contractual amounts is recognised as income on the straight-line basis, unless payments are structured to increase in line with expected general inflation, or another systematic basis is better representative of the time pattern of the user's benefit.
- **Sale and lease-back**
  - If a sale and lease-back results in a finance lease, the seller should not recognise any excess as a profit, but recognise the excess over the lease term.
  - If a sale and lease-back results in an operating lease, and the transaction was at fair value, the seller must recognise any profits or losses immediately.

Chapter 19
Share-based payment

Contents

19.1 Scope

This chapter applies to the accounting for all share-based payment transactions including transactions in which an entity:

- Acquires goods or services in return for the issue of equity instruments in itself. Such equity instruments may include shares and share options.
- Acquires goods or services by incurring liabilities to the supplier of those goods or services, the value of which services are based on the price (or value) of the acquiring company's shares or other equity instruments. Such liabilities will then be settled in cash rather than equity instruments as above.
- Receives or acquires goods or services, and the terms of the arrangement entered into provide either the entity or the supplier of those goods or services with a choice of whether the entity settles the transaction in cash (or other assets) or by issuing equity instruments.

It also applies in group situations where a share-based payment transaction may be settled by another group entity (or a shareholder of any group entity) on behalf of the entity that receives the goods or services. This section of the Standard also applies to 1) an entity that receives goods or services when another entity in the same group (or a shareholder of any group entity) has the obligation to settle the share-based payment transaction, or 2) when another entity has an obligation to settle a share-based payment transaction when an entity in the same group receives the goods or services unless the transaction is clearly for a purpose other than the payment for goods or services supplied to the entity receiving them.

19.2 Definitions

A **share-based payment transaction.** 1) The entity receives goods or services (including services from employees) as consideration for equity instruments of the entity, or 2) it acquires goods or services by incurring liabilities to the supplier of those goods or services for amounts that are based on the price of the entity's shares or other equity instruments of the entity.

An **equity-settled share-based payment transaction.** The entity receives goods or services as consideration for equity instruments of the entity (including shares, share options and equity-settled appreciation rights).

A **cash-settled share-based payment transaction.** The entity acquires goods or services by incurring a liability to transfer cash or other assets to the supplier of those goods or services for amounts that are based on the price (or value) of the entity's shares or other equity instruments of the entity.

Cash-settled share-based payment transactions are often in the form of **share appreciation rights**. For example, an entity may grant rights to its employees as part of their remuneration package, whereby the employees will become entitled to a future cash payment (rather than an equity instrument), based on the increase in the entity's share price from a specified level over a specified period of time. Alternatively, the entity may grant its employees a right to receive a future cash payment by granting them a right to shares (including shares to be issued upon the exercise of share options) that are redeemable, either mandatorily (eg upon cessation of employment) or at the employee's option. The rights granted are, in effect, share appreciation rights.

19.3 When to recognise a share-based payment transaction

An entity recognises the goods or services received or acquired in a share-based payment transaction when ownership of the goods passes, or the services have been rendered. A corresponding increase in equity is recognised if the goods or services were received in a transaction that was settled through the issue of shares, or as an increase in liabilities if the goods or services were acquired in a cash-settled share-based payment transaction.

> Goods or services received or acquired are recognised as they are received and result in a corresponding increase in equity or liability.

If the goods or services acquired do not meet the qualification criteria for recognition as an asset, the transaction should be recognised as an expense.

Example 19-1: Construction services settled by issuing shares

A contractor has been appointed to complete alterations to buildings owned by Bangkok. The contract price is fixed at CU2,200,000. After completion of specific milestones, the work is certified by independent quantity surveyors. On receipt of a certificate, 50% of the amount certified is payable in cash, and the balance by issuing shares at their market value to settle the remaining 50% balance. The shares have a nominal value of CU5. On 31 March 20X1, Bangkok received a certificate of CU2,200,000 when the fair value of the shares was CU40. The number of shares to be issued is 27,500 shares ((CU2,200,000 x 50%)/CU40).

Required
Provide the journal entry to account for the expansion of the building of Bangkok.

Suggested solution
Journal
31 March 20X1

Dr	Building under construction (SFP)	2,200,000	
Cr	Bank (SFP)		1,100,000
Cr	Share capital (Equity)		137,500
Cr	Share premium (Equity)		962,500

Recognition of payments in respect of the expansion of the building.
(27,500 x CU5) and (27,500 x CU35)

In the absence of the receipt of specifically identifiable goods or services, other circumstances may indicate that goods or services have been, or will be, received. This typically involves the issuance of equity instruments to employees or, as some jurisdictions require, to people other than employees without those people providing any specifically identifiable goods and services to the entity. If the identifiable consideration received appears to be less than the fair value of the equity instruments granted or the liability incurred, this situation typically indicates that other consideration (ie unidentifiable goods or services) has been or will be received. This is dealt with in more detail under *19.9*.

19.4 Recognition when there are vesting conditions

A grant of equity instruments may be conditional on employees satisfying specified conditions that are related to their service or performance. Such conditions are termed vesting conditions. An example of a vesting condition relating to service is when a grant of shares or share options to employees is conditional on the employees remaining in the entity's employ for a specified period of time. If there are no conditions attached to the employees continued employment, then the equity instruments granted accrue to the employees immediately. In essence, this means that the employees are not required to provide any additional service to the entity before they are unconditionally entitled to those equity instruments. In the absence of facts that contradict this position, the entity is required to recognise the service in full with a corresponding increase in equity. It is presumed that the services rendered by the employee as consideration for the equity instruments had been received by the grant date.

> For instruments that vest immediately, the assumption is that they relate to past service and should be expensed immediately in full, unless information to the contrary exists.

With equity instruments that do not vest until the employee completes a specified period of service, the entity assumes that the services rendered by the employee as consideration for those equity instruments, will only be received in the future. As such, the entity accounts for those services as they are rendered over the length of the vesting period with a corresponding increase in equity. An example of a vesting condition relating to performance is when a grant of shares or share options is conditional on a specified period of service and on 1) the entity achieving a specified growth in profit (which is termed a non-market vesting condition as it is entirely dependent on the company itself and its performance), or 2) a specified increase in the entity's share price (which is termed a market vesting condition as it is dependent on the market's view of the value of the underlying assets).

All vesting conditions related to employee service or to a non-market performance condition are taken into account when estimating the number of equity instruments that are expected to vest. After the initial measurement, the entity is required to revise the initial estimate if new information becomes available that indicates that the number of equity instruments that are expected to vest differs from that estimate or any of the subsequent estimates that may be carried out. On the vesting date, the entity is required to revise the estimate to equal the number of equity instruments that will ultimately vest. Vesting conditions related to employee service or to a non-market performance condition are not considered when estimating the fair value of the shares, share options or other equity instruments at the measurement date.

Market vesting conditions and non-vesting conditions are taken into account when estimating the fair value of the shares, share options, or other equity instruments, at the measurement date, with no subsequent adjustment to the estimated fair value, irrespective of the outcome of the market or non-vesting condition, provided that all other vesting conditions are satisfied. The accounting treatment of vesting conditions is addressed in more detail under *19.5.2*.

Example 19-2: Vesting conditions

The eight directors of San Francisco each received an option at 1 January 20X1 to take up 100 CU1 shares in San Francisco for a purchase consideration of CU30 per share after the completion of a two-year service period. San Francisco obtained the services of a valuation expert who calculated the fair value of the share options provided to the directors to be CU15, on 1 January 20X1.

Required

Provide the journal entry to account for the transaction for the period ended 31 December 20X1 by **San Francisco.**

Suggested solution

The benefits do not vest immediately since the benefits have a two-year vesting period. The transaction should be accounted for as an equity-settled share-based payment in the accounting records (refer to *19.5*).

The transaction is a share-based payment transaction with an employee and should be measured at the fair value of the equity instruments (options) at the grant date (refer to *19.5.2*). This value should not be adjusted over the life of the share-based payment transaction.

Calculation for 20X1

8 directors x 100 options each x CU15 fair value of options at grant date x ½ completed service period = CU6,000

Journal

1 January 20X1

Dr	Employment cost (P/L)	6, 000	
Cr	Equity reserve (Equity)		6,000

Accounting for the 20X1 share-based payments to directors.

19.5   Equity-settled share-based payment transactions

19.5.1   Goods and services

An entity is required to measure the goods or services received (debit) and the corresponding increase in equity (credit) based on the fair value of the goods or services received. In some instances, the fair value of the goods or services received cannot be estimated reliably, and in such a situation, the entity should measure the value of the goods or services and the related increase in equity based on the fair value of the equity instruments that were granted.   Fair value is determined as of the date when the entity obtains the goods or the service is rendered (refer to *Example 19-1*).

> ⚠ Transactions are measured based on the value of the goods or services. If this value is not reliable, value is based on the fair value of the instruments issued.

> 👁 Shares issued in a black economic empowerment (BEE) arrangement should be treated in the same manner as if the fair value of the goods and services received cannot be determined.

19.5.2 Employees

In respect of transactions with employees and other providers of similar services, the entity should determine the fair value of the services based on the fair value of the instruments issued. The presumption in such an instance is that one cannot reliably estimate the fair value of the services received.

The value of the instruments is determined at the grant date of such instruments. Service and non-market performance conditions are considered when estimating the number of shares that are expected to vest. Market conditions and non-vesting conditions are considered when the fair value of the instrument is calculated on the grant date with no subsequent adjustment if there is a different outcome.

19.5.2.1 Service conditions

A service condition is when a grant of shares or share options to an employee is conditional on the employee remaining in the entity's employment for a specified period of time. Service conditions are considered in determining the number of shares or share options at the grant date. They are not taken into consideration in determining the fair value of the instruments. At each measurement date, the estimate of the number of equity instruments should be revised to equal the amount that will actually be issued to the employees or other parties. At the vesting date, the actual number of shares that vest is taken into consideration in the final estimation.

Example 19-3: Vesting service conditions

On 1 January 20X1, Lisbon grants 20 share options to each of its 100 employees. Each grant is subject to the condition that the employees must work for another two years. Lisbon estimates that 80% of the employees will fulfil the condition to stay for two years. During 20X1, 10 employees left, and Lisbon still estimated that 20% of the original employees will leave over the two-year period. During 20X2, another 15 employees left before the maturity date. The fair value of each option is estimated to be CU10 at the grant date.

Required

Provide the journal entries to account for the transaction for the periods ended 31 December 20X1 and 20X2 by Lisbon.

Example 19-3: Vesting service conditions *(continued)*

Suggested solution

Journals

1 January 20X1

Dr	Employment cost (P/L)	8, 000	
Cr	Equity reserve (Equity)		8,000

Accounting for the 20X1 share-based payment employment cost.
(20 options x 100 employees x 80% (estimated) x CU10 x ½ years)

31 December 20X2

Dr	Employment cost (P/L)	7, 000	
Cr	Equity reserve (Equity)		7,000

Accounting for the 20X2 share-based payment employment cost.
((20 options x 75 employees (actual) x CU10) = 15,000 - 8,000 = 7,000)

19.5.2.2 Market and non-market performance conditions

Market and non-market performance (or vesting) conditions may be included in the share-based transaction. An example of a market performance condition is a specified increase in the entity's credit rating. Market conditions are included in the estimation of the fair value on the grant date.

Example 19-4: Market performance (or vesting) conditions

At 1 January 20x1, Boston grants a senior executive 1,000 share options with no service conditions. The share options are exercisable on 31 December 20X1. The share options may only be exercised on 31 December 20X1 if the credit rating of Boston increases from BB to BB+ during 20X1.

Boston applied a binomial option pricing model to estimate the fair value of the options at the grant date to be CU20.

Required

Provide the journal entry to account for the transaction for the period ended 31 December 20X1 by Boston.

Suggested solution

The credit rating condition is a market condition and is considered in the valuation on the grant date.

Since no further vesting conditions are included, the share-based transaction is recognised at the grant date.

Journal

1 January 20X1

Dr	Employment cost (P/L)	20, 000	
Cr	Equity reserve (Equity)		20,000

Accounting for the 20X1 employment cost.
(1,000 shares x CU20)

A non-market performance condition is for example an entity achieving a specified growth in revenue. Non-market conditions are taken into account in determining the quantity of the instruments that will be issued and not in the fair value of the instrument on the grant date.

Example 19-5: Non-market performance conditions

On 1 January 20X1, Calgary grants 40 shares to 200 employees subject to the condition that the employees remain in the employment of the entity for the vesting period. The shares will vest on 31 December 20X1 if the earnings of the entity increase by 10%, and on 31 December 20X2 if the earnings increase by an average of 8% per year over the two years. The shares had a fair value of CU25 at the grant date.

On 31 December 20X1, the earnings only increased by 9%, 30 employees left and Calgary expects that another 20 employees will leave during the 20X2 financial period. Calgary expects that the vesting conditions will be met during the 20X2 financial period.

On 31 December 20X2, the vesting conditions are met since the earnings increased by 10% during 20X2. 15 employees left employment during the 20X2 financial period before the shares vested.

Required

Provide the journal entries to account for the transaction for the periods ended 31 December 20X1 and 20X2 by Calgary. The journal for the issue of the shares is not required.

Suggested solution
Journals
20X1

Dr	Employment cost (P/L)	75, 000	
Cr	Equity reserve (Equity)		75,000

Accounting for the 20X1 share-based payment employment cost.
(40 shares x 150 (200 - 30 - 20) employees (expected) x CU25 x ½ years)

20X2

Dr	Employment cost (P/L)	80, 000	
Cr	Equity reserve (Equity)		80,000

Accounting for the 20X2 share-based payment employment cost.
(40 shares x 155 (200 - 30 - 15) employees (actual) x CU25) = 155,000 - 75,000 = 80,000

19.5.3   Measurement of fair value

If the fair value of the goods or services received cannot be measured reliably, the fair value of the shares, share options or equity-settled share appreciation rights must be determined using the three-tier measurement hierarchy included in *Figure 19-1*.

Figure 19-1: Fair value hierarchy

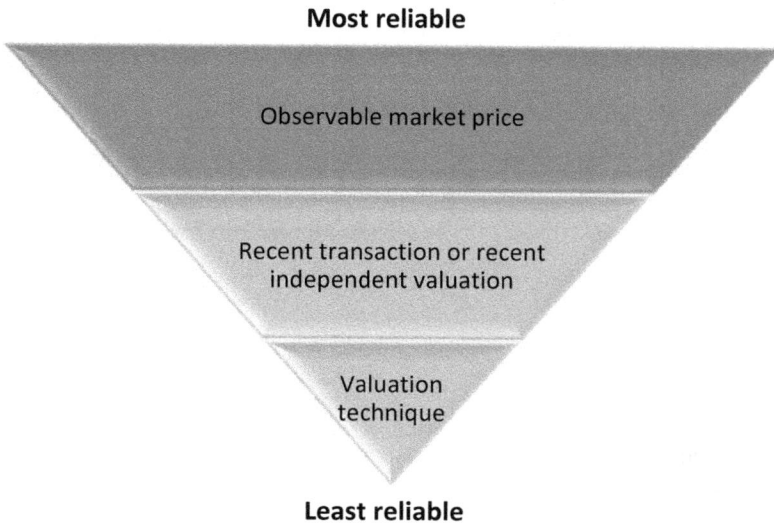

Most reliable

Observable market price

Recent transaction or recent independent valuation

Valuation technique

Least reliable

An observable market price of the equity instruments granted is only used if such a price is available. This is unlikely to be applicable as an SME will not be listed on a stock exchange. In the absence of observable market prices, observable market data may be used, such as:

- A recent transaction in the entity's shares.
- A recent independent fair valuation of the entity or its principal assets.

If the value of shares cannot be measured by an observable market price, or reliable measurement under level two is impractical, the shares are measured indirectly by using a valuation method. A valuation method uses, to the greatest practicable extent possible, market data that can be externally verified to arrive at a position that the equity instruments under consideration would be exchanged at the grant date between knowledgeable willing parties. Similarly, share options and share appreciation rights are valued under level three of the hierarchy by using an option pricing model. This would, in effect, be a directors' valuation, and as such the directors should apply their judgement in determining the amount. The valuation method should, however, comply with generally accepted methodologies for valuing equity instruments.

19.5.4 Modifications and cancellations to the terms and conditions

Changes in the economic conditions or circumstance of the entity may sometimes make an entity change the terms and conditions that are attached to employee share ownership schemes. The entity may modify the terms and conditions in a manner that is beneficial to the employee (for example, by reducing the exercise price of an option, or reducing the vesting period, or by modifying or eliminating a performance condition). Changes of terms and conditions are only considered if they are beneficial to the employers.

Such changes should be taken into account in accounting for the share-based payment transaction as illustrated in *Figure 19-2*.

Figure 19-2: Modifications and cancellations to the terms and conditions

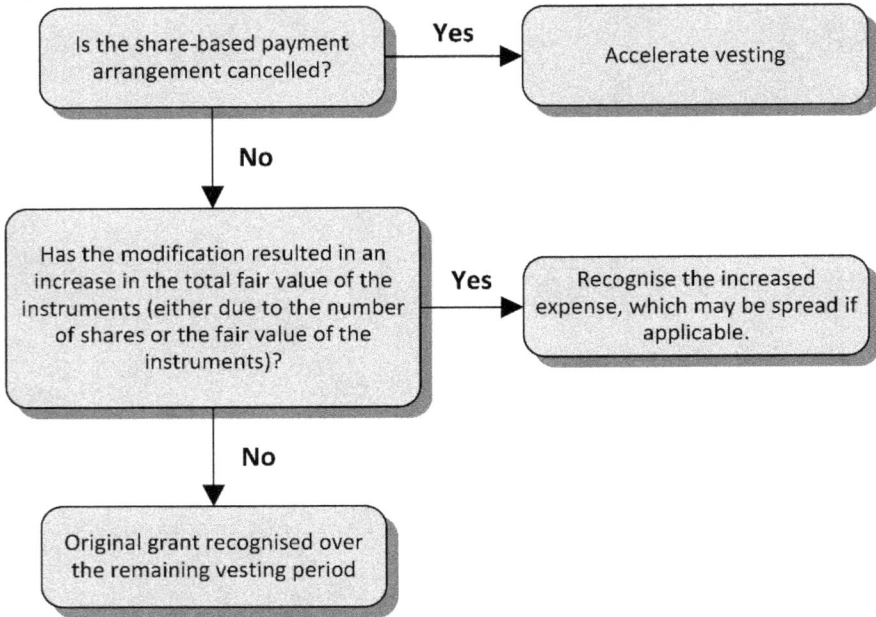

19.5.4.1   If the modification increases the fair value

If the modification to the scheme increases the fair value of the equity instruments granted, or the number of equity instruments granted, the entity should account for the incremental total fair value equity instruments granted as a share-based payment expense. The incremental fair value is the difference between the fair value of the modified equity instrument and the original equity instrument on the date of the modification. The balance of the original equity instrument granted is recognised over the remainder of the original vesting period.

Example 19-6: Modification of a share-based payment transaction

The 10 directors of Brno received options on 1 January 20X1 to take up 100 CU1 shares in Brno for a purchase consideration of CU20 per share after the completion of a two-year service period. Brno obtained the services of a valuation expert who calculated the fair value of the share options provided to the directors to be CU11 on 1 January 20X1.

The amount recognised as a share-based expense during 20X1 amounted to:
(100 options x 10 employees x CU11 x ½ years) = CU5,500

On 1 January 20X2 the share price of Brno shares decreased to CU18. The directors expressed concern that their options carried no value, and requested that the entity decrease the consideration price to be paid to CU15. The entity decreased the purchase consideration from CU20 to CU15; a valuation expert calculated the fair value of the CU20 share option to be CU2 and a CU15 share option to be CU8 as at 1 January 20X1. All the directors exercised their options on 31 December 20X2.

Required
Provide the journal entry to account for the transaction for the period ended 31 December 20X2 including the issue of the shares.

Suggested solution
Calculation
Original issue

Total benefit	11,000
(10 directors x 100 options each x CU11)	
Previously recognised	5,500
Amount still to be recognised	5,500

Modification
Since the incremental fair value is positive (CU8 - CU2), the value of the modification based on the incremental fair value is included in the share-based payment expense. The value is CU6,000 (10 directors x 100 options each x (CU8 - CU2) incremental fair value of options at modification date x 1/1 completed service period).

Current year expense
CU11,000 (original issue) + CU6,000 (modification) - CU5,500 (prior year) = CU11,500

Journals
31 December 20X2

Dr	Employment cost (P/L)	11,500	
Cr	Equity reserve (Equity)		11,500
Accounting for the 20X2 employment cost.			
Dr	Bank (SFP)	15,000	
(10 directors x 100 share x CU15)			
Dr	Equity reserve (Equity)	17,000	
(CU5,500 (20X1) + CU11,500 (20X2))			
Cr	Share capital (Equity)		1,000
(10 directors x 100 Brno shares)			
Cr	Share premium (Equity)		31,000
Accounting for the issue of the share capital to honour the shares issued.			

19.5.4.2 If the modification decreases the fair value

If the modification reduces the total fair value of the share-based payment arrangement, or the terms are changed in such a way that the arrangement is no longer for the benefit of the employee, the entity is still required to account for the services received as consideration for the equity instruments granted as if that modification had not occurred. No changes are therefore made to the accounting for the share-based payment arrangement. Therefore, in *Example 19-6*, only the CU11,000 expense relating to the original issue will be recognised over the vesting period.

19.5.4.3 Cancellations and settlements

Where an entity cancels or settles an equity-settled share-based payment award, it accounts for such cancellation or settlement as an acceleration of vesting. The entity, therefore, recognises immediately in profit or loss the amount that otherwise would have been recognised for services received over the remainder of the vesting period.

Example 19-7: Vesting service conditions

On 1 January 20X1, Baghdad grants 30 share options to each of its 200 employees. Each grant is subject to the condition that the employees must work for Baghdad for another three years. The fair value of each option is estimated to be CU10 at the grant date. Baghdad estimates that 80% of the employees will fulfil the condition to stay for three years. Based on the estimation, the following was recognised during the 20X1 financial period:

Dr	Employment cost (P/L)	16,000
Cr	Equity reserve (Equity)	16,000

Accounting for the 20X1 employment cost.
(30 options x 200 employees x 80% (estimated) x CU10 x 1/3 years)

During 20X2 the share-based transaction was cancelled because the options are out of the money.

Required
Provide the journal entry to account for the transaction during the period ended 31 December 20X2 by Baghdad.

Suggested solution
The vesting period is accelerated and any outstanding balance is recognised.

Dr	Employment cost (P/L)	32,000
Cr	Equity reserve (Equity)	32,000

Accounting for the 20X2 employment cost.
(30 options x 200 employees x 80% x CU10) = 48,000 - 16,000 = 32,000

19.5.4.4 Applicability to share-based payment transactions with parties other than employees

The requirements above are provided in the context of share-based payment transactions with employees. The requirements also apply to share-based payment transactions with parties other than employees if these transactions are measured by reference to the fair value of the equity instruments granted, but reference to the grant date refers to the date that the entity obtains the goods or the counterparty renders service.

19.6   Cash-settled share-based payment transactions

For cash-settled share-based payment transactions, an entity is required to measure the goods or services acquired and the liability incurred at the fair value of the liability. Thereafter, the liability is remeasured to its fair value at each reporting date until such time that it is settled. Any movements in the fair value of the liability are recognised in profit or loss for the period.

> The Standard does not prescribe the method for measuring the liability. It can be assumed that the fair value of the liability is the present value of the amount that is likely to be payable, taking into account all the conditions attached to the transaction.

Example 19-8: Cash-settled share-based payment

At 1 January 20X1, Casablanca grants a cash-settled share-based payment transaction to 100 employees. In terms of the transaction, each employee is entitled to receive the increase of the independent value of the 10 shares of Casablanca above CU20, in cash, after a vesting period of two years service.

On 1 January 20X1, it was expected that 90% of the employees will still be in service on the vesting date. The actual number of employees in service on 31 December 20X2 was 88.

The independent expert valued the right attached to one share as follows:

31 December 20X1   CU6

31 December 20X2   CU9

The full liability was settled on 31 December 20X2.

Required

Provide the journal entries to account for the transaction for the periods ended 31 December 20X1 and 20X2 by Casablanca.

Suggested solution

Journals

31 December 20X1

Dr	Employment cost (P/L)	2,700	
Cr	Share-based payment liability (SFP)		2,700

Accounting for the 20X1 share-based payment employment cost.
(10 shares x 100 employees x 90% x CU6 x ½ years)

31 December 20X2

Dr	Employment cost (P/L)	5,220	
Cr	Share-based payment liability (SFP)		5,220

Accounting for the 20X2 employment cost.
(10 shares x 88 employees (actual) x CU9) = 7,920 - 2,700 = 5,220

19.7 Share-based payment transactions with cash alternatives

The share-based payment agreements entered into may give the parties to the agreement a choice of settling the transaction in cash or through the transfer of equity instruments. Where such a choice exists, the transaction is accounted for as a cash-settled share-based payment transaction unless either of the following criteria is met:

- There has been a past practice of settling obligations by issuing equity instruments (which can be demonstrated).
- The option has no commercial substance because the cash settlement amount bears no relationship to, and is likely to be lower in value than, the fair value of the equity instrument. As such, the likelihood of the settlement taking place in cash is, at best, very remote.

If either of these two criteria is met, then the entity can account for the transaction as an equity-settled share-based payment transaction.

Example 19-9: Settlement alternatives

On 1 January 20X1, Brighton grants 1,000 shares to a senior executive, subject to service condition of two years. Each share has a fair value of CU25 at the grant date. The executive can choose to receive the 1,000 shares, or cash equal to the value of 1,000 shares, on the vesting date. The fair value of the shares are:

31 December 20X1	CU27
31 December 20X2	CU31

Required
Provide the journal entries to account for the transaction for the periods ended 31 December 20X1 and 20X2 by Brighton.

Suggested solution
The transaction is recorded as a cash-settled share-based payment because the executive has a choice of settlement.

1 January 20X1

Dr	Employment cost (P/L)	13,500	
Cr	Share-based payment liability (SFP)		13,500

Accounting for the 20X1 employment cost.
(1,000 shares x CU27 x ½ years)

31 December 20X2

Dr	Employment cost (P/L)	17,500	
Cr	Share-based payment liability (SFP)		17,500

Accounting for the 20X2 employment cost.
((1,000 shares x CU31) = 31,000 - 13,500 = 17,500)

19.8   Group share-based payment plans

> ♪ Expenses in a group situation are allocated to each company in the group on a reasonable basis.

If a share-based payment award is granted by a parent entity to the employees of one or more entities in the group, and the parent presents consolidated financial statements using either the IFRS for SMEs or full IFRS, such subsidiaries are permitted as an alternative to the foregoing, to measure share-based payment expense based on a reasonable allocation of the expense recognised for the group. In practice, such allocation may be based on the proportion of share-based payment awards granted to individual employees employed at the subsidiary to the total of the share-based payment awards granted across the entire group. The calculation will generally be carried out at a central position, and the numbers disseminated to the subsidiaries to facilitate consistency of application, and elimination of overlaps on consolidation.

Other methods may also be used provided that the allocation of the expense is done on a reasonable and rational basis.

19.9   Unidentifiable goods or services

Some countries have programmes by which equity investors (such as employees) are able to acquire equity without providing goods or services that can be specifically identified (or by providing goods or services that are clearly less than the fair value of the equity instruments granted). This indicates that other consideration has been or will be received (such as past or future services from the employee). As such, the entity is required to measure the unidentifiable goods or services received (or to be received) as the difference between the fair value of the share-based payment, and the fair value of any identifiable goods or services received (or to be received), measured at the grant date. The related amounts are either expensed immediately in the case of past receipt of goods or services, or are recognised on an ongoing basis into the future for goods or services still to be received or rendered. Where a transaction is cash-settled, the liability is remeasured at the end of each reporting period until it is settled.

19.10   Disclosure

The following information about the nature and extent of share-based payment arrangements that existed during the period is required to be disclosed in the financial statements in terms of this Section:

- A description of each type of share-based payment arrangement that existed at any time during the period, including the general terms and conditions of each arrangement, such as vesting requirements, the maximum term of options granted, and the method of settlement (eg whether in cash or equity). An entity with substantially similar types of share-based payment arrangements may aggregate this information for its arrangements.

- The number and weighted average exercise prices of share options for each of the following groups of options:
  - Outstanding at the beginning of the period.
  - Granted during the period.
  - Forfeited during the period.
  - Exercised during the period.
  - Expired during the period.
  - Outstanding at the end of the period.
  - Exercisable at the end of the period.
- For equity-settled share-based payment arrangements, an entity is required to disclose information about how it measured the fair value of goods or services received or the value of the equity instruments granted. If a valuation methodology was used, the entity is required to disclose the method used and its reason for choosing that particular method.
- For cash-settled share-based payment arrangements, an entity is required to disclose information about how the liability was measured.
- For share-based payment arrangements that were modified during the period, an entity is required to disclose an explanation of those modifications.
- If the entity is part of a group share-based payment plan, and it measures its share-based payment expense on the basis of a reasonable allocation of the expense recognised for the group, it is required to disclose that fact and the basis for the allocation.
- The entity is also required to disclose the effect of the share-based payment transactions on its profit or loss for the period, and on its financial position. The following information is to be disclosed:
  - The total expense recognised in profit or loss for the period.
  - The total carrying amount at the end of the period of the liabilities arising from share-based payment transactions.

19.11   Summary

This chapter covers all share-based payment transactions, being either cash or equity settled.

- **Equity settled**
  - These transactions must be recorded at the fair value of the goods and services received, if this can be estimated reliably.
  - For transactions with employees or where the fair value of goods and services received cannot be measured reliably, these should be measured with reference to the fair value of the equity instruments granted.
- **Cash settled**
  - A liability is to be measured at fair value on grant date and subsequently at each reporting date as well as settlement date, with each adjustment being recognised in profit or loss for the period.

- **Cash alternatives**
  - Account for all such transactions as cash settled unless the entity has a past practice of settling by issuing equity instruments, or the option has no commercial substance because the cash settlement amount bears no relationship to, and is likely to be lower in value than, the fair value of the equity instrument.
- Where shares only vest after a specific period of service has been completed, the expense must be recognised as the service is rendered.
- In certain instances, share-based payment plans provide for owners (such as employees) to acquire equity without providing goods or services that can be specifically identified (or by providing goods or services that are clearly less than the fair value of the equity instruments granted). These are share-based payment transactions that are within the scope of this chapter.

Chapter 20
Employee benefits

Contents

20.1 Scope

The Standard provides guidance on how to account for the consideration given by an entity to its employees in return for their service. All benefits provided to employees are covered under this chapter with the exception of share-based payment transactions, which are dealt with in terms of *Chapter 19* on Share-Based Payment.

20.2 Definitions

Employee benefits are made up of four types of remuneration, which are defined in the Standard as illustrated in *Figure 20-1*:

Figure 20-1: Classification of employee benefits

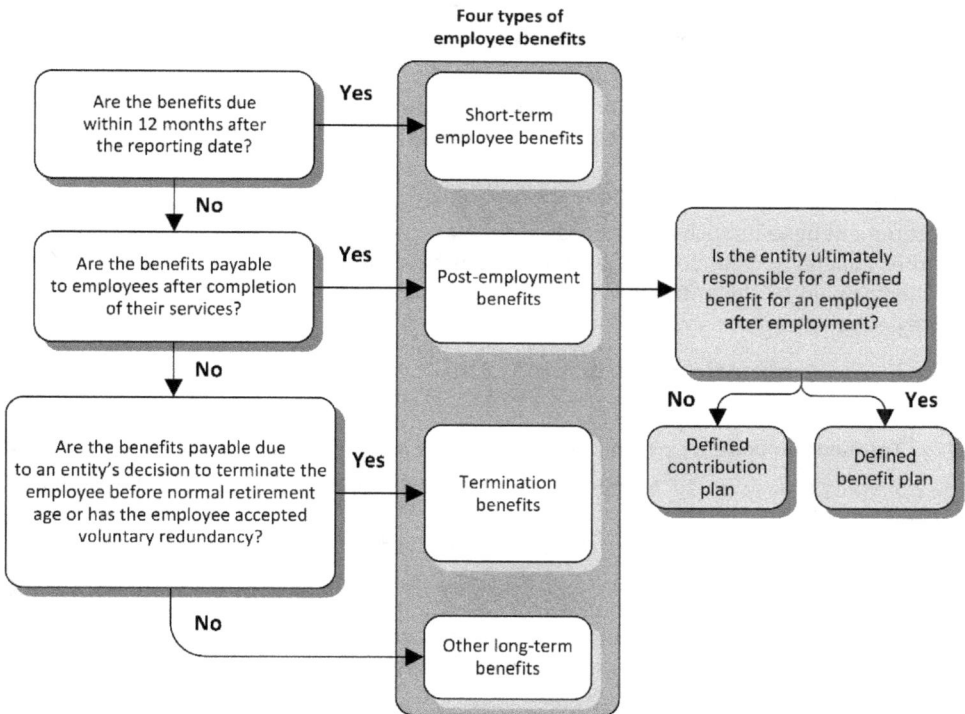

20.2.1 Short-term employee benefits

Short-term employee benefits are employee benefits (other than termination benefits) that are wholly due within 12 months after the reporting date in which the employees render the related service.

Short-term benefits generally consist of such items as:

- Salaries and wages.
- Canteen subsidies.
- Leave pay.
- Medical aid contributions.
- Social security contributions.
- Pension contributions.
- Other fringe benefits (such as access to the use of free or subsidised entity assets, eg vehicles, accommodation, goods and services).

Short-term benefits, as defined, do not include any costs relating to the termination of the employees' contracts of employment with the entity.

20.2.2   Post-employment benefits

Post-employment benefits are employee benefits (other than termination benefits) that are payable after the completion of employment.

Post-employment benefits may include the following:

- Retirement benefits such as pensions.
- Other benefits such as continued contributions to life insurance policies and medical aid schemes paid by the entity that former employees may be entitled to in terms of their previous employment arrangements.

20.2.3   Termination benefits

Termination benefits are employee benefits payable as a result of either:

- An entity's decision to terminate an employee's employment before the normal retirement date; or
- An employee's decision to accept voluntary redundancy in exchange for those benefits.

There are certain criteria that should be met before termination benefit obligations can be recognised. These criteria are covered later in this chapter.

20.2.4   Other long-term employee benefits

Other long-term employee benefits are employee benefits (other than post-employment benefits and termination benefits) that are not wholly due within 12 months after the end of the period in which the employees render the related service.

Other long-term employee benefits include the following:

- Long-term compensated absences such as long-service or sabbatical leave.
- Benefits payable in respect of long-service achieved.
- Long-term disability benefits.
- Profit-sharing and bonuses payable 12 months or more after the end of the period in which the employees render the related service.
- Deferred compensation paid 12 months or more after the end of the period in which it is earned.

20.3   General recognition principle

Employee benefits are recognised when the employee becomes entitled to the benefits as a result of services rendered, or termination. On the recognition date, a liability is recognised for the entitlement (this obligation may be paid immediately reducing assets, eg bank) and the contra-entry is an expense, except where the amount is permitted to be capitalised in terms of the Standard.

The liability recognised is reduced with amounts that have been paid directly to the employee, paid on behalf of the employee or by the subsequent re-measurement of the obligation.

When the amount paid exceeds the obligation that the employer has to the employee, the excess is recognised as an asset to the extent that the amount will result in a reduction of future payments or is refundable in cash.

Example 20-1: Amount of employee benefits paid in advance
Tunisia has incurred employment costs amounting to CU4,000,000 for the year ended 31 December 20X1. At the beginning of the same year, a housing scheme for the benefit of the company's employees was established. The terms of the housing scheme state that Tunisia is obliged to pay 10% of the employee costs as a contribution to the housing scheme on behalf of the employees. Tunisia had paid in an amount of CU500,000 at 31 December 20X1.
Required
Describe the accounting treatment in Tunisia's accounting records for the year ended 31 December 20X1.
Suggested solution
The CU400,000 should be expensed in the 31 December 20X1 statement of comprehensive income. In addition to this amount, Tunisia paid CU100,000 more than its obligation in terms of its employment contracts with staff. The excess amount of CU100,000 should therefore be recognised as an asset to the extent that the excess amount will offset future years' contributions to the employees' housing scheme.

20.4 Short-term employee benefits

20.4.1 Recognition and measurement

Short-term employee benefits are recognised when the related service is rendered. The recognition of short-term employee benefits may be based on employment contracts. However, employment may also be non-contractual, often referred to as *casual labour*.

Short-term employee benefits are measured at the **undiscounted amount** expected to be paid in exchange for the service rendered.

| ♩ Short-term employee benefits are not discounted. |

20.4.2 Exceptions

There are three exceptions to the basic measurement and recognition regarding short-term employee benefits, which are detailed below.

20.4.2.1 Accumulated short-term compensated absences

The treatment of short-term compensated absences depends on whether the absence accumulates. Short-term compensated absences accumulate when any unused portion of the benefit accruing can be carried forward and used in future periods. Accumulating compensated absences are recognised when employees render service that increases their claim to future compensated absences. The expected cost of accumulating compensated absences is measured at the undiscounted additional amount that is expected to be paid by the entity to discharge its obligation to the employees. *Additional* in this instance refers to amounts that are payable in addition to the normal salary of the employees concerned. Accumulated compensated absences are presented as a current liability.

20.4.2.2 Non-accumulated short-term compensated absences

The cost of non-accumulating compensated absences is recognised when the absences occur, and are measured at the undiscounted amount of salaries and wages paid or payable for the period of absence.

Example 20-2: Non-accumulated short-term compensated absences

Madrid's employment contracts with employees provide that employees are entitled to one day of sick leave for every month worked. Sick leave accumulated over the financial period resets to zero on the last day of the financial period. Unutilised sick leave cannot be cashed or used for any other purpose. At 31 December 20X1, 15 of the 20 employees of the entity had not taken any sick leave during the year.

Required

Describe the accounting treatment in Madrid's accounting records for the period ended 31 December 20X1.

Suggested solution

As the sick leave entitlement falls away at the end of the reporting period, and it does not result in any additional obligation for Madrid, Madrid should reverse the unutilised provision for sick leave accumulated during the reporting period on 31 December 20X1, ie for the 15 employees.

20.4.2.3   Profit-sharing and bonus payments

The expected cost of profit-sharing and bonus payments is recognised when the entity has a present legal or constructive obligation, at the reporting date, to make such payments as a result of past events, and a reliable estimate of the obligation can be made. Similar to a provision, a constructive obligation arises when the entity has no realistic alternative but to make the payments.

Example 20-3: Bonus payments

Aswan entered into performance contracts with its staff in terms of which the staff are entitled to bonuses amounting to 15% of their annual salaries upon the achievement of certain predetermined operational performance targets during the reporting period. The bonuses are payable 11 months after the reporting period to staff still in the employment of the entity at that date. Entities that operate in the same environment as Aswan generally find that they lose 20% of their staff 11 months after reporting periods. The performance targets agreed have been met for the reporting period.

Required
Discuss the measurement of the bonus at the reporting date.

Suggested solution
Bonuses should be measured at the end of the reporting period based on the expected cost that Aswan expects to pay to its employees in 11 months time, thus only based on 80% of the employees. No discounting of the amount payable is required.

20.4.3   Disclosure and classification

No specific disclosure requirements are necessary for short-term employee benefits. But, in terms of financial statement presentation (refer to *Chapter 3*), provisions for employee benefits must be shown separately on the face of the statement of financial position, with other provisions, if applicable.

20.5   Post-employment benefit classification

Post-employment benefits are employee benefits that an entity is obliged to pay to its employees, or on their behalf, after the termination or completion of employment. Post-employment benefits are normally provided through special vehicles established for this purpose, although the establishment of separate entities is not a pre-requisite. Post-employment benefit arrangements may include the setting up of provident, pension, medical and other insurance plans that facilitate the settlement of obligations of the entity to its employees after they have left its employment.

20.5.1   Defined contribution plans

In a defined contribution plan, the entity assumes no further risks after settlement of contributions.

Defined contribution plans are benefit plans under which an entity pays a pre-determined sum of money (usually based on a percentage of the employees' salaries) into a separate entity (a fund); it is up to the fund to invest the funds. As such, the entity will have no further exposure to any risks associated with the fund. It also does not have any further legal or constructive obligation to make good any shortfalls that may exist should the fund not hold sufficient assets to settle claims from employees.

The amount of the post-employment benefits received by the employee is thus determined by the amount of the contributions made, and the related returns or net income earned from the accumulated contributions made by the entity.

20.5.2   Defined benefit plans

> In a defined benefit plan, the entity assumes additional risks.

Defined benefit plans are defined simply as "post-employment benefit plans other than defined contribution plans". The employer is required to underwrite the fund should the fund not hold sufficient assets to pay the promised employee benefits. The entity is, therefore, legally obliged to ensure that the benefits due to the current and former employees are sufficiently provided for, and in so doing, the entity assumes, in substance, both the actuarial and investment risks of the fund.

Actuarial risk is the risk that the benefits ascribed to the participants in the fund will cost more or less than is expected. Investment risk is the risk that the return earned on assets purchased by the fund will not be sufficient to cover the cost of the anticipated benefits to participants.

20.6   Multi-employer plans and state plans

Multi-employer plans are benefit plans where a group of employers come together to provide benefits to all their employees. The plan is then administered by a nominated party with each individual employer making contributions on behalf of their staff. Trustees may be appointed to oversee the day-to-day functioning of the benefit vehicle. The obligation of each employer to the benefit fund (ie defined contribution plan or defined benefit plan) will then be determined based on its principal terms and conditions, and the principles of accounting for the particular type of plan as set out in this chapter. The conditions may include constructive obligations that go beyond the formal terms of the plan.

> A fund may be treated as a defined contribution plan if insufficient information is available.

Where a fund is determined to be defined benefit in nature, but insufficient information is available to apply defined benefit accounting for the plan as required, the plan is accounted for as a defined contribution plan. The entity must disclose the fact that the plan is a defined benefit plan, and the reasons why it has applied defined contribution plan accounting. Any available information about the plan's surplus or deficit position and its related implications must also be disclosed.

20.7   Insured benefits

Post-employment benefits may also be funded by taking out insurance contracts to cover the obligation.

> 👁 This may be a function of the date when the arrangement was put in place. In practice, insurers will not insure entities and individuals retrospectively unless the premiums payable are loaded to reflect the "risk" attached to the past activities. Such premiums will tend to be quite exorbitant, and as such, entities may look to self-insure. In such instances, the entities will therefore carry the risk attached to all services that were rendered by its employees, possibly up to the point at which the insurance contracts take effect.

Insurance plans are normally treated as defined contribution plans since the entity normally assumes no further risk past the payment of the premiums due. However, there are instances when such plans are treated as defined benefit plans. These are as follows:

- When the entity has an obligation to pay the employee benefits directly as they fall due. The entity thus assumes the full liability for all future payments, irrespective of whether such payments are fully refundable through the insurance contract.
- When the entity has an obligation to pay further amounts to the beneficiaries of the plan in the event that the insurer does not pay all future benefits relating to services rendered in the current and prior period.

Despite having put in place an insurance contract to cover any future obligations, a constructive obligation to settle the employee benefits may arise in the following circumstances:

- An arrangement exists between the entity and the insurer through which future premiums are determined.
- There is a relationship between the entity and the insurer. The relationship referred to here is a relationship as defined in the chapter on related parties (refer to *Chapter 28*).

Example 20-4: Post-employment benefit plan's relationships with related parties

Djibouti has a related party relationship with Gaborone Insurance Company (Gaborone). It entered into an arrangement requiring Gaborone to establish a post-employment benefit plan, using insurance contracts, for all the employees of the company.

The post-employment benefit plan should be accounted for as a defined benefit plan in the financial statements of Djibouti due to the related party relationship and based on all the facts detailed above. If Gaborone had been an unrelated entity, the risk relating to the pension plan may not have resulted in a constructive obligation for Djibouti, and as such, would be accounted for as a defined contribution plan.

20.8 Defined contribution plans

20.8.1 Recognition and measurement

A liability and related expense are recognised for defined contribution plans in terms of the general recognition principle. The expense may also be capitalised in the cost of another asset, if permitted. The liability is reduced by amounts already paid. However, an asset is recognised for the full amount of the excess when the contribution payments exceed the contributions due for services rendered.

Example 20-5: Defined contribution plans

50% of the employees of Dar Es Salaam currently subscribe to a defined contribution plan to which Dar Es Salaam makes contributions on behalf of the employees. During 20X1, Dar Es Salaam was required to make contributions to the amount of CU400,000 to the fund. This amount was paid in cash during 20X1.

Dar Es Salaam is only required to make the payments to the fund and has no further responsibility to either the employees or the fund regarding the future benefits payable to the employees.

Required

Provide the journal entries required to account for the termination benefits in the accounting records of Dar Es Salaam.

Suggested solution

Dar Es Salaam only has an obligation to make the contributions to the fund when they become payable. Dar Es Salaam is therefore only required to account for all the payments that were paid or became due during the 20X1 reporting period.

Journals required for 20X1:

Dr	Employment cost (P/L)	400,000	
Cr	Bank (SFP)		400,000

Accounting for the contributions paid during the 20X1 financial period.

20.8.2 Disclosure

The expense recognised in profit or loss for defined contribution plans must be disclosed.

20.9 Defined benefit plans

👁 A defined benefit plan is highly unlikely to be implemented by an SME. If an SME provides for employees' post-employment benefits it is much more likely to be a defined contribution plan (refer to *20.8*).

The following eight steps are recommended to determine the defined benefit obligation and plan assets, at the reporting date, as well as any related gains and/or losses during the period due to valuations, and other factors (refer to *21.9.1* to *21.9.7*).

- Calculate the present value of the defined benefit obligation by following these steps:
    - Apply the projected credit unit method if the entity can obtain such a valuation without undue cost or effort, otherwise any other method deemed appropriate to determine the expected future payments.
    - Consider the impact of any plan introductions, changes, curtailments and settlements.
    - Discount the future payments.
- Calculate the fair value of the plan assets at the reporting date.
- Calculate the defined benefit liability, which is defined benefit obligation (*Step 1*) less the plan assets (*Step 2*).
- If the amount is negative, an asset is created. Then apply limitation to the defined benefit asset, if any (refer to *20.9.6*).
- Determine the cost or income of the defined benefit plan, ie current period gain or loss.
- Apply the accounting policy selection for actuarial gains and losses.
- Consider the recognition of any reimbursement rights that may exist.
- Present and disclose the resulting defined benefit plan asset or obligation.

20.9.1   Recognition

In applying the general recognition principle to defined benefit plans, a liability and an expense are also recognised for defined benefit plans. However, the liability is recognised for the entity's obligations under the defined benefit plan after deducting the value of the related plan assets.

20.9.2   Measurement of the defined benefit liability

The defined benefit liability is defined as the present value of the defined benefit obligation at the reporting date, minus the fair value at the reporting date, of any plan assets out of which the obligations are to be settled directly. Therefore, the defined benefit liability is measured at the reporting date as the net total of the present value of the defined benefit obligation, less the fair value of the related plan assets (refer to *Figure 20-2*).

Figure 20-2: Calculation of the defined-benefit obligation

20.9.2.1 The present value of the defined benefit obligation

The present value of the defined benefit obligation is the present value of the future payments required to settle the post-employment benefits that have resulted from employee service in the current and prior periods, before taking into account any plan assets that may be available to the entity.

Therefore the obligation reflects the estimate of the amount of benefits that employees have earned up to the reporting date.

The benefits earned also take into account those amounts that have not yet vested, and the effects of benefit formulas that give employees greater benefits for later years of service. Non-vested benefits result when the service is rendered but the benefits are conditional on future employment. The same principle is applicable to post-employment medical benefits. Although the benefits are only payable after retirement when events requiring the settlement of the participants' medical costs occur, the obligation is recognised as and when the related service is rendered. The probability that the event may not occur is also included in the measurement.

The determination of the defined benefit obligation starts with the plan's benefit formula and is based on estimates called actuarial assumptions. The actuarial assumptions include demographic and financial variables. Demographic variables are such items as turnover and life expectancy of employees. Financial variables consist of such items as changes in future salaries and interest rates. The Standard specifically states that the actuarial assumptions should be unbiased, mutually compatible, and selected to result in the best estimate of the plan's future cash flows.

> ♪ The calculation starts with the plan's benefit formula adjusted for actuarial assumptions.

20.9.2.2 Discounting

The defined benefit obligation is measured at its discounted present value. The discount rate used is based on the market yields achieved on high quality corporate bonds. Essentially, when one looks at high quality corporate bonds, one is dealing with debt instruments that are considered to be of high quality but are not entirely risk-free (unlike, for instance, government bonds which will probably be seen to be risk-free). If such market yields are not available, the market yields of government bonds may be used. In addition, the currency and term of the bond considered must be consistent with the currency and estimated period of the future payments of the plan.

> Discounting is based on the yield applicable to high quality corporate bonds.

20.9.2.3   Actuarial valuation method

The benchmark treatment is used to measure the defined benefit obligation and the related expense is the projected unit credit method, provided it can be used without the entity incurring undue cost or effort in the determination and application of the necessary data. Under the projected unit credit method, each period of service gives rise to an additional unit of benefit entitlement that is accumulated to build up to the eventual obligation. In some instances, the payment of future benefits is based on future salaries, and as such, estimates of such future salary increases are incorporated in the calculation. Other actuarial assumptions (such as mortality rates, rate of turnover of employees, discount rates, and expected rates of return on plan assets that are deemed to be relevant to the determination of the amounts in question) are also used.

> The projected unit credit method is used as the valuation method provided it can be done without undue cost or effort. If not, three simplifications may be used.

When the projected unit credit method cannot be used without undue cost or effort, the entity is allowed to make some modifications to the method. The modifications will then ignore the following items:

- **Estimated future salary increases.** The assumption that is made here is that there will not be a change in the salaries currently being paid until all current employees are expected to begin receiving post-employment benefits.
- **Future service of current and new employees.** The assumption is that there will be no additional contributions made into the fund by current employees, and that the plan is not available to any future employees of the entity.
- **Any in-service-mortality of current employees before retirement.** The assumption is that the number of beneficiaries of the plan will continue unchanged between the reporting date and the date that the employees of the entity will start receiving benefits. After-service mortality must be considered, ie the life expectancy of retired employees.

The application of these simplifications in determining the amount of the defined benefit obligation does not preclude the consideration of both vested and unvested benefits. Such benefits must still be considered in arriving at the quantum of the obligation of the entity at the reporting date.

The use of independent actuaries to perform a comprehensive actuarial valuation to determine the defined benefit obligation is not required by the Standard, nor is there a requirement to have a comprehensive actuarial valuation carried out annually. The entity is permitted to have such valuations periodically. In years where such valuations are not carried out, the entity would be entitled to calculate the defined benefit obligation by taking into account changes in employee demographics (such as number of employees and salary levels), assuming that there have not been any significant changes in the principal actuarial assumptions made at the last valuation.

20.9.3   Plan introductions, changes, curtailments and settlements

In some instances, the rights of the beneficiaries or the obligations of the participating entity in a plan may change. When such a change happens, it has an impact on the defined benefit liability of the entity; this impact is recognised in profit or loss. Plan introductions result in a situation where the beneficiaries are provided with additional or enhanced benefits, effectively increasing the entity's expense. Taking the same principle to curtailments and settlements, the defined benefit obligation of the entity is decreased or eliminated for curtailments of settlements and the resulting gain or loss recognised in profit or loss. A curtailment occurs when benefits to groups of employees are reduced while a settlement is where the obligation is discharged in total. All gains and losses are recognised in profit or loss in the current period.

20.9.3.1   Plan assets

Plan assets include the assets held by a long-term employee benefit fund. Normally, the plan assets of a fund will only include the assets held by the fund directly. However, in some instances, the fund takes out insurance policies to underwrite its risks, and as such, these insurance policies must be taken into account in the determination of assets held, provided that the qualify as assets. In the case of insured benefits discussed in *20.7*, the plan assets will include the fair value of the insurance policies held.

Plan assets include the assets of the fund plus qualifying insurance policies.

Example 20-6: Defined-benefit plans

50% of the employees of Libreville currently subscribe to a defined benefit plan. It is Libreville's responsibility to ensure the employees receive a minimum amount of benefits after retirement.

The valuation specialist of the defined benefit plan provided the following information for the financial period ended 31 December 20X1:

Defined benefit obligation – 31 December 20X0	23,250
Current service cost	1,700
Interest paid	1,400
Actuarial gains for the year	(600)
Payments made to employees	(1,700)
Defined benefit obligation – 31 December 20X1	24,050
Fair value of plan assets – 31 December 20X0	22,900
Expected return on assets	1,700
Actuarial (loss)/gain	(200)
Contributions received from entity	1,200
Payments made to employees (as per obligation)	(1,700)
Fair value of plan assets – 31 December 20X1	23,900

Required

Provide the journal entries required to account for the defined benefit plan in the accounting records of Libreville for the period ended 31 December 20X1.

Suggested solution

Dr	Employee benefits (P/L)	1,700	
Cr	Defined benefit obligation (SFP)		1,700

Recognise current service cost for 20X1.

Dr	Interest expense (financing cost) (P/L)	1,400	
Cr	Defined benefit obligation (SFP)		1,400

Recognise interest accrued on outstanding employee benefits for 20X1.

Dr	Defined benefit obligation (SFP)	600	
Cr	Employee benefits (P/L)		600

Actuarial gains/losses on the defined benefit liability are recognised immediately in profit or loss.

Dr	Plan assets (SFP)	1,700	
Cr	Employee benefits (P/L)		1,700

Recognise the expected return on plan assets for 20X1.

Dr	Employee benefits (P/L)	200	
Cr	Plan assets (SFP)		200

Actuarial gains/losses are recognised immediately in profit or loss in 20X1.

Dr	Plan assets (SFP)	1,200	
Cr	Bank (SFP)		1,200

Recognise the contributions made by Libreville in 20X1.

Note: The difference between the defined benefit obligation and the plan assets will create either a net defined benefit liability or a net defined benefit asset.

20.9.3.2 Defined benefit asset

The plan has a surplus when the fair value of the plan assets exceeds the present value of the defined benefit obligation (refer to *Figure 20-3*). The plan surplus is only recognised as a defined benefit plan asset to the extent that the amount is recoverable. Recoverability in this instance refers to the reduction of future contributions or through direct refunds of the amounts paid to the plan.

Figure 20-3: Calculation of the defined-benefit obligation

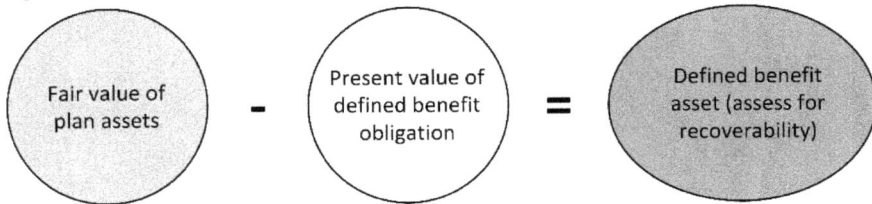

Fair value of plan assets - Present value of defined benefit obligation = Defined benefit asset (assess for recoverability)

A surplus is recognised to the extent that it is recoverable.

Example 20-7: Recognition of defined benefit asset/surplus

Blantyre Group established a pension fund, Blantyre Pension Fund, for the benefit of all the group's employees 25 years ago. The last comprehensive actuarial valuation was carried out at 31 December 20X1, and revealed that the fund had a deficit of CU250,000.

On 1 January 20X2, the Blantyre Group settled this deficit by paying in the deficit amount, and at the same time, decided that as some of its employees were nearing retirement age, it did not want to face a recurrence of a similar deficit. As such, the rate of contributions was increased from 6% of pensionable salary to 10% of pensionable salary.

At 31 December 20X3 Blantyre Group's management carried out a valuation of the fund. It considered the principal actuarial assumptions made in the last valuation, and was satisfied that there had not been any significant changes in the assumptions. It also considered the impact that employees nearing retirement would have on the fund, the current salary levels of the staff as well as other criteria that it thought appropriate.

Having taken all these factors into account, management determined that the fund has a surplus of CU600,000. As this surplus is not repayable to the Blantyre Group, management decided to be prudent, and not reduce payment to the pension fund.

Required

Determine the accounting required by the Blantyre Group in 20X1.

Suggested solution

The surplus must be recognised as an asset only to the extent management determined that it is recoverable either directly through repayment to Blantyre Group or to be offset against future contributions to be made to the Blantyre Pension Fund.

In this case it would seem that the Blantyre Group will not be able to recognise the surplus as an asset but may disclose it as a contingent asset.

20.9.4   Cost of a defined benefit plan

The net change in the defined benefit liability or asset for the period is recognised as the cost or income of the defined benefit plan. This excludes changes due to benefits paid or contributions received for the period.   Normally, all changes except benefits paid or contributions received are recognised in profit or loss. However, actuarial gains may be recognised in other comprehensive income and the cost may be capitalised in the carrying value of other assets, if allowed. For instance, defined benefit cost of staff working in the production process of goods sold by the entity may be capitalised to inventories.

> Normally, all changes except for cash receipt and payments are recognised in profit or loss.

The cost of a defined benefit plan consists of the following:

- Service rendered.
- Interest on the defined benefit obligation.
- Returns earned on plan assets including fair value changes.
- Fair value of recognised reimbursement rights.
- Actuarial gains and losses. Increases or decreases in the defined benefit obligations arising due to introductions, changes to, curtailments or settlement of plans.

20.9.5   Election for actuarial gains and losses

Actuarial gains and losses for a period are recognised either in profit or loss or other comprehensive income. This is an accounting policy election that must be applied consistently to all the entity's defined benefit plans.

> Actuarial gains and losses may be recognised in profit or loss or OCI.

20.9.6   Reimbursements

A reimbursement right is only recognised as a separate asset if an entity is virtually certain that another party will reimburse the benefit expenditure. Reimbursement assets are measured at fair value. The cost of the defined benefit plan may be reduced with the reimbursement credit and presented on a net basis.

20.9.7   Disclosure

The following is disclosed separately for each defined benefit plan, in total for all plans, or in useful groupings of different plans:

- A general description of the type of plan and funding policy.
- The accounting policy used for recognising actuarial gains and losses and the amount of actuarial gains and losses recognised.
- A narrative explanation of any measurement simplifications used.
- The date of the most recent comprehensive actuarial valuation and description of the adjustments that were made since such valuation.

- A reconciliation of opening and closing balances of the defined benefit obligation showing separately benefits paid and all other changes.
- A reconciliation of the opening and closing balances of the fair value of plan assets and separately for any recognised reimbursement right, showing separately contributions, benefits paid and other changes in the plan assets held.
- The total cost of the defined benefit plans for the period, showing separately the amounts recognised in profit or loss as an expense and capitalised in the cost of an asset.
- The fair value of the total plan assets and for each major class of plan asset the percentage or amount that each major class constitutes. Major classes may include equity instruments, debt instruments, property, and all other assets. A distinction must be made between the entity's own financial instruments and any property occupied or other assets used.
- The actual return on plan assets.
- The principal actuarial assumptions used, which may include the discount rates, the expected rates of return on any plan assets, the expected rates of salary increases, medical cost trend rates (if applicable), and any other material actuarial assumptions.

All the required reconciliations are only presented for the current year.

20.10   Other long-term employee benefits

20.10.1   Recognition and measurement

Other long-term employee benefits are due later than 12 months after the reporting date in which the related service was rendered. This excludes post-employment and termination benefits. For example, long-service awards, sabbatical leave, disability benefits, profit-sharing and bonuses – if they are payable later than 12 months after the reporting date.

> The liability for other long-term employee benefits is measured at the reporting date, at the net amount of the present value of the future obligation, minus the fair value at the reporting date of any related plan assets. Since a fund is normally not created for long-term employee benefits, the plan assets could consist of qualifying insurance contracts. The net change in the liability, other than changes due to employer contributions or benefits paid to employees, shall be recognised in profit or loss as an expense (unless it may be capitalised to the cost of an asset in terms of another section) during the period.

20.10.2   Disclosure

Disclosures are required for each category of other long-term benefits that are provided to employees, noting the nature of the benefit, the amount of the entity's obligation and whether the obligation is funded at the reporting date.

20.11   Termination benefits

Termination benefits could arise from legal and constructive obligations between the entity and its employees, and may arise due to two situations:

- Where a termination benefit is payable as a result of an entity's decision to terminate an employee's contract of employment before the normal retirement age.
- As a result of a voluntary redundancy package that may have been offered.

Any payments that do not fall in any of these two situations are not regarded as termination benefits.

20.11.1   Recognition

The recognition of termination benefits is not linked to services rendered. Termination benefits are only recognised when the entity is demonstrably committed to fulfil either the termination of employment before the normal retirement date or where an offer made to encourage voluntary redundancy was accepted by the employee.

Termination benefits are immediately expensed in profit or loss because they do not represent future economic benefits. The recognition of termination benefits may trigger the curtailment of retirement or other employee benefits.

Specifically, an entity is demonstrably committed to a termination only when the entity has a detailed formal plan for the termination and there is no realistic possibility of withdrawing from such a plan.

Example 20-8: Termination benefits

On 1 December 20X1, Jakarta decided to terminate the services of two of its employees due to the prevailing negative economic environment.

This, as well as an offer of CU200,000 per employee as compensation for terminating their employment in January 20X2, was communicated to the two employees on 20 December 20X1. The employees accepted the offer before 31 December 20X1.

Required
Provide the journal entries required to account for the termination benefits in the accounting records of Jakarta in the year ending 31 December 20X1.

Suggested solution
Jakarta has a constructive obligation to pay an amount of termination benefits at the reporting date, ie 31 December 20X1. This is because Jakarta had created a valid expectation with the affected employees. As the amount is payable within the following financial period, the amount should not be discounted.

Journal
31 December 20X1

Dr	Employment cost (P/L)	400,000	
Cr	Provision for termination benefits (SFP)		400,000

Provision made for the obligation to pay termination benefits.

20.11.2   Measurement

Termination benefits are measured at the reporting date at the best estimate of the expenditure that would be required to settle the obligation. Where an offer made to encourage voluntary redundancy is made, the measurement of termination benefits are based on the number of employees expected to accept the offer.

Termination benefits are discounted when they are due more than 12 months after the reporting date.

20.11.3 Disclosure

Disclosures are required for each category of termination benefits, stating the nature of the benefits accruing, the amount of the obligation and the extent of funding provided. A contingent liability arises when there is uncertainty about the number of employees who will accept an offer of termination.

20.12 Group plans

When a parent provides benefits to the employees of its subsidiaries, the group employee benefits may be allocated amongst the subsidiaries on a reasonable basis. This provision is only available if the parent presents consolidated financial statements using either the Standard or full IFRS.

20.13 Summary

- **Short-term benefits**
  - Measured at an undiscounted rate and recognised as the services are rendered. Other costs (such as annual leave) are recognised as the related services are rendered if the costs accumulate, otherwise the cost is expensed when the leave is taken or used. Bonus payments are only recognised when an obligation exists and the amount can be reliably estimated.
- **Post-employment benefits – Defined contribution plans**
  - Contributions are recognised as a liability and expensed when the contributions are due. Any pre-payments of contributions made must be recognised as assets.
- **Post-employment benefits – Defined benefit plans**
  - Recognise a liability based on the net of, present value of defined benefit obligations less the fair value of any plan assets, at balance sheet date.
  - The projected unit credit method is required, provided it does not entail undue cost or effort. Simplifications are incorporated to overcome the requirement to use the projected unit credit method.
  - An alternative accounting policy option is allowed for actuarial gains and losses. The alternative allows the recognition in other comprehensive income.
- **Other long-term benefits**
  - The entity must recognise a liability at the present value of the benefit obligation, less any fair value of plan assets.
- **Termination benefits**
  - These are recognised in profit or loss immediately when certain requirements are met, as there are no future economic benefits to the entity.

Chapter 21
Income tax

Contents

21.1   Scope

Current and future tax consequences of transactions and other events that are recognised in the financial statements give rise to income tax, which represents current and deferred tax. This chapter deals with both current and deferred tax. This chapter does not deal with the methods of accounting for government grants but with the accounting of temporary differences arising from such grants.

21.2   Definitions

21.2.1   Income tax definitions

Income tax is defined as all domestic and foreign taxes that are based on taxable profits. Income tax also includes taxes, such as withholding taxes, that are payable by a subsidiary, associate or joint ventures on distributions to the reporting entity. *Figure 21-1* identifies the different taxes included in income tax.

Figure 21-1: Different income taxes

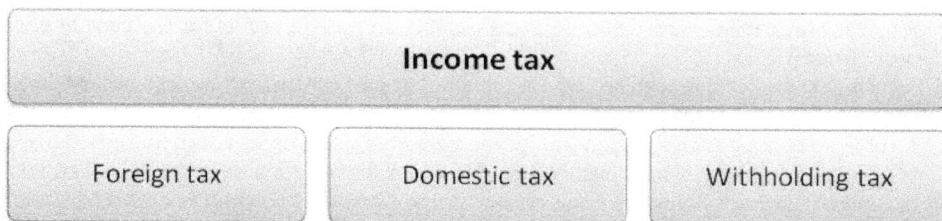

Taxable profit (tax loss) is defined as the profit (loss) for a reporting period upon which income taxes are payable or recoverable, determined in accordance with the rules established by the taxation authorities. Taxable profit equals taxable income less amounts deductible from taxable income.

Current tax is defined as the amount of income tax payable (recoverable) in respect of taxable profits (tax losses) for the current or past periods.

Tax expense is defined as the aggregate amount included in total comprehensive income or equity for the reporting period in respect of current tax and deferred tax.

21.2.2   Deferred tax definitions

Deferred tax is defined as income tax payable (recoverable) in future periods, generally as a result of the entity recovering or settling its assets and liabilities for their carrying amount, and the tax effect of the carry forward of currently unused tax losses and credits.

Temporary differences are defined as the differences between the carrying amount of an asset or liability in the statement of financial position and its tax base.

Deductible temporary differences are defined as temporary differences that will result in amounts that are deductible in determining taxable profit (tax loss) of future periods when the carrying amount of the asset or liability is recovered or settled.

Tax base of an asset or liability is defined as the amount attributed to that asset or liability for tax purposes.

Deferred tax assets are defined as the amount of income tax recoverable in future periods in respect of:

- Deductible temporary differences;
- The carry-forward of unutilised tax losses; and
- The carry-forward of unutilised tax credits.

Deferred tax liabilities are defined as the amount of income tax payable in future periods in respect of taxable temporary differences.

21.3 Current tax

21.3.1 Recognition

Current tax is the tax due on taxable profit for both current and prior periods. Current tax is recognised as follows:

- A current tax liability is recognised for tax payable on taxable profits for the current and past periods.
- A current tax asset is recognised where the amount paid for the current and past periods exceeds the amount payable.
- A current tax asset is also recognised for the benefit of a tax loss that can be carried back to recover tax paid in a previous period. This is specifically not a deferred tax asset. For example, if a previous period's tax return has been revised by the tax authorities and resulted in a reduction of taxable profits (or increase of taxable losses), and the amount is recoverable from the tax authorities in the current period.

Changes in current tax liabilities or current tax assets for the reporting period are included in the tax expense in profit or loss. However, if the changes relate to income or expense recognised as other comprehensive income or in equity, the tax effect is directly included in other comprehensive income or in equity.

Example 21-1: Tax on dividends payable
Berkley's local tax authority levies a tax on dividends that is payable by the entity declaring the dividend, and not the shareholder. The financial director was uncertain how the transaction should be treated for accounting purposes.
Required
Advise the financial director of the accounting implications of the transaction in Berkley's financial statements.
Suggested solution
In this case, the tax does not represent a withholding tax (refer to 21.6). Such dividend tax is a tax expense of the reporting entity. Since dividends payable are recognised in equity, the tax levied on the dividends payable must also be recognised in equity, except if the tax legislation specifically identifies that the tax on dividends form part of the current tax of the entity for the period.

21.3.2   Measurement

Current tax liabilities (or assets) are measured at the amounts that are expected to be paid (or recovered) by using the tax rates and laws that have been enacted or substantively enacted at the reporting date. Tax rates are regarded to be substantively enacted when the remaining steps in the enactment process have not affected the outcome in the past, and are unlikely to do so.

Example 21-2: Substantively enacted

The tax rate applicable to Bangalore for the 20X1 reporting period is 30%. Before the end of the 20X1 reporting period, the Minister of Finance announced a new rate of 28% that will be applicable for the 20X2 reporting period. Tax rates announced preliminarily by the Minister of Finance have never been changed in the past and have subsequently been passed into law.

Required

Provide guidance on which tax rates should be used in the 20X1 and 20X2 periods.

Suggested solution

The new rate is deemed to be substantively enacted at the end of 20X1 since an announced rate has never been changed in the past. Although a new rate of 28% has been announced, the current tax for 20X1 will still be calculated at 30%, because the taxable profit of 20X1 is still subject to the old tax rate of 30%. Taxable profit will be calculated at 28% from the beginning of 20X2.

> 👁 The tax rate used to calculate deferred tax must be based on the rate enacted or substantively enacted at the reporting date, even though the tax rate for the reporting period may differ.

21.4   Deferred tax

21.4.1   Recognition and measurement

A deferred tax asset or liability is recognised for tax recoverable or payable in future periods as a result of past transactions or events. Deferred tax arises from temporary differences. Temporary differences are differences between the carrying amounts of assets and liabilities in the statement of financial position and their tax bases. Deferred tax assets are also recognised for the carry-forward of unutilised tax losses and unutilised tax credits. *Figure 21-2* provides the steps that must be followed to identify, calculate and recognise the amount of deferred tax relating to future tax payable or recoverable at the reporting date.

The related deferred tax expense (or income) is allocated in the same manner as current tax to the components of profit or loss, other comprehensive income and equity. The steps of the process to recognise deferred tax are explained below:

Figure 21-2: Process to recognise and measure deferred tax

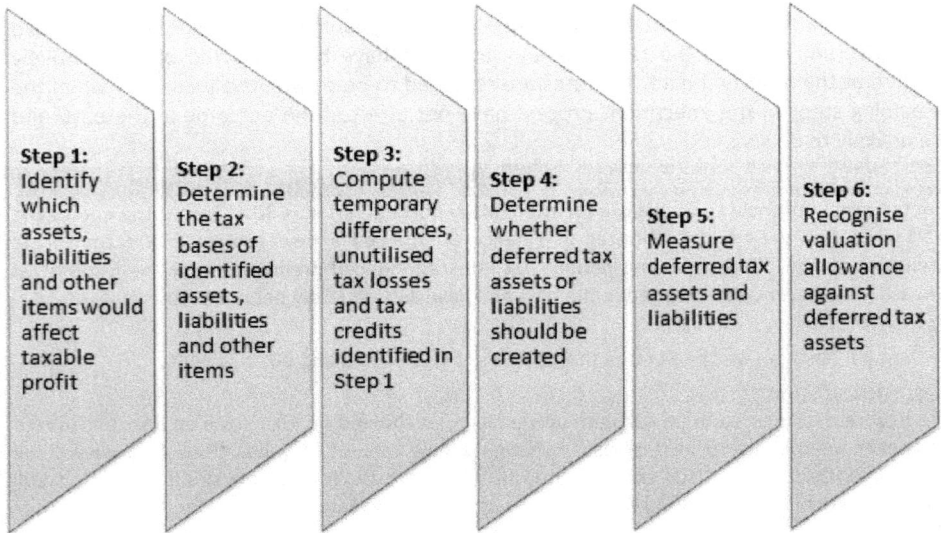

Step 1: Identify which assets, liabilities and other items would affect taxable profit

Step 2: Determine the tax bases of identified assets, liabilities and other items

Step 3: Compute temporary differences, unutilised tax losses and tax credits identified in Step 1

Step 4: Determine whether deferred tax assets or liabilities should be created

Step 5: Measure deferred tax assets and liabilities

Step 6: Recognise valuation allowance against deferred tax assets

21.4.2 Step 1: Identify assets and liabilities affecting taxable profits (taxable losses)

The first step is to identify which assets or liabilities would affect taxable profits (losses) if the assets are recovered or liabilities settled at their present carrying amount, at the reporting date. Where it is expected that the recovery of an asset or settlement of a liability will not affect taxable profits (taxable losses), no deferred tax is recognised for the asset or liability.

> 👁 If the recovery of an asset or settlement of a liability will not affect taxable profits or losses, their tax bases are assumed to be equal to their carrying amounts, and no temporary difference is created. This effectively creates an exemption from recognising deferred tax.

If the deemed recovery or settlement of an asset or liability will affect taxable profits (losses), the tax base of the asset or liability is determined as described in *Step 2*.

Example 21-3: Exception – Where no temporary difference is created

Chicago holds an office building with a cost price of CU2 million. At the reporting date, the office building was depreciated to CU1.6 million. The tax authority grants no tax allowance on the office building for normal tax purposes.

Required

Discuss whether deferred tax should be calculated on the office building, under both of the following situations:

1. A Capital Gains Tax (CGT) is applicable to capital gains and losses.
2. No CGT is applicable to capital gains and losses.

Suggested solution

To determine whether deferred tax should be calculated, the tax effect must be considered if the asset is sold at the reporting date for CU1.6 million. No normal tax consequences are applicable since the office building is a capital asset.

1. CGT

If CGT is applicable to the capital loss of CU400,000, then any related deferred tax should be calculated using the next step.

2. No CGT

If no CGT is applicable, the exemption will apply, and the tax base of the office building will be regarded to be CU1.6 million.

21.4.3 Step 2: Determine the tax base of identified assets, liabilities and other items

The tax base determines the amounts that will be included in taxable profits (losses) on the recovery of an asset or the settlement of a liability, at the reporting date. The tax base is defined as the measurement of an asset, liability or equity instrument under applicable substantively enacted tax law. The tax base therefore calculates the value of an asset or liability for tax purposes.

The tax base must be determined for all assets and liabilities, except for those excluded in *Step 1*. Since deferred tax is based on past transactions, the existence of any tax base resulting from items recognised as expenses, income and equity instruments, must also be considered. For example, research and development cost expensed for accounting purposes but deducted for tax purposes over a period of time.

21.4.3.1 Assets

The tax base of an asset represents the amount that would be deductible for tax purposes against any taxable economic benefits that will flow to an entity when it recovers the carrying amount of the asset. As explained in *Example 21-3*, if the economic benefits from an asset are not taxable, the tax base is equal to the carrying amount of the asset.

Example 21-4: Tax base of an asset

Frankfurt purchases a machine on 1 January 20X1 for CU500,000, which is depreciated over five years on a straight-line basis. Frankfurt's reporting period ends on 31 December 20X1. The carrying value of the machine at 31 December 20X1 is CU400,000 (CU500,000 - CU100,000 depreciation). The tax authorities allow an accelerated wear and tear allowance of 30% for the first period.

Required
Determine the tax base of the asset on 31 December 20X1.

Suggested solution
The tax base of an asset is the amount deducted for tax purposes if the asset is sold for its carrying value at the reporting date. The tax base of the asset at 31 December 20X1 is therefore **CU350,000** (CU500,000 - (30% x CU500,000)). The tax value of CU350,000 will be deductible for tax purposes if the machine is sold.

21.4.3.2   Liabilities

The tax base of a liability equals its carrying amount less the amount that would be deductible for tax purposes in respect of that liability in future periods.

Example 21-5: Tax base of a liability

Alexandria created a provision for restructuring costs of CU500,000 at 31 December 20X1, which is its reporting date. The provision will only be deducted for tax purposes in the future when the actual restructuring cost is incurred.

Required
Determine the tax base of the provision at 31 December 20X1.

Suggested solution
The full restructuring costs of CU500,000 will be deducted for tax purposes if the restructuring cost is settled on 31 December 20X1. Therefore the tax base of the provision is zero (CU500,000 carrying amount - CU500,000 deemed amount deductible from taxable profit).

21.4.3.3   Revenue received in advance

The tax base of revenue received in advance is the carrying amount, less any amount of revenue that will not be taxable in future periods.

Example 21-6: Deferred income

At 31 December 20X1, an amount of CU200,000 received has been recognised in the accounting records of Casablanca as deferred income under liabilities. At 31 December 20X1, the full amount of CU200,000 was included in taxable profit, since the amount was received.

Required
Determine the tax base of the deferred income at 31 December 20X1.

Suggested solution
Since the full amount was taxable during 20X1, no amount will be taxable in future periods. The tax base is zero (CU200,000 carrying value - CU200,000 taxable in the current year).

21.4.3.4   Expenses

The tax base of an expense, for which no related asset or liability is recognised in the financial statements, is the amount deducted against future taxable profits (losses). The difference between the tax base and the carrying amount of nil is a deductible temporary difference.

Example 21-7: Expenses only deductible in subsequent periods for tax purposes

Research and development costs incurred of CU100,000 were expensed in profit or loss. For tax purposes, the expense will only be deducted in future years when certain requirements are met.

Required
Determine the tax base of the expense at the reporting date.

Suggested solution
The tax base is CU100,000, being the amount deductible in future periods for tax purposes.

21.4.3.5   Income

The tax base of income, for which no related asset or liability is recognised in the financial statements, is the future taxable amount.

Example 21-8: Income not yet included in taxable profits (taxable losses)

Income received during the year of CU100,000 is recognised in profit or loss. For tax purposes, 50% is taxable in the current year and 50% the next year.

Required
Determine the tax base of the income at the reporting date.

Suggested solution
The tax base is CU50,000 (50%), being the amount taxable in the next year.

21.4.3.6   Equity instruments

The tax base of an equity instrument is the amount that may be deducted for tax purposes in the future.

Example 21-9: Equity instrument

Ho Chi Minh City issued a convertible instrument that may be converted into equity if certain conditions are met. In terms of the compound financial instruments' requirements, an amount of CU300,000 of the issue price of CU900,000 was recognised in equity.

Required
Determine the tax base of the amount recognised in equity.

Suggested solution
If the amount of CU300,000 is deductible in the future for tax purposes, the tax base will be CU300,000.

The above illustrates that the tax base is determined by considering the consequences of the sale of assets or settlement of liabilities, at their present carrying amounts, at the reporting date. The actual deemed tax consequences of sale or settlement at the reporting date, and not the possibility that the entity intends to use the asset or liability, determines the tax base.

The tax base of an asset, liability or other item is also determined in accordance with enacted or substantively enacted law. In consolidated financial statements, the tax base of assets and liabilities are determined by applying the tax law applicable to each entity separately. Thus, deferred tax is determined separately in each entity before consolidation. When the group files a consolidated tax return, the tax base is determined by the tax law governing the consolidated tax return if it differs.

21.4.4 Step 3: Compute any temporary differences, unutilised tax losses and tax credits

This step involves two separate guidelines for the treatment of:

- Temporary differences.
- Unutilised tax losses and credits.

21.4.4.1 Temporary differences

Temporary differences are defined as differences between the carrying amounts of assets and liabilities in the statement of financial position and their tax base. The differences are only calculated if the entity expects that the assets, liabilities or other items will affect future taxable profits (taxable losses).

In consolidated financial statements, temporary differences are determined by comparing the carrying amount in the consolidated financial statements with the tax base. The tax base is determined by reference to the individual tax return of each entity in the group, except if consolidated tax returns are applicable.

The Standard provides the following examples of temporary differences:

- The difference between the carrying amounts and tax base on the initial recognition of assets and liabilities.
- Assets and liabilities acquired in a business combination at fair value but such an adjustment is not made for tax purposes.
- Remeasurements, such as revaluations, not adjusted for tax purposes.
- Items that have a tax base, but are not recognised as assets and liabilities in the financial statements.
- Income or expenses are recognised in different periods for accounting and tax purposes.
- If the tax bases of assets or liabilities change, but such changes are not recognised in the assets' or liabilities' carrying amounts.

Example 21-10: Temporary differences

At 31 December 20X1, the assets and liabilities of Athens consist of:

Property, plant and equipment	400,000
Investment in shares	120,000
Inventories	200,000
Trade and other receivables	300,000
Long-term liabilities	180,000
Trade and other payables	220,000

The tax bases of the assets and liabilities at 31 December 20X1 are:

Property, plant and equipment	350,000
Investment in shares	120,000
Inventories	210,000
Trade and other receivables	280,000
Long-term liabilities	180,000
Trade and other payables	210,000

Research and development cost of CU15,000 was expensed during the 20X1 reporting period but is only deductible for tax purposes in future periods.

Required

Calculate the temporary differences of Athens at 31 December 20X1.

Suggested solution

The temporary differences of Athens at 31 December 20X1 are:

	Carrying value	Tax base	Temporary difference
Property, plant and equipment	400,000	350,000	50,000
Investment in shares	120,000	120,000	0
Inventories	200,000	210,000	(10,000)
Trade and other receivables	300,000	280,000	20,000
Long-term liabilities	(180,000)	(180,000)	0
Trade and other payables	(220,000)	(210,000)	(10,000)
Research and development cost	0	15,000	(15,000)

21.4.4.2   Unutilised tax losses and unutilised tax credits

The existence of unutilised tax losses and tax credits must be determined at the reporting date. The recognition of the deferred tax asset is limited to the probability of recoverability as discussed in *21.4.5.3*.

Example 21-11: Unutilised tax losses (assessed losses)

Santo Domingo has a calculated tax loss of CU300,000 at the reporting date, which has been assessed, and has been appropriately acknowledged by the tax authorities. In Santa Domingo's jurisdiction, the tax rate applicable on profits is 28%.

Required

Discuss the accounting treatment of the transaction.

Suggested solution

A deferred tax asset of CU84,000 (CU300,000 x 28%) could be recognised.

The probability that the deferred tax asset can be utilised must be assessed at the reporting date. Only the probable portion must be recognised.

Example 21-12: Unutilised tax credits

Santiago has accrued tax benefits (credits) of CU300,000, which the government granted to it for engaging in social development activities. In Santiago's jurisdiction, the tax rate applicable on profits is 35%.

Required

Discuss the accounting treatment of the transaction.

Suggested solution

These tax credits may be subtracted from taxes payable in the future. A deferred tax asset of CU105,000 (CU300,000 x 28%) is recognised.

The recovery of the deferred tax asset must be assessed at the reporting date as described in *21.4.5.3*.

21.4.5 Step 4: Determine whether deferred tax assets or liabilities should be created

Deferred tax assets and liabilities are recognised for accumulated temporary differences, unutilised tax losses and unutilised tax credits, identified in *Step 3*, as follows:

- A deferred tax liability is recognised for a taxable temporary difference.
- A deferred tax asset is recognised for deductible temporary differences.
- Deferred tax assets are also recognised for the probable portion of unused tax losses and tax credits.

21.4.5.1 Taxable temporary difference

Taxable temporary differences are temporary differences that will result in taxable amounts in determining taxable profit (tax loss) of future periods when the carrying amount of the asset or liability is recovered or settled. Examples of taxable temporary differences are:

- Interest revenue accounted on a time-proportion basis but is only taxed when the interest is received. This is a taxable temporary difference since the recognised interest is taxable in the future.

- Tax depreciation that is accelerated by deducting an amount earlier for tax purposes. The carrying amount would be higher than the tax base, resulting in that catch-up depreciation would not be deducted for tax purposes when the catch-up depreciation is recognised for accounting purposes.

21.4.5.2   Deductible temporary differences

Deductible temporary differences are temporary differences that will result in amounts that are deductible in determining taxable profit (tax loss) of future periods when the carrying amount of the asset or liability is recovered or settled. Examples of deductible temporary differences are:

- Tax depreciation that occurs at a slower pace than the accounting depreciation, resulting in an amount that will be deductible for tax purposes in the future after the accounting depreciation has ceased.
- Retirement benefits cost is deducted for accounting purposes when the related services are rendered, but only deducted for tax purposes when the contributions are paid to the fund or the retirement benefits are paid.

A deferred tax asset is only recognised for deductible temporary differences to the extent that taxable profits will be available against which the deductible temporary difference can be utilised. This probability test follows a two-step approach. 1) It should be probable that taxable profits will be available to utilise the deductible temporary differences when there are sufficient taxable temporary differences available that are expected to reverse:

- In the same period as the expected reversal of the deductible temporary differences; or
- In periods into which a tax loss arising from the deferred tax asset can be carried back or forward.

2) Where there are insufficient taxable temporary differences available to utilise the deductible temporary differences, the deferred tax asset is recognised to the extent that:

- It is probable that the entity will have future taxable profits available; or
- Tax planning opportunities are available to create the required taxable profits.

The probability test is applied to the same tax authority and the same tax entity. Therefore entities with businesses that are taxed in different countries must apply the probability test for each such business separately.

Example 21-13: Determine taxable or deductible temporary differences and whether a deferred tax asset or liability should be created

The example is based on temporary differences identified for tax purposes of Athens, as determined in *Example 21-10.*

Required

Determine whether a deferred tax asset or liability should be created by Athens at 31 December 20X1, and the effect on taxable profits.

Suggested solution

	Temporary difference	Nature of difference	Increase/decrease of future taxable profits
Property, plant and equipment		Taxable	
	50,000	(Liability)	Increase
Investment in shares	0	None	None
Inventories		Deductible	
	(10,000)	(Asset)	Decrease
Trade and other receivables		Taxable	
	20,000	(Liability)	Increase
Long-term liabilities	0	None	None
Trade and other payables		Deductible	
	(10,000)	(Asset)	Increase
Research and development cost		Deductible	
	(15,000)	(Asset)	Increase

21.4.5.3 Limitation on the recognition of unused tax losses and unused tax credits

A deferred tax asset is only recognised for the carry-forward of unused tax losses and unused tax credits to the extent that it is probable that future taxable profit will be available against which the unused tax losses and unused tax credits can be utilised. To assess the probability of future taxable profits available, the Standard states that the following are considered:

- Whether the entity has sufficient taxable temporary differences relating to the same taxation authority and the same taxable entity, which will result in taxable amounts against which the unused tax losses or unused tax credits can be utilised before they expire.
- Whether it is probable that the entity will have taxable profits before the unused tax losses or unused tax credits expire.
- Whether the unused tax losses result from identifiable causes, which are unlikely to recur.
- Whether tax planning opportunities are available to the entity that will create taxable profit in the period in which the unused tax losses or unused tax credits can be utilised.

21.4.5.4 Reassessment of deferred tax assets

Unrecognised deferred tax assets must be reassessed at the end of each reporting period by applying the probability criteria discussed above to assess the recoverability of the deferred tax asset. A recognised deferred tax asset is also reduced if the recovery is no longer probable.

21.4.5.5 Exceptions to general rules

Three exceptions are applicable to the general principles that deferred tax should be recognised for all temporary differences, unutilised tax losses and credits:

- A deferred tax liability is not recognised for the initial recognition of goodwill.
- A deferred tax asset or liability is not recognised in a transaction that is not a business combination, and at the time of the transaction does not affect the accounting profit or taxable profit.
- An exception for temporary differences of investment in subsidiaries, branches and associates as discussed in *21.4.5.6*.

21.4.5.6 Investments in subsidiaries, branches and associates and interest in joint ventures

Temporary differences arise when the carrying amounts of investments in subsidiaries, branches and associates and interest in joint ventures differ from their related tax bases.

The Standard also provides the following examples of why differences may exist between the carrying amount and tax base of these investments:

- The existence of undistributed profits of subsidiaries, branches, associates and joint ventures.
- Changes in foreign exchange rates when a parent and its subsidiary are based in different countries.
- A reduction in the carrying amount of an investment in an associate to its recoverable amount.

An exception in the recognition of deferred tax on the difference between the carrying value and tax base of these investments is applicable to both deferred tax liabilities and deferred tax assets. A deferred tax liability is recognised on all taxable temporary difference, except to the extent the following conditions are met:

- The parent, investor or venturer is able to control the timing of the reversal of the temporary difference.
- It is probable that the temporary difference will not reverse in the foreseeable future.

A deferred tax asset is, however, only recognised for deductible temporary differences to the extent that it is probable that:

- The temporary difference will reverse in the foreseeable future.
- Taxable profit will be available against which the temporary difference can be utilised.

Example 21-14: Investment in associates

Dallas has an investment in a foreign associate that is recognised using the equity accounting method. The carrying amount of the investment in the associate is increased with the unremitted earnings of the associate from the date of acquisition. If the associate is sold at the reporting date for the carrying value, the amount capitalised above the cost price will be subject to CGT.

Dallas has no intention to sell the associate.

Required

Determine whether a deferred tax asset or liability should be recognised.

Suggested solution

Since Dallas can decide when to sell the foreign associate, it can control the timing of the reversal of the temporary difference. Since it did not make a selling decision, it is probable that the temporary difference will not reverse in the foreseeable future. Therefore, no deferred tax is recognised on the difference between the carrying value and cost price of the investment in the associate. However, if Dallas changes its intention and decides to sell the associate, deferred tax should be recognised on the difference between the carrying amount and the cost of the investment based on the CGT rate.

21.4.6 Step 5: Measure deferred tax assets and deferred tax liabilities

The applicable tax rates are based on enacted or substantively enacted tax law, at the reporting date, that are expected to apply when the deferred tax asset is realised or the liability is settled. Tax rates and tax laws are regarded as substantively enacted when the remaining steps in the enactment process that is followed have not affected the outcome in the past and are unlikely to do so in the future. Applicable future tax rates that are enacted or substantively enacted at the reporting date may thus be used to measure deferred tax.

> Although the IFRS does not preclude the use of the usage rate, our option is that for consistency, it is better to apply the same principles used for the tax base to measure the deferred tax.

When different tax rates apply to different levels of taxable profit, the deferred tax expense (income) and related deferred tax liabilities (assets) may be determined by using the average rates that are expected to be applicable to the taxable profit (loss) of the periods in which the deferred tax is expected to be realised or settled.

The measurement of deferred tax liabilities and assets must reflect the tax consequences that would follow from the way in which the entity expects, at the reporting date, to recover or settle the carrying amount of the related assets and liabilities.

The tax rate and tax base that are consistent with the expected manner of recovery or settlement are therefore used, which could result in the application of different rates of tax that are dependent on whether the settlement or recovery of the transaction will culminate in a tax rate that is based on usage, sale, or a combination.

If a deferred tax liability or deferred tax asset arises from a non-depreciable asset that is measured using the revaluation model, the measurement of the resultant deferred tax liability or asset should reflect the tax consequences of recovering the carrying amount of the asset through sale. If the deferred tax liability or asset arises from investment property that is measured at fair value, then there is a rebuttable presumption that the carrying amount of the investment property will be recovered through sale. As such, the measurement of the deferred tax liability or asset reflects the tax consequences of recovering the carrying amount of the investment property through sale. This presumption is rebutted if the investment property is depreciable and is held within a business model whose objective is to consume substantially all of the economic benefits that are embodied in the investment property over time, rather than through sale. In such a situation, the deferred tax liability or asset resulting should reflect the tax consequences that would follow from the manner in which the entity expects, at the reporting date, to recover or settle the carrying amount of the related assets and liabilities.

21.5 Other issues affecting the measurement of current and deferred tax

21.5.1 Discounting of current and deferred tax
The Standard specifically does not permit the discounting of current or deferred tax.

21.5.2 Tax on undistributed profits
If profits are distributed, eg as dividends, income tax may be payable at a higher or lower rate, or additional tax may be payable or refundable. Current and deferred taxes are measured at the tax rate applicable to undistributed profits until the entity recognises the liability to pay the related dividend. Only when the liability for the dividend is recognised, must an adjustment be made.

Example 21-15: Additional tax on distribution of dividends

The income tax legislation of a country states that current tax of 30% is payable on undistributed taxable income, but that the tax rate increases to 40% for all distributed profits.

Required
Determine the tax rate that should be used to determine current and deferred tax.

Suggested solution
Current tax of 30% is recognised on the taxable profit for the period. Only when a dividend is recognised is the additional tax of 10% recognised on the amount of the dividend.

21.6 Withholding tax on dividends
Withholding tax on dividends is applicable when a portion of dividends payable is paid to taxation authorities on behalf of shareholders. This type of tax is a tax on the shareholder and is included in equity as part of the total dividend payable.

Example 21-16: Withholding tax in dividends

A dividend of CU300,000 is payable to foreign shareholders. 20% of the amount must be withheld and paid to the tax authorities on behalf of the shareholders.

Required

Provide the relevant journal entry to recognise the dividend payable.

Suggested solution

Dr	Dividend (Equity)	300,000	
Cr	Dividend payable (SFP) (80%)		240,000
Cr	Withholding tax payable (SFP) (20%)		60,000

Recognise dividend and withholding tax payable.

21.7 Presentation

The tax expense is presented in the same component of total comprehensive income or equity as the transaction or other event that gives rise to it. Therefore, a distinction is normally made between profit or loss and items recognised in other comprehensive income. The tax expense related to continued and discontinued operations must also be presented separately.

Deferred tax assets and liabilities are not classified as current assets or liabilities.

21.8 Offsetting

Current tax assets and liabilities, or deferred tax assets and liabilities are only offset when a legally enforceable right to offset the amounts exists and the entity can demonstrate without undue cost and effort that it plans either to settle them on a net basis or to realise the asset and settle the liability simultaneously. If the undue cost or effort exemption is used, the amounts that have not been offset, and the reasons why applying the requirement would involve undue cost or effort must be disclosed.

21.9 Disclosure

Information that enables users of financial statements to evaluate the nature and financial effect of the current and deferred tax consequences of recognised transactions and other events is disclosed, including:

- The major components of tax expense, including:
  - Current tax expense (income).
  - Adjustments of current tax for prior periods.
  - The amount of deferred tax relating to the origination and reversal of temporary differences.
  - The amount of deferred tax relating to changes in tax rates or the imposition of new taxes.
  - The amount of the benefit arising from a previously unrecognised tax loss, tax credit or temporary difference of a prior period that is used to reduce tax expense.

- Adjustments to deferred tax arising from a change in the tax status of the entity or its shareholders.
- Deferred tax expense (income) arising from the write-down, or reversal of a previous write-down, of a deferred tax asset. The amount of tax expense relating to changes in accounting policies and errors.

- The aggregate current and deferred tax relating to items that are recognised in other comprehensive income or directly in equity.
- An explanation of the significant differences in amounts presented in the statement of comprehensive income and amounts reported to tax authorities.
- An explanation of changes in the applicable tax rate(s) compared with the previous reporting period – this is the tax rate reconciliation.
- For each type of temporary difference and tax losses and credits, the amount of the deferred asset or liability at the end of the reporting period and an analyses of the changes during the year.
- The amount and expiry date of temporary differences, unutilised tax losses and credits for which no deferred tax asset was recognised.
- An explanation of the nature of the potential income tax consequences that would result from the payment of dividends to its shareholders.

21.10   Summary

- **Current tax**
  - An entity recognises a current tax liability if the current tax payable exceeds the current tax paid at that time. A current tax asset is recognised when current tax paid exceeds current tax payable. A current tax asset is also recognised for the benefit of a tax loss that can be carried back to recover tax paid in a previous period.
  - Current tax assets and liabilities for current and prior periods must be measured at the actual amounts that are owed or owing using the applicable tax rates enacted or substantively enacted at the reporting date.
- **Deferred tax**
  - A temporary difference is a difference between the carrying amount of an asset, liability and its tax base that will result in a taxable or deductible amount in the future.
  - The tax base is the measurement of an asset, liability or equity instrument under applicable substantively enacted tax law at the reporting date. A notional tax balance sheet is created.
  - Deferred tax is based on the recovery or settlement of assets and liabilities at their current carrying amounts.
  - A deferred tax liability is recognised for income tax payable in the future reporting periods in respect of taxable temporary differences.
  - Deferred tax assets are recognised for deductible temporary differences to the extent that it is probable that taxable profit will be available against which the deductible temporary difference can be utilised.

- Three exemptions are available. Deferred tax is not recognised for the initial recognition of goodwill. Deferred tax is also not recognised if at the time of the transaction, the transaction does not affect accounting profit or taxable profit. Deferred tax is also not recognised for temporary differences associated with unremitted earnings from foreign subsidiaries, branches, associates and JVs, in certain instances.
- Recognition of changes in current or deferred tax must be allocated to the related components of profit or loss, other comprehensive income and equity.
- No discounting of deferred tax balances is allowed.

Chapter 22
Revenue

Contents

22.1   Scope

This chapter deals with the recognition, measurement and disclosure of revenue from:

- The sale of goods.
- The rendering of services.
- Construction contracts in which the entity is the contractor.
- The use by others of entity assets yielding interest, royalties, or dividends.

Revenue transactions that are covered by other chapters are not dealt with in this chapter. These revenue transactions are:

- Lease agreements (refer to *Chapter 18*).
- Dividends and other income arising from investments that are accounted for using the equity method (refer to *Chapters 9* and *10*).
- Changes in the fair value of financial assets and liabilities or their disposal (refer to *Chapter 17*).
- Changes in the fair value of investment property (refer to *Chapter 11*).
- Initial recognition of biological assets and agricultural produce, as well as changes in the fair value of biological assets related to agricultural activity (refer to *Chapter 29*).

22.2   Definitions

- **Revenue** is defined as the gross inflow of economic benefits during the course of the ordinary activities of an entity, when those inflows result in increases in equity other than increases relating to contributions from equity participants. *Note: Increases relating to contributions from equity participants are dealt with in Chapter 16.*
- **Construction contracts** are defined as contracts specifically negotiated for the construction of an asset, or a combination of assets, that are closely inter-related or inter-dependent in terms of their design, technology and function, or their ultimate purpose or use.

22.3   Measurement

Revenue is measured at the fair value of the consideration received or receivable by the entity. Fair value is calculated by taking into account the amount of any trade discounts, prompt settlement discounts and volume rebates allowed by the entity. These are deducted when measuring the revenue from a transaction.

Example 22-1: Measurement of revenue

Amsterdam sells goods to Paris for CU114. Included in the sale amount is 14% Value-Added Tax. Paris always pays within 30 days of invoice and receives a 5% prompt settlement discount on the net of VAT amount, which it can redeem against a future purchase. Amsterdam has no reason to believe that Paris will not pay within 30 days of this invoice.

Example 22-1: Measurement of revenue *(continued)*

Amsterdam will recognise revenue of CU95 on the transaction calculated as follows:

Gross cash inflow due to Amsterdam	114
Less VAT portion (14%)	(14)
Net cash inflow due to Amsterdam	100
Less expected prompt settlement discount (5%)	(5)
Revenue to be recognised by Amsterdam	95

> The Standard does not indicate whether a probability-weighted value should be determined if there are various different outcomes, or a large amount of transactions, at special terms.
>
> We suggest that an entity make an estimate based on all information available, including a probability-weighted calculation, if appropriate and reliable.

22.3.1   Principal or agent

The Standard also requires that in an agency relationship, an entity recognise revenue to the extent of its commission. The Standard does not define an agency relationship. The agency versus the principal is a very important concept given that it can materially alter the revenue recognised by an entity should the entity get this assessment wrong. Where an entity is the principal in a revenue transaction, it will recognise the full amount in revenue, with the associated costs recognised in cost of sales. Agents only recognise their commission or fee as revenue.

> As the Standard gives no detailed guidance on the agency versus principal relationship, an entity may choose to look at the principles in full IFRS. In the examples to *IAS 18 – Revenue*, an entity is acting as a principal when it has exposure to the significant risks and rewards associated with the revenue transaction. The following features of a principal relationship are identified:
>
> - The entity has the primary responsibility for the rendering of services, or provision of the goods.
> - The entity has the risk of holding inventories at some point in the transaction.
> - The entity has latitude in establishing prices.
> - The entity bears customer credit risk (ie risk of the customer not paying for the goods or services).
>
> Whereas the above are not rules, they are indicative of a principal relationship, and may be taken into account when making an assessment of a revenue transaction. *Note: Where an entity does not have any exposure to the significant risks and rewards in a transaction, it is most likely an agent.*

22.3.2   Deferred payment

Where an entity enters into a revenue transaction, which includes a financing element, the entity should account for the effect of the financing separately from the revenue arising from the sale of the goods or rendering of services. A financing arrangement may be indicated by an entity providing interest-free or below-market interest rate credit to the customer.

> The Standard states that an entity needs to discount a deferred revenue transaction when such a transaction contains a financing element.
>
> This will be required when the impact of the discounting on the financial statements of the entity is material. This clearly is a judgment call that the directors of an entity will need to make.
>
> The chapter on basic financial instruments (refer to *Chapter 17*) provides other indicators of a financing transaction. These are where either of the following credit terms is present:
> - Where payment terms are over a period that is deemed to be beyond normal business terms.
> - Where a transaction is financed at a below market rate of interest.

The fair value of the revenue element, as distinct from the financing element, represents the **present value** of all future receipts determined using an **imputed rate of interest**. The imputed rate of interest is either:

- The prevailing rate for a similar instrument of an issuer with a similar credit rating.
- A rate of interest that discounts the nominal amount of the instrument to the current cash sale price of the goods or services.

The difference between the present value of all future receipts and the nominal amount of the consideration (ie amounts to be received) is accounted for as interest revenue based on the imputed rate of interest.

Example 22-2: A financing transaction

Prague sells clothing to the public on six-month interest-free terms, on 1 January 20X1. Assuming Prague sold CU240,000 of merchandise, it would be recognised as revenue, as follows:

Sales	240,000	(Payable in CU40,000 payments over six months)
Imputed rate of interest (%)	10	
Discounted value	233,153	(Present value of payments = 40,000; Periods = 6 and interest at 0.833% (10%/12)

The amortisation table is as follows:

Opening balance (CU)	Interest (CU)	Capital payment (CU)	Closing balance (CU)
233,153	1,943	-40,000	195,096
195,096	1,626	-40,000	156,721
156,721	1,306	-40,000	118,027
118,027	984	-40,000	79,011
79,011	658	-40,000	39,669
39,669	331	-40,000	0

On 1 January 20X1, Prague will recognise revenue of CU233,153 and a debtor of the same amount. Thereafter, Prague will recognise interest every month on the debtors' balance at 10% pa.

Required

Provide the journal entries at 31 January 20X1.

Suggested solution

31 January 20X1

Dr	Trade and other receivables (SFP)	1,943	
Cr	Interest revenue (SCI)		1,943

Interest for the first month (refer to amortisation profile below).
(233,153 x 0.833%)

Dr	Bank (SFP)	40,000	
Cr	Trade and other receivables (SFP)		40,000

Payment received.

22.3.3 Exchanges of goods or services

The Standard states that revenue arises when an entity enters into an exchange transaction for dissimilar goods or services (refer to *Figure 22-1*). Where the goods or services are exchanged for goods or services that are of a similar nature and value, or where the exchange is for dissimilar goods or services, but the transaction lacks commercial substance, no revenue arises. Refer to *Chapter 12.4.3.2* for guidance as to what constitutes commercial substance from the full IFRS.

Figure 22-1: Exchange of goods

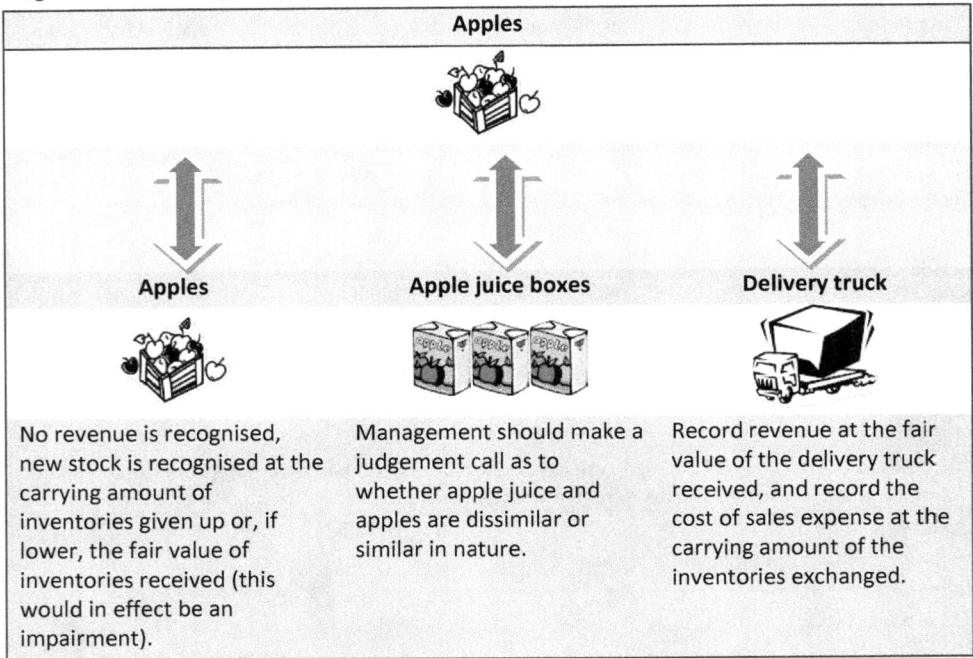

Apples		
Apples	**Apple juice boxes**	**Delivery truck**
No revenue is recognised, new stock is recognised at the carrying amount of inventories given up or, if lower, the fair value of inventories received (this would in effect be an impairment).	Management should make a judgement call as to whether apple juice and apples are dissimilar or similar in nature.	Record revenue at the fair value of the delivery truck received, and record the cost of sales expense at the carrying amount of the inventories exchanged.

Where an exchange transaction is for dissimilar goods or services, and has commercial substance, revenue is measured at the fair value of the goods or services received, adjusted for any amount of cash or cash paid/received.

Where the fair value of the goods received cannot be measured reliably, the transaction is measured at the fair value of the goods or services given up, adjusted by any cash or cash equivalents paid/received. If neither fair value can be measured reliably, then the transaction is measured at the carrying amount of the asset given up, adjusted for any cash or cash equivalents paid/received.

Figure 22-2 provides a detailed illustration of the recognition and measurement of an exchange transaction.

Figure 22-2: Exchange transactions

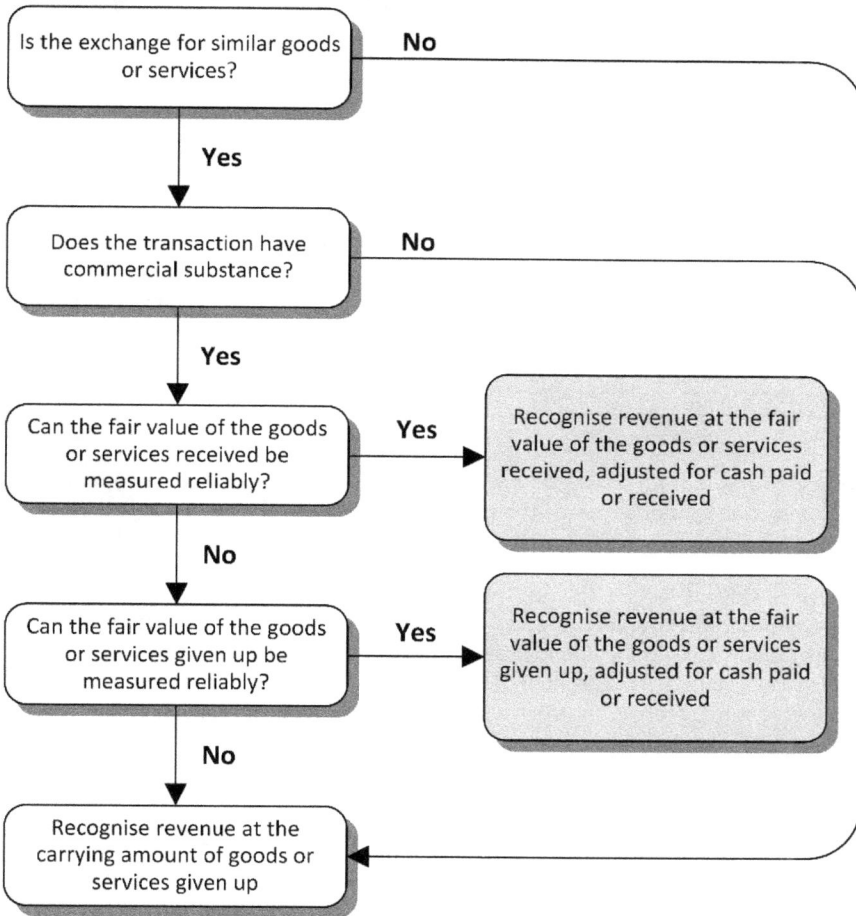

22.4 Identification of the revenue transaction

22.4.1 Separate components

Where a revenue transaction has multiple components, it should apply the revenue recognition criteria separately to each component.

> 👁 *Chapter 15: Provisions and Contingencies* determines that a provision should be created for warranties in a revenue contract. Warranties are therefore not regarded as a separate revenue component of a revenue contract.

Example 22-3: Multiple components to a sales contract

Moscow sells machinery to clients for CU5 million. Included within that price is a contract to service the machine for four years. Should the client not require Moscow to service the machine, the client can purchase the machine for CU4 million.

Required
Provide advice to Moscow's management on the timing of recognising the revenue from this transaction.

Suggested solution
Moscow must account for the sale of the machine at CU4 million, ie the normal selling price without any service contract. The service component of CU1 million must be deferred as a revenue received in advance in the statement of financial position, and recognised over the period the service is rendered, by applying the state of completion or straight-line method.

If the straight-line method is used, CU250,000 of deferred revenue will be recognised as revenue per year for four years.

22.4.2   Combined transactions

However, where two or more transactions are connected in such a way that the commercial effect of the transaction cannot be understood without looking at the transaction as a whole, then the revenue recognition criteria needs to be applied to the transaction as a whole.

22.4.3   Customer loyalty programs

Customer loyalty programs are very popular marketing tools used globally. These include schemes where customers receive points or credits every time they shop at a certain store or fly on a particular airline. These can then be redeemed in the future for free or discounted goods or services. Where an entity has such a scheme, the revenue transaction giving rise to the award needs to be split into two components:

- The sale of the good or rendering of service.
- The award of credit.

The value of the award credits will be measured at their fair value. This is the amount for which the award could be sold separately. This amount will normally be deferred on the statement of financial position as deferred revenue until appropriate recognition criteria are met.

👁 The Standard does not give any guidance as to when to release the deferred revenue into profit or loss.

An entity should develop an accounting policy based on the nature of the loyalty agreement with their customers.

Full IFRS provides further guidance in which the amount deferred is released on redemption of the award or on the expiry of the award. It is important to note, however, that an entity is not bound by the accounting treatment in full IFRS in the absence of guidance in the IFRS for SMEs and may therefore develop its own accounting policy in this regard in terms of the guidance in *Chapter 7*.

For instance, in the example below, the revenue allocated to the energy bar may either immediately be recognised as revenue, or as deferred revenue in the statement of financial position based on the substance of the arrangement. If deferred, the revenue may be recognised based on when the award is redeemed or expires. This would be an accounting policy choice that must be disclosed and consistently applied.

Example 22-4: Award credits provided to clients

Oslo sells bottles of a health drink for CU50. Customers who purchase the health drink receive an award credit enabling them to purchase an energy bar in the future for CU5. The normal cost of the energy bar is CU9. Based on history, Oslo estimates that 40% of its customers will use its awards. Oslo normally sells health drinks for CU46.50 without the award. There is no market price for the reward credit.

Oslo developed an accounting policy of deferring the reward credit until redemption or expiry of the award credits.

Required

Provide the journal entry for the sale of a health drink by Oslo in the following scenarios:

1. The estimate of the fair value of the award credit is based on the difference between the sales price with, or without, the award credit.
2. The estimate of the fair value of the award credit is based on the estimated percentage of customers that will use the award.

Suggested solution

1. Oslo calculates the fair value as the increased price due to the reward credits.
   (50.00 - 46.50) = CU3.50

   Oslo will account for the revenue on the sale of each health drink by using the fair value as per its accounting policy :

Dr	Bank/Cash/Debtor (SFP)	50.00	
Cr	Deferred revenue – Award credits (SFP)		3.50
Cr	Revenue – Health drinks (P/L)		46.50

   Recognition of sale of health drink.

Example 22-4: Award credits provided to clients *(continued)*

2. Oslo calculates the fair value of the award based on the estimated percentage of customers that would uses the awards:

   40% × (9.00 – 5.00) = CU1.60

   Oslo will therefore account for the revenue on the sale of each health drink by using the fair value as per its accounting policy:

Dr	Bank/Cash/Debtor (SFP)	50.00	
Cr	Deferred revenue – Award credits (SFP)		1.60
Cr	Revenue – Health drink (P/L)		48.40

   Recognition of sale of health drink.

This deferred revenue will be released when the energy bar is sold or the award expires.

22.5   Sale of goods

22.5.1   Recognition of sale

Sales of goods are revenue transactions where actual goods, as opposed to services, are transferred to the customer. The Standard requires an entity to recognise revenue from the sale of goods when **all** the following conditions have been met:

- The entity has transferred to the buyer the significant risks and rewards of ownership of the goods;
- The entity retains neither continuing managerial involvement to the degree usually associated with ownership nor effective control over the goods sold;
- The amount of revenue can be measured reliably;
- It is probable that the economic benefits associated with the transaction will flow to the entity; and
- The costs incurred or to be incurred in respect of the transaction can be measured reliably.

The assessment of when an entity has met the above criteria is a matter of judgment. Management will need to consider all the facts and circumstances in a transaction to determine when a sale should be recognised. In most cases, the transfer of the risks and rewards of ownership coincides with the transfer of the legal title or the passing of possession to the buyer. If only insignificant risks are retained by the entity, then the entity may recognise the revenue.

The Standard provides examples on the application of the recognition of revenue when selling goods on different terms (refer to *Table 22-1*). The Standard states that the law in different countries may cause the recognition criteria to be met at different times – this must be considered at all times.

Table 22-1: Sale of goods recognition guidance

Nature of transaction	Recognition guidance
Bill and hold sales – delivery is delayed at the buyer's request, but buyer takes title and accepts billing	Revenue is recognised when the buyer takes title, if all of the following is applicable: ▪ The delivery is probable; ▪ The item is on hand, identified and ready for delivery; ▪ The buyer specifically acknowledged the deferred delivery; and ▪ The usual payment terms apply.
Goods shipped subject to conditions: installation and inspection	Revenue is normally recognised when installation and inspection are completed, but revenue is recognised on delivery when: ▪ The installation process is simple; or ▪ Inspection is performed to determine the final contract price.
Goods shipped subject to conditions: a limited right of return	When there is uncertainty about a possible return, revenue is recognised when the shipment is formally accepted or the period of rejection has elapsed.
Goods shipped subject to conditions: consignment sales	Revenue is recognised when the recipient sold the goods to a third party.
Goods shipped subject to conditions: cash on delivery sales	Revenue is recognised when delivery is made and cash received.
Lay-away sales: delivery is subject to a final payment or part-payments	Revenue is recognised when the goods are delivered. However, based on experience, revenue might be recognised earlier if most sales are consummated and a significant deposit is received, provided the goods are on hand, identified and ready for delivery.
Payment or partial payments in advance of delivery for goods not on hand	Recognise revenue when goods are delivered to the buyer.
Sale and repurchase agreements	For non-financial assets, the terms of the agreement must be analysed to establish whether risks and rewards of ownership are transferred. If risks and rewards are retained, the transaction is a financing arrangement and no revenue is recognised.

Table 22-1: Sale of goods recognition guidance *(continued)*

Nature of transaction	Recognition guidance
Sales to intermediate parties	Revenue is recognised based on the normal principles except if the intermediate party acts as an agent.
Subscriptions to publications and similar items	If the value is similar for each period, a straight-line basis of revenue recognition is used. If not, revenue is allocated based on the dispatched values to the total estimated value.
Instalment sales	Revenue is recognised based on the sale price – the present value of the consideration by discounting the instalments at the imputed rate of interest.
Agreements for the construction of real estate where the entity enters into agreements with buyers before construction is completed	The agreement is regarded as a service if one of the following conditions are met: • The buyer is able to specify the major structural elements of the design before or during construction; or • The buyer acquires and supplies the construction materials. Otherwise, the sale is only recognised on the delivery of the completed real estate since the buyer does not obtain control or significant risks and rewards of ownership before delivery. This is when the entity provides services together with the construction material.
Customer loyalty awards	The reward credit should be allocated as discussed under *22.4.3*.

Example 22-5: Risks and rewards – Sale of goods

St Petersburg sells televisions to customers who have 60 days to pay. The customer takes the television home on conclusion of the sale, on day one. St Petersburg retains legal title to the television for the period until the customer settles the account to protect itself against non-payment of the account. St Petersburg has a very strict credit policy and as a result has only immaterial cases of non-payment. In this situation, St Petersburg could recognise the sale on day one as the risks it has retained are insignificant, and the other criteria detailed above for recognition of the sale have been met.

22.5.2   Retention of risks and rewards

An entity should not recognise revenue if it retains significant risks of ownership. The Standard provides the following examples of where an entity may retain significant risks and rewards of ownership:

Table 22-2: Examples of risks and rewards retained

Entity retains an obligation for unsatisfactory performance not covered by normal warranties.
Receipt of the revenue from a particular sale is contingent on the buyer selling the goods.
Goods are shipped subject to installation and the installation is a significant part of the contract that has not yet been completed.
Buyer has the right to rescind the purchase for a reason specified in the sales contract, or at the buyer's sole discretion without any reason, and the entity is uncertain about the probability of return.

Where an entity allows for returns for any reason, it should recognise a provision (refer to *Chapter 15*) against revenue for such returns, because the risks the entity has retained are insignificant.

22.6   Rendering of services

22.6.1   Recognition

Where an entity provides services to a customer, as opposed to selling goods, the Standard requires it to recognise revenue by reference to the stage of completion of the transaction at the reporting date. This is sometimes referred to as the 'percentage of completion method'. Refer to *22.8* for guidance on the percentage of completion method.

The Standard states that the outcome of a transaction where services are rendered can be estimated reliably when all the following conditions are satisfied:

- The amount of revenue can be measured reliably.
- It is probable that the economic benefits associated with the transaction will flow to the entity.
- The stage of completion of the transaction at the reporting date can be measured reliably.
- The costs incurred for the transaction and the costs to complete the transaction can be measured reliably.

The Standard provides the following examples on the application of the recognition of revenue when rendering services.

Table 22-3: Rendering of services recognition guidance

Nature of transaction	Recognition guidance
Installation fees	Recognition is based on the stage of completion unless the installation is incidental to the sale of a product.
Servicing fees included in the price of a product	Any identifiable amount for subsequent service must be deferred and recognised over the period of the service. The amount deferred is the expected cost of the service plus a reasonable profit.
Advertising commission	Media commissions are recognised when the advertisement or commercial appears before the public. Production commissions are recognised based on the stage of completion.
Insurance agency commissions	Recognise revenue on the effective commencement or renewal dates if no further service is required by the agent. If further service is required, the commission is deferred over the period the policy is in force.
Admission fees for artistic performances, banquets or special events	Recognise revenue when the event occurs. Subscriptions for a number of events are allocated based on the performance of each event.
Tuition fees	Recognise revenue over the period of instruction.
Initiation, entrance, and membership fees	Recognition depends on the nature of the service rendered. Revenue is recognised when no significant uncertainty of collection exists, when all other services or products are paid for separately, or a separate annual subscription is applied. Otherwise, revenue is recognised on a basis that reflects the timing, nature and value of the benefits provided.

The Standard provides the following examples on the application of the recognition of revenue in franchising arrangements.

Table 22-4: Franchise fees recognition guidance

Nature of franchise fees	Recognition guidance
Supply of equipment and other tangible assets	Revenue is recognised at the fair value of the assets sold when the items are delivered or title passes.
Supply of initial or subsequent services	Recognise revenue for continuing services when the service is rendered, whether part of the initial or a separate fee. When the separate fee does not cover the cost plus a reasonable profit for such fees, a portion of the initial fee is allocated to the continuing fees.
	A part of the initial fee is also deferred if the agreement provides for the delivery of goods below the normal selling price. The initial fee and other obligations must also be allocated to different outlets.
	If there is significant uncertainty as to whether the initial fee will be recovered, these fees are recognised on a cash basis, ie when they are received.
Continuing rights and other services in the agreement	Recognise revenue as services are rendered or the rights used.
Agency transactions	Transactions in which the franchisor acts as agent for which no fees are charged do not give rise to revenue.
Development of customised software	The software developer recognises revenue based on the stage of completion, including post-delivery services.

Example 22-6: Stage of completion – Rendering of services
Stockholm is providing a two-year project management service to a mining company. At the reporting date, the following facts are given:

Total contract price	**1,000,000**
Total costs to date	270,000
Further costs to complete	130,000
Total expected costs	**400,000**

Example 22-6: Stage of completion – Rendering of services *(continued)*

The amount of revenue that should be recognised at reporting date is as follows:

Percentage completion	67.5	(270,000 / 400,000)
Revenue	675,000	(67.5% x 1,000,000)
Cost of sales	270,000	(actual costs incurred)
Gross profit	405,000	

When services are performed by an indeterminable number of acts over a specified period of time, revenue should be recognised on a straight-line basis over the period of the service, unless there is evidence that some other method better represents the stage of completion. If there is one significant act in a contract, revenue should be postponed until this act has been performed.

22.6.2 Uncertainty regarding outcome

When the outcome of the transaction cannot be estimated reliably, revenue should be recognised only to the extent of the expenses recognised and deemed recoverable.

Example 22-7: Uncertainty – Rendering of services

Ankara has a contract for managing a farming project. The fee for this project is CU500,000. Ankara has never completed a contract of this nature, and is unsure how much longer it will take to complete. At the reporting date, the stage of completion is difficult to estimate, but the contract is regarded to be profitable. The information available to date is:

Total costs to date	150,000
Costs to complete	Unsure

The amount of revenue that should be recognised at the reporting date is limited to the costs incurred and is reflected as follows:

Revenue	150,000
Cost of sales	150,000
Gross profit	0

22.7 Construction contracts

Construction contracts are defined as contracts specifically negotiated for the construction of an asset or a combination of assets that are closely inter-related or inter-dependent in terms of their design, technology and function, or their ultimate purpose or use.

22.7.1 Reliable measurement

The recognition of revenue on construction contracts depends on whether the outcome of the construction contract could be reliably estimated. The possibilities are:

- When the outcome of the contract could be estimated reliably, revenue and expenses are recognised respectively by reference to the percentage of completion method (refer to *22.8* for a discussion of the method).

- When the outcome of a construction contract cannot be estimated reliably, revenue is only recognised to the extent of contract costs incurred that will be recoverable. Contract costs are recognised as an expense in the period in which they are incurred.
- When it is probable that total contract costs will exceed total contract revenue, the expected loss must be recognised immediately as an expense with a corresponding provision for an onerous contract (refer to *Chapter 15*).

22.7.2 Separate or combined recognition

Revenue recognition is normally applied to each construction contract separately.

However, the guidance could be applied to separate identifiable components of a single contract, or a group of contracts, based on the substance of the contract or group of contracts.

22.7.2.1 Separation of a single contract

Different assets in a single contract should, however, be separated when the contract meets all of the following criteria:

- A separate proposal was submitted for each asset.
- Each asset has been subject to separate negotiation, and the contractor and customer are able to accept or reject that part of the contract relating to each asset.
- The costs and revenues of each asset can be identified separately.

22.7.2.2 Combination of contracts

A group of contracts should be treated as a single construction contract when the contract meets all of the following criteria:

- The group of contracts is negotiated as a single package.
- The contracts are so closely inter-related that they are, in effect, part of a single project with an overall profit margin.
- The contracts are performed concurrently or in a continuous sequence.

The Standard provides the following examples of the application of the recognition of revenue in franchising arrangements.

22.7.3 Agreements for the construction of real estate

Where the entity enters into an agreement with buyers for the construction of real estate before construction is completed, the agreement is only regarded as a construction or service contract (ie to which the percentage of completion should be applied) if one of the following conditions are met:

- The buyer is able to specify the major structural elements of the design before or during construction; or
- The buyer acquires and supplies the construction materials, while the reporting entity only provides, for example labour (rendering of service, refer to *22.6*).

Otherwise the agreement is regarded as a sale as explained in *Table 22-1*.

👁 If an agreement for the construction of real estate is performed on property owned by the client, the agreement is usually regarded as a construction contract.

If one or both of the following questions can be answered in the positive to the question of 'contractually what will happen if the contract is cancelled?', the contract is probably a construction contract in terms of *22.7.3*:

- Does the work-in-progress transfer to the client?
- Is the construction entity entitled to the revenue from the work completed?

22.8   Percentage of completion method

There are various methods that can be used to determine the percentage of completion (or stage of completion) of a construction contract. Possible methods include:

- The proportion of costs incurred in relation to the estimated total costs. Costs incurred for work performed to date do not include pre-payments or other costs that relate to future activity.
- Surveys of work performed.
- Completion of a specified physical proportion of the work in terms of the contract.

In determining the percentage of completion, an entity must use whatever method it believes measures the work performed most reliably. Progress payments and advances received from customers often do not reflect the work performed.

The following should be taken into account when determining the percentage of completion:

- An entity must recognise costs that relate to future activity on the transaction or contract (such as for materials or pre-payments) as an asset, if it is probable that the costs will be recovered.
- An entity must immediately recognise as an expense any costs whose recovery is not probable.
- If the collectability of an amount already recognised as contract revenue is no longer probable, the entity must recognise the uncollectible amount as an expense rather than as an adjustment of the amount of contract revenue.

If it is no longer probable that an amount already recognised as contract revenue will be collectable, the entity must recognise the uncollectible amount as an expense rather than as an adjustment of the amount of contract revenue.

22.9   Interest, royalties and dividends

Interest, royalties and dividends should be recognised as stated in *Table 22.5* when the normal recognition criteria are met:

- It is probable that the economic benefits associated with the transaction will flow to the entity.
- The revenue amount can be measured reliably.

Table 22-5: Recognition of interest, royalties and dividends

Interest must be recognised using the effective interest method.
Royalties must be recognised on an accrual basis in accordance with the substance of the relevant agreement.
Dividends must be recognised when the shareholder's right to receive payment is established.

22.9.1   Interest

Interest is recognised using the effective interest method. Refer to *Chapter 17.8.3* for an explanation of this method of calculation.

Example 22-8: Interest revenue

Paris loans CU100 million to one of its clients. It will get back CU130 million at 31 December 20X3. No interest payments will be made during the three years.

Required
Determine the journal entry for the year ending 31 December 20X1.

Suggested solution
Under the effective interest rate method, it will have to account for the effective interest on the loan as follows:

Amortisation schedule

CU thousands	Interest	Balance
1 January 20X1	-	100,000
31 December 20X1	9,139	109,139
31 December 20X2	9,975	119,114
31 December 20X3	10,886	130,000

The rate of 9.14% is calculated by determining the IRR of an outflow of CU100 million at the beginning of year 1, and an inflow of CU130 million at 31 December 20X3.

The required journal entry at 31 December 20X1 is:

Dr	Loan (SFP)	9,139	
Cr	Interest received (SCI)		9,139

22.9.2   Royalties

Royalties are recognised on an accrual basis, in accordance with the substance of the relevant agreement. As a practical matter, this might be on a straight-line basis over the duration of the agreement. The appendix to the Standard clarifies that an assignment of rights for a fixed fee or non-refundable guarantee under a non-cancellable contract that allows the licensee to exploit the rights freely where no remaining obligations to perform exists, is in substance a sale, and should be treated as a sale. When licence fees or royalties are contingent on the occurrence of a future event, the revenue is only recognised when it is probable that the revenue will be received, which is normally when the event occurs.

Example 22-9: Royalty revenue

London sells the exclusive rights to one of its novels to an internet company for two years for an amount of CU500,000. The internet company will publish it online for its users. It is unclear how many users will access the book during the two years as the internet company does not track its users.

London must recognise the revenue over the two years on a straight-line basis, ie CU250,000 revenue per year.

22.9.3   Dividends

Dividends must be recognised when the shareholders' right to receive payment is established.

Example 22-10: Dividend revenue

Madrid owns shares in Glasgow. Madrid has a 31 December reporting date. Glasgow's management proposed a dividend on 30 November 20X1; its shareholders approved the dividend at the annual general meeting held on 21 January 20X2.

In the jurisdiction Glasgow operates, only shareholders may legally authorise payment of dividends.

Required

Should Madrid recognise the dividend revenue and the related dividend receivable at 31 December 20X1?

Suggested solution

No, as Glasgow is only legally bound to pay the dividends on 21 January 20X2. Glasgow's shareholders have an alternative not to pay the dividend, or pay a different amount. Therefore, Madrid will not be able to recognise the dividend revenue, and the related dividend receivable at 31 December 20X1. It may, however, disclose it in its notes.

Madrid may recognise the dividend revenue, and the related dividend receivable in its accounts on the 21 January 20X2, as this is the date the shareholders have an unconditional legal right to receive the dividends.

22.10   Disclosure

22.10.1   General disclosures about revenue

The Standard requires the following to be disclosed:

- The accounting policies related to the various items of revenue.
- The method used to determine the stage of completion of transactions involving the rendering of services.
- The amount of each category of revenue recognised during the period, showing separately, at a minimum, revenue arising from:
  - The sale of goods.
  - The rendering of services.
  - Interest.
  - Royalties.
  - Dividends.

- Commissions.
- Government grants.
- Any other significant types of revenue.

22.10.2   Disclosures relating to revenue from construction contracts

The Standard requires the following to be disclosed:

- The amount of contract revenue recognised as revenue in the period.
- The methods used to determine the contract revenue recognised in the period.
- The methods used to determine the stage of completion of contracts in progress.
- The gross amount due from customers for contract work as an asset.
- The gross amount due to customers for contract work as a liability.

22.11   Summary

- Revenue results from the sale of goods, services being rendered, construction contracts by the contractor, and the use by others of assets, yielding interest, royalties or dividends.
- The following are excluded from this chapter and dealt with elsewhere: leases *(Chapter 18)*, dividends from equity accounted entities *(Chapters 9 and 10)*, changes in fair value of financial instruments *(Chapter 17)*, initial recognition and subsequent re-measurement of biological assets *(Chapter 29)*, and initial recognition of agricultural produce *(Chapter 29)*.
- Measurement of revenue must be the fair value of the consideration received, taking into account any possible trade discounts or rebates, including volume rebates and prompt settlement discounts.
- Deferred payment terms result in a financing transaction where the fair value of the consideration is the present value of all future receipts. The difference is recognised as interest revenue.
- Sale of goods is recognised when: 1) the significant risks and rewards have passed, 2) no managerial involvement remains, 3) the amount of revenue and costs can be measured reliably, 4) it is probable that benefits will flow to the entity, and 5) costs can be measured reliably.
- Rendering of services is recognised based on the stage of completion basis when: 1) the amount can be estimated reliably, 2) there is a probable inflow of benefits, 3) the stage of completion can be measured, and 4) costs incurred and that will be incurred can be estimated reliably. If the outcome is unreliable, then revenue should be recognised to the extent of the expenses incurred.
- Award credits or other customer loyalty plan awards need to be accounted for separately, and therefore reduce the amount of revenue that is recognised upfront. The revenue related to the award credits is deferred and recognised when the awards are redeemed.
- Interest, royalties and dividends are recognised when it is probable an inflow of economic benefits will occur and it can be measured reliably. Interest is recognised using the effective interest method, royalties on an accrual basis per the agreement, and dividends when the right to receive the dividend is established.

- Construction contracts result in revenue when it can be estimated reliably, and an inflow of economic benefits is probable. Revenue is then recognised based on the stage of completion. An estimation of the stage of completion requires estimates of future costs, billings and time frames to completion.
- For construction contracts, revenue recognition is usually applied to each contract, but it may be necessary to apply it to each separately identifiable component of a contract, or group of contracts collectively.

Chapter 23
Government grants

Contents

23.1   Scope

The guidance applies to the accounting for all government grants, except for the following:

- Government grants in the form of government assistance that cannot reliably be valued.
- Transactions with government that cannot be distinguished from an entity's normal trading transactions.

Disclosures, and not recognition and measurement, are provided for government assistance (refer to 23.5). Government assistance excludes benefits available in determining taxable profit or tax loss, or the income tax liability. Such income tax benefits include tax exceptions or holidays, tax credits, accelerated write-offs and lower income tax rates. Refer to *Chapter 21* for guidance in accounting for taxes based on income.

23.2   Definitions

A **government grant** is assistance by government in the form of a transfer of resources to an entity, in return for past or future compliance with specified conditions, relating to the operating activities of the entity.

Government assistance is action by government designed to provide an economic benefit specific to an entity or range of entities qualifying under specified criteria. This could be in the form of free advice or consultation, guarantees, and low interest rate loans.

> Government grants must be reliably measurable, otherwise they are regarded as government assistance.

The recognition and measurement principles apply to assistance from government included in the definition of government grants, while certain disclosure is required for government assistance as defined. The crucial distinction is that a government grant is a transfer of resources. If that transfer of resources cannot be measured reliably, it will fall under the definition of government assistance.

23.3   Recognition and measurement

The recognition and measurement of government grants is determined by the performance conditions included (refer to *Table 23-1*). When no performance obligation is included, the grants are recognised as income when the proceeds are receivable. However, when future performance conditions are included, the grants are only recognised as income when the performance conditions are met.

> Recognition is based on the performance conditions.

Deferred income is recognised as a liability for grants received for which the recognition of income is deferred as the performance conditions have not yet been fulfilled.

Table 23-1: Performance conditions and related recognition guidance

Performance conditions	Recognition guidance
No specified future performance conditions imposed.	Recognise income when the grant proceeds are receivable.
Specified future performance conditions imposed.	Recognise income only when the performance conditions are met.
Grants received before the above revenue recognition criteria are satisfied.	Recognise as a liability.

Non-monetary grants must be measured at fair value. Such grants are measured at the fair value of the asset received or receivable. However, assistance that cannot be measured reliably is excluded.

Example 23-1: Recognition and measurement of a government grant

Istanbul is an ultimate holding company of a diverse group of entities, with a reporting date of 31 December. On 1 January 20X1, Istanbul decided to build a nursery school for its employees' children. Government approved a cash grant of CU500,000 provided the building is completed by 31 March 20X2, and is used as a nursery school for at least 10 years. A pro-rata portion is refundable if the building is not used as a nursery school for 10 years. Istanbul received the cash grant on 1 November 20X1. It completed the school on 31 January 20X2 at a total cost of CU1,000,000, and immediately started to use the building as a nursery school. CU800,000 of the amount was incurred at 31 December 20X1.

Required

Provide the journal entries to account for the cost of the nursery school and the government grant for the financial periods ending 31 December 20X1 and 31 December 20X2. Assume buildings are depreciated over 20 years.

Suggested solution

1 November 20X1

Dr	Bank (SFP)	500,000	
Cr	Deferred government grant – liability (SFP)		500,000

Recognise government grant subject to future performance.

31 December 20X1

Dr	Property, plant and equipment (SFP)	800,000	
Cr	Bank / Creditor (SFP)		800,000

Recognise cost of nursery school incurred to date.

31 January 20X2

Dr	Property, plant and equipment (SFP)	200,000	
Cr	Bank / Creditor (SFP)		200,000

Recognise additional cost to complete the nursery school.

Example 23-1: Recognition and measurement of a government grant *(continued)*		
31 December 20X2		
Dr Depreciation (P/L)	45,833	
Cr Accumulated depreciation (SFP)		45,833
Accounting for the depreciation charge for 11 months.		
(CU1,000,000/ 20 years) x 11/12 months)		
Dr Deferred government grant – liability (SFP)	45,833	
Cr Government grant income (P/L)		45,833
Recognition of government grant.		
Recognise the deferred grant income over 10 years – 11 months in current year (CU500,000/10 years x 11/12 months).		

23.4   Disclosure related to government grants

The following disclosure is required:

- The nature and amounts of government grants recognised.
- Unfulfilled conditions and other contingencies attached to government grants that have been deferred as liabilities.

23.5   Disclosure related to government assistance

An entity must disclose indications of other forms of government assistance from which it has directly benefited.

23.6   Summary

- Income tax benefits are excluded from the scope.
- Grants are measured at the fair value of the assets received or receivable.
- Grants without future performance conditions should be recognised when proceeds are receivable. However, if there are conditions, they should only be recognised when the conditions are met.

Chapter 24
Borrowing costs

Contents

24.1   Definition

Borrowing costs are interest and other costs that an entity incurs in connection with the borrowing of funds.

Types of borrowing costs include:
- Interest expense calculated using the effective interest method.
- Finance charges in respect of finance leases.
- Exchange differences arising from foreign currency borrowings to the extent that they are regarded as an adjustment to interest costs.

24.2   Recognition

Borrowing costs must be expensed in profit or loss in the period in which they are incurred.

24.3   Disclosure

There are no specific disclosures relating to borrowing costs.

Refer to *Chapter 3* for the disclosure of total finance costs and *Chapter 17* for the disclosure of total interest expense relating to financial liabilities not carried at fair value.

24.4   Summary

- Borrowing costs are interest and other costs arising from an entity's financial liabilities and finance lease obligations.
- All borrowing costs should be expensed, even when the costs relate to an asset that takes a substantial period of time to construct as there is no option to capitalise borrowing costs.

Chapter 25
Foreign currency translation

Contents

25.1   Scope

The Standard provides guidance on foreign currency translation, and more specifically specifies how to account for the following:

- Incorporation of foreign currency transactions, and the resulting balances in the reporting entity's accounts.
- Incorporation of foreign operations, ie subsidiaries, branches, associates, or JVs into the individual or consolidated financial statements.
- Translation of financial statements into a presentation currency other than its functional currency.

Special guidance is also provided for the identification and changes in functional currency, and the treatment of exchange rate differences relating to net investments in foreign operations.

Guidance on the treatment of hedge accounting of foreign currency risks and the foreign translation guidance applicable to financial instruments that derive their value from the change in a specified foreign exchange rate (eg foreign currency forward exchange contracts) is provided in *Chapter 17* on financial instruments.

25.2   Definitions

The following definitions are provided in the Standard:

- **Functional currency** is defined as the currency of the primary economic environment in which the entity operates.
- **Monetary items** are defined as units of currency held and assets and liabilities to be received or paid in a fixed or determinable number of units of currency.
- **Presentation currency** is defined as the currency in which the financial statements are presented.
- The Standard does not explicitly define a **foreign operation**, but it refers to it as subsidiaries (refer to *Chapter 5*), branches, associates (refer to *Chapter 9*), or JVs (refer to *Chapter 10*) of the reporting entity.

25.3   Determination of functional currency

General purpose financial statements are normally prepared in the functional currency of an entity. Every entity must identify and disclose its functional currency, even if financial statements are not prepared in the functional currency. The functional currency is defined as the currency of the primary economic environment in which the entity operates. In principle, this is the one in which the entity primarily generates and expends cash. Judgement is applied to determine the functional currency based on primary and secondary factors.

25.3.1   Primary factors

The functional currency is thus based on both an assessment of where revenue is predominantly generated, and where expenses related to that revenue are incurred.

Based on the revenue factors, the functional currency is determined by considering the following:

- The currency that predominantly **influences sales prices**, which will normally be the currency in which sales prices are denominated and settled.
- The currency of the **country whose competitive forces** and regulations mainly determine the sales prices of its goods and services.

In assessing expenses, the functional currency is based on the currency that **mainly influences labour, material, and other costs** of providing goods or services. This is normally the currency in which such costs are denominated and settled.

These are referred to as the primary indicators.

25.3.2   Secondary factors

Additional factors may be considered in determining the functional currency. These are referred to as secondary indicators, and are the following currencies:

- The currency in which funds are generated to finance the activities of the entity. This includes equity and debt transactions.
- The currency in which receipts from operating activities are usually retained, such as bank, investments, and property.

These secondary indicators are employed, for example, when the functional currency decision is ambiguous due to more than one dominant currency influencing the revenue and cost lines of the entity, or where consideration of the primary indicators is not conclusive in the determination of the functional currency.

25.3.3   Functional currency of a foreign operation

Determine whether the functional currency of a foreign operation is different from that of the reporting entity.

The functional currency of a foreign operation (ie subsidiaries, branches, associates, or JVs) is determined in relation to the reporting entity. Therefore, to determine the functional currency of a foreign operation, and to assess whether it is different from the reporting entity, the following criteria and questions must also be considered, in addition to the primary and secondary indicators:

- The degree of autonomy of the foreign operation. Are the activities of the foreign operation carried out as an extension of the reporting entity or with a significant degree of autonomy?
- The extent of the transactions between the parent and the foreign operation. Are transactions with the reporting entity a high or a low proportion of the foreign operation's activities?
- The degree to which the cash flows of the foreign operation impacts the cash flows of the reporting entity. Do the cash flows from the activities of the foreign operation affect the cash flows of the reporting entity directly, and are they readily available for remittance?

- The funding needed from the reporting entity. Are the cash flows from the activities of the foreign operation sufficient to service existing and normally expected debt obligations without having to resort to the reporting entity to secure additional funding?

Based on these additional criteria, a foreign entity whose activities appear to be integrated with that of the reporting entity will normally have the same functional currency. A foreign operation whose activities are independent will normally determine its functional currency separately.

Example 25-1: Foreign branch

Seoul has a foreign branch that is responsible for the sale of Seoul's products in the foreign country. The transfer price for the goods is similar to the normal transfer price that is applicable to third parties that sell the product in other countries. The foreign branch is responsible for its own bank account. It funds itself from loans obtained in the foreign country at inception, and cash flows from its operations in the foreign currency.

Based on the criteria above, it seems that the foreign branch operates independently from Seoul and should therefore determine its functional currency independently from Seoul.

25.4   Change in the functional currency

A functional currency can only be changed when the underlying transactions, events and conditions on which the functional currency was based have changed. The change could be as a result of a shift in the relative currency that has the main influence on the sales prices of goods or services supplied by the entity, or a change in the currency that influences the labour, material and other costs of providing the goods and services.

> No profit or loss is recognised since all items are translated at the same rate.

All items are translated to the new functional currency using the foreign currency exchange rate at the date of the change. The effect of a change in functional currency is thus always applied prospectively. Since all items (ie income, expenses, assets, liabilities and equity) in the financial statements are translated at the same rate, no profit or loss results. The translated amounts for non-monetary items become their new historical cost.

25.5   Translation of foreign currency transactions and balances

25.5.1   General

The basic principle is that foreign currency transactions are recorded on the transaction date and restated subsequently for any changes in the relevant foreign currency exchange rate.

The translation procedures are only applicable to entities whose functional currency is not the currency of a hyperinflationary economy. If an entity's functional currency is that of a hyperinflationary economy, the guidance in *Chapter 26* must be followed.

The financial performance, cash flows and position of an entity is translated (refer to *Figure 25-1*) to a different presentation currency as follows:

- **Assets and liabilities**, irrespective of whether they are monetary or non-monetary, are translated at the closing rate at the reporting date.
- **Income and expenses** are translated at foreign currency exchange rates at the respective transaction dates.
- **Cash inflows** and **outflows** are translated at foreign currency exchange rates at the respective transaction dates.
- **Equity items** at the dates of the transaction, including dividends deducted in equity.
- The resulting **exchange differences** are recognised as other comprehensive income in equity commonly referred to as a foreign currency translation reserve (FCTR). The amount is never subsequently reclassified to profit or loss.

Figure 25-1: Applicable foreign currency exchange rates

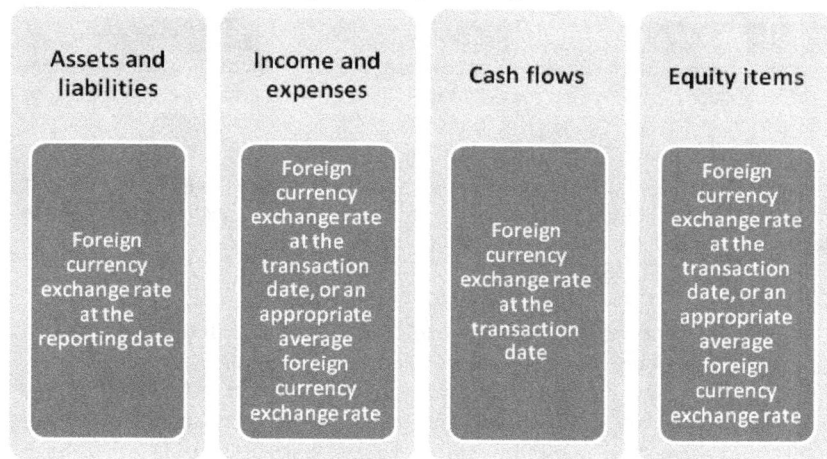

Assets and liabilities	Income and expenses	Cash flows	Equity items
Foreign currency exchange rate at the reporting date	Foreign currency exchange rate at the transaction date, or an appropriate average foreign currency exchange rate	Foreign currency exchange rate at the transaction date	Foreign currency exchange rate at the transaction date, or an appropriate average foreign currency exchange rate

The translation must be done for each reporting date presented. Therefore, comparatives should also be translated at the comparative period(s) foreign currency exchange rates. The rate used for translating the comparative(s) will differ from the current period, unless the rates are pegged or remained unchanged over the period(s).

25.5.2   Initial recognition

A foreign currency transaction is translated into the functional currency of the reporting entity by applying the spot exchange rate ruling at the transaction date.

Figure 25-2: Initial translation

The date of a transaction is the date on which the transaction qualifies for recognition in terms of the Standard. A rate that approximates the actual rate is often used, provided that the foreign currency exchange rate does not fluctuate significantly. An approximate rate could include weekly or monthly average rates. Where the average rate does not approximate the actual rate ruling on the transaction date, the actual rate should be used.

Example 25-2: Date of foreign currency exchange rate to be used

Roma, with a functional currency of CU imports goods from the USA. Goods of USD10,000 were imported. The shipping date is determined to be 1 March 20X1, and the goods were available for collection by the entity on 1 August 20X1. The foreign currency exchange rates at the shipping and delivery dates were USD1=CU7.78 and USD1=CU7.24, respectively.

If the shipping was made free-on-board, the transaction must be recognised on 1 March 20X1 at CU77,800 (USD10,000 x CU7.78). If the shipping was made cost-insurance-freight, the transaction must be recognised on 1 August 20X1 at CU72,400 (USD10,000 x CU7.24).

25.5.3   Subsequent reporting periods

Monetary and non-monetary items (refer to *Figure 25-3*) are translated at different rates at the reporting date (refer to *Figure 25-4*). Foreign currency monetary items are translated by using the closing rate. Foreign currency non-monetary items are translated differently depending on whether they are recognised at historical cost or fair value. If they are recognised at historical cost, the non-monetary items are translated using the foreign currency exchange rate at the date of the original transaction. If the non-monetary items are measured at fair value in a foreign currency, the foreign currency exchange rate at the date when the fair value was determined is used.

Figure 25-3: Monetary and non-monetary items

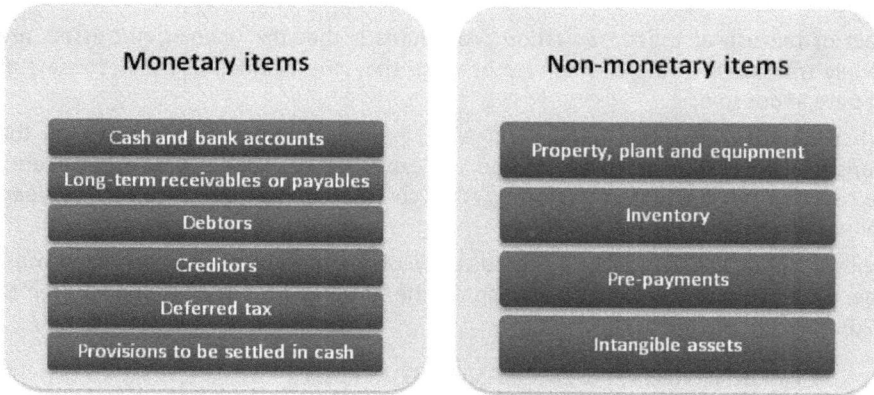

Monetary items	Non-monetary items
Cash and bank accounts	Property, plant and equipment
Long-term receivables or payables	Inventory
Debtors	Pre-payments
Creditors	
Deferred tax	Intangible assets
Provisions to be settled in cash	

No further guidance is provided for items such as pre-payments and deferred tax. In full IFRS, deferred tax and provisions to be settled in cash are monetary items, while pre-payments are non-monetary items.

Figure 25-4: Applicable translation rates

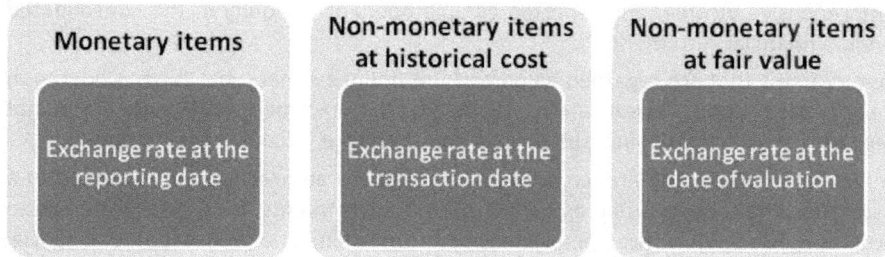

Monetary items	Non-monetary items at historical cost	Non-monetary items at fair value
Exchange rate at the reporting date	Exchange rate at the transaction date	Exchange rate at the date of valuation

25.5.4 Translation differences

All foreign currency exchange differences on the translation and settlement of transactions are recognised in profit or loss. There are exemptions for certain exchange differences related to a net investment in a foreign entity, discussed in 25.6.

When gains and losses on non-monetary items are presented in other comprehensive income, the related exchange component is also presented in other comprehensive income. For example, a post-employment defined benefit plan obligation to be settled in a foreign currency or cash flow hedge accounting.

The resulting exchange differences may be due to:

- The translation of income and expenses at the foreign currency exchange rates at the dates of the transactions, and certain related assets and liabilities at the closing rate.

- The translation of the opening net assets at a closing rate that differs from the previous closing rate.

The impact of the use of these translation procedures is that the opening net assets are automatically translated to the closing rate because they are included in the net assets at reporting date, if not sold.

A rate that approximates the foreign currency exchange rates at the dates of the transactions may be used to translate income and expenses, provided the foreign currency exchange rates do not fluctuate significantly. This could be an **average rate for the year, month, or week**.

Entities whose functional currency is the currency of a hyperinflationary economy must follow the translation procedures prescribed in the chapter on *Hyperinflation* (refer to *Chapter 26*).

25.6 Translation of a net investment in a foreign operation

Foreign operations are translated for consolidation, equity accounting or fair valuation purposes by translating **all** assets and liabilities, but not equity, at the foreign currency exchange rates, at the reporting date.

25.6.1 Consolidated and individual financial statements

Exchange differences that arise on the translation of monetary items that are deemed to form part of a reporting entity's net investment in a foreign operation are reclassified to other comprehensive income, and reported as a component of equity in the **consolidated and individual financial statements**.

The monetary items that are regarded as part of the net investment in a foreign operation will be eliminated upon consolidation. However, the exchange differences are not eliminated, but form part of the investment and are, therefore, accounted for in equity.

For example, any exchange difference on non-current loans and receivables extended to a foreign operation that are regarded as part of the net investments, must be transferred to equity, ie recognised in other comprehensive income. In the consolidated financial statements, the amounts will not be eliminated (refer to *Example 25-3*).

25.6.2 Separate financial statements

Exchange differences that arise on the translation of monetary items that are deemed to form part of a reporting entity's net investment in a foreign operation are recognised in profit or loss in the **separate** financial statement of the reporting entity.

Example 25-3: Net investment in a foreign subsidiary – Separate and consolidated financial statements

Yokohama, with CU as its functional currency, has a net investment in a foreign subsidiary in Europe. A loan granted to the foreign subsidiary of EUR100,000 is regarded as part of the net investment in the foreign subsidiary since there are no fixed repayment terms for the loan, but repayment is expected. The loan was granted when Yokohama obtained a 100% interest in the subsidiary in a previous period. The foreign currency exchange rates applicable for the current year are:

31 January 20X1	EUR1 = CU7.52
31 December 20X1	EUR1 = CU8.02

Required
Provide the journals for the exchange difference in Yokohama's **separate** and **consolidated** financial statements at 31 December 20X1.

Suggested solution
Journal entry in Yokohama's separate accounts
31 December 20X1

Dr	Loan to foreign subsidiary (SFP)	50,000	
Cr	Exchange difference (P/L)		50,000

Recognise the exchange difference in profit or loss.
EUR100,000 x (8.02 - 7.52)

Journal entry in Yokohama's consolidated financial statements

Dr	Exchange difference (P/L)	50,000	
Cr	Exchange difference reserve (Equity/OCI)		50,000

Transfer the exchange difference to other comprehensive income, as an exchange difference reserve in a net investment in a foreign operation (CU100,000 x (8.02 - 7.52)).

> No guidance is provided in the Standard on how to account for the FCTR after a disposal of a subsidiary. The accumulated reserve may, therefore, be transferred to retained earnings or included in the statement of comprehensive income.

25.6.3 Consolidation procedures applicable to foreign operations

A foreign operation is translated by translating all assets and liabilities, irrespective of whether they are monetary or non-monetary, at the foreign currency exchange rate at the reporting date. Thereafter, the normal consolidation or equity accounting procedures are followed. However, certain transactions that may have resulted should be considered separately in performing the consolidation.

25.6.3.1 Deemed net investment in a foreign operation

Certain monetary items that are long-term receivables or payables with a foreign operation, and for which there are no set repayment terms in place, may be considered, in substance, to be part of the net investment of the foreign operation. Settlement must also neither be planned nor likely to occur in the foreseeable future.

In the **consolidated or individual** financial statements, exchange differences on monetary items that are deemed to be part of the net investment of the foreign operation must be recognised in **other comprehensive income** and reported as a **component of equity**. The accumulated exchange differences may not be recognised in profit or loss on disposal of the net investment.

In the **separate financial statements** of the reporting entity or the individual financial statements of the foreign operation exchange, differences arising on a monetary item that is deemed to form part of a reporting entity's net investment in a foreign operation must be recognised in **profit or loss**.

Trade receivables and trade payables are not deemed to form part of the net investment in a foreign operation.

25.6.3.2   Inter-group balances

In the consolidated financial statements, inter-group monetary assets or liabilities cannot be eliminated against the corresponding inter-group liability or asset without taking into account the impact of currency fluctuations that may have occurred. To eliminate them the exchange differences are recognised in the financial statements of the entity whose reporting currency differs from the currency in which the transaction is dominated.

Only the inter-group monetary items are eliminated and not the related exchange differences, and such exchange differences must therefore be shown in the consolidated financial statements. Exchange differences are recognised in profit or loss and are thus included in the consolidated profit or loss with no adjustment, except for the effect of any non-controlling interest.

Exchange differences on inter-group transactions are not eliminated.

25.6.3.3   Goodwill and fair value adjustments

Any goodwill created on the acquisition of a foreign operation and any fair value adjustments to the carrying amounts of assets and liabilities on the date of the acquisition are regarded as assets and liabilities of the foreign operation. Therefore, all the goodwill and fair value adjustment calculations must be performed in the functional currency of the foreign operation and translated at the closing rate as part of the normal translation procedures.

Goodwill and initial fair value adjustments are regarded as belonging to the foreign operation, ie an asset, gain or loss of the foreign operation, and should be translated accordingly.

25.6.3.4   Non-controlling interest

Any portion of the exchange differences resulting from the translation of a foreign operation that is not wholly-owned must be allocated to non-controlling interests.

25.7 Translation to another presentation currency

25.7.1 Selection of presentation currency

An entity may present its financial statements in any currency it wishes. In doing so it translates the information recorded in its functional currency to the presentation currency of its choice. In the preparation of consolidated financial statements, the financial statements and/or information of any individual entity that is prepared in a currency that differs from the selected presentation currency of the group is translated to this selected presentation currency.

> 👁 Although an entity can choose to use any presentation currency, due consideration must be taken of the applicable laws and other requirements of the jurisdiction in which the entity operates.

25.7.2 Translation to a presentation currency

The same principles as translating a foreign operation are applied when translating financial statements from a functional currency into a different presentation currency.

Example 25-4: Translation to a different presentation currency

The condensed statement of financial position of Milan on 31 December 20X1, presented in EUR.

Statement of financial position

	EUR
Property, plant and equipment	30,000
Investments at fair value	20,000
Inventories	15,000
Trade and other receivables	10,000
Cash and cash equivalents	10,000
	85,000
Trade and other payables	(5,000)
Long-term loan	(25,000)
Share capital	(30,000)
Retained earnings	(25,000)
	(85,000)

Required

Translate Milan's statement of financial position to the presentation currency (CU) at 31 December 20X1.

Additional information

The foreign currency exchange rate at 31 December 20X1 was EUR1 = CU7.50.

The share capital was issued when a foreign currency exchange rate of EUR1 = CU6.50 was applicable.

Example 25-4: Translation to a different presentation currency *(continued)*

Retained earnings consist of the retained earnings at 1 January 20X1 of CU85,200, which has been translated over the years at the appropriate foreign currency exchange rates for the respective periods.

The statement of comprehensive income for the year ended 31 December 20X1 was evenly distributed, and the foreign currency exchange rate was relatively stable. The average foreign currency exchange rate for the year ended 31 December 20X1 was EUR1 = CU7.20.

Suggested solution

All assets and liabilities are translated at the closing rate. The share capital is recorded at the historical rate of EUR1 = CU6.50. As the items of income and expenses for the year ended 31 December 20X1 were evenly distributed, the average foreign currency exchange rate for 20X1 would be an appropriate substitute for the actual foreign currency exchange rates' ruling at the transaction dates.

Property, plant and equipment *(EUR30,000 x CU7.50)*	225,000
Investments at fair value *(EUR20,000 x CU7.50)*	150,000
Inventories *(EUR15,000 x CU7.50)*	112,500
Trade and other receivables *(EUR10,000 x CU7.50)*	75,000
Cash and cash equivalents *(EUR10,000 x CU7.50)*	75,000
Total assets	**637,500**
Trade and other payables *(EUR5,000 x CU7.50)*	(37,500)
Long-term loan *(EUR25,000 x CU7.50)*	(187,500)
Share capital *(EUR30,000 x CU6.50)*	(195,000)
Retained earnings – 31 December 20X1 (refer to calculation below)	(178,800)
Foreign currency translation difference (balancing figure)	(38,700)
Total equity and liabilities	**(637,500)**

Calculation of retained earnings

Profit for the year *(EUR13,000 x CU7.20)*	(93,600)
Retained earnings – 1 January 20X1	(85,200)
Retained earnings – 31 December 20X1	(178,800)

The translation difference of CU38,700 is recognised in other comprehensive income as a credit entry to equity, commonly known as the Foreign Currency Translation Reserve.

25.8   Disclosure

Disclose the following for the reporting period:

- Exchange differences recognised in profit or loss, except for those arising on financial instruments measured at fair value through profit or loss.
- Exchange differences recognised and classified in a separate component of equity.
- The presentation currency must be disclosed. When the presentation currency is different from the functional currency, the fact must be stated along with the reason for using a different presentation currency.

When the functional currency of the reporting entity (or a significant foreign operation) changes, the fact and the reason for the change must be disclosed.

25.9   Summary

- Each entity should identify its functional currency, ie the currency of the primary economic environment in which it operates. A change in functional currency is applied prospectively from the date of the change.
- Recording transaction in an entity's functional currency:
  - On initial recognition, an entity must record the transaction by applying the spot rate at the date of the transaction. An average rate may be used, unless there are significant fluctuations in the rate.
  - At reporting date, the entity must translate foreign currency monetary items using the closing rate. Translation of non-monetary items depends on if they are recognised at historical cost or fair value. For non-monetary items measured using historical cost, the exchange rate at the date of the transaction must be used. For non-monetary items measured using fair value, the exchange rate at the date when the fair value was determined must be used.
- Exchange differences are normally recognised in profit or loss. The only exemptions are for monetary items that form part of the investment in foreign operations, and the translation into a different presentation currency.
- Exchange differences arising from a monetary item that forms part of the net investment in a foreign operation are recognised in profit or loss in the financial statements of the individual entities. However, in the consolidated financial statements, such exchange differences are recognised in other comprehensive income.
- Exchange differences on translation to a different presentation currency are recorded in other comprehensive income. This will include the translation of foreign subsidiaries.
- Goodwill arising on the acquisition of a foreign operation is deemed to be an asset of the foreign operation, and translated at the closing rate at the reporting date.
- When a foreign operation is disposed of, any cumulative amount recognised in equity is included in the calculation of the profit or loss, on disposal.

Chapter 26
Hyperinflation

Contents

26.1   Scope

The guidance on hyperinflation applies to all entities whose functional currency (refer to *Chapter 25*) is the currency of a hyperinflationary economy. These entities must adjust their financial statements for the effect of hyperinflation by applying the restatement procedures provided (refer to *26.4*).

26.2   Identification of a hyperinflationary economy

The Standard does not establish an absolute inflation rate to identify a hyperinflationary economy. The identification criteria employed are subjective, and all available information must be considered in making the assessment. The Standard provides five possible indicators on which the assessment is based. However, it should be noted that the assessment can be widened to include other indicators that may be considered relevant. The indicators noted in the Standard are based on the actions of the general population in the economy concerned, and are as follows:

- Wealth is maintained in non-monetary assets or in relatively stable foreign currencies. The general population uses their local currency to purchase other assets such as property, plant and equipment, and inventories, which maintain their value. Such assets are liquidated when cash is required.
- Monetary amounts are not considered in terms of the local currency, but rather in a relatively stable foreign currency or currencies. Generally, one may find that the prices of goods and services are quoted in a stable currency. However, the local currency may be accepted using rates of exchange that are determined on a frequent basis. The acceptance of the local currency by merchants may also be limited, as they generally face the risk that it will depreciate before they replace the goods sold.
- Credit sales and purchase prices compensate for the expected loss of purchasing power during the credit period, even for short periods. This generally manifests itself in high interest charges for the period that the debt is outstanding, or alternatively, the prices are determined in a way that the margins achieved will enable the seller to replace the inventories on sale.
- Interest rates, wages and prices are linked to a price index. In economies of relative stability, interest rates, wages and prices are generally reviewed perhaps on an annual basis. In a hyperinflationary economy, the review of levels of prices occur on a more regular basis. In some instances, merchants may resort to pricing goods and services in a stable currency, which is then converted to the local currency at the rate ruling, at the time of the transaction.
- The cumulative inflation rate over three years is approaching or exceeds the 100 percent mark.

26.3   Measuring unit in the financial statements

The principle of restatement for hyperinflation is that all amounts in the financial statements must be stated in terms of the measuring units which are current at the reporting date. This process entails *revaluing* transactions based on an acceptable index such as a general price index (measure of inflation) that reflects changes in general purchasing power. Comparative amounts and any other information presented are similarly restated.

The presentation currency is the hyperinflation currency in which the financial statements are presented. Specifically, this guidance may not be overcome by selecting a presentation currency that is not in hyperinflation, if the functional currency of the entity is affected by hyperinflation.

Where a general price index is not available or reliable, other measures that are available and reliable, such as foreign currency exchange rates, may be used.

26.4 Procedures for restating financial statements

> ◊ Restatement is applied to historical cost financial statements using a general price index.

Restatement procedures are carried out on all historical amounts reflected in the financial statements of an entity. As the Standard primarily provides for the preparation of historical cost financial statements, most items that are carried on the statement of financial position are stated at historical cost. There are some limited exceptions such as certain biological assets, investment property and financial instruments measured at fair value, at the reporting date.

26.4.1 Statement of financial position

> ◊ Assets and liabilities are restated separately from equity. Equity is the net result of the restated assets and liabilities.

Monetary items consist of money held and items to be received, or paid in money and are not restated (with the exception of the comparative amounts) as they are already shown in terms of the measuring unit that is current at the reporting date. All non-monetary assets and liabilities that are carried at historical cost, at the reporting date, must be restated by applying the general price index.

The restatement procedures are:

- Assets and liabilities (including monetary items) linked by agreement to changes in prices are adjusted in accordance with the agreement and recorded at the adjusted amount. For example, an index-linked debt agreement.
- Non-monetary items carried at current amounts at the reporting date, for example investment property measured at fair value and inventory items measured at fair value less cost to sell, are not restated. These are items recorded at their fair value or recoverable amount. Some non-monetary items are carried at amounts that are current at dates other than that of their acquisition or the reporting date (eg property, plant and

equipment that was revalued at some earlier date). In such cases, the carrying amounts are restated from the date of the revaluation.

- Non-monetary items carried at cost, or cost less depreciation, are adjusted by applying the general price index to both the historical cost and accumulated depreciation. The price index is applied from the date of acquisition and restated every year from the previous index.

Comparative amounts of all the above items, including items measured at fair value and monetary items must be restated using the official inflation index over the period.

After restatement, a non-monetary item must be assessed to determine if the restated amount exceeds the asset's recoverable amount. If the restated amount exceeds the recoverable amount, this is indicative of an impairment of the asset, which must now be recognised in profit or loss to reduce the carrying value of the asset to its recoverable amount (refer to *Chapter 14*).

Special restatement procedures apply to equity. When the hyperinflation adjustments are applied for the first time (in the opening restated statement of financial position), the various components of equity, except retained earnings and any revaluation surplus, are restated by applying the general price index to the date that the capital was contributed, or first arose. In other words, at the end of the period, components of equity are restated by applying the general price index from the beginning of the period or, if the equity arose during the year, the date the component of equity was recognised.

The restated retained earnings amount is a function of all other restatements and is determined after all other restatements have been carried out. When the Standard is applied for the first time, the retained earnings' amount will be the balancing figure with any revaluation surplus that arose in previous periods eliminated in the process.

26.4.2   Statement of comprehensive income and income statement

All amounts in the statement of comprehensive income must also be recorded at the measuring unit that is current at the reporting date. These amounts are therefore restated by applying the general price index from the dates when they were initially recorded. An average rate of inflation may be used, if both general inflation and the recording of income and expenses arose more or less evenly throughout the period. Where the application of an average rate of inflation is deemed inappropriate, more detailed calculations may be necessary. The calculations may need to be carried out using monthly, quarterly or six-monthly averages of the general price index as appropriate. The appropriateness of the measure to be applied is judgmental and will be determined by the extent of inflation faced in the economy.

26.4.3   Statement of cash flows

All items in the statement of cash flows must also be presented in terms of the presentation currency at the reporting date. The various components of the statement of cash flows will be determined based on the restated statement of financial position and the statement of comprehensive income. Where components included in the statement of cash flows are not necessarily separately disclosed in any of these statements, such components are restated using the same procedures as applied to the statement of the financial statements to which they apply.

Example 26-1: Restating financial statements in a hyperinflationary economy

Honolulu's economy is regarded as a hyperinflationary environment. The condensed statement of financial position of Honolulu on 31 December 20X2, presented in local currency of CU before any hyperinflationary adjustments for the year, is as follows:

Statement of financial position (before adjustments for a general price index)

Property, plant and equipment	40,000
Investments at fair value	10,000
Inventories	12,000
Trade receivables	18,000
Cash	10,000
	90,000
Trade payables	(13,000)
Long-term loan	(22,000)
Share capital	(26,000)
Retained earnings	(29,000)
	(90,000)

Required

Translate Honolulu's statement of financial position to the measuring unit current at 31 December 20X2.

Additional information

The measuring unit's general price indices were as follows:

31 December 20X1	1.25
30 September 20X2	1.43
31 October 20X2	1.46
31 December 20X2	1.52
Average for the year	1.36

No property, plant and equipment was purchased during the year and the balance shown is recorded at the measurement unit at the beginning of the year. The investments are recorded at the fair value at the end of the year. Inventories was, on average, purchased three months before the end of the period. Trade receivables are on average outstanding for the last three months, and trade payables for two months. The long-term loan was secured in the previous period and is recorded at the measuring unit at the end of the previous period.

The share capital and retained earnings at the beginning of the period are recorded at the measuring unit at the end of the previous year. Retained earnings consist of the retained earnings at the beginning of the year of CU10,000 and the balance of the profit for the year. The profit was earned evenly throughout the period.

Suggested solution

All assets, liabilities and equity items are translated to the measuring unit at the reporting date.

Example 26-1: Restating financial statements in a hyperinflationary economy *(continued)*

Statement of financial position (after adjustments for a general price index)

Property, plant and equipment *(CU40,000 x 1.52/1.25)*	48,640
Investments at fair value (fair value at reporting date)	10,000
Inventories *(CU12,000 x 1.52/1.43)*	12,755
Trade receivables (reporting date value)	18,000
Cash (reporting date value)	10,000
	99,395
Trade payables (reporting date value)	(13,000)
Long-term loan (reporting date value)	(22,000)
Share capital *(CU26,000 x 1.52/1.25)*	(31,616)
Retained earnings (calculation below)	(33,395)
	(100,011)
Measurement difference	(616)
	99,395

Calculation of retained earnings at 31 December 20X2

Retained earnings – beginning *(CU10,000 x 1.52/1.25)*	12,160
Profit for the year *(CU19.000 x 1.52/1.36)*	21,235
	33,395

The measurement difference represents a monetary loss of CU616 and is deducted from the profit for the year to create an adjusted profit of CU20,619 (refer to *26.5*), which will in turn reduce retained earnings to 32,779 (33,395 - 616).

26.5 Gain or loss on net monetary position

In inflationary environments, an entity can lose or gain purchasing power, based on the mix of assets and liabilities that it carries and their nature – monetary or non-monetary. Purchasing power is lost when monetary assets exceed monetary liabilities, and the reverse applies when monetary liabilities exceed monetary assets.

The profit or loss on the net monetary position is included in profit or loss. In practice, the profit or loss on the net monetary position is determined as the balancing figure that is required to be processed to the income statement to reconcile the movements in equity from one period to the next, and thus balance the statement of financial position. The amount so determined should take into account the impact of those assets and liabilities linked by agreement to changes in prices.

26.6 Economies ceasing to be hyperinflationary

When an economy ceases to be hyperinflationary, the application of the general price index in the financial statements stops. The carrying amounts recorded in the presentation currency at the previous reporting date become the opening carrying amounts in the reporting entity's subsequent financial statements.

26.7 Disclosure

- The fact that financial statements and other prior period data are restated for changes in the general purchasing power of the presentation currency.
- The identity and level of the price index at the reporting date and changes during the current and previous reporting periods.
- The gain or loss on monetary items.

26.8 Summary

- No absolute rate at which an economy is deemed hyperinflationary is given. Certain indicators are provided, including where:
  - A country's cumulative inflation rate approaches or exceeds 100% over a three-year period;
  - Wealth is maintained in non-monetary assets or foreign currencies; and
  - Where interest rates, wages and prices are linked to a price index.
- All amounts in the financial statements must be stated in terms of the presentation currency at the reporting date. The presentation currency is the hyperinflation currency in which the financial statements are presented. Comparative information and any information presented in respect of earlier periods must also be restated in the presentation currency using the most recent index.
- The restatement of financial statements is performed by using a general price index that reflects changes in general purchasing power. If available, a general price index, which may be produced by the government, is used.
- All assets and liabilities not recorded in the presentation currency at the reporting date must be restated by applying the general price index. Different restatement procedures are provided for monetary and other items. Special restatement procedures apply to equity and retained earnings.
- All amounts in the statement of comprehensive income and statement of cash flows must also be recorded at the presentation currency at the reporting date. These amounts are restated by applying the general price index from the dates when they were recorded.
- The profit or loss on the net monetary position is included in profit or loss. The profit or loss is adjusted by those assets and liabilities linked by agreement to changes in prices.

Chapter 27
Events after the end of the reporting period

Contents

27.1 Scope

This chapter clarifies the principles for recognising, measuring and disclosing events after the reporting date.

27.2 Definition

Events after the end of the reporting period (reporting date) are defined in the Standard as favourable and unfavourable events that occur between the reporting date and the date the financial statements are authorised for issue.

The Standard groups such events into two types:

- **Adjusting events.** Events that provide evidence of conditions that existed at the reporting date.
- **Non-adjusting events.** Events that are indicative of conditions that arose after the reporting date.

Events after the end of the reporting period are defined as all events up to the date when the financial statements are authorised for issue, even if those events occur after the public announcement of certain financial information, such as profit or loss.

27.3 Adjusting events

The amount recognised in the financial statements, as well as the related disclosures are amended to reflect the effect of adjusting events.

Examples of adjusting events after the reporting date that require an entity to adjust the amounts recognised in its financial statements are listed in *Table 27-1*:

Table 27-1: Adjusting events

Nature of event	Recognition guidance
A court case settled after the reporting date	A court case settled after the reporting date may confirm that an entity had a present obligation at the reporting date.
Bankruptcy of a debtor	Bankruptcy of a debtor that occurs after the reporting date usually serves as additional confirmation that the debtor was impaired at the reporting date.
Sale of inventories	The sale of inventories after the reporting date below the carrying value may indicate that the inventories was impaired at the reporting date.
Purchase and sale of assets	Additional information obtained after the reporting date may confirm the purchase or sale prices of the item purchased or sold before the reporting date.
Profit sharing or bonus payments	If a legal or constructive obligation exists at the reporting date to make such payments, all information obtained after the reporting date to confirm the amount of the payments must be included in the measurement.
Errors	Discovery of fraud or errors that reveal the financial statements are incorrect (refer to *Chapter 7*).

Example 27-1: Adjusting event after the end of the reporting date

Vancouver has a reporting date of 31 December. The board of directors approved the financial statements for issue on 28 February 20X2. The financial director was uncertain if the following transaction should be accounted for in the 20X1 financial period:

Debtor under liquidation

It came to the attention of the board that a debtor owing CU2 million was liquidated after 31 December 20X1. The company received notice on 10 January 20X2 that it will only receive 10% of the outstanding amount from the liquidation, therefore only CU200,000. The liquidator indicated that the debtor has had financial difficulties for the past six months.

Required

Advise the financial director of the implications of the transaction in Vancouver's financial statements for the period ending 31 December 20X1.

Suggested solution

The notice received about liquidation after the reporting date provided more information about the fact that the debtor could not pay Vancouver the full amount as at 31 December 20X1. The transaction is seen as an adjusting event that took place after the reporting date as it provided more information about an unrecoverable amount that already existed at 31 December 20X1.

Example 27-1: Adjusting event after the end of the reporting date *(continued)*
Vancouver is therefore required to process the following journal entry for the unrecoverable amount in the 20X1 financial statements:

Dr	Unrecoverable amount (P/L)	1,800,000	
Cr	Debtor (SFP)		1,800,000

Accounting for the unrecoverable amount.

27.4   Non-adjusting events

No adjustments to the amounts recognised in the financial statements are required for non-adjusting events after the end of the reporting period.

Examples of non-adjusting events after the reporting date, where the amounts recognised in its financial statements may not be adjusted, are included in *Table 27-2*.

Table 27-2: Non-adjusting events

Nature of event	Recognition guidance
A decline in market value of an investment	A decline in the market value of an investment after the reporting date does not normally relate to the condition of the investments at the reporting date, but rather reflects circumstances that have subsequently arisen.
A favourable judgement or settlement of a court case delivered after the reporting date	A favourable judgement or settlement of a court case must be disclosed as a contingent asset at the reporting date, except if an agreement was reached before the reporting date that an amount is receivable.

Example 27-2: Non-adjusting event after the end of the reporting date
Toronto has a 31 December reporting date. The financial director was uncertain if the following transactions should be accounted for in the 20X1 financial period:
A warehouse burned down on 1 January 20X2. The fire was caused by an electrical fault that was caused by a lightning storm that afternoon. The damage to inventories was estimated at CU400,000.
Required
Advise the financial director of the implications of the transaction in Toronto's financial statements for the period ending 31 December 20X1.
Suggested solution
As the fire at the warehouse took place after the reporting date, it is seen as a non-adjusting post balance sheet event as it does not provide information about the condition of the warehouse and the value of the inventories at 31 December 20X1.
Toronto should, however, make the following disclosure:
▪ The fact that the warehouse was destroyed in a fire, and the inventories was damaged.
▪ The estimate of an impairment of CU400,000 of inventories.

27.5 Dividends

If an entity declares dividends to holders of its equity instruments after the reporting date, the entity must not recognise those dividends as a liability at the reporting date. The amount of the dividend may, however, be presented as a separate component of retained earnings at the reporting date.

Example 27-3: Dividend declaration after the reporting date

Halifax has a 31 December reporting date. The financial director was uncertain if the following transactions should be accounted for in the 20X1 financial period:

Dividend declared

The board of directors proposed a dividend on 31 December 20X1 based on a fixed dividend policy of 20% of profit after-tax. The company had a past history of complying with this dividend policy every year since incorporation, and a valid expectation was created with the shareholders that a dividend of 20% of profit after-tax will be declared annually. The shareholders approved the dividend of 20% of profit after-tax on 22 February 20X2.

Required

Advise the financial director of the implications of the transaction in Halifax's financial statements for the period ending 31 December 20X1.

Suggested solution

The Standard clearly states that "if an entity declares dividends to holders of its equity instruments after the reporting date, the entity must not recognise those dividends as a liability at the reporting date. The amount of the dividend may be presented as a segregated component of retained earnings at the reporting date".

Therefore, Halifax should not provide for the dividend payment even though a valid expectation was created and there is a formal dividend policy in place requiring a dividend payment.

Halifax should, however, disclose the fact that it declared a dividend after the reporting period.

27.6 Disclosure

27.6.1 Date of authorisation for issue

The date when the financial statements were authorised for issue and who gave that authorisation must be disclosed. If the entity's owners or others have the power to amend the financial statements after issue, that fact must be disclosed.

27.6.2 Non-adjusting events after the reporting date

For each non-adjusting event after the reporting date, the following must be disclosed:

- The nature of the event.
- An estimate of its financial effect, or a statement that such an estimate cannot be made.

The following are examples of non-adjusting events after the reporting date that would generally result in disclosure; the disclosures will reflect information that becomes known after the reporting date but before the financial statements are authorised for issue:

- A major business combination or disposal of a major subsidiary.

- Announcement of a plan to discontinue an operation.
- Major purchases of assets, disposals or plans to dispose of assets, or expropriation of major assets by government.
- The destruction of a major production plant by a fire.
- Announcement or commencement of the implementation of a major restructuring.
- Issues or repurchases of an entity's debt or equity instruments.
- Abnormally large changes in asset prices or foreign exchange rates.
- Changes in tax rates or tax laws enacted or announced that have a significant effect on current and deferred tax assets and liabilities.
- Entering into significant commitments or contingent liabilities, for example, by issuing significant guarantees.
- Commencement of major litigation arising solely as a result of events that occurred after the reporting date.

27.7   Summary

- **Adjusting events.** An entity should adjust amounts recognised in the financial statements to reflect events that provide evidence of conditions that existed at the reporting date.
- **Non-adjusting events.** No adjustment is made for events that are indicative of events that arose after the reporting date. The entity must disclose the nature of the event and an estimate of its financial effect.
- Dividends approved after the statement of financial position date must not be recognised as a liability at year-end.

Chapter 28
Related party disclosures

Contents

28.1   Scope

This chapter sets out the disclosure requirements for transactions with related parties. As dealings and transactions with related parties may have a significant impact on the financial position and results of the reporting entity, a disclosure is necessary in the understanding of financial statements presented.

28.2   Definitions

28.2.1   Related parties

A related party is a person or entity that is related to the entity that is preparing and reporting its financial statements. The Standard defines the reporting entity as related to another party in the following instances.

28.2.1.1   A person

In the case of a person or a close member of that person's family, if that person meets any of the conditions in *Table 28-1*:

Table 28-1: Related persons

Condition	Example
The person is a member of the key management of the reporting entity, or of a parent of the reporting entity.	A director of the parent of the reporting entity.
The person has control or joint control over the reporting entity.	The controlling shareholder of an entity (refer to *Chapter 5*). The person that has joint control in terms of a joint arrangement.
The person has significant influence over the reporting entity.	A shareholder with between 20-50% voting rights in the reporting entity (refer to *Chapter 9*).

28.2.1.2   An entity

The entities in *Table 28-2* are regarded to be related:

Table 28-2: Related entities

Condition	Example
Members of the same group.	Parent, subsidiaries and fellow subsidiaries.
Associates or JVs of the same investor (also associates and JVs of members of a group).	Two associates of an investor. Two joint ventures of the same entity. An associate or JV of the same investor. An associate of one of the fellow subsidiaries of the reporting entity (refer to *Chapter 9* and *10*).

Table 28-2: Related entities *(continued)*

Condition	Example
A post-employment benefit plan for the benefit of employees of either the reporting entity or an entity related to the reporting entity. If the reporting entity is itself is a post-employment benefit plan, the sponsoring employers are deemed to be related to the reporting entity.	An entity that houses a defined benefit plan for a group or any subsidiary of the group (refer to *Chapter 20*).
A separate entity that is controlled or jointly controlled by a person identified as being related to the reporting entity (refer to *28.2.1.1.*).	An entity controlled by the executive manager of the reporting entity (refer to *Chapter 5*).
A separate entity, or any member of a group of which it is a part, provides key management personnel services to the reporting entity or to the parent of the reporting entity (refer to *28.2.1.1.*).	An entity over which the executive manager of the reporting entity has significant influence (refer to *Chapter 9*).
An entity over which a member or close family member of the key management personnel of the entity, or a parent of the entity, that has control or joint control over the reporting entity. An entity over which a person or a close family member of that person has control or joint control and significant influence over the entity.	An entity over which the managing director's wife has control.

In considering a related party relationship, the entity is required to take into consideration the **substance** of the relationship between the parties concerned, and **not merely the legal form of the relationship**. Certain relationships, which might otherwise have been construed as related party relationships because of agreements that have been put in place to meet regulatory or other requirements, do not always necessarily meet the criteria. In addition, some relationships exist merely by coincidence or circumstance, and should not be construed as establishing a relationship between two or more parties that would otherwise have been deemed to be unrelated.

Example 28-1: Joint ventures

Different parties tender for the construction of a road to the local roads department. The department decided to grant the tender to **two** different parties. However, the roads department requires that the parties must adhere to a joint control agreement.

Required
Determine whether the two parties granted the tender are related.

Suggested solution
Normally, jointly controlled parties are related. However, due to the creation of the JV by a regulatory requirement, all the facts must be considered to establish whether the contributing parties are in substance related.

28.2.2   Possible exceptions

The Standard provides examples of relationships that may not necessarily result in a related party relationship:

- Two entities simply because they have a director or other member of key management personnel in common.
- Two **venturers** simply because they share **joint control** over a JV.
- Any of the following simply by virtue of their normal dealings with an entity (even though they may affect the freedom of action of an entity or participate in its decision-making process):
  - Providers of finance.
  - Trade unions.
  - Public utilities.
  - Government departments and agencies.
- A customer, supplier, franchisor, distributor or general agent with whom an entity transacts a significant volume of business, merely by virtue of the resulting economic dependence.

The nature of the relationship should, therefore, be analysed in more detail and the underpinning issues around the relationship taken into account before arriving at a conclusion.

28.2.3   Key management personnel

The Standard defines **key management personnel** as those individuals that have authority and responsibility for planning, directing and controlling the activities of the entity.

This also includes non-executive directors of the entity who may not necessarily have direct control over the entity. The compensation defined includes all benefits provided to employees, including those that are in the form of share-based payments, in return for services rendered.

28.3   Disclosure

28.3.1   Disclosure of parent-subsidiary relationships

The Standard requires that all relationships between a parent and its subsidiaries be disclosed in the financial statements of the entity, irrespective of whether there have been any transactions in the period under review. The entity is also required to disclose the following information in its financial statements:

- Name of its parent.
- The ultimate controlling party but only if this party is different from the parent named above.

If neither the entity's parent nor its ultimate controlling party produces financial statements that are made available for public use, the name of the entity in the group that produces such financial statements should be disclosed.

28.3.2   Disclosure of key management personnel compensation

The reporting entity is required to disclose the compensation paid to key management personnel as one total amount. There is no requirement to disclose compensation based on the five major categories – short-term, post-employment, other long-term, termination and share-based payment benefits.

Example 28-2: Key management personnel

An entity has seven staff members that are regarded to be key management personnel. The total compensation payable to them only needs to be disclosed as one total amount, for example:

Remuneration payable to key management   CU2,400,000

28.3.3   Disclosure of related party transactions

28.3.3.1   Transactions and balances

Transactions with related parties entail the transfer of resources, services or obligations between a reporting entity and a related party, regardless of whether a price is charged.

28.3.3.2   Specific related-party transactions

Specific related party transactions that must be disclosed may include the following:

- Transactions between an entity and its owners.
- Transactions between entities that are both under the common control of a single entity or person.
- Transactions in which an entity or person that controls the reporting entity incurs expenses directly that otherwise would have been borne by the reporting entity.

28.3.3.3   Details to disclose

If an entity has related party transactions, it is required to disclose the nature of the relationship with the related party. It must also provide information about the transactions, outstanding balances and commitments, and other information that may be necessary for the user of the financial statements to obtain an understanding of the potential effect of the relationship on the results achieved as well as the financial position of the reporting entity.

The disclosure of related party transactions is in addition to the disclosure made around the compensation of key management personnel and includes, at a minimum, the following:

- The value of the transaction.
- The balances outstanding.
    - Their terms and conditions, ie any security held, and the nature of the consideration to be provided in settlement.
    - Details of any guarantees given or received.
- Whether any provisions have been raised against uncollectible receivables that are included as part of the balances due to the reporting entity.
- The expense recognised during the period in respect of bad or doubtful debts due from related parties.

Such transactions may include purchases, sales or transfers of goods or services, leases, the provision of guarantees to or by related parties, and the settlement of amounts due to third-parties by the entity on behalf of a related party, or the settlement by a related party of amounts due by the entity to a third party.

The entity is required to show the items described above separately for each of the following categories:

- Entities with control, joint control or significant influence over the entity.
- Entities over which the entity itself has control, joint control or significant influence.
- Key management personnel of the entity or its parent (in aggregate).
- Other related parties.

As a result of the relationships, sometimes trade is undertaken on terms that are more favourable than with third parties. Sometimes, despite this relationship, the terms of trade are such that no preference is offered to the related parties of the entity. In such instances, the entity is permitted to disclose that the transactions undertaken with related parties are on an arm's length basis. However, if such terms cannot be substantiated, the entity is prohibited from making such a statement in its financial statements.

28.3.3.4   State-controlled entities

Entities are exempt from making disclosures around the amount of the transactions, balances outstanding and provisions made against uncollectible debts if the transactions are with:

- The state, including national, regional or local government, if the state has control, joint control or significant influence over the reporting entity.
- Another entity that is a related party because the same state has control, joint control or significant influence over both the reporting entity and the other entity.

> If an entity is controlled by the government (either local, regional or national), such a state-controlled entity should disclose the related party relationship with the state, but need not disclose the nature of the related transactions, any outstanding balances, or provision relating to the amounts with the state or other state-controlled entities.

However, the entity is still required to disclose the parent-subsidiary relationship in the manner that is described earlier in this chapter.

The entity is also permitted to disclose, in aggregate, items that are of a similar nature unless the nature and circumstances around the items is such that their disclosure as separate items will facilitate a better understanding of the effects of related party transactions undertaken on the financial statements reported.

28.4   Summary

- Relationships between parent entities and subsidiaries must always be disclosed, including the ultimate controlling party.
- Disclosure is required of key management's short-term, post-employment, other long-term and termination benefits, and share-based payments as one total amount. Key management personnel are persons responsible for planning, directing and controlling the activities of an entity, and include executive and non-executive directors.
- For transactions between related parties, an entity must disclose:
  - The nature of the relationship;
  - Information about the transactions and outstanding balances necessary to understand the potential impact on the financial statements;
  - The amount of the transaction;
  - Provisions for uncollectible receivables; and
  - Any expense recognised during the period in respect of an amount owed by a related party.

Chapter 29
Specialised activities

Contents

29.1 Scope

The chapter applies to the following activities:

- Agriculture.
- Extractive activities.
- Service concessions.

29.2 Agriculture

29.2.1 Definitions

The following definitions are provided in the Standard:

- **Agricultural activity** is the management, by an entity, of the biological transformation of biological assets for sale into agricultural produce or into additional biological assets.
- **Agricultural produce** is the harvested product of the entity's biological assets. For example, felled trees, harvested fruit or other crop, cattle carcasses, wool or milk.
- **Biological asset** is a living animal or plant. For example, cattle, standing crops, plantations, fruit trees and certain wildlife.
- A **class of biological asset** is a grouping of biological assets of a similar nature and use in an entity's operations.

Table 29-1: Examples of biological assets, agricultural produce and processed produce

Biological assets	Agricultural produce	Produce that are the result of processing after harvest
Sugar cane plantation	Harvested sugar cane	Sugar and molasses
Goats	Goat's milk	Goat's cheese
Chickens (free-range)	Chicken carcasses	Processed chicken pieces
Sheep	Wool	Yarn, carpet
Herb plantation	Picked herbs	Dried herbs
Orange trees	Oranges	Orange juice

29.2.2 Recognition

To recognise a biological asset or agricultural produce, an entity must show that all of the following criteria are met:

- The asset is controlled as a result of a past event.
- It is probable that future economic benefits will flow to the entity.
- The cost or fair value of the asset can be measured reliably without undue cost or effort.

29.2.3 Measurement

Different accounting treatments are applied to biological assets and agricultural produce.

Figure 29-1: Measurement bases of biological assets and agricultural produce

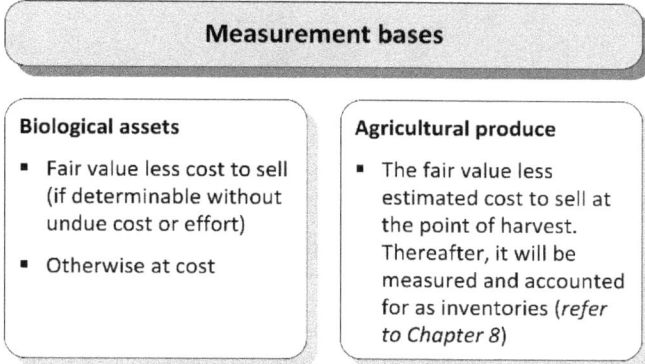

Measurement bases

Biological assets

- Fair value less cost to sell (if determinable without undue cost or effort)

- Otherwise at cost

Agricultural produce

- The fair value less estimated cost to sell at the point of harvest. Thereafter, it will be measured and accounted for as inventories (*refer to Chapter 8*)

For biological assets, the fair value or cost model is applied to each class of biological asset depending on whether fair value is readily determinable without undue cost or effort. The fair value is the default measurement basis for biological assets. However, if the fair value is not readily determinable without undue cost or effort, then the entity may use the cost model. The bases of measurement may, therefore, be different for different classes of biological assets.

Agricultural produce harvested from an entity's biological assets is initially measured at fair value less cost to sell at the point of harvest. The measurement at fair value less cost to sell becomes the cost under the guidance on inventories (refer to *Chapter 8*) or any another applicable guidance in exceptional cases. From the date the agricultural produce is harvested, it is not regarded to be part of the agricultural activities. There is no option to measure agricultural produce at cost.

Example 29-1: Agricultural activities

Standing cane is measured at fair value. The fair value of standing cane at the beginning of the period was CU560,000 and at the reporting date CU450,000. The fair value of agricultural produce harvested during the period was CU420,000, on the respective dates of harvest.

Required

Determine the movement in the fair value of biological assets for the period and provide the journal entries to recognise the transactions and events for the period.

Suggested solution

Determine the movement in fair value of biological assets for the period.

Fair value at the beginning of the period	560,000
Less: Transfer of agricultural produce to inventories during the period at fair value	(420,000)
Biological assets before fair value adjustment at reporting date	140,000
Fair value at the reporting date	450,000
Less: Fair value of biological assets before fair value adjustment	140,000
Fair value movement in biological assets for the period	310,000

Example 29-1: Agricultural activities *(continued)*		
Dr	Biological assets (closing fair value) (SFP)	450,000	
Cr	Biological assets (opening fair value) (SFP)		560,000
Dr	Inventories (agricultural produce) (SFP)	420,000	
Cr	Fair value adjustment (P/L)		310,000
Recognise the agricultural produce harvested and movement in fair value of biological assets for the period.		

29.2.4 Application of the fair value model

At initial measurement biological assets are measured at fair value less cost to sell (for example, the purchase or the birth of a calf). At each subsequent reporting date biological assets are also recognised at fair value less cost to sell. Changes in fair value less cost to sell are recognised in profit or loss.

Agricultural produce must be measured at fair value only at the point of harvest.

> No undue cost or effort exemption applies to the measurement of agricultural produce.

Example 29-2: Fair value model		
During the period under review Toronto purchased four breeding bulls at CU500,000 each. This is deemed to be their fair values at the dates of purchase. During the same period 20 calves were born with a fair value of CU35,000 each.		
Required		
Provide the journal entries to recognise the transactions and events during the period.		
Suggested solution		
Dr	Biological assets (SFP)	2,000,000	
Cr	Bank/Cash (SFP)		2,000,000
Purchase of breeding bulls.		
Dr	Biological assets (SFP)	700,000	
Cr	Fair value adjustment (P/L)		700,000
	(35,000 x 20)		
Recognition of calves born during the period.		

29.2.4.1 Fair value hierarchy

Figure 29-2 provides the fair value hierarchy applicable to biological assets and agricultural produce.

Figure 29-2: Fair value hierarchy

Most reliable

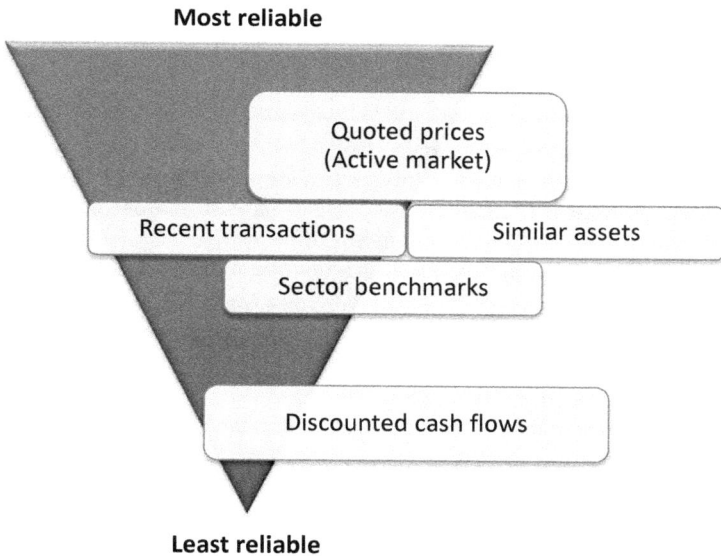

Quoted prices
(Active market)

Recent transactions | Similar assets

Sector benchmarks

Discounted cash flows

Least reliable

29.2.4.2   Active market

When an active market exists for biological assets or agricultural produce in their present location and condition, fair value is based on the quoted price in that market. When an entity has access to different active markets, the quoted prices in the market that the entity expects to transact in should be used.

⎧ ♪ If an active market exists, the quoted price must be used.   ⎫

29.2.4.3   No active market

Where there is no active market, fair value is based on the following:

- Most recent market prices of the asset, provided that there has not been a significant change in economic circumstances.
- Market prices for similar assets with appropriate adjustments.
- Sector benchmarks.

Management should use its judgement to determine the most appropriate base to use in determining the fair value of biological assets.

29.2.4.4   Discounted cash flows

Even though market prices of biological assets in their present condition are not available (based on quoted prices or deemed prices), their fair value may still be readily determinable without undue cost or effort.

An entity must consider whether the present value of expected net cash flows from an asset discounted at appropriate current market rates results in a reliable measure of fair value, provided it is determinable without undue cost or effort.

29.2.4.5   Disclosure – fair value model

The following is disclosed in respect to the fair value model:

- A description of the biological assets.
- The methods and significant assumptions applied in determining the fair value of each category of agricultural produce at the point of harvest and each category of biological assets.
- A reconciliation of changes in the carrying amount of biological assets, which include:
  - Gain or loss on changes in fair value less cost to sell.
  - Purchases.
  - Decreases resulting from harvest or sale.
  - Increases resulting from business combinations.
  - Net exchange differences on the translation of financial statements.
  - Other changes.

  The reconciliation is not required to be presented for prior periods.

29.2.5   Cost model

The cost model is only used when the fair value cannot be readily determined without undue cost and effort.   Under the cost model biological assets are measured at cost less any accumulated depreciation and any accumulated impairment.

> No guidance or examples of cost are given in the Standard. The principles to determine costs for other similar assets such as inventories (refer to *Chapter 8*) may be used to determine the cost of biological assets.
>
> Examples of cost could include the purchase price of livestock and other costs necessary to bring the biological asset to the location and into the condition necessary for it to be capable to produce income.
>
> Therefore, all the costs directly incurred up to the point at which, for example, a hen is able to produce eggs, eg feed, may be capitalised as part of the cost of the biological asset, but after the hen is capable of producing eggs, the costs to maintain the production are expensed.
>
> Similarly, where a plantation (for logging) is grown, all costs to get the plantation ready for logging, such as water and fertiliser, may form part of cost. General overheads, administrative and similar expenses, which cannot be directly allocated to a specific biological asset, are normally expensed.

29.2.5.1   Disclosure – cost model

The following disclosure is required:

- A description of the biological assets.
- An explanation as to why fair value cannot be measured reliably without undue cost or effort.
- The depreciation method used.
- The useful lives or the depreciation rates used.
- The gross **carrying amount** and the accumulated depreciation (aggregated with accumulated impairment losses) at the beginning and end of the period.

29.3 Exploration for and evaluation of mineral resources

This Standard includes activities for the exploration or evaluation of mineral resources.

The Standard states that an entity must use its judgement in developing and applying an accounting policy that specifies which expenditures are recognised as exploration and evaluation assets, and apply this policy consistently. In making these judgements, management must refer to the qualitative characteristics' requirements and guidance in *Chapter 7.2.2* but is exempt from applying the definitions and recognition criteria of assets, liabilities, income and expenses that are discussed in detail in *Chapter 2*.

The Standard gives examples of expenditures that might be included in the initial measurement of exploration and evaluation assets:

- Acquisition of rights to explore.
- Topographical, geological, geochemical and geophysical studies.
- Exploratory drilling, sampling and trenching.
- Activities in relation to evaluating the technical feasibility and commercial viability of extracting a mineral resource.

29.3.1 Initial measurement

Exploration and evaluation assets must be initially measured at cost. If an entity has an obligation to dismantle or remove an item, or to restore the site, such obligations and costs are accounted for in accordance with *Chapter 12: Property, plant and equipment* and *Chapter 15: Provisions and contingencies*.

29.3.2 Measurement after initial recognition

After initial recognition, expenditure on the acquisition or development of exploration and evaluation assets must be accounted for by applying other sections of the Standard (eg intangible assets and property, plant and equipment). Where an obligation to dismantle or remove an item, or to restore a site, these obligations and costs must be accounted for as described in *Chapter 12: Property, plant and equipment* and *Chapter 15: Provisions and contingencies*.

29.3.3 Impairment

Exploration and evaluation assets need to be impaired only when there is an indication of impairment for these assets. The indicators noted in *Chapter 14* should not be applied, but rather these below:

- The period that the company has the right to explore the specific area has or will expire shortly and is not expected to be renewed.
- Further expenditure towards exploration and evaluation of mineral resources in a specific area is neither budgeted nor planned.
- Exploration and evaluation of mineral resources in a mining specific area have not led to the discovery of commercially viable quantities of mineral resources, and the company has thus discontinued further exploration and evaluation in the specific area.
- Where the development of a specific area will proceed, if additional exploration and evaluation costs were to be incurred on this site and these further costs would not likely be recovered from this development or sale.

29.3.3.1   Cash-generating units

The first step in the impairment of a cash-generating unit (CGU) is to identify the unit. To assess exploration and evaluation assets for impairment, the company must develop its own accounting policy to allocate exploration and evaluation assets to cash-generating units or groups of cash-generating units.

29.3.3.2   Measurement and disclosure of impairment

The requirements for measuring impairment losses and the reversal thereof as well as the presentation and disclosures, noted in *Chapter 14*, must be applied to exploration and evaluation assets.

29.4   Service concession arrangements

The operator either recognises a financial asset or an intangible asset, depending on whether the grantor has provided an unconditional guarantee of payment or not. *Note: Accounting guidance is only provided for the operator.*

29.4.1   Definitions

The Standard defines a **service concession arrangement** as an arrangement whereby a government or other public sector body (**the grantor**) contracts with a private operator (**the operator**) to develop (or upgrade), operate and maintain the grantor's infrastructure assets such as sports stadiums, railways, roads, shipping ports, energy distribution networks or hospitals.

29.4.2   Identification

For a service concession arrangement to be applicable, the grantor must be able to control certain aspects (refer to *Figure 29-4*). The grantor must be able to control or regulate the type of services the operator must provide by using the assets. This control or regulation must also include the persons to whom and the price at which the services may be provided. The grantor must control any significant residual interest in the assets at the end of the arrangement.

Figure 29-4: Control or regulating requirements

Grantor controls or regulates

| Type of service | Users of infrastructure |
| Price charged for use | Residual interest |

There are two types of service concession arrangements – 1) where the operator recognises a financial asset, and 2) where an intangible asset is recognised. Both types of service concession arrangements normally include constructing or upgrading a public sector asset and then operating and maintaining the asset for a specified period of time. *Figure 29-5* provides a decision tree to determine whether a service concession arrangement exists or whether the arrangement must recognise a financial asset or an intangible asset.

Examples of service concession arrangements include toll roads, car parks, tunnels, airports, and water treatment and supply facilities.

Figure 29-5: Identification and classification of a service concession arrangement

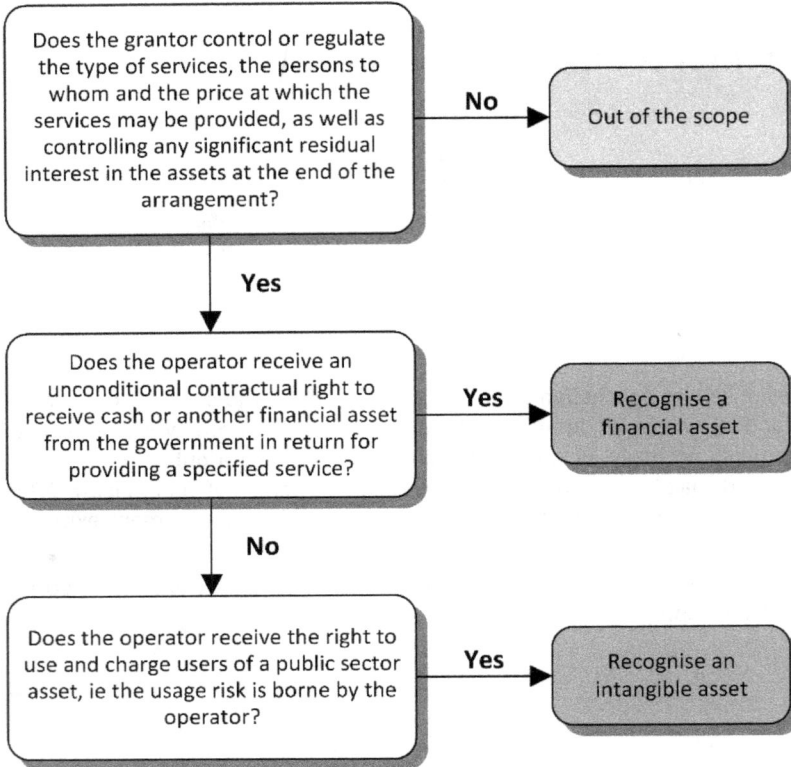

29.4.3   Financial asset model

Under the financial asset model, the operator receives an unconditional contractual right to receive a specified or determinable amount of cash or another financial asset from the government in return for the service. Normally, guarantees are provided by the government for any shortfall between amounts received from users of the public service and specified or determinable amounts. The crucial factor is whether an unconditional right to receive cash is created.

A financial asset is recognised to the extent that the operator has an unconditional contractual right to receive cash or another financial asset. The operator measures the financial asset initially at fair value (which will be the present value of the discounted unconditional contractual cash flows), and thereafter, follows the guidance applicable to financial instruments (refer to *Chapter 17*).

Example 29-4: Service concession arrangement – financial and possible intangible asset

Dusseldorf receives a concession to build and operate a new toll road between two major cities in Germany. Dusseldorf will construct and operate the road for 30 years after which it will pass to the German government. The cost of the construction was CU150 million.

The government guarantees Dusseldorf that it will receive a minimum amount per week in tolls from the public utilising the toll road. Should there be a short-fall, the government will pay the difference to Dusseldorf. The present value of the minimum amounts receivable discounted at an appropriate discount rate to reflect the time value of money, amounts to CU150 million.

Required

Determine whether the service concession asset should be classified and accounted for as an intangible asset, financial asset, a combination, or not at all. Also indicate the amounts.

Suggested solution

Dusseldorf accounts for the expenditure on the toll road by capitalising a financial asset of CU150 million. It may also recognise an intangible asset for the fair value of the right to charge the public in excess of the guaranteed amount of CU150 million, if reliably determinable.

29.4.4   Intangible asset model

Under the intangible asset option, a right to charge for use of a public sector asset is provided. A right to charge users is not an unconditional right to receive cash because the outcome depends on the extent of usage by the public. The usage risk is borne by the operator.

An intangible asset is recognised to the extent that the operator receives a right or licence to charge users for the public service. The operator also measures the intangible asset initially at fair value, but subsequently follows the guidance on intangible assets to account for the intangible asset (refer to *Chapter 13*).

Example 29-5: Service concession arrangement – intangible asset

Ankara receives the concession to upgrade and operate a government hospital in Turkey. The Turkish government will not fund any of the upgrade but grants Ankara the right to operate the hospital and charge for healthcare for 10 years. The costs incurred to upgrade the hospital amount to CU12 million. The fair value of the intangible asset is determined to be CU15 million at the date Ankara has the right to operate the hospital.

Required

Determine whether the service concession asset should be classified and accounted for as an intangible asset, financial asset, a combination, or not at all.

Suggested solution

As the government does not guarantee any of the revenues, Ankara does not have an unconditional right to receive cash and therefore does not have a financial asset. As a result, Ankara will capitalise CU15 million, the fair value of the right to operate and charge customers as an intangible asset. This intangible asset will represent the right to charge the public for healthcare over the 10 years. The CU3 million may be deemed to be a government grant and therefore accounted for in terms of *Chapter 23*. If not, an accounting policy regarding the treatment of the CU3 million gain must be developed, as per the guidelines in *Chapter 7.2.2*.

29.4.5   Combined model

A single contract may contain both a financial and intangible asset. The contract is then divided between the following components:

- To the extent that an unconditional guarantee of payment for the construction of the public sector asset is given, a financial asset is recorded.
- To the extent that the operator has to rely on the public using the service to obtain payment, an intangible asset is recorded.

Example 29-6: Service concession arrangement – combination of financial and intangible asset

Houston receives a concession to run a new train service from Houston to Dallas in the USA for 20 years. Houston will run the train service for the public, and the ticket prices will be set by the government.

The cost of building and running the new train service is CU100 million. The government has guaranteed a minimum number of users on the train line over the period, and also has contractually agreed to subsidise the reporting entity in the event of a short-fall. The fair value of the guarantee from the government is CU80 million.

Required
Provide the journal entries to account for the arrangement.

Suggested solution
Houston will account for the transaction as follows:

Dr	Financial asset (SFP)	80,000,000	
Dr	Intangible asset (SFP)	20,000,000	
Cr	Bank (SFP)		100,000,000

Recognition of service concession received.

The measurement of the intangible asset is calculated as the difference between the cost incurred and fair value of the financial asset.

The financial asset is the value of the guaranteed amount.

29.4.6   Operating revenue

The operator of a service concession arrangement must recognise, measure and disclose revenue for the service it renders in accordance with guidance on Revenue (refer to *Chapter 22*).

29.4.7   Recognition – Other assets used and obligations arising

The Standard does not provide specific guidance for additional assets received to operate the infrastructure, such as plant and equipment.

The Standard does not provide specific guidance on other contractual obligations arising from the service concession arrangement.

> Judgement should be applied in developing accounting policies for assets used and obligations arising from service concession arrangements. *Chapter 12* on Property plant and equipment and *Chapter 15 on* Provisions and contingencies should be considered.

29.4.8   Disclosure

The Standard does not prescribe disclosure requirements for service concessions. The following chapters' disclosure requirements may be required:

- Basic financial instruments or other financial instruments (refer to *Chapter 17*).
- Intangible assets other than goodwill (refer to *Chapter 13*).
- Provisions and contingencies (refer to *Chapter 15*).
- Property, plant and equipment (refer to *Chapter 12*).
- Impairment of assets (refer to *Chapter 14*).

29.5   Summary

- **Agriculture**
  - Where the fair value of each biological asset is readily determinable without undue cost or effort, an entity engaged in agricultural activity must apply the fair value through profit or loss.
  - Where the fair value is not readily determinable, or is determinable only with undue cost or effort, the entity must measure its biological assets at cost less accumulated depreciation and impairment.
  - At harvest, agricultural produce must be measured at fair value less estimated costs to sell.

- **Extractive industries**
  - Accounting policies must be developed for the accounting of expenditure on tangible and intangible exploration and evaluation assets, and judgement must be applied in developing these policies. Once determined, these policies must be applied consistently.
  - Requirements to dismantle or remove items, or restore sites, must be accounted for using *Chapter 12* (Property, plant and equipment) and *Chapter 15* (Provisions and contingencies) of the Standard.
  - Specific indicators for impairment have been described in this chapter for exploration and evaluation assets.
  - All other exploration costs must be expensed.

- **Service concession arrangements**
  - Guidance is provided on how the operator accounts for a service concession arrangement. The operator should either recognise a financial asset or an intangible asset depending on whether the grantor has provided an unconditional guarantee of payment.

- A financial asset is recognised to the extent that the operator has an unconditional contractual right to receive cash or another financial asset from, or at the direction of, the grantor for the construction services.
- An intangible asset is recognised to the extent that the operator receives a right or licence to charge users for the public service.

Chapter 30
Transition to the IFRS for SMEs

Contents

30.1   Scope

The transition rules apply to a first-time adopter of the Standard. A first-time adopter is defined as an entity that presents its first annual financial statements that conform to the IFRS for SMEs, regardless of whether its previous accounting framework was full IFRS or another accounting framework.

An entity that has applied the Standard in a previous reporting period, but in its most recent prior period not fully complied with the Standard (applied another GAAP) may either apply:

- The transitional procedures in this Chapter; or
- IFRS for SMEs retrospectively (in accordance with *Chapter 7.2.6*) as if the entity had never stopped applying the Standard.

30.2   Definition

The date of transition to the Standard is defined as the beginning of the earliest period for which the entity presents full comparative information in accordance with the Standard. Normally this will be at the beginning of the comparative period, but the Standard allows that information may be provided for more than one comparative year.

> The date of transition is the beginning of the earliest period for which comparatives are presented. This would normally be exactly two years before the reporting date, assuming one year's comparatives are presented and the periods presented are for 12 months.

Example 30-1: Date of transition

Chicago is a company that produces and sells various products. Management decided to apply the IFRS for SMEs for the first time in preparing its financial statements for the year ended 31 December 20X3.

To date, Chicago applied its own accounting policies. The company's policy is to present one year's comparative information.

Required
Determine the date of Chicago's transition.

Suggested solution
The date of transition to the Standard is 1 January 20X2, which is the beginning of the earliest period, ie the year ended 31 December 20X2, for which the entity prepares comparative information.

30.3   First-time adoption

A first-time adopter may apply the transitional procedures in its first financial statements that conform to the Standard. An entity's first financial statements that conform to the Standard are the first annual financial statements in which the entity makes an explicit and unreserved statement in those financial statements that it complies with the IFRS for SMEs.

A first-time adoption will occur when an entity previously presented financial statements applying another national accounting framework, accounting standards or full IFRS. However, if an entity has used the Standard but either did not make an explicit and unreserved statement or did not apply all the requirements, a first-time adoption is required when the explicit or unreserved statement of compliance is made for the first time.

30.4 Procedures for preparing financial statements at the date of transition

30.4.1 Retrospective application

The entity may choose to entirely apply IFRS for SMEs retrospectively in accordance with *Chapter 7*, if it previously had applied IFRS for SMEs (but not in its most recent prior period). Retrospective application means that the new accounting policy is applied to comparative information as if the new accounting policy had always been applied.

The entity may instead choose to apply the transitional procedures, which begin with the restatement of the opening statement of financial position at the date of transition to the Standard, which is the beginning of the earliest period presented. The following main procedures are required:

- Recognise all assets and liabilities as required by the Standard.
- Derecognise any asset or liability not permitted by the Standard.
- Reclassify items that need reclassification in terms of the Standard.
- Apply the measurement principles of the Standard to all recognised assets and liabilities.

> The transition procedures begin by restating the opening statement of financial position on the date of transition.

Any changes in accounting policies used in the opening statement of financial position, resulting from the use of different accounting policies before the date of transition to the Standard, are recognised directly in retained earnings (or another category of equity) at the date of transition to the Standard.

30.4.2 Limitations and restrictions

When the Standard is adopted for the first time, the accounting of transactions listed in *Table 30-1* may not be adjusted retrospectively (or may only be adjusted as indicated). They are also referred to as mandatory exemptions.

> 👁 The transitional procedures are performed at the date of transition. Accordingly, the limitation on retrospective application is not applicable to the comparative figures, except if specifically allowed or required.
>
> In other words, the comparative amounts need to be adjusted to comply with the Standard, where necessary.

Table 30-1: Limitations on retrospective adjustments

Transitional limitations	Interpretations
Derecognition of financial assets and liabilities	
Financial assets and liabilities derecognised under a previous accounting framework should not be recognised on adoption. For financial assets and liabilities not derecognised under the previous accounting framework, that should have been derecognised under the Standard, the entity may choose to derecognise them on adoption of the Standard, or to continue to recognise them until disposed of or settled.	Financial assets and liabilities derecognised under a previous framework that should be recognised under the Standard are only adjusted in the current period, ie not as part of the transitional procedures (refer to *Chapter 17*). An entity may choose to continue to recognise financial assets and financial liabilities that should be derecognised under the Standard until the items are disposed of or settled (refer to *Chapter 17*).
Hedge accounting	
Hedge accounting for hedging relationships that no longer exist at the date of transition may not be changed. For hedging relationships that exist at the date of transition, the hedging requirements of the Standard must be followed, including the requirements for discontinuing hedge accounting for hedging relationships that do not meet the hedge accounting conditions.	The Standard's hedge accounting guidance must be applied for all hedging accounting relationships that exist on the date of transition (refer to *Chapter 17*). However, if the reporting entity did not document or designate the hedge relationship before the date of transition, the entity is not **required** to designate the relationship, but the option to designate a hedge relationship remains.
Accounting estimates	Accounting estimates may only be adjusted at the end of the current period, ie not as part of the transitional procedures (refer to *Chapter 7*).
Discontinued operations	Previous accounting policies applied to discontinued operations may not be adjusted at the date of the transition. Discontinued operations must be presented in accordance with the Standard after the transition date (refer to *Chapter 3.5.2*)

Table 30-1: Limitations on retrospective adjustments *(continued)*

Transitional limitations	Interpretations
Government loans	Government loans recognised under a previous framework at the date of transition to IFRS for SMEs must apply the requirements of this Standard (refer to *Chapter 17* and *Chapter 23*) prospectively. However, if the entity did not previously recognise and measure the benefit of a government loan at a below-market rate of interest and treat it as a government grant, that carrying amount of the loan in accordance to the previous GAAP at the date of transition to this IFRS must be used as the carrying amount of the loan at that date and must not recognise the benefit of any government loan at a below-market rate of interest as a government grant.
Measuring non-controlling interests	
The requirements to allocate profit or loss and total comprehensive income between non-controlling interest and owners of the parent shall be applied prospectively from the date of transition to the Standard (or from such earlier date as the Standard is applied to restate business combinations).	The measurement and allocation of the non-controlling interest may not be changed from the previous accounting policies at the date of transition. If the optional business combination exemption is applied, this limitation applies to the earlier date (refer to *Table 30-2*). The allocation of profit or loss and total comprehensive income between the non-controlling interest and the owners of the parent are presented in the comparative figures (refer to *Chapter 3.5.1*).

30.4.3   Optional exemptions

A first-time adopter may use one or more of the exemptions in *Table 30-2* in preparing its first financial statements that conform to the Standard.

Table 30-2: Optional transition exemptions

Exemptions	Interpretations
Business combinations	
An entity may elect not to apply the guidance in *Chapter 6* on business combinations and goodwill to business combinations that were effected before the date of transition. However, if a business combination is restated, all subsequent business combinations must be restated.	This is only a once-off election for business combinations effected before the date of transition. The term *effected* is not explained. We believe sufficient evidence, such as contracts, must be available to demonstrate that the business combination was effected (refer to *Chapter 6*).
Share-based payment transactions	
An entity is not required to apply the guidance on share-based payment in *Chapter 19* to: ▪ **Equity instruments** granted before the date of transition or ▪ **Liabilities** arising from share-based payment transactions that were settled before the date of transition.	Equity instruments are normally granted when the related service is delivered, including vesting and non-vesting conditions (refer to *Chapter 19*). Any equity instrument recognised before the date of transition need not be changed, but **all liabilities outstanding on the date of transition are recognised or restated,** if needed.
Fair value as deemed cost	
An entity may elect to measure an item of **property, plant and equipment**, an **investment property**, or an **intangible asset** on the date of transition at its fair value. This fair value is then its deemed cost at the date of transition.	The fair value on the date of transition becomes the initial measurement amount on the date of transition, on which the relevant subsequent measurement of the related assets, such as cost less depreciation, is applied.
Event-driven fair value measurement as deemed cost	
An entity may elect to use a previously determined event-driven fair value to establish deemed cost for assets and liabilities **at or before the date of transition** as its deemed cost at the revaluation date. If the event-driven fair value measurement is determined **after the date of transition but during the first periods covered** by the first financial statements that conform to IFRS for SMEs, these may be used as its deemed cost at the time of that event.	The carrying amount of the fair valued asset becomes the initial measurement amount on the date of transition. If the valuation was done before the date of transition, adjustments, such as depreciation, may be required. If the fair value is determined after the date of transition but during the first periods covered, the resulting adjustments are recognised directly in retained earnings at the measurement date.

Table 30-2: Optional transition exemptions *(continued)*

Exemptions	Interpretations
Revaluation as deemed cost	
An entity may elect to use a previous accounting policy revaluation of an item of **property, plant and equipment**, an **investment property**, or an **intangible asset** at, or before, the date of transition as its deemed cost at the revaluation date.	The carrying amount of the revaluated asset becomes the initial measurement amount on the date of transition. If the valuation was done before the date of transition, adjustments, such as depreciation, may be required.
Cumulative translation differences	
An entity may elect to deem the cumulative translation differences, also known as a foreign currency translation reserve (FCTR), for all **foreign operations** to be zero at the date of transition (ie a *fresh start*).	Any FCTRs may be adjusted to zero at the date of transition. Only foreign currency translation differences arising after the date of transition are recognised (refer to *Chapter 25*).
Separate financial statements	
If **investments in subsidiaries, associates, and jointly controlled entities** are measured at **cost** in the separate financial statements, such investments may be measured at the date of transition at cost, or deemed cost, which shall be either fair value at the date of transition or previous accounting policy's carrying amount on that date.	This exemption is only applicable to the separate financial statements as defined (refer to *Chapter 5*). On the date of transition such investments may be recognised at cost, fair value, the previous accounting policy's amount, or using the equity method (refer to *Chapter 9.6*).
Compound financial instruments	
An entity is not required to separate a compound financial instrument into its liability and equity components if the **liability component** is not outstanding at the date of transition.	If any liability component is outstanding at the date of transition, the equity and liability component of a compound financial instrument must be separated (refer to *Chapter 16.8*).
Deferred income tax	
An entity may apply the requirements of *Chapter 21: Income Tax*, prospectively from the date of transition to IFRS for SMEs.	Refer to *Chapter 21* for further detail on recognition, measurement, and offsetting of current income taxes and deferred taxes.

Table 30-2: Optional transition exemptions *(continued)*

Exemptions	Interpretations
Service concession arrangements	
An entity is not required to apply the Standard's guidance on service concessions to arrangements entered into **before** the date of transition.	An election is available not to apply the guidance on service concessions (refer to *Chapter 29*), and therefore continue to apply their previous accounting policy to service concession arrangements entered into before the date of transition.
Extractive activities	
If **full cost accounting** was used under the previous accounting policy, the adopter may elect to measure **oil and gas assets** (those used in the exploration, evaluation, development or production of oil and gas), on the date of transition, at the amount determined under the previous accounting policy. Those assets must, however, be tested for impairment at the date of transition.	The election to measure exploration, evaluation and extraction costs as per the entity's previous accounting policy is only available for oil and gas assets, provided full cost accounting was used. The full cost accounting method allows for all exploration, evaluation and extraction costs to be capitalised. Refer to *Chapter 29* for guidance on extractive industries.
Arrangement containing a lease	
May elect to determine whether an arrangement existing at the date of transition contains a lease on the basis of facts and circumstances existing at the date of transition, rather than when the arrangement was entered into.	At the date of transition any agreements still in place at the date of transition, may be assessed to identify arrangements containing leases (refer to *Chapter 18.1.2*). This assessment may be done on the date of transition only. After the transition date all arrangements must be examined for a lease component.

Table 30-2: Optional transition exemptions *(continued)*

Exemptions	Interpretations
Decommissioning liabilities	
An entity may elect to measure the decommissioning component of the **cost of an item of property, plant and equipment** at the date of transition, rather than on the date when the obligation initially arose.	The estimation of the amount of the decommissioning, dismantlement or restoration cost relating to property, plant and equipment, which should be capitalised, may be done on the date of transition. Where the estimation is not performed at the date of transition, the estimated obligation must be measured and accounted for retrospectively. Refer to *Chapter 12* for guidance on initial estimate of the costs of dismantling and removing the item and restoring the site on which it is located.
Operations subject to rate regulation	
An entity may elect to measure all items of **property, plant and equipment** or all **intangible assets** on the date of transition at the previous GAAP carrying amount as its new deemed cost. Provided that the entity operates in an industry where prices (established by an authorised body) are set for the goods and services provided from the use of those assets. These assets must be tested for impairment at the date of transition in accordance with the requirements of *Chapter 14*. The previous carrying amount of the asset becomes the initial measurement amount on the date of transition.	The previous carrying amount of the asset becomes the initial measurement amount on the date of transition.
Severe hyperinflation	

If an entity's functional currency is subject to hyperinflation and:
- Its date of transition is on or after the functional currency normalisation date, the entity may elect to use that previously determined fair value as the deemed cost for assets and liabilities.
- The functional currency normalisation date is within a 12-month comparative period, the entity may use a comparative of less than 12 months, provided a complete set of financial statements is provided for that shorter comparative period.

30.4.4 Impracticability exemption

If it is impracticable for an entity to make any of the transitional procedures at the date of transition, the entity must apply the transitional procedures in the earliest period for which it is practicable to do so. Applying a requirement is regarded to be impractical when the entity cannot apply it after making every reasonable effort to do so.

> 👁 To apply the impractical exemption an entity must demonstrate why a reasonable effort to re-state the opening statement of financial position cannot be made.
>
> The Standard does not give guidance on whether an item, which is re-stated after the date of transition, will actually require all re-statements to be done at the later date. The entity may therefore develop an accounting policy that the later date (at which it becomes practicable to apply an exemption) is the date at which all exemptions may be applied, ie the date of transition.

If the impracticability exemption is applied, the date of transition and the amounts that have not been restated and are not comparable must be disclosed. When it is impracticable to provide any disclosures required for previous periods, the omission must also be disclosed.

30.5 Disclosure

When an entity has previously applied the Standard (but not in its most recent prior period), and in the current period returned to the Standard, the following must be explained:

- The reason it departed from the Standard previously.
- The reason it is resuming the application of the Standard.
- Whether it has applied the transitional provisions in this chapter or applied the Standard retrospectively.

If the entity has chosen to retrospectively apply the IFRS for SMEs Standard, the disclosures in *Chapter 7* relating to such retrospective application of IFRS for SMEs must be adhered to.

The effect on the reported financial position, financial performance and cash flows of the transition from the previous financial reporting framework to the IFRS for SMEs must be explained. The explanation includes:

- A description of the nature of each change in accounting policy.
- Reconciliations of the equity determined in accordance with the previous financial reporting framework to equity determined in accordance with this Standard for both of the following dates:
  - The date of transition to the IFRS for SMEs.
  - The end of the latest period presented in the entity's most recent annual financial statements determined in accordance with its previous financial reporting framework.
- A reconciliation between the entity's profit or loss for the comparative period, as previously reported in accordance with its previous financial reporting, to the restated profit or loss as determined in accordance with the Standard.

An entity must distinguish between the correction of errors and changes in accounting policies in the above reconciliations.

When financial statements are not presented for previous periods, this fact must be disclosed in the first financial statements that conform to the IFRS for SMEs.

30.6   Summary

- This section is to be applied by first time adopters of the IFRS for SMEs and may be applied by those returning to IFRS for SMEs, regardless of whether their previous reporting was under full IFRS or another GAAP, including the Exposure Draft of IFRS for SMEs, which was adopted as a Statement of Generally Accepted Accounting Practice for Small and Medium-Sized Entities in South Africa.
- The opening balance sheet for the comparative period shall be adjusted for:
  - Recognition of assets and liabilities required under IFRS for SMEs
  - Not recognise items as assets or liabilities if the Standard does not permit such recognition
  - Derecognition of assets and liabilities not permitted under Standard
  - Reclassification of assets, liabilities or equity under the Standard, and
  - Any adjustments to the measurement of any assets and liabilities arising from application of the Standard.
- The following transactions shall not be amended on adoption of the Standard:
  - Derecognition of financial assets and liabilities
  - Hedge accounting
  - Accounting estimates
  - Discontinued operations
  - Measuring non-controlling interests
  - Government loans and
  - Assets classified as held for sale or discontinued operations.
- An entity's date of transition to the Standard is the beginning of the earliest period for which the entity presents full comparative information in accordance with this standard in its first financial statements that conform to the Standard.
- Optional exemptions exist on first-time adoption for business combinations, share-based payments, fair value, event-driven fair value or revaluation as deemed cost, separate financial statements, service concession arrangements, extractive industries, arrangements containing a lease, cumulative translation differences, decommissioning assets, compound financial instruments, rate regulated operations, entities subject to severe hyperinflation, share-based payment transactions and deferred income taxes.
- Disclosure of the impact or the retrospective application of the Standard is required (if the transition provisions are not applied).
- Disclosure of the impact of the transition on the financial position, financial performance and cash flows is required. In addition, reconciliations of equity and profit or loss as previously reported must be given. Any errors in the application of the previous reporting framework must be separately disclosed.